Great Monuments

of

India, Bhutan, Nepal, Pakistan and Shri Lanka

Great Monuments

of

India, Bhutan, Nepal, Pakistan and Shri Lanka

Shobita Punja

Photographs by Fredrik Arvidsson

Dr. Shobita Punja was born in South India and studied in various schools in India, Beirut, and London. She has a Bachelor's Degree in Art History, a Master's Degree in Ancient Indian History, another Master's Degree in Art Education from Stanford University, California. Her doctoral research was also in the field of Art Education. She has written several books; Museums of India was published by The Guidebook Company, Hong Kong in 1989. Her recent study has been in the interpretation of the temples of Khajuraho. Her innovative analysis, Divine Ecstasy was published by Viking in 1992.

Fredrik Arvidsson was born in Stockholm, Sweden and attended several private schools in Sweden, Greece, and France. He has travelled extensively in south-east Asia, America, and Europe. Since 1990 he has been travelling with his wife through India, Pakistan, Nepal, and Shri Lanka on his 500 cc Enfield motorcycle taking photographs.

First published in 1994 by The Guidebook Company Limited, Hong Kong
3/F., 20 Hollywood Road, Hong Kong

ISBN: 962-217-354-3

Photographs by Fredrik Arvidsson.
Additional Photographs by:
Fotomedia (Aditya Arya, pp. 275, 282; P.K. De, pp. 188, 189; Marie D'Souza, pp. 43, 45; Joanna Van Gruisen, pp. 327)
Aditya Patankar, pp. 2, 97, 111, 264, 266, 268
Kamal Sahai, pp. 35, 129 (both), 146, 296
Pankaj Shah, pp. 261
Toby Sinclair, pp. 26, 28, 42, 151, 256, 270, 279, 280, 283, 313, 316, 322, 323, 324, 326
Maps: Bai Yiliang

Publisher: Bikram Grewal.
Designed and produced by Gulmohur Press, New Delhi.
Production House: Twin Age Limited, Hong Kong

Printed in China

To my parents

Naomi Meadows Ramesh Punja
Ian Meadows Premalata Punja

who introduced me to beautiful places

Contents

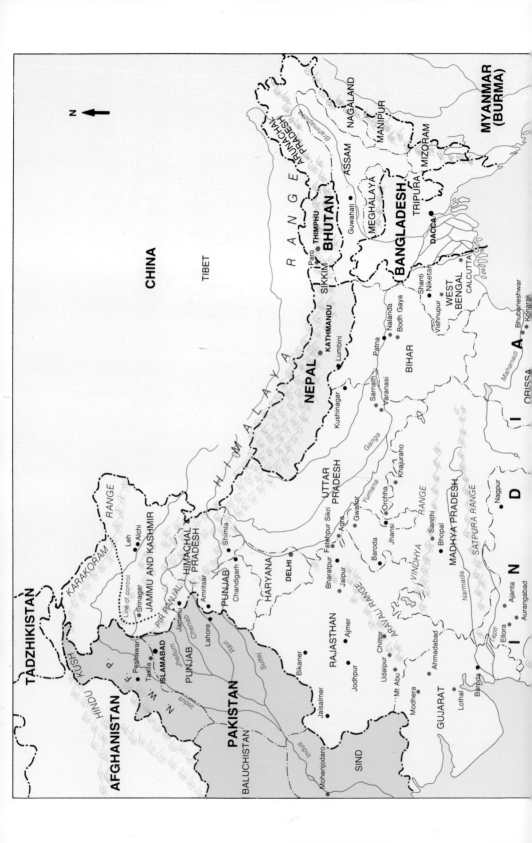

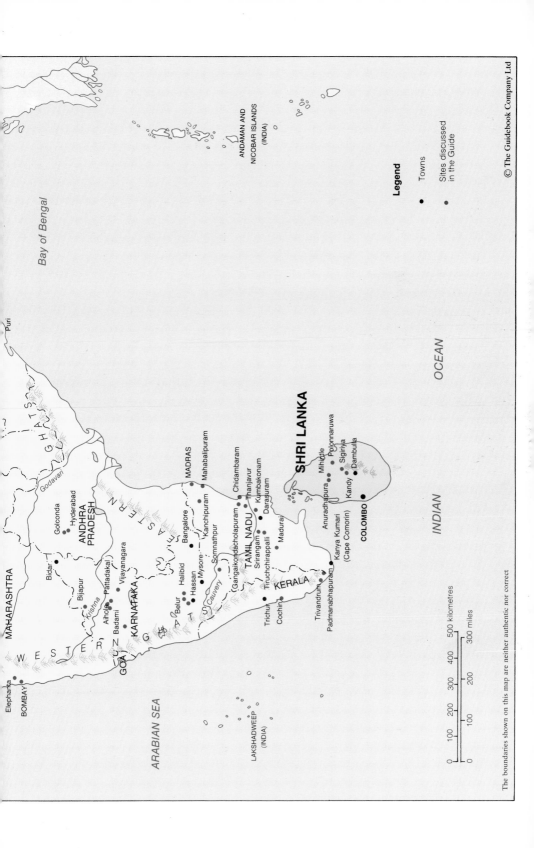

Puri

Bay of Bengal

ANDAMAN AND
NICOBAR ISLANDS
(INDIA)

Legend

● Towns

● Sites discussed
in the Guide

© The Guidebook Company Ltd

MAHARASHTRA

GHATS

Godavari

Hyderabad

Golconda

ANDHRA
PRADESH

Bidar

Bijapur

Krishna

Aihole

Badami

Pattadakal

Vijayanagara

KARNATAKA

GOA

Belur

Halibid

Hassan

Mysore

Somnathpur

Cauvery

Bangalore

Kanchipuram

Gangaikondacholapuram

TAMIL NADU

Srirangam

Tiruchirappalli

Madurai

KERALA

Trichur

Cochin

Trivandrum

Padmanabhapuram

Kanya Kumari
(Cape Comorin)

MADRAS

Mahabalipuram

Chidambaram

Thanjavur

Kumbakonam

Darasuram

SHRI LANKA

Anuradhapura

Mihintle

Polonnaruwa

Sigiriya

Kandy

Dambula

COLOMBO

INDIAN

OCEAN

WESTER

ARABIAN SEA

Elephanta

BOMBAY

LAKSHADWEEP
(INDIA)

0   100   200   300   400   500 kilometres

0   100   200   300 miles

The boundaries shown on this map are neither authentic nor correct

Acknowledgements

The author would like to thank The Guidebook Company, Hong Kong, and Gulmohur Press, New Delhi, for their support.

I am specially thankful to Fredrik Arvidsson for contributing his spectacular photographs for this guidebook.

Other photographers I wish to thank are Toby Sinclair, Kamal Sahai, Aditya Patankar, Pankaj Shah, and Fotomedia, New Delhi for their contributions to this book.

While designing the layout of the book in Gulmohur Press, I was greatly helped by Ajay Verma.

I am extremely grateful to the Archaeological Survey of India for permissions to photograph the historical sites.

I wish to thank my gurus with whom I studied Indian art. They inspired in me a deep love for art and also the need for conservation of these monuments, a sentiment that lies within every sentence of this book.

A special note of gratitude to my editor, not merely for working on the manuscript, but always nurturing my passion for architecture and defending my hatred for all forms of violence.

Preface

This illustrated guide to the **Great Monuments** of the Indian subcontinent has been written for the general reader, visitor, and tourist. The aim is to provide background information on places and historical monuments supported by photographs, maps, and plans in order to present a whole view of the scale and grandeur of the monuments of the subcontinent.

The guidebook covers historical buildings in places of cultural importance in India, Bhutan, Nepal, Pakistan, and Shri Lanka. This region has been treated as an integrated unit for, in the course of history, they were bound by cultural ties that were unconstricted by contemporary national boundaries.

Lord Curzon once referred to the architectural heritage of the region as 'the greatest galaxy of monuments in the world'. This overwhelming abundance has made the process of selection of 'star monuments' to include in this guide extremely difficult. It was a question of deciding whether to cover a larger number of places and limit each description to a sketch or to select a few favourite buildings and give them fuller coverage. Aware that my personal predilections might not correspond entirely with anyone else's selection of what to eliminate and include, I eventually chose a representative sample of monuments spread over various historical periods, from ancient to modern; and from diverse geographical zones, from the desert forts of Rajasthan to the temperate valleys of the Himalaya. I have, by so doing, covered the customary tourist itinerary and to that list added sites I personally cherish, such as Badami and Aihole, which are not regular tourist destinations but deserve to be.

The book begins with an **Introduction** to the monuments of the subcontinent. This section outlines the evolution of the artistic traditions in the region, covering historical monuments, religious buildings, forts, palaces, and a few secular structures. Most ancient building sites that have survived the ravages of time are those built out of permanent, durable material such as stone. Stone construction is an elaborate process requiring the sponsorship of wealthy patrons and extravagant resources (of material, time, and labour), which were often only available for very important religious and royal buildings. While the Indian subcontinent has an ancient tradition of building in other materials, such as bamboo, clay, and wood, these buildings have not always weathered the passage of time. An exception to this are the timber and brick constructions of the Kathmandu

Valley, where both religious, royal, and domestic architecture
have been preserved and are discussed here. For the most part,
however, the history of the monuments of the region tends to be
a two dimensional account of the development of religious
(Buddhist, Jain, Hindu, and Islamic) and royal stone architecture,
and perforce has to bypass the no less interesting third dimension
of buildings which ordinary people lived in and used.

The **Introduction** thus outlines the evolution of stone architecture as it developed in different geographical climates, regions, and historical periods. In some respects this portion is a
review of the monuments described later in the book. Here the
monuments are studied in historical and architectural perspective, ignoring modern political boundaries, as in the case of
Buddhist art that evolved in Nepal, India, Pakistan, and Shri
Lanka over a span of over two thousand years. I have tried to
familiarise the reader with various facets of a Hindu temple, an
Islamic mosque, and a Buddhist stupa, and to describe the
evolution of architecture and their all-pervading symbolism.

Most of the monuments described in this book are signposts
of national heritage and are no longer 'living buildings'. Their
empty walls, rooms, and corridors no longer reverberate with
purposeful activity or echo their original splendour. Yet a
Mughal palace, for instance, is magnificent even today, though
bare and stark, and one has only to look at some miniature

Painting of City
Palace, Jaipur.

paintings of the time to visualise its contemporary context. The lush gardens that once surrounded it, the interiors adorned with carpets that reflected the glory of the flowers and trees outside, as fragrant perfumed water channels and fountains cooled the rooms, driving away the intense heat of the Indian summer. The carpets have gone and the fountains have lost their musical cadence, but the splendour of the palaces can still be recreated in the imagination of the visitor. One of my principal concerns is therefore to kindle this by providing visitors with an informed perspective of how the monuments were designed to serve the social and religious functions of their time and the historical personalities associated with them.

The main text follows the preliminary Introduction with a detailed description of each selected monument. The reader is invited to see the monuments through the eyes of the author, to move through the buildings and to simulate in the mind's eye the atmosphere of the particular historical period. The maps, plans, and photographs accompanying each section provide useful visual information about the layout of the site and significant pictorial highlights. Wherever a monument or a site is referred to more then once in the text, it has been cross-referenced through bold lettering.

At the end of each section is a sub-section entitled WHAT'S IN THE NEIGHBOURHOOD. Here I have cited museums, other monuments and places of interest in the vicinity. In this way I have been able to cover many more places of historical interest than are listed in the Contents. For instance, **Ahmadabad** in Gujarat is an important city with several medieval tombs and mosques. But from **Ahmadabad** one can take day trips to **Lothal**, one of India's oldest cities (5000 years old), the beautiful Sun temple of **Modhera** (c. AD 1000) to which one can trace the tradition of fine carving for which the monuments of Ahmadabad are famous. Suggestions have also been made on HOW TO GET THERE, the best time of the year to visit the monument, and the kinds of local accommodation available.

Important information about photography and filming permissions are given in the **Travel Information** section. General tips for internal travel within a country, visas, travel within the subcontinent, health, accomodation, and communication have been provided for the convenience of the reader.

This is an unconventional travel book, going beyond the merely 'how-to-do-it' concept by taking the reader on an illustrated historical and architectural guided tour of some of the most spectacular monuments of the Indian subcontinent.

Introduction

Many factors have shaped the course of history in the Indian
subcontinent, a principal one among them being the physical
character of the land. This geographical region of great diversity
includes the world's highest and youngest mountains, some of
the oldest geographical formations, deserts, rain forests, tropical
islands, fertile river valleys and an extensive coastline.

The northern boundary of the subcontinent is formed by
interlocking mountain ranges. The Hindu-Kush, Karakoram,
and the Himalaya sweep in from Afghanistan and culminate on
the Burma–China border separating the subcontinent from the
Central Asian (Eurasian) plateau. This great mountain chain
harbours the world's highest peaks that rise in Pakistan, India,
and Nepal. While most of these peaks were scaled only in this
century or towards the end of the last, it was the passes and
mountain valleys around them that linked the subcontinent to
Persia and the countries bordering the Mediterranean to the
west, Tibet and Mongolia to the north, China, Burma, and
south-east Asia to the east. These routes brought trade, ideas,
and invading armies for over 3000 years.

Himalaya, the abode
of snow.

These dramatic mountain ranges are
of deep philosophical significance. In Buddhist and Hindu mythology the pure snow
white regions are the abode of the gods
and the central axis of the universe. The
pristine mountain landscape became the
retreat for religious sages and saints. Huge
monasteries and pilgrim centres were
established along the mountain regions. In
Bamiyan in Afganisthan, Takti-Bahi in the
Swat Valley in Pakistan, Kashmir, Ladakh,
and the Spiti region of India, Nepal's
Kathmandu Valley, and Bhutan lie ancient Buddhist centres protected by these
formidable mountain ranges.

From these magnificent mountains
flow great rivers that enrich the plains
below. In the west the Indus and its five
tributaries descend from the northern
mountains through the 2400 kilometre
length of Pakistan till they reach the south
where they merge with the Arabian sea.

The mighty Indus river was the home of the earliest urban civilisation built over 5000 years ago. This river was forded by the invading armies of Alexander of Macedon in the third century BC and later, in the fourteenth century AD by Timur (Tamerlane), the Mongol invader, and two centuries later by Babur, the founder of the Mughal dynasty. It was from the river that the names Hindu, Sind, and India are all derived, referring to the land and people of the Indus.

The Ganga (Ganges) and her tributaries flow from the north in an easterly sweep parallel to the Himalaya, till they join the Brahmaputra river and flow into the Bay of Bengal. Other rivers, like the Narmada and the Godavari, criss-cross from east to west, and west to east along the expanse of the peninsula. Rivers moving from their source on a meandering journey towards the sea have always provided vital fertility to the plains of greater India, bathing their banks with alluvial soil and cleansing the land with each monsoon. In the Hindu tradition these life-sustaining rivers assumed sacred properties of prosperity and purity. Their passage from their source to the great oceans came to represent the cycle of life, death, and reunion. The sources of rivers, such as Gomukh and Amarkantak, soon became places of pilgrimage and the entire length of the rivers were dotted with temples and religious centres. Thus, cremation of the dead on the banks of these rivers is believed to expedite the passage of the soul to its reunion with the ocean of universal creation.

Varanasi, on the banks of the Ganga.

The rivers and mountain ranges of the Indian peninsula form one of the oldest networks of communication, enabling communities to maintain cultural and economic contact with far-flung regions to the east and west. Through the course of 5,000 years of historical evolution, these rivers sustained the growth of myriad kingdoms, republics, and empires. The natural vegetation and mineral wealth of the subcontinent supported the development of some of the wealthiest kingdoms of their time, whose reputation and trade, and occasionally even empire, spread far beyond the boundaries of the subcontinent. Trade from the earliest times was in timber, spices, gold, and diamonds, which were taken across the lands and seas to Europe, Africa, and south-east Asia. The wide sweep of coastline with natural harbours and ports was conducive to maritime trade, which began almost five thousand years ago. Over the centuries, as sailors braved the oceans, they came to rely on the seasonal cycle of the monsoon winds. The seasonal winds facilitated faster travel, regulated their schedule of travel and rest, and their journeys to countries to the east and to the west.

The climate and the distinctive seasons lent their hand in shaping the natural heritage of the subcontinent. Migratory birds made their annual visitations, and the once exuberant forests were the home of exotic species of animals and birds, enticing the visitor and trader to revel and wonder.

The Stone Age

There was an exciting discovery this century in the Himalayan foothills. Here remains of Ramapithecus were found, indicating that human beings had lived and roamed the subcontinent 600,000 years ago. The wonder of nature and the natural curiosity of human beings is, perhaps, best expressed in the paintings of the stone age. Habitation of the subcontinent began in the distant past, perhaps more than ten thousand years ago. There are sites in Pakistan and India which mark that period when *Homo sapiens* had learnt to domesticate animals and to plant crops. In India there are several sites (**Bhimbetka**, Madhya Pradesh) where these early dwellers lived. There, natural caves in the hillsides are littered with remnants of their tools and flints made of stone. The walls and ceilings of the caves are painted with dramatic hunting scenes and what appear to be the earliest records of elaborate rituals; these works of energetic artistic expression are still to be seen 8,000 years later.

Indus Valley Civilisation

Until the 1920s it was believed that the history of the Indian subcontinent dated back only as far as the third century BC when Alexander of Macedon led his army into the plains of north-west India. While Hindus and Buddhists claimed that their history and culture was far more ancient, there was no historical evidence of the antiquity of human culture in the subcontinent. When a railway line was being laid in Sind (now a province of Pakistan) in the late nineteenth century, officers noticed that the never-ending supply of bricks came from strange looking mounds along the path of the Indus. The first site to be explored was Harappa, but the significance of the findings was not realised till several years later. In 1920, R.D. Banerji visited a site near the mouth of the Indus which the villagers called **Mohenjodaro**, the 'Mound of the Dead'. Excavations continued and in 1924 John Marshall, Director of the Archaeological Survey of India, realised the amazing similarity between the pottery, seals, and bricks of two cities separated by over 400 miles. The excitement of his discovery resounds in his report:[1]

> Not often has it been given to archaeologists, as it was given to Schliemann at Tiryns and Mycenae, or to Stein in the deserts of Turkestan, to light upon the remains of a forgotten civilization. It looks, however, at this moment, as if we are on the threshold of such a discovery in the plains of the Indus.

As excavations continued over the years it became apparent that these cities represented a culture that had flowered five thousand years ago. Their discovery served to push back the history of the

Plan of the city of Mohenjodaro.

© The Guidebook Company Ltd

subcontinent by several millenia and confirmed that this was a civilisation contemporaneous to those of Mesopotamia and Egypt. There was evidence of trade between Mesopotamia and the Indus Valley Civilisation from these ancient times. The civilisation also appeared to have spread over a much larger area than its contemporaries, beyond the Indus plains to the east in Rajasthan, towards the south in Gujarat, and along the Yamuna river near Delhi in India. These urban cities suggested two things. First, that human culture in the subcontinent had by 2500 BC reached an astonishing level of sophistication necessary to construct well-planned cites and to administer them for more than a thousand years. Second, the appearance of cities so early in the history of the region also suggested that, for some centuries prior to this, human societies had made striding advances in agriculture and metallurgy to enable them to support such large-scale urban developments.

The cities first excavated lay along the Indus river, and the culture came to be known as the Indus Valley Civilisation, with two magnificent sites at **Mohenjodaro** and Harappa (Pakistan). The cities were well planned with an orderly grid scheme, roads and service lanes meeting at right angles to form uniform blocks of buildings, with an efficient drainage system. Each city had identifiable trade and residential areas and a few prominent locations that were termed administrative or civic. The residential areas were lined with rows of houses, often two storeys high. All the buildings were made out of bricks of uniform size. The standardised size of bricks used in the cities of the Indus Valley amazed historians for it suggested that an extremely efficient or autocratic administrative system must have controlled industrial production and regulated the size of the bricks, weighing scales, and other commercial instruments and tools.

Within private houses excavators discovered a vast collection of elegant wheel-thrown pottery, finely chiselled semi-precious stone jewellery, delightful toys, household items, and animal and human figures. This culture heralded in the bronze age with its labour-intensive and sophisticated technology of mining, casting, and forging of metal implements.

Amongst the ruins were found thousands of small seals, often just an inch square. Each seal bears a legend in a pictorial script that has yet to be deciphered. The remaining space bears an emblem: a figure of an animal, or a motif, a human figure or a divine form. The script, when it is deciphered, will open up new avenues of investigation and perhaps provide answers to some enticing questions. Who were the original inhabitants? Were they the indigenous Dravidian population? Who ruled and regulated the construction of these cities that conform so well to a pattern and a discipline and are so modern in conception?

What was the religion of these city dwellers? Why did this culture, which prospered for over a thousand years, gradually disappear? Was it an earthquake, that changed the course of the river; was there some natural calamity, were there dramatic ecological changes; or did the central authority finally lose its power and hold over these magnificent ancient cities?

The Iron Age

Coinciding with the gradual disappearance of the Indus sites around 1500 BC was the arrival of nomadic tribes from Central Asia. They moved in groups towards Europe in the west, to the south to Iraq, Iran, and India. Certain generic terms, like mother and father, can be traced back from contemporary languages to a common linguistic heritage that is said to have derived from those ancient communities. Excavations have revealed that these communities settled wherever they found a congenial environment. Amongst the remains were found iron implements which appear to have changed the lives of the people, enabling them to tame the forests, convert them into agricultural lands, and build villages. With the passage of time these villages supported the growth of towns, market centres, political formations, and a complex structured society based on professions. It was during this period that the sacred Vedic texts evolved, describing rituals, social practices, and the secrets of the universe. Mention is made of the nature gods, upon whom so much of the agricultural life seemed to depend: Agni the lord of fire, Indra the lord of the skies who brought rain and prosperity to the land, Vayu the wind god, and many others. These texts and epic poems, like the Ramayana and the Mahabharata, were not written down but passed from one generation to the next by word of mouth. Sacred texts, classical and folk literature formed the rich oral tradition, which remains one of the most pervasive characteristics of the subcontinent.

The Path of the Buddha

By the sixth century BC a large part of the subcontinent had fallen under the control of republics and small kingdoms. It was at this time that an important religion gained momentum and new commemorative monuments were constructed throughout the subcontinent. The Buddha, as he came to be known, was born into a princely family of Nepal. The legend of his birth appears often in Buddhist sculpture and depicts how his mother, Maya, dreamt of a white elephant. The dream was interpreted by the court astrologer as signifiying the birth of a child who would be a gift to mankind, a universal sovereign or saint. Maya, on her way to her parental home for her confinement, gave birth to a male child while resting in a grove of Ashoka trees at Lumbini.

The child was called Siddhartha or by his family name Gautam, later to be known as Shakya-muni (the sage of the Shakyas), Gautam Buddha or the Buddha, the Enlightened One.

Siddhartha's father belonged to a *kshatriya* (warrior) clan of the Shakyas and was keen to rear a warrior-ruler not a saint, as prophesied, so he prevented the young boy from wandering outside the palace. Siddhartha eventually managed to escape from his luxurious prison and encountered on his sojourn an old man, a sick man, a dead man, and a holy ascetic. Struck by the experience of pain and suffering, the young prince was consumed by a desire to renounce his royal inheritance and search for the true meaning of life. The prince, aged not more than twenty-nine years, decided to leave his palace, his young wife, son Rahul, all his wealth and possessions, and start on a long journey of self-discovery. His philosophic quest took him to holy places like **Varanasi** (India) where he held discussions with Hindu philosophers and sages but was not content with the explanations they gave. Finally he wandered to a ancient centre in Bihar (India) where he spent forty-nine days and nights meditating under a large pipal tree. Eventually, withstanding the temptations of the sensual world, he attained the wisdom (*buddhi*) to understand the meaning of life and came to be called **The Buddha**, the Enlightened one. The tree was called the **Bodhi Tree** and the site where he attained this universal wisdom was called **Bodh Gaya**.

Worship of the Bodhi Tree, Sanchi.

Having found the wisdom to comprehend the wonder of creation, the Buddha wished to pass his days in prayer and meditation but a few disciples, keen to benefit from his learning, persuaded him to teach them. The Buddha came to a quiet forest, called **Sarnath**, referred to as the Deer Park, just outside the city of **Varanasi** (Uttar Pradesh, India), where he delivered his first sermon and set up the first Sangha or order of Buddhists. At Lumbini, **Bodh Gaya**, and **Sarnath** beautiful monasteries and shrines were built in subsequent centuries to mark the holiest places associated with the Buddha. No original buildings from the time of the Buddha exist today. The lovely flowering Ashoka tree and the regal Bodhi Tree (pipal tree) associated with his spiritual evolution still play an important part in the landscape and layout of Buddhist sites and are venerated by Buddhists throughout the subcontinent.

The Buddha, after forty years of spreading his message of peace, came to a place called Kusinagar (Uttar Pradesh, India) where he died and attained eternal life, his final or great Awakening, *Parinirvana*. His bodily remains were cremated and the ashes enshrined. After his death, a council of five hundred Buddhists congregated at Rajgir (Bihar, India) to compile the main corpus of the Buddha's teachings.

The essence of his analysis of human life is contained in the 'Four Noble Truths' which begins by proclaiming that: (1) All life is sorrowful. (2) The cause of suffering is ignorant craving and desire, for it is material wealth and transient pleasures that bind us to this physical life. Then by way of a cure it is suggested, (3) The suppression of suffering can be achieved by following, (4) the Noble Eightfold Path of right perception, right aspiration, right speech, right conduct, right means of living with lofty endeavours, mindfulness, and contemplation. Such practices would cleanse the body and mind of ego-perpetuating desires. True awakening, *nirvana*, would end the endless cycle of life and the misery caused by desire.

The Buddha, by example, spent all his previous lives or incarnations, in selfless service and generous action for the benefit of others. **Jataka Tales** became a popular theme of painting and sculpture in Buddhist monuments. They are didactic tales that relate how the Buddha in each previous incarnation,

Buddhists at prayer.

even when born as an elephant or a monkey, served the needs of others. The Jataka tales poetically describe how in each life he was cleansed of egotistical cravings, thus preparing himself for nirvana.

The second Buddhist council was held nearly a hundred years after the Parinirvana of the Buddha at Vaishali (Bihar, India). At this meeting of various Buddhist orders there was a major schism. Each group had their own version of the Buddhist sacred law and their own interpretation of the doctrine of the Buddha. The path prescribed by the Buddha was a way to salvation and liberation from suffering, and the two major modes of reaching 'that other shore' were termed the lesser vehicle (ferry) **Hinayana** and the greater (*maha*) vehicle (or ferry), the **Mahayana**. The Mahayana tradition suggests that Buddhahood was available to all and incorporates a whole pantheon of Bodhisattvas or potential Buddhas, who out of compassion for humanity remain present to direct human beings to that other shore, so that all may attain True Liberation.

By the third century BC a large portion of central and northern India came under the administrative control of the Mauryan dynasty with their capital in Pataliputra (Patna, Bihar, India). Emperor Ashoka, who ruled in the third century BC, extended the Mauryan empire and, as the story goes, was converted to Buddha's way after a terrible, bloody battle at Kalinga in Orissa (India). Emperor Ashoka is said to have made a royal pilgrimage to all the sites associated with the Buddha and at each place erected monuments, columns, and edicts that proclaimed his faith and new found belief. He visited the Lumbini garden, Kapilavastu, the site of the great renunciation, and paid his respects to the great **Bodhi Tree** at **Bodh Gaya**, to **Sarnath** and at Kusinagar, the site of the Parinirvana. The emperor is said to have supported several thousand monks, erected several thousand

Stupa No. 1 with toran, Sanchi.

stupas and countless monasteries during the height of the Hinayana period. Ashoka's son (or brother in some versions) and daughter, carried a branch of the holy Bodhi Tree, from **Bodh Gaya** to **Shri Lanka**. Ambassadors to **Taxila** and **Nepal**, teachers to Syria and Macedonia were dispatched by routes that ran through Afghanistan, Baluchistan, and Sind. Along these routes he ordered the building of roads, wells, and gardens for pilgrims to rest in, stupas and shrines for prayer.

After the fall of the Mauryan empire Buddhism continued to receive royal or court patronage under the rule of the Kushanas of Gandhara (north-west Pakistan) and Mathura in northern India in the first to third century AD and in the third and fifth centuries under the Gupta empire which encompassed large portions of central and northern India. Great Mahayana universities were established at **Taxila** (Pakistan) and **Nalanda** (Bihar, India). Scholars from all parts of the ancient world came to study the great Buddhist texts from venerable masters, after making their pilgrimage to the holy sites associated with the Buddha.

It was through the movement of pilgrims and traders that these routes across difficult terrain were kept open and Mahayana Buddhism spread to western and southern India, and across the Himalaya, to Nepal, Bhutan, on to Tibet, and finally to the Far East, China, Korea, and Japan. By the twelfth and thirteenth centuries Mahayana Buddhism began to fade in northern and central India, and was preserved only in the remote Himalayan valleys of Tibet, **Ladakh**, **Bhutan**, and **Nepal** where splendid monasteries and *gompa*s continued to be built and rebuilt up to the present century. Pilgrims and scholars continue to come to visit the original holy Buddhist sites and much of the revival and new construction at places like **Bodh Gaya** and **Dhauli** have received financial and spiritual patronage from Buddhists in Japan, neighbouring Burma and Shri Lanka. Important festivals at these sites attracts large crowds from all corners of the world.

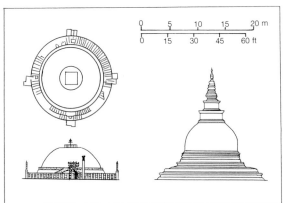

Stupa at Sanchi,
and Anuradhapura,
Shri Lanka.

Buddhist Monuments

The holiest of all Buddhist shrines is the *stupa*, the funerary mound. The evolution of the stupa began with small hemispherical mud mounds built over the remains of Buddhist saints and teachers. To preserve the sanctity of the mound a wooden or bamboo fencing was built around it. Gradually, as the influence of Buddhism spread, these mud mounds were enlarged and sheathed with stone. The wooden fencing was replaced with elaborate stone railings and ornate gateways, *toran*s. The stupa railing for centuries after carried the marks of their humble wooden origin and craftsman imitated the wooden joints and buttresses even when they were no longer necessary. The sculptured panels on the torans depict some scenes of contemporary secular architecture which appears to have been predominantly bamboo and wooden constructions. The torans are principally decorated with panels depicting the life of Buddha and other Jataka tales. The Stupa at Bharut, in Madhya Pradesh (India) was one of the oldest monuments of this kind but unfortunately was destroyed by local villagers. Only a few magnificent sculptures from the railing and toran can be seen of this early Hinayana monument at the Indian Museum in Calcutta. Some splendid early Hinayana stupas can be seen at **Sanchi** (Madhya Pradesh, India). Over several centuries, starting from the time of Emperor Ashoka, the main Stupa (No. 1) was renovated and enlarged, and the present diameter of the hemispherical mound is over 36 metres. This stupa has been raised off the ground on a huge cylindrical base and there are two levels of railings, one along the ground, the other along the upper part of the base. The enclosure railing has four magnificent torans facing the cardinal directions. Stupas were also built in south India between the second century BC and the second century AD, and the transition from Hinayana to

Mahayana Buddhism can be traced at the sites of Amaravati and Nagarjunakonda. The stupa was gradually adorned with the graceful and peaceful image of the Buddha, replacing sculptural panels of the Hinayana period in which the Buddha was only represented by symbols such as the empty throne, the Bodhi Tree, the impressions of his feet, and the sovereign umbrella.

In plan the stupa maintained its hemispherical shape and was a large solid structure with no entrance, but encased within the mound were the earthly remains of a religious leader. The stupa developed over a circular plan, grew in height, and in different regions of the subcontinent assumed varying proportions. The *dagoba* in Shri Lanka and *chorten* in Bhutan and Ladakh continued to have a ground plan that resembled a circle, a wheel with many spokes, that was filled in to create the mound. The symbolism of the wheel in Buddhist lore is of great significance. It is called the wheel of dharma, the *Dharmachakra*. It incorporates the principles of the four noble truths of suffering and existence, and progressive movement towards nirvana, the eventual enlightenment of humankind.

In Buddhist monasteries situated in far-flung areas where there were no commemorative burial mounds, symbolic votive stupas (dagobas, chortens, gompas) were constructed. At the rock-cut caves of **Ajanta** (Maharashtra, India) where a large community of Buddhist monks resided replica votive stupas, images, halls and shrines were carved out of the hillside.

Evolution of the stupa, Nepal.

The *Chaitya* is a large hall for Buddhist congregational worship, at one end is the central image and other sacred objects. In the early caves the Chaitya hall was dominated by a plain votive form of the stupa, the symbolic image of the Buddha. In the Mahayana period the stupa became just a backdrop for the seated or standing image of the Buddha. The faithful would enter the stupa enclosure or the Chaitya hall, perform a pradakshina and walk around the stupa. They would make offerings of flowers, water, and incense to the stupa or image.

The ritual circumambulation of the stupa (or votive stupa in a Chaitya hall) required the devotee to walk around the object of worship, keeping it always parallel with the right shoulder. This *pradakshinapatha*, path of circumambulation, was incorporated in the free-standing stupa plan and the Chaitya hall. The *pradakshina* is a symbolic circumambulation of the universe and the stupa with its hemispherical mound came to represent the dome of the earth. In Shri Lanka the processional path around the stupa was covered, as in a *vatadage*.

On the summit of the stupa was placed a *harmika*, a small railing around a many-tiered umbrella symbolic of the levels of heavenly existence. The stupas of Kathmandu have stylised harmikas with an exaggerated finial of tiers.

In Shri Lanka and Nepal the stupa assumed enormous proportions (over 100 metres in diameter) and images of the Buddha and Boddhisattvas were added to the symbolic earth mound. Gradually the votive stupa became a mere symbol and the image of the Buddha, progressively grew in importance and size, and soon dominated the Chaitya hall. These early images are forerunners of the gigantic images of the Buddha to be found in subsequent centuries and characterise the Buddhist art of Shri Lanka, Burma, Thailand, Japan, and China.

*Vihara*s are monasteries for Buddhist monks. The early viharas of **Sarnath** and **Ajanta** (India) consist of small cells for monks to sleep in, large halls for communal meetings and dining areas, and a small shrine with an image for community prayer within the residential quarters. The concept of the vihara was further elaborated and huge establishments and *bahal*s and *gompa*s were constructed in Bhutan, Nepal, and Shri Lanka. Here the monastery became the nucleus for Buddhist learning, with vast libraries, virtual storehouses of Buddhist knowledge and wisdom in such diverse fields as medicine and philosophy. The viharas were adorned with paintings and decorations, the dedicated expression of Buddhist monks and devotees. The mural paintings of **Ajanta** and the profusely adorned monasteries of **Nepal, Bhutan**, and Tibet suggest how change and continuity of tradition occurred in the development of Buddhist art and how it spread to every corner of the subcontinent.

The Hindu Way

In the early centuries of the Christian era, while Buddhism spread its influence through the subcontinent, temples to gods of the Hindu pantheon were being built in brick and wood. The development of Buddhist art and the expansion of secular architecture had a substantial effect on the evolution of the temple form. During the Gupta era (third to fifth century AD) a large part of India came under a unified administrative umbrella.

It was during this period that the earliest surviving examples of the Hindu temple can be dated. After the break up of this vast empire, the region was divided into countless kingdoms whose boundaries varied with each ruler and successive generation. The arts, including architecture, sculpture, painting, music, dance, and literature, that once developed under the Gupta empire now blossomed and evolved into regional styles. It was the creation of a culture with a thousand manifestations.

In the next thousand years regional styles matured to such a degree that a Jain and Hindu temple built in the same area had much more in common with each other than with their equivalents in other regions. Besides, the continual blending and amalgamation of boundaries this historical period saw the synthesis of local styles and the merger of ideas. Throughout, court art patronised by one dynasty also inspired diverse and similar artistic trends amongst rivals and neighbours. The monuments of the Pallava dynasty in **Mahabalipuram** and **Kanchipuram** (Tamil Nadu) during conquests inspired Chalukyan temple construction at **Aihole** and **Pattadakal** in northern Karnataka. The Cholas erected vast temples in the **Thanjavur** district and the Gangas built temples in **Orissa**, while the Chandellas built their stupendous temples at **Khajuraho**. The history of the monuments and cultural development from the fifth century AD to the present day is a wonderful story of creativity, synthesis and diversity, continuity and change.

Worship of the elements of nature, Pushkar, Rajasthan.

The Hindu Temple

Both the Hindu temple and the Buddhist shrine derive much of their form and decoration from their mythology and philosophy. Unlike a Buddhist stupa, a Hindu temple is not a funerary, commemorative monument. It is conceived as an abode of the gods or *devalaya*, and to construct such an abode 'which the gods love to visit' required unerring accuracy in spiritual symbolism in every feature and detail. The Indian subcontinent is unified by a strange and wonderful mythical geography which binds distant places together in the context of a myth or legend. Where the gods fought and frolicked became sacred pilgrimage centres, and throughout the length and breadth of the land these centres are linked in the minds of devotees. The sanctity of the site is of utmost importance because in mythological time it has already been blessed by the visitation of the gods.

The origins of a temple began (as it still does) with a modest shelter under a tree or on the banks of a tank or river that marks a sacred spot. Water is important in the layout of the temple as it symbolises the *tirth*, a place for the spiritual 'crossing over' to the other shore of wisdom. As the shrine attained importance and acquired financial resources, it expanded into a fully-fledged building. Since the temple is an abode of the gods it was built as a miniature reflection of the cosmos. The structure was aligned to the cardinal directions. The region of constancy is the east where the sun rises. Where the sun sets is the region of Varun, the Lord of the eternal ocean. The north star determines the region of permanence and the opposite southern direction is, understandably, one of change and decay, the kingdom of Yama, the Lord of Death. Depending on the presiding deity and the season when the temple is built, it will face one of the cardinal directions, but most often the temple faces the auspicious region of the east. The configuration of the stars and planets is also determined and their paths are plotted into the plan and foundation of the temple so that the gods can recognise the reconstruction of the universe in the order and layout of the temple and ensure blessings to the builders and worshippers. These rules were adhered to whether the temple was built in India or Nepal, in the desert or the hills.

When royal patrons and courtiers provided financial assistance and commissioned a temple or a sculpture it was always for a particular reason: to mark a political victory, the conquest of land and territory, or in memory of some loved one and the perpetual glorification of their own family name.

A temple consists of a single, often square, sacred sanctum called the *garbha griha*, or the womb chamber. Within the dark unadorned garbha griha is installed the main idol of worship and the temple is usually named after it. The most famous temple at **Varanasi** is called **Vishvanatha**, The Lord of the entire Universe (an appellation of Shiva, after the central image).

The sacred square garbha griha, with its equal faces directed toward the cardinal points of change and permanence (with four open doors, as found in the temples of the Kathmandu Valley), was in later centuries elaborated to form more intriguing designs and proportions. The sacred square of the sanctum could be rotated to create a star-like plan, as in the temples of **Belur** and **Halebid** (Karnataka, India) or the round shrines of Kerala and the undulating walls of the temples of **Khajuraho** (Madhya Pradesh, India).

During the elementary stages of development, the temple was often just a single-roomed shrine with a humble flat roof.

There are still many temples in India where the shrine is constructed in wood and brick with these humble proportions. As patronage to these places of worship grew the temple was redesigned in stone, a more durable and expensive material. The garbha griha was surmounted by a prominent roof called the *shikhara*, which over the centuries assumed monumental, awe-inspiring proportions, and dominated the surroundings so that the tower of the temple was visible to all.

Temple architecture has been classified by the form and shape of the shikhara and the distinctiveness of its decoration. The shikharas of southern India tend to be made up of distinct horizontal levels that diminish to form a rough pyramid. Each level is decorated with miniature temple roof-tops. The temples of north and central India have by contrast shikharas resembling an upturned cone that is decorated and buttressed with miniature conical shikharas. Those of **Bhubaneshwar** (Orissa, India) evolved their own form and are made up of many minute horizontal levels of decorated stonework that rise like a huge column straight above the garbha griha and only curve inward on reaching the tip of the tower.

The roofs of the subsidiary halls of Central Indian and Orissan temples developed a distinct pyramidal shape made up of several diminishing layers. The profile of these temples, as they matured, began to resemble a range of mountains with

Style of shikhara, Thanjavur and Somnathpur.

roof-tops of subsidiary halls rising up towards the highest reaches of the shikhara, thus adding to the symbolism of the temple as the residence of the gods amidst the Himalaya. In the Kathmandu Valley (due to the climatic conditions) timber architecture of temples attained a pagoda-like roof design with many levels. Wooden temples of Kerala and Goa also had grand sloping roofs covered with tiles.

At the apex of all shikharas is the *kalash*, the water pot-shaped emblem. Found throughout the subcontinent, the kalash is the symbolic pot of ambrosia, the ultimate goal of prayer, the promise of eternal life free from change and death.

The sculptural decorations on the outer walls of the garbha griha and the halls was also a matter of convention and regional taste. Although the *Vastu-shastras*, the quasi sacred texts on temple architecture, described the art and symbolism of construction, each region interpreted the codes and norms to their own advantage. The garbha griha which houses the central image of the temple was enclosed on three sides. The entrance doorway to the shrine, from the earliest Gupta examples, was elaborately carved with images of the river goddesses on either side, ensuring the purity of all who passed between the portals, and with other auspicious figurines along the border of the doorway. The central position on the lintel across the doorway was carved with a figure of the deity to whom the temple was

Style of shikhara, Khajuraho and Orissa.

dedicated. Niches on the outer walls of the garbha griha were installed with images that reflected the manifestations of the deity within. The walls of the temple could narrate themes from mythology, or have figures of the other gods and goddesses of the pantheon. To this vast decorative scheme was added a host of semi-demi gods and mythical creatures who protected and safeguarded the temple from evil forces. The quantity and proportion of these temple motifs was a matter of convention and varied from region to region, ranging from the sparsely decorated temples of **Hampi** to the profusely congested decoration of the temples at **Belur** and **Halebid** within the same region of Karnataka (India).

Worship at a Temple

One enters a temple after a ritual bath at the nearby tank or river. Physical cleansing was necessary to the notion of worship and spiritual cleansing. The tank was incorporated into the temple scheme and elaborate rituals were performed there. Over the centuries the tank developed elaborate architectural features.

On entering the temple one is expected to approach the building carrying offerings and to perform a *pradakshina* or circumambulation of the main building. This rite (similar to the Buddhist pradakshina) around the sacred structure takes the devotee symbolically around a miniature reconstruction of the cosmos. As the devotee moves slowly around the shrine, respect is paid to idols installed along the way and to the figures set in the niches of the temple, all manifestations of the image within. The figures on the temple wall, the shastras constantly remind us, have been created to aid the devotee in prayer, to provide an image of a superior, omnipotent, formless, and unmanifest power.

Decorated image within the garbha griha.

Like the child of a house, the idol within the temple is woken every morning and dressed and fed with offerings by brahmin priests of the temple. They are often hereditary priests, appointed centuries ago to maintain the temple, who were awarded lands and gifts for their subsistence by kings and patrons. Each season the gods are dressed in different clothes and in colours that symbolise the festive celebration. In some wealthy temples, like that at Tirupati (Andhra Pradesh, India), the jewellery that is worn by the principal deity costs many millions of rupees while in a village shrine the deity is content with a string of beads.

Once the deity is dressed the doors or curtain of the temple are opened to the devotee who comes with offerings of fruit and flowers. Each offering to the idol has a significance which voices the spiritual advancement of the devotee. Lighting of lamps holds great symbolic value in the Hindu view of life. For light is wisdom that eliminates darkness or ignorance which is understood as the only source of evil in the world. It is eternal wisdom to comprehend the oneness of nature, which is the central theme of prayer and worship in Hindu temples. Lamps, like the beautiful, many-tiered brass oil lamps of the southern Indian temples are of many shapes and sizes. The lamps are lit and waved before the idol to evoke wisdom in the devotee to receive *darshan*, 'to see' the ultimate truth of life. The play of light on the bejewelled idol within the dark inner chamber of the grabha griha served to enhance the concept of the inner divinity sheathed within each individual. Symbolic offerings of the five elements of nature (also representing the five senses) are made to the idol: water, from which all life on earth is sustained; flowers, which carry the scent of growth and prosperity; fruit, the notion of fulfilment and reward for labour; incense, which fills the life-giving air with sweet fragrances; and the sound of pealing bells which awakens the gods and resounds through that common space in which we all coexist.

Each deity has a favourite flower and offering. The goddess in her more virile form loves the smell of blood and such sacrifices are still made in some temples of Nepal and India. Today, blood has been replaced by vermilion powder which is smeared on the forehead of the devotee to signify the power of the deity to reproduce and sustain life. Shiva loves offerings of milk and being bathed with water: such offerings are made in accordance with the norms and the needs of the devotee. After the prayers the brahmin will distribute *prasad*, which are the blessings from the deity in the form of vermilion powder (from the goddess) or ash from Shiva, along with other items like sweets or fruit which are returned to the devotee as a symbol of the abundant grace of the deity.

When blessings are received from the gods the devotee can make offerings either of a jewel or clothes for the deity to wear, or some service like singing or playing a musical instrument during festive occasions. In a temple that is still in worship you will see many such offerings being made: a person sitting in a corner singing for the gods, or rushing in on his way to office to garland the deity with an especially favoured flower wreath, or performing a number of elaborate rituals.

As the temple grew in popularity, so did the demands of the devotees and the deity. With donations new pavilions or *mandap*s were constructed, often open halls for special ceremonies and services. The *vahana* or animal vehicle of the deity was given pride of place in front of the shrine. Either perched on a column in front of the temples of the Kathmandu Valley or in a separate shrine, as was common practise in parts of south India. A tall lamp pillar was erected in front of the main doorway and lit on special occasions. The ancient temples of Orissa and southern India have a *nat* or dance mandap, a *bhoga* mandap and for distribution of food to devotees, a *kalyana* mandap to conduct the marriage ceremony of the gods and for other festivals for which the temple is famous. Smaller shrines were built within the compound for the other related deities. A Shiva temple would also have subsidiary shrines for his wife, Parvati, and his two sons Ganesh and Kartikkeya.

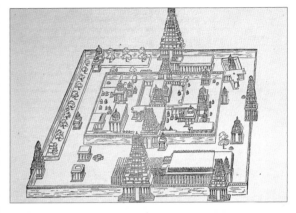

In southern India, by the thirteenth century the temple became the heart and nucleus of the city. Around the temple compound there was accommodation for the brahmins to live in, and a boundary wall demarcated the separation of the temple precinct from the world of commerce. The temple, drawing pilgrims from the countryside, soon became a commercial centre for produce that was brought from neighbouring villages. At temple cities like **Kanchipuram** and **Thanjavur** (Tamil Nadu,

India) everything is available along the temple boundary walls: cloth, utensils, flowers, and other offerings, food stalls; and soon potters and metal-workers set up their craft-shops to meet the requirements of the visiting pilgrim. **Thanjavur** (Tamil Nadu, India) is still famous for its handmade metalware, bronze cast idols for worship, and jewelled paintings on glass of deities that could be installed in the home. The temple city of **Kanchipuram** (Tamil Nadu, India) is best known for its silk and cotton handloom industry. The dividing line between commerce and worship vanished, a popular pilgrim centre and rural market place soon became one.

Drawing of a south Indian temple complex. (below) Temple complex.

The Jain Temple

Typically, a Jain temple follows the pattern of its Hindu counterpart. The principle deity is enshrined within the central garbha griha above which rises a shikhara. The halls in front of the grabha griha serve the ritual needs of the assembly of devotees. However, in the early stages of development, when monastic orders were formed in remote rock-cut shelters, they resembled contemporary Buddhist centres. Several Hindu kings converted to Jainism, and royal patrons and wealthy merchants were responsible for the development of monasteries and temples. Sites at **Udayagiri** and **Khandagiri** (first century BC, Orissa, India) and the older shelters at Lomas Rishi (Bihar, India) with rooms and halls for prayer have been carved out of the hillside in accordance with the ancient practices of rock-cut architecture while elaborate temples were built in other regions.

Jain temple complex, Rajasthan.

The holiest images in a Jain temple are the figures of the twenty-four **Tirthankara**s (makers of the 'crossing over' or tirth) which are placed in niches along the inner boundary wall of the temple or within the temple hall. In the popular belief of Jains and Buddhists, worldly wants and supplications are on a plane that neither the Buddha nor the Tirthankaras could sanction or approve of. So Hindu deities like Lakshmi, the goddess of wealth, found their way into the sculptural scheme of their temples. Devotees were advised to worship these Hindu deities when they required things that would sustain and perpetuate life on earth, while the Tirthankaras represent the ultimate goal of human beings: absolute release from the cycle of life and death.

Vardhamana Mahavir, a contemporary of the Buddha, is regarded as the last of the Tirthankaras that have so far descended to earth. **Parshvanatha** preceded him and the first of the Tirthankaras was **Adhinatha**. The story of Mahavir is exemplary of the main tenets of Jain philosophy. He, like the Buddha, grew up in a royal home but departed from his palace in search of truth. Renouncing worldly existence and becoming an ascetic or *vir* (hero) he achieved the greatest human victory (*mahavir*) which is the subjugation of desire and worldly pursuits. From the term *jina*, the victor, comes the word *Jaina* or *Jain*, meaning followers or sons of the victor.

In the early days Jain monks wore nothing, in accordance with their belief, but as time went on two branches of Jainas were formed. One, called **Svetambara** or the white clothed ones, wore pure white garments and the other, the **Digambara** sect, were clothed by the sky—wore nothing. Many of the Tirthankara images are therefore depicted nude or with a minimum of clothing. The great 17.7 metres stone image of **Gommateshvara** (**Shravanabelagola**, Karnataka, India) is depicted standing unadorned with clothing. It is said he stood so still in perfect meditation for a whole year that creepers clambered around over his body. The images of the Tirthankara are represented with no facial expression and have been criticised for their often dead-pan appearance. Yet this expression was an artistic rendering of the total equilibrium of the mind, free from the anger, greed, and desires that bind us to this earthly existence of suffering and pain.

A majority are traders and from their widespread popularity in the early centuries of the Christian era, the Jain community have been concentrated in port and trading centres of the subcontinent such as Bombay, Gujarat, Rajasthan, Orissa, and a few places in central and south India. Apart from temples, the Jain community adhering to the concept of **ahimsa** or non-violence, is well-known for its charitable work, and hospitals, ashrams, and shelters for the poor and sick are to be found all over India. In Delhi there is a Jain bird hospital that cares exclusively for wounded and helpless birds. The architecture of these semi-religious structures varies from region to region and they are functional rather than memorable works of art.

Image of Gommateshvara, Shravanabelagola.

It is the marble Jain temples of Rajasthan (**Ranakapur** and **Mount Abu**) that are truly remarkable and have no rival in the profusion of their rich sculptural ornamentation. Marble is such a pristine material that the temple interiors have a pure ascetic quality about them. At the same time the hard stone allowed for the most intricate workmanship. In these 1000 year old structures the ceilings, pillars, and walls are actually teeming with religious images and sculptural decorations, patterns, and figurines.

Inspirations from Islam

In the seventh century AD, from the centre of the ancient world, Islam spread with conquests along time-worn trade routes to Spain, Africa, Middle and Central Asia, China, and Java. In the subcontinent, trade and cultural contact with the Middle East had long been established and the new religion and way of life brought in demands for particular structures and buildings. While Islamic buildings throughout the world share a common philosophical heritage, within each country where Islamic influences were felt, a new style and form emerged. Islamic mosques in Spain, North Africa, Saudi Arabia, Iran, Pakistan, India and through to South East Asia are examples of a perfect synthesis with indigenous cultures. In Islamic art, the blend of mutual influences of both the newcomer and the native is far more pronounced than in the art of any other religion.

Masjid: a place of prayer

Central to Islamic belief is the concept of communal equality and community worship. There are three kinds of mosques or masjids which serve the need for prayer: **Id-gah** for mass congregation during Id and other religious festivals; the **Jumma** or **Jama** or **Jami** mosque for mass Friday (*jumma*) worship, and lastly for private prayer five times a day a small space, where the worshipper could kneel on a prayer rug

Nineteenth century rendition of Jama Masjid, Delhi.

facing Mecca and the Kaa'ba, the *axis mundi* of Islamic cosmology. To create a tranquil space for prayer, a mosque consists of an enclosed courtyard with the central area wide open for the devotees to assemble. One wall of the courtyard is aligned towards Mecca, the direction of prayer. This wall or *quibla* unadorned with images is given prominence by the construction of a niche called the *mirhab*, decorated usually with borders of Quranic verse. The open courtyard, in front of the quibla, has a tank or fountain for ritual washing of hands, feet, and face before

Calligraphy on Wazir Khan's Mosque, Lahore.

prayer. The quibla, over the centuries, attained greater distinction and grandeur with the addition of domes, pillared halls, and a splendid façade of arches. Communal worship in a mosque made the construction of *minar*s or minarets indispensable to the plan. The priest would ascend the stairs of the minar and his lilting voice announce the commencement of prayer to the world of roof-tops below. To provide symmetry to the mosque, one minar was replaced by two or even four minarets at the corners of the boundary wall of the mosque. The evolution of the minaret from the Middle East, Egypt and Iran, can be traced from simple square towers to elaborate circular, star-shaped, and many-sided ones. In Pakistan one finds minars clothed in colourful ceramic tiles; in India there are examples of those dressed in red sandstone and marble with intricate inlay-work.

Tombs for the Saint and Ruler

Within the category of religious architecture the tomb plays an important role in the Islamic way of life. Throughout the Islamic world the dead are buried in graves with a low tombstone aligned to Mecca to await Judgement Day. The tomb is raised above the ground and covered by the 'canopy of the sky'. Later, for tombs of important people, the metaphor of the 'canopy of the sky' was converted into huge masonry domes.

To visit a tomb of a saint or poet was to commune with their spirit of goodness and faith, and soon these tombs attracted thousands of pilgrims. To celebrate the life of a saint, an annual *urs* and other such religious festivals were organised and the vicinity of the tomb became a meeting ground for devotional music and poetry. Markets selling items for worship at the tomb and adjoining mosque, shelters for pilgrims from afar, and schools of learning, *madrassas* accompanied the development of these centres of pilgrimage. A *dargah*, an Islamic tomb complex, is not similar to a silent Christian graveyard but resounds with the bustle of pilgrims, the song of devotees, and call of the priest for *namaz*. The tomb of Khwaja Moin-ud-Din Chisti in Ajmer and of Hazrat Nizam-ud-Din in Delhi (India) are perhaps the most important pilgrimage centres in this region, and devotees from every part of the subcontinent are drawn to their doors.

Royal tombs in the subcontinent, from the twelfth century to those of the eighteenth, reveal a curious pattern of development and change from simple, square-domed structures to buildings of spectacular proportions. For royalty, the tomb was often conceived and built within their lifetimes as monuments to their lives and deeds, leaving no scope for misinterpretation by the next generation of rulers! The tomb, from its primary function as a resting place till Judgement Day, began to resemble paradise, the heavenly goal of the just and the faithful. Paradise in Islamic literature is described in poetic terms as a garden of exotic evergreen trees, flowers, and birds. A perennial stream flows past, enhancing the beauty of the heavenly garden and nourishing it with the water of life. The **Taj Mahal** (**Agra**, India) is a seventeenth century tomb of an earthly queen of Shah Jahan, the fifth Mughal emperor. The layout of the tomb is within a garden divided into square garden plots and fruit-trees intersected by water channels and beautiful fountains. The marble and inlay work decorations on the building are evocative of this poetic metaphor of paradise, and everywhere there are patterns of the tree of life, flowers, animals, birds and butterflies. Prayer carpets used in the mosque and palace also took over this symbolism of the Garden of Paradise, and layer upon layer of meaning was added to each artistic detail. The extensive integration of water in the plan of the tomb is a reminder of the promise of eternal rest, far from the turmoil and dust of earthly existence.

Painting of charbagh garden design, Akbar's tomb, Sikandra.

Ornamentation of religious buildings and tombs proved no difficulty in the subcontinent which was noted for its abundant supply and variety of materials. In the desert regions of its origin, where stone was not available, tombs were decorated with stucco, plaster-work, and coloured tiles. The art of making tiles of turquoise, midnight blue, leaf green, sunlight yellow, and brick red was perfected in this region. The tiles were cut to size and assembled to create intricate patterns, ranging from geometric designs of interwoven squares, stars, circles, and lines or stylised motifs of the evergreen cyprus tree, sweet-smelling flowers, and birds and butterflies. In **Wazir Khan's Mosque** (**Lahore**, Pakistan) one can see the finest examples of ceramic tile-work in the region. In India tile-work was gradually replaced by the use of coloured stones and precious gems. The transition can be witnessed in the sixteenth century tomb of Humayun, the second Mughal emperor (**Delhi**) where there is a combination of tile-and inlay-work in the internal and external decoration of the gateway and tomb building.

Fortified Palaces

Apart from the striking cities of the Harappan period, there are few examples of domestic and secular architecture in the subcontinent till the twelfth century. One of the greatest examples is the stately township of **Hampi** (Karnataka, India) with fortress

Tree of life motif: inlay from Agra and ceramic mosaic from Lahore.

walls, royal temples and palaces that belong to the Vijayanagar kingdom. Here one can see that majestic secular architecture often competed with religious structures in gracefulness of form and opulence of ornamentation.

In northern India and Pakistan, with the arrival of Islamic rulers from the eleventh and twelfth centuries, palatial structures were built for their residence and establishment of new courts. The fundamentals of the domestic architecture of this period lie in the clear demarcation of private and public areas. Private areas were placed at a distance from the entrance and public eye by the use of doorways, trellised windows, and screens of cloth and stone. The private room of audience, into which only family members and close relatives were allowed was called the *Diwan-e-Khas*, and there were other palace rooms for sleeping and entertainment, *hamam* for bathing, and kitchens and quarters for the servants. The hall of public audience, the *Diwan-e-Am*, was where kings and ambassadors bearing gifts and supplications assembled to meet the emperor. Ordinary citizens and lower-ranking officials rarely came before the emperor, except perhaps for judgement and execution!

Contemporary paintings reveal that the rooms of palaces had little furniture apart from carpets, bolsters, cushions, and screens. These could be rearranged at will, a style reminiscent of the tented life with which most of these dynasties were familiar. The Mughal emperors built their capitals at **Delhi**, **Agra** (India), and **Lahore** (Pakistan). These multiple capitals, strategically placed along rivers or trade routes and power centres, were not blessed with a climate conducive to living, and Babur, the founder of the Mughal empire, complained bitterly about the heat and dust of Hindustan. The palace buildings in these capitals needed to protect the royal occupants against the bitter cold winds of winter and the intemperate, intolerable heat of summer. While the royal inmates often escaped in summer to places like **Kashmir** and Kabul, the rooms of their palaces were cooled by large open doors, scented fountains, and water channels. The intense summer light was defused and scattered by the use of stone lattice screens called *jalis*. The sixteenth century palaces of the Mughals in **Lahore**, **Delhi**, **Agra**, and **Fatehpur Sikri** have beautiful jali windows that allow the breeze to waft into the rooms but pattern and tame the sunlight.

The forts of **Lahore**, Shekapura (Pakistan), **Delhi**, and **Agra** do not have many buildings within them, despite the number of people who lived within the fort walls. The Mughals, like their predecessors, were accustomed to an outdoor nomadic life in beautiful coloured, embroidered tents and appliquéd pavilions set up in the gardens where they could enjoy the cool perfumed evenings of summer and the warmth of a winter's day amidst the flowers and trees. The flowers planted in these palace gardens were those that held some romantic and symbolic value. Roses, irises, and the lovely narcissi that appear in Mughal paintings must definitely have thrived in the gardens amidst the water channels, fountains, and pavilions.

Beyond the fortified palace lay the homes of the nobility, the common folk, and the markets. The old cities of **Lahore** and **Delhi** still retain the flavour of an Arab *caravanserai* with special areas assigned to the sale of a particular commodity and specialised craft: like Chandni Chowk (in Delhi), the exclusive lane of silversmiths and jewellery shops.

A typical town of the medieval period would have had a dargah of a saint, a place of pilgrimage and worship like the mosque, royal palaces, water reservoirs, all enclosed by the fort walls. The markets and residential areas for the remaining population were protected by outer fortification walls.

All a Matter of Engineering

If an engineer was asked to define the difference between a Hindu structure and an Islamic one the answer would most surely be one of engineering principles used in construction. A Hindu temple is built on the beam and pillar principle, where the space between two pillars or two walls of a room are bridged by a single slab of stone or beam. The space between two pillar

Pillared-look of a Hindu Temple.

supports has to be relatively narrow or else the beam will break and collapse in the centre. It is therefore common to find in Hindu temples narrow doorways, low ceilings, and halls clustered with hundreds of pillars.

The hall or mandap of a thousand pillars in a southern Indian temple (**Chidambaram**, Tamil Nadu) is a good example of the concentrated 'pillared look' so prevalent in *trabeate* (pillar and beam) architecture. The roof above the pillars is flat and a shikhara was constructed by placing levels of pillars and beams one upon the other until the required height was reached. The staggered horizontal, pyramidal and conical shikharas of the temples were constructed in this manner, with each level carefully balanced and joined to the next like a pack of cards. Hindu architecture also discouraged the use of cement and mortar, so joints and brackets, the balance and placement of the stone blocks was an integral part of the design.

Concurrent with the introduction of Islam in the Indian subcontinent, building technology incorporated the use of the arch. This engineering principle employed the use of wooden scaffolding so that the bridge between two pillars or walls can be made of small blocks of stone placed in an arc and held together by cement and mortar. The span of the doorway and window was no longer restricted by the size of the beam, and huge wide openings were now possible. The roof of the building

Arch and squinch principle.

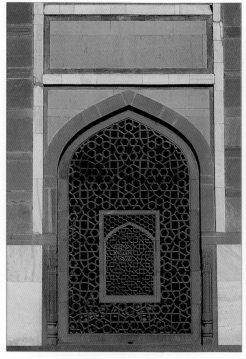

could also be framed by a series of arches to form a dome over the room below. To convert a square room into a circular base for a round dome required the use of squinches. These were decorated or plain and cut the corners of the rooms, converting a four-sided room into an eight-sided, then a sixteen, thirty-two, and finally sixty-four cornered form. This sixty-four sided base, virtually a circle, formed the platform from which sprang the grand arches of the dome. To provide additional height to the dome, in order to create a dramatic exterior, the dome was often raised on a high platform or drum above the wall of the room. An interior false dome ceiling was made to compensate for the excessive height of the exterior. The wide open doorways and the bulbous onion-shaped roof made buildings built on this architectural principle completely unlike those that employed the beam and pillar principle.

Artisans who had worked for generations with the pillar, bracket, and the beam were at first hesitant to use the arch. In the first Islamic structure in India, the **Quwwat-ul-Islam Masjid** in **Delhi**, the local artisans have often provided additional support with brackets, beams, and in some cases, filled in the area of the arch! With experience the arches and domes in the subcontinent lost their hesitant form and a new confidence appears in lofty arches spanning wide areas undisturbed by pillars and posts, and soon the rooms were filled with airy spaces and muted

Combination of arch and trabeate principles.

light. During the sixteenth century, under Mughal rule, successful experiments in combining the pillar and beam with the arch were made. The fort of **Agra** and **Fatehpur Sikri**, built by Emperor Akbar, the third great Mughal ruler, are perfect examples of how the pillar and flat roof was made to blend in design with the arch and the dome, an exemplary marriage of Hindu and Islamic styles. The **Diwan-e-Am**, **Red Fort**, **Delhi** is a flat-roofed building with pillars and an assembly of beautiful cusped arches, adorned on all four corners with small domed kiosks. This elegant blend was termed Indo-Islamic architecture, where fusion of Hindu and Islamic motifs and engineering designs came to rest in perfect harmony.

What followed was a period of great amalgamation of styles. In the seventeenth and eighteenth centuries the palaces of Rajasthan presented a curious blend of Islamic ideals and traditional Hindu architectural practices. With the foundation of the Sikh faith, a philosophical blend of the core of Hindu beliefs and Islamic principles of equality, their religious buildings (*gurudwara*), also took on an eclectic form.

Colonial Rule

It was during the period of Mughal rule in northern India and several centuries earlier in southern India that western traders, merchants, and ambassadors visited the subcontinent to try to establish trade contacts. When permission was accorded to foreign investors to trade they acquired, or were granted, areas to set up their trading posts and warehouses. The Portuguese in Goa and Kerala, the French in the southern states, and the British in Bombay, Surat, and Madras set up their trading centres and factories. The architecture of this phase was commercial, functional, and unostentatious. The early structures in **Madras** and **Calcutta** were confined within fort walls segregating the 'natives' from the foreigners.

After the rebellion of 1857, when British interests in India were no longer merely commercial but imperial, the style of architecture changed significantly. Madras, Bombay, and Calcutta developed their own style of architecture over the years. Handsome forts, imposing administrative buildings, government houses, post offices, and courts were built carrying a certain stately grandeur about them. British architects who came to India to work sought to establish the imperial impression through the use of neo-classical architecture derived from Imperial Rome and Greece.

Residential homes in India and the greater subcontinent, as in Burma, had to be built to suit the climate and began with the introduction of traditional techniques for cooling and comfort, like verandahs and high ceilings. Gardens with flowers—

hollyhock, geraniums, sweet peas, carnations, a variety of roses—were all brought out from Europe to transform the Indian environment. The introduction of ideas from abroad also had their impact on local architecture. Eighteenth century palaces of Rajasthan and Mysore, for example, bear testimony to this two way movement of ideas. Churches were no longer modest structures and competed in magnificence with the religious edifices of the subcontinent.

At this time the changes in modes of transportation necessitated the construction of broad city roads and railway stations. The railway system was crucial to the administration of the Raj, moving troops and commercial goods. Railway stations were constructed with care and invested with stylistic elegance, and small Indian towns were gifted with charming imitation European railway stations.

Finally, in 1911 **Delhi**—not Calcutta, the London of the East, nor Bombay, the commercial heart of the empire—was chosen as the capital of the British empire in India. The architecture of New Delhi is dissimilar to that of any other major British–Indian cities and far less beautiful. In the Imperial capital a style emerged that attempted to blend components of Indian architecture (like the Islamic arch) with the grand imperial orders of Rome and Greece, and at the same time took inspiration from the great administrative and palatial buildings of Europe. It was a cocktail that few purists relished.

Victoria Memorial Hall, Calcutta.

Today a city like Delhi, Madras, or Lahore incorporates the old and the new: splendid monuments of the Raj with contemporary monstrosities. In the post-Independence era colonial architecture and foreign ideals continued to permeate the subcontinent. It is only in recent years that creative architects, drawing inspiration from the indigenous tradition have evolved new forms of self-expression in monumental architecture.

Alchi

In the high cold desert region of Ladakh, enveloped in the western Himalaya with its severe climate and barren topography, stands one of the world's most beautiful Buddhist monuments. The exuberant painted shrines at Alchi, some of which date back to the late eleventh century, are considered by scholars to be the rarest and most extensive examples of Buddhist art in Kashmir. This region was once vital for trade and cultural contact, and when Islamic armies entered the subcontinent it was Buddhist monuments and idols that they first encountered. Islam disallows idol worship and their word for idol was in fact derived from the term, Buddha. It was therefore Buddhist monuments and monasteries in this region that suffered most under the hand of iconolasm. Alchi, set amidst the barren gorges of the Indus river and desolate mountains, escaped destruction and some of the 900-year old paintings and murals are so well preserved and luminous that they appear to have been painted just yesterday.

The **Choskor** (religious enclave) at Alchi consists of five temples with *chorten*s (votive stupas) and residential complexes for the monks. Central to this complex is the **Du-khang**, or temple, that enshrines Mahayana images. Beside it to the east is **Sum-tsek**, unsurpassed for the glory of its sculptures, paintings, and unique architectural features. Further east is **Lha-khang Soma** and to the north-west of the Du-khang are the shrines **Lotsawa Lha-khang** and **Manjushri Lha-khang**.

Du-khang

According to inscriptional information, **Du-khang** is the earliest temple at Alchi, founded by the Kal-dan Shes-rab of Tibetan descent around the eleventh century AD. Entrance to the temple is through a courtyard and an elaborately carved doorway with panels of tiny Bodhisattvas and guardian figures. Within the temple is a niche housing a plaster image of Vairochana, the Resplendent Buddha. The walls are adorned with *mandala*s and sacred forms that illustrate the structure of Buddhist Cosmology, levels of heavenly existence and manifestations of Buddhahood. A mandala is an aid to prayer, its geometric shape is a visualisation of the universe and an art unique to the region. On the south wall above the doorway is a magnificent depiction of Mahakala, Great time, Timelessness, Deathlessness, or Eternity, surrounded by attendant figures, animals and sacred symbols.

(opposite) : General view of Alchi.

Sum-tsek

This is a triple-storeyed temple with a carved wooden façade consisting of pillars, carved brackets, and capitals. Every feature of the construction, whether it is the beam or the bracket, is incorporated in the design of the temple. Form and function are clothed in artistic detail. This tradition of painting, carving beams, pillars and other architectural members of a building, is still prevalent in the hill states of the Himalayan region.

The three-storeyed temple has an open shaft through the centre of each floor to allow light to penetrate from the roof down to each level. The walls of the halls are covered with mandalas in vibrant colours, a kaleidoscope of blues, reds, and whites. Most noteworthy are the double-height niches on three sides which house large (four metre high) standing figures of Bodhisattvas, whose legs and torsos are visible from the ground floor while their heads extend to the ceiling of the first floor. These gigantic figures represent the Bodhisattvas, important in Mahayana Dhayani Buddhism. It is these Bodhisattvas who, out of compassion for human beings, have not taken their final liberation or nirvana in order to lead everyone on earth to the path of eternal salvation. In the eastern niche is the figure of **Manjushri**, the embodiment of wisdom, whose garments are painted with images of the 84 Masters of the Tantra. The figure in the western niche is **Avalokiteshvara** who is, in some ways, the personification of the greatest Mahayana ideals. He is depicted adorned with brightly painted headgear and costume. On his robes is a sacred map of shrines and sites of Buddhist pilgrimage and faith, as if to personify in his person the path of wisdom.

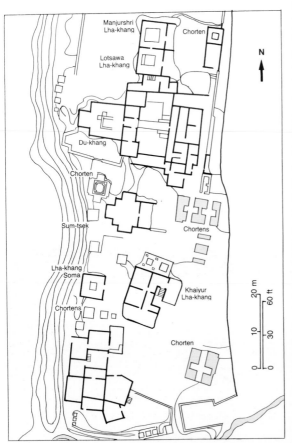

Plan of Alchi.

In the northern niche is **Maitreya**, the Buddha of the age yet to come. In Mahayana art, the Thousand Buddhas represents the popular theme of the Buddhas that came or will come down to earth in each age or period. Gautam Buddha is the historical Buddha of our age and the Maitreya Buddha represents the

Buddha who is yet to come. In Sum-tsek, the image of Maitreya is decorated with round frames, each containing stories from the life of the last historical Buddha.

Lotsawa Lha-khang and Manjushri Lha-khang

These are two small adjoining shrines that share a similar plan. The square shrine has four central columns that hold up the raised roof. Within the shrine of Manjushri are four large plaster images of the Bodhisattva, of no great antiquity. The murals of the temple follow the theme of the Thousand Buddhas, while goddesses and guardians dominate the wall space.

The Lotsawa Lha-khang is one of the few temples found dedicated to Rinchen Zang-po, the venerated teacher and renowned translator of Buddhist lore.

Lha-khang Soma

This structure is of a later date than the other shrines at Alchi. Within the small square room is a chorten or votive stupa. Columns that support the roof have wonderful carved brackets with lion faces. On the western wall of the shrine are three large painted mandalas, on the northern is the image of Vairochana, and on the eastern the image of the Buddha surrounded by Bodhisattvas and guardian figures. The doorway is decorated and protected as usual with the image of Mahakala.

Shrine and mural, Alchi.

WHAT'S IN THE NEIGHBOURHOOD

Ladakh has several spectacular monasteries that seem to grow out of the rugged escarpments and mountain ridges. Monasteries at Shey, Thikse, and Hemis are close to Leh and have an abundant wealth of Buddhist images, murals, and carvings. There is a small museum at Stok.

HOW TO GET THERE

Leh is the capital of Ladakh, tucked away in the Himalaya at 3,440 metres, nestling in the valley of the Indus river along an ancient trade route. Flights from Delhi operate throughout the year. From Srinagar, via Chandigarh and Jammu, flights are available during the season. Leh has hotels that meet the needs of budget travellers of all kinds. From Leh a half hour road ride brings you to Alchi. The 434 kilometre road journey from Srinagar to Leh takes two days and the 477 kilometre journey from Manali in Himachal Pradesh takes three. Both journeys are only possible in the short summer spell when the passes are clear of snow.

The winter cold prevents easy access to Leh. The best period is from May to September. A visit to Alchi in June, to coincide with the three-day Hemis festival, provides a spectacle of Ladakhi culture and living traditions.

Srinagar

Jahangir, the fourth Mughal emperor, wrote of Kashmir as 'a garden of eternal spring, an iron fort to a palace of kings—a delightful flower-bed, and a heart-expanding hermitage for the mendicant'[3]. In some ways Srinagar was the loveliest part of the Mughal empire. Cherished for its location amidst the Himalayan mountains where beautiful wild flowers grow, where the streams are always bubbling with crystal clear water, and the gentle breeze is scented with the aroma of mountain herbs. Akbar brought this region into his empire in 1586 and he, his sons, and grandsons spent time and money in building gardens and palaces to enhance the natural splendour of the valley.

Srinagar is today the summer capital of the state of Jammu and Kashmir and lies 1730 metres above sea level in the centre of the Kashmir valley. The name Srinagar implies a city (*nagar*) marked by distinctive beauty and dignity, abundance, and affluence (*Shri*). The city is situated amidst a ring of mountains, with three lakes, the **Dal, Sona,** and the **Nagin**, and the river Jhelum gently meanders through it on its course to the wide plains below the valley. It is not one monument or building but the natural location of the city and the distinctive quality of the architecture that claims the attention and admiration of visitor and tourist.

It is the natural beauty of the valley, the lakes with its houseboats and floating flower gardens, the formal yet exquisitely laid-out formal Mughal gardens, the ancient buildings and quaint wooden architecture of Kashmir, that capture the romance of Srinagar.

The city has grown around the three lakes which lie in the central basin of the valley. To the north and north-east of the lakes are the Mughal gardens, **Nazim, Shalimar,** and **Nishat**. To the west of the lakes is the **Hariparbat Hill** on which Akbar built a splendid fort that overlooks the entire city. On the eastern side of the Dal lake is the Shankaracharya Hill atop which stands one of the most ancient temples of Srinagar. Due east is another popular garden called **Chashma-i-Shahi** and the Pari Mahal with its commanding location. South-east (five kilometres) of the town is **Pandrethan** where a lovely Shiva temple still stands. To the south-west of the lakes, amidst the old city, is the magnificent old **Jami Masjid** and the **Patthar Masjid** (literally the stone mosque).

Shankaracharya Temple

This is perhaps the oldest known site in Srinagar and a motorable road up to its summit provides a captivating view of the city below with its maze of streets, peaked roof-tops, and shimmering lakes. On top of the hill is a small Hindu temple associated with Shankaracharya, a ninth century philosopher who is said to have travelled from Kerala to Kashmir holding discourses and discussions along the way to revitalise Hindu philosophy. Even today his commentaries and discourses are an invaluable means of understanding the abstract and intricate beauty of Hindu thought. Excavations at this site have suggested that there may have been a Buddhist monument here erected during the third century BC in the reign of Emperor Ashoka.

Hariparbat

On the opposite side, between Srinagar city and Nagin lake, is a low hill held sacred by the goddess Durga with the Chakradhara temple on the north-western side which has a mosque that replaced the original structure on one side. Crowning the hill is the Hariparbat Fort built between 1592 and 1598. The outer walls and gateways, though much restored, bear evidence that the Mughal emperor Akbar also contributed to the construction of this fort situated at this dramatic vantage point overlooking the lovely city of Srinagar. In accordance with the style of the day, the fort once contained many palace buildings, ceremonial halls, apartments for royalty, quarters for servants, but nothing of this Mughal past remains today.

Hariparbat, Srinagar.

On the southern side of the fort is the **Shrine of Makhdum Sahib** and a relatively new mosque. The shrine draws hundreds of pilgrims as it is reputed for its healing powers. Below it is the **Mosque of Akhund Mulla Shah** built by Shah Jahan's favourite son Dara Shikoh. Like his great grandfather, the Mughal emperor Akbar, Dara Shikoh delighted in the study of religions and sacred texts of the ancient world. Unfortunately he was executed in 1659 by his brother Aurangzeb who succeeded Shah Jahan to the throne, so little of Dara Shikoh's architectural heritage remains today. When Mohammed Dara Shikoh returned from Hijra (in 1640) he went to Kashmir and met Mulla Shah whom he called 'the most perfect of the perfect, the flower of the gnostics, the tutor of tutors, a sage amongst sages'. Dara Shikoh held several discourses with this great Sufi teacher in his quest to find a unifying philosophy that would bind all the religions of the world together. The mosque built by Dara Shikoh is dedicated to Mulla Shah and is a unique structure built in stone rather than in wood. The grey limestone mosque stands in a quiet garden surrounded by a stone wall.

At the foot of the Hariparbat hill stands the **Gurudwara** of Guru Hargobind Singh, the sixth guru of the Sikhs. The shrine commemorates the visit of the sixth Guru to Kashmir during the reign of the Mughal Emperor, Aurangzeb.

Jama Masjid

A ten minute walk from the shrine of Makhdum Sahib is the great Friday mosque called Jama Masjid or Jami Masjid. The peaceful inner courtyard of the mosque is entered through arched openings at the centre of each side of the rectangular enclosure wall. The arched doorway is crowned not by the usual domed roof so characteristic of Islamic architecture, but with tall pyramid-shaped pagoda-type towers that dominate the landscape of Srinagar. The sloping roof of the enclosure is held up by over 370 pillars, each one an entire tree-trunk of deodar (a distinctive, local, evergreen tree).

The mosque was originally built at the end of the fourteenth century but suffered great damage after fires in 1479 and 1674.

Jama Masjid, Srinagar.

In 1841, in the reign of Maharaja Sher Singh, it was rebuilt and enlarged to its present proportions and remains one of the best examples of the cross-cultural fertilisation of the architecture of Kashmir.

Shah Hamadan Mosque to the south is another fine example of the wooden architecture of Kashmir. Though it was built in the fourteenth century it has also been renovated several times. The elegant so-called **Patthar Masjid** across the river is a stone mosque built in 1623 by the empress Nur Jahan, the legendary beauty and wife of the fourth Mughal Emperor, Jahangir.

Royal gardens

Srinagar was developed by the Mughal rulers as a retreat from their capitals— **Agra**, **Delhi**, and **Lahore**. When the heat of the plains became intolerable they found cool comfort in the garden palaces of Kashmir. **Nazim Bagh**, the Garden of the Morning Breeze, was the earliest garden

built by the Mughals. It was constructed to the west of the Dal lake by emperor Akbar, but unfortunately very little of it remains. **Nishat Bagh**, the Garden of Happiness, was built during the reign of Jahangir. Situated to the north-east of the Dal lake it affords a spectacular view of the hills and the water. The **Chashma-i-Shahi**, the Royal Spring, is an exquisite garden designed around a natural spring. It was built for the Mughal Emperor Shah Jahan by his provincial governor.

    Shalimar Bagh, situated on the north-eastern end of the Dal lake, is perhaps the most beautiful of all the Mughal gardens of the Indian subcontinent. The garden was constructed by Nur Jahan, wife of Jahangir, though renovated and supplemented by subsequent rulers. The plan of the garden is based on the Persian *charbagh* design in which a square garden is divided into four equal parts by water channels laid out to form a cross. The garden were constructed at three levels. The lowest was a public garden with a pavilion, the Diwan-e-Am, with a black marble throne where the emperor is said to have sat in public audience. The middle level was the Emperor's garden, and above it is the *zenana* garden for the private pleasure of the ladies of the harem. From this exalted place they enjoyed the best view of the location. At the centre of the cross-shaped water channel of the zenana is the Black pavilion added by Shah Jahan in 1630. It is a beautiful, curious hybrid structure with a three-tiered sloping roof that conforms to indigenous wooden architecture, with stone pillars and carved brackets comparable to the ones seen in the Mughal forts of Agra and Delhi. The water channels were once filled with fragrant water which cascaded down from one garden level to the next. Oil lamps were placed in the *chini-kana*s (trellised pigeon-holes), and as water flowed over them a fairy light effect of shimmering cascades was created. The gardens were once adorned with trees and plants that the Mughals and their wives adored. There was an assortment of evergreen trees and blossoming fruit trees: the stately chinar or oriental plane tree, the straight and regal cypress, fruit trees like the apple and plum which brought forth bouquets of lovely bright blossoms in spring. The blend of seasonal (temporal) and evergreen (constant) trees was symbolic and aesthetically pleasing.

    Among the favourite spring flowers were the iris, narcissi, and bright torches of tulips, while the summer brought cascades of sweet-smelling jasmine and roses, brilliant sprays of peonies and delphiniums. Between May and October a *son et lumiere* is held at Shalimar Bagh in the evenings to capture the fairyland effect of this lovely garden palace of the Mughal princes.

WHAT'S IN THE NEIGHBOURHOOD

A stroll through the old city of Srinagar can be an interesting experience, for the Kashmiri is also a talented artist and salesman. There are woollen and silk carpets that echo the carpets of old, embroidered clothes and *firen*s (the baggy over-shirt worn over even baggier trousers by men and women), and brightly painted objects made out of papier mâché. The **Shri Pratap Singh Museum** near Raj Bagh has an interesting collection of stone sculptures from Hindu temples of the region, samples of handicrafts and textiles, especially some exquisite shawls. There are some archaeological objects from places like **Burzahom** (16 kilometres from Srinagar) where a neolithic site dating back to 2400 BC was recently unearthed. At **Pandrethan**, a twelfth century Shiva temple has been constructed at the centre of a spring tank. This temple made of limestone has a delightful sloping Kashmiri roof, gabled porches, and classical columns. Of the ancient Buddhist and Hindu architectural heritage of Kashmir little remains except for two superb examples at **Avantipur** (28 kilometres from Srinagar) and the ancient **Sun Temple of Martand** at Matan (101 kilometres from Srinagar). These are classic eighth–ninth century examples of local stone architecture reflecting influences from Gandharan art and indigenous wooden prototypes. The ruins of the Martand temple are located in a beautiful setting against the backdrop of the hills on a high plateau overlooking the plains. Though ruined, the massive proportion of the temple with colonnades and sculptured details is very impressive. Conforming to the wooden model, the temple has steep sloping roofs as a precaution against heavy snowfall. The Martand temple is unique in form other notable examples of the Sun Temple are those of **Konarak** (Orissa) and **Modhera** (Gujarat).

Sun Temple, Martand.

HOW TO GET THERE

Srinagar is linked by road and air from Delhi and Jammu. The nearest railhead is 283 kilometres to the south. Srinagar is well-equipped for the traveller with an assortment of hotels, though many people would prefer to experiment with a stay in the well-furnished house-boats on the Dal and Nagin lakes.

In Srinagar summertime begins with the festival of Baisakhi (13-14 April). Visits to the resort of Gulmarg, camping and trekking are very popular during this time of year. Entry to Ladakh is also possible by road during the summer months when the roads are open.

Golden Temple

The Golden Temple at Amritsar is perhaps one of the most serene religious buildings in the world. As a building it blends fundamental concepts of the faith with architectural excellence. All along the enclosure of the Temple there are shops and rest-houses to meet the needs of pilgrims. The small winding roads are crammed with wares that spill out of the shops, making it difficult to move. The massive walls enclosing the Temple block out this hustle and bustle of the city and protect the sanctity of the quiet area of peace and tranquillity within. A tall clock tower and four large gateways facing the four cardinal directions mark the entrance to the Temple, and these doors are open to members of all religions, faiths, and walks of life, echoing the poetry of the Jaap Sahib prayer[2]:

> *Des aur na bhes jakar, rup rekh na rag*
> *Jattra tattra disa visa, hue phaileo anurag.*

> The Almighty has no country, no traditional costume, no mark, no form and favours no one in particular.
> The Almighty is present in every place, on every side and in every corner; this universal Love exists everywhere.

Once inside the Golden temple complex the space is dominated by the white marble walls of the enclosure wall and the broad pavement that frames a tank. The floor of the pavement is patterned with marble inlay in a variety of designs. Pilgrims enter the complex and wash their feet and do a clockwise *parikrama* (a processional walk around the tank). There are many small shrines and sacred spots where the pilgrims break their processional walk to stop and pay their respect to martyrs and great teachers. In the middle of the tank is the spectacular vision of the Golden temple, like a jewelled casket floating in tranquil waters. The tank is called *amrit* (the waters of immortality) *sarovar* (pool). Those who drink of the philosophy of the faith are promised immortal life, a promise held by the water of the tank and temple that it holds up in the centre like a tiny jewel. Throughout the day people from all walks of life come to the temple and bathe in the tank, and symbolically drink of its waters, while others take a holy dip as part of a spiritual baptismal ritual. Amritsar, the name of the city in the state of Punjab (India) also derives its name from this sacred tank of *amrit* and immortality of the Golden Temple.

(opposite) : The Golden Temple, Amritsar.

The amrit pool is 150 metres square and on the western side a long marble causeway leads pilgrims across the water into the **Harmandir Sahib**. The temple stands on a (52 metre) square platform. It rises three storeys high. The first floor is covered with white marble decorated with sculpted panels, and the next two levels are covered with plates of gilded copper. Entry to the temple is from one doorway, which regulates the immense surge of pilgrims into this holy site. Within, on the ground floor, is the sanctum, an open space with richly painted walls. Above is the Shish Mahal, the hall of mirrors with gold and coloured painted panels. The roof of the shrine consists of a low gilded dome with kiosks and parapets surmounted by miniature domes.

Absorbed in the serenity of the site, it is hard to believe the history of violence and bloodshed that is associated with this beautiful and holy temple. Tradition has it that the site where the temple stands today was an ancient retreat where the heroes of the Hindu epic poem the Ramayana once visited. The pool of amrit is famed for its healing powers and miraculous restoration of health and vitality.

The foundation of the Golden Temple was laid during the period of the fifth Guru Arjan Dev (1581-1606). The shrine became one of paramount importance to the Sikh community for several reasons, not least because it houses the original Guru Granth Sahib, the holy book compiled by the fifth Guru. The

Worship of the Guru Granth Sahib.

Guru Granth contains over 7000 hymns composed by five gurus and saints of different religions and castes inspired by the principal tenets of the faith.

Each day at dawn the sacred book is ceremoniously carried in a golden palanquin and installed in the sanctum of the Golden Temple. There is no image within the shrine, for the centre of all worship is the holy book placed under a gem-studded canopy. Throughout the day passages are recited as pilgrims file past, bow and pay their respects to the word of the gurus. It was the Guru Granth Sahib that was declared the Guru Eternal after the last mortal guru.

It is said that the Mughal emperor Akbar visited the site and was greatly impressed by the *langar*: the practice of feeding people of all castes and walks of life from a common kitchen in a community feeding area. (A direct protest at that time against the awful Hindu caste system that prohibits such communal eating.) Even today the community kitchen has hundreds of volunteers who work each day preparing and feeding everyone who visits the temple complex.

Soon afterwards, politics entered the temple precincts as Mughal rulers like Jahangir began to feel threatened by the power inherent in the popularity of the Sikh faith. One story tells of how the emperor's son had been given refuge here. The fifth Guru Arjan Dev, the founder of this temple, was then tortured and put to death in 1606. The next Guru Hari Gobind built the **Akal Takhat**, the seat of temporal and civil justice within the premises of the temple. An elected committee was established which exercised authority over all religious and political matters that related to the Sikh community. In 1761, Ahmad Shah Durrani from Afganistan sacked the city of Amritsar and razed the temple to the ground. The temple was rebuilt by community effort but continued to attract the wrath of the Mughal rulers and several massacres took place when the faithful defended it. During the reign of Maharaja Ranjit Singh (1799-1838), who established a principal-

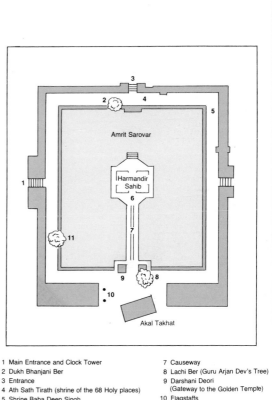

1 Main Entrance and Clock Tower
2 Dukh Bhanjani Ber
3 Entrance
4 Ath Sath Tirath (shrine of the 68 Holy places)
5 Shrine Baba Deep Singh
6 Entrances to the Golden Temple
7 Causeway
8 Lachi Ber (Guru Arjan Dev's Tree)
9 Darshani Deori
  (Gateway to the Golden Temple)
10 Flagstaffs
11 Ber Baba Buddha (Three Shrine)

Plan of the Golden Temple complex.

ity independent of the enfeebled Mughal rulers of the time, the temple was renovated and the Akal Takhat was given four new storeys. Donations to the temple included sheets of gilded copper to adorn the upper storeys of the temple. When these shimmering golden sheets were added to the walls and dome of the shrine, it was then that the temple came to be known as **Swaran Mandir** or the Golden Temple.

During the period of British rule the temple fell into the hands of corrupt management and it was only after 1925 that a reform movement from within the community restored the temple to its rightful status, and the community gathered together to offer their services to clean and maintain it. *Kar sewa* or voluntary labour has become an honoured code amongst the Sikhs, when rich and poor alike volunteer to take up the brush and broom to serve the temple. In recent years a group of terrorists occupied the temple and the sacred building was stormed by the Indian army on orders from the government headed by Mrs Indira Gandhi. This Operation Blue Star wounded the sentiment of the Sikh community and once again the Golden Temple was heroically repaired by the kar sewa of the faithful.

WHAT'S IN THE NEIGHBOURHOOD

Inlay detail, the Golden Temple.

The city of Amritsar is crowded and congested, with some remnants of colonial architecture—Khalsa College, the railway station, and a few churches. There are several memorials of historical significance such as the **Saragarhi Memorial** that commemorates the brave Sikh soldiers who died defending Saragarhi Fort on the North-West Frontier in 1897.

Jallianwalla Bagh is a memorial to the abominable massacre of innocent people on 13 April 1919 at the command of General Dyer of the British army. It was the eve of Baisakhi, a grand festival of rejoicing to celebrate the harvest and the coming of summer. Thousands had gathered together on that day, though the state was under martial law. General Dyer signalled to disperse the crowd and as the shooting began the crowds scattered. Thousands of people, women and children, confined within a relatively small enclosure unable to escape, died in the cross-fire.

Ranjit Singh (1799-1838), who donated much to the Golden Temple during his rule, also built the **Rambagh Public Garden** in Amritsar. The garden was garnished with fountains and ornamental flower-beds. He also completed the **Govindgarh Fort** (to the south-west of Amritsar).

HOW TO GET THERE

Amritsar, in the Punjab, is well linked by air, road, and rail to Delhi. There is a daily train from Amritsar to Lahore (Pakistan). The city is not particularly attractive and is quite congested in parts. Amritsar has ample accommodation and tourist facilities to meet the needs of travellers with all kinds of budgets. Cars and taxis, rickshaws and buses are available for travel in the city.

The best time to visit the Golden Temple is in winter, preferably at dawn when the temple is peaceful. One can sit and listen to the soothing recitation of the Gurbani, and watch the devotees offer their devotional service. The most important festivals which attract crowds of pilgrims to the Golden Temple are Baisakhi, the spring festival held on 13 and 14 April; Guru Nanak's birth anniversary which falls on the full moon night of *Kartik Purnima* between the months of October and November. The Hindu festival of Divali, the festival of lights and fireworks in celebration of the triumph of good over evil, is a holiday throughout India (between the months October and November), is a heady time at Amritsar. For the festival the Golden Temple is bedecked with thousands of tiny lamps and fairy-light.

Painted ceiling, Golden Temple.

Delhi

Dihli, Dilli, Dhillika, Dhilli, and now Delhi are some of the names of this historic city, the capital of the Indian Republic. There are many stories about this fabulous city whose origins are traced back to mythological times, and Indraprastha, the capital the heroes of the Mahabharata epic built beside the sacred Yamuna (Jamuna) river. The river flows down from the northern Himalaya towards the south, and the city, or several (seven it is believed) cities that flourished here, were all situated on the west bank. The river at that time was an essential route for transport, a prerequisite for trade. The territory of Delhi nestles between the river and the ridge of the Aravalli hill range on the western side. While the hills and the river afforded protection, the hills also dominated a major ford and crossroad of communication over much of northern India. When Delhi was first inhabited it was predominately in the south where the early cities were built. In the seventeenth century, when the great Red Fort of Shah Jahan was built, it was located further north of the older habitations and modern Delhi, encompassing both the old and the new.

Excavations in the area of Purana Qila, below the sixteenth century fortifications, revealed pottery and artifacts dating to *c.* 1000 BC. To say that this city was inhabited for more than 3000 years would have been achievement enough but in 1992 archaeologists were investigating the possibility of a stone age culture which suggests that human occupation in the vicinity has lasted for more than 15,000 years. Recorded history and inscriptions (of the third century BC) indicate that the region of Delhi was part of the Mauryan empire of emperor Ashok. Delhi was then occupied by successive Hindu rulers, the last of whom were the Chauhans at Qila Rai Pithora. The remains of buildings and temples were used to construct the **Quwwat-ul-Islam** mosque, the first important Islamic structure in India.

Qutub area

Delhi became the capital of the first Islamic dynasty when Mohammed Ghori (who was responsible for several raids and looting expeditions in the region from his principality of Herat in Afghanistan) appointed Qutub-ud-Din as his viceroy, in 1193. Having secured his territory Qutub-ud-Din set about constructing a mosque in Delhi appropriately called 'the might of Islam', **Quwwat-ul-Islam**. The mosque follows the traditional

(opposite) : Iron pillar, Qutub Area, Delhi.

design evolved in Central Asia with an enclosure wall and entrance gateway with the *mirhab* and striking archways marking the western side. There are several features of this mosque that distinguish it from all later buildings. The new conquerors had first to rely on local craftsmen. With their previous experience of Hindu architecture the artisans introduced elements of decoration that paved the way for the synthesis of both cultures in the very first building of its kind on Indian soil. The very concept of the arch was a novelty but the indigenous artists hid their inexperience and created corbelled arches that looked more or less like the real thing. Obviously built in a hurry, the colonnade around the mosque was composed of pillars taken from broken temples, set often one on top of the other, to arrive at the required height. The famous Hindu **Iron pillar** (7.20 metres of pure rust-resistant iron) dated to the fourth century AD proved such a curiosity and technical masterpiece that the early Islamic rulers installed it in the courtyard of the mosque.

A gigantic 72.5 metres free-standing minar was raised to the south-east of the mosque, obstensibly to call people to prayer and to serve as a mighty tower of victory for all to see. The **Qutub Minar** is perhaps the most beautifully conceived building in this complex. Its great height and the simplistic design of a three (later five)-storeyed tower would have been quite monotonous if the architect had not used an ingenious idea of creating each storey with a different plan. The first floor has pointed and circular flutings, those of the next are round, and of the third star-shaped. Each level is separated by ornate projecting balconies with honeycomb-like supporting brackets and the entire tower, except the additional top two levels, is sheathed in warm red sandstone.

Qutub-ud-Din died in a polo (*chaughan*) accident and was buried in **Lahore** (Pakistan) but his building projects were completed by his son-in-law and successor Shams-ud-Din Iltutmish. The mosque was doubled in size with the addition of

Historical cities of Delhi.

screens and archways with exquisite calligraphy and geometric decoration. A tomb of modest proportions with elaborate stone carving on every inch of the wall surface (perhaps once tiled or coloured with stucco work) was built for Iltutmish on the north-west extension of the Qutub mosque.

Following a line of weak successors, Delhi was conquered by the Khalji tribe in 1290. Ala-ud-Din Khalji introduced architectural developments in the Qutub complex. In 1311, he ordered the construction of the **Ala-i-Darwaza**, an ornamental gateway to the mosque with true arches framed with fringes of lotus buds and many toned decorative panels of inlaid marble and sandstone. Ala-ud-Din Khalji also had visions of grandeur and had planned to build a second minar that would have been twice the height of the Qutub Minar. The unfinished 24.5 metres stump of **Alai Minar** still stands at the north-eastern corner of the complex near the present entrance. Behind the mosque on the south-western side are the remains of a madrassa or college with rows of (now ruined) arched alcoves and rooms, and a plain tomb with no distinguishing accents that are attributed to Ala-ud-Din Khalji.

Drawing of Ghiyas-ud-Din Tughluq's Tomb.

Tughluqabad

A grand fortified capital was built by the Tughluq ruler, Ghiyas-ud-Din, who overthrew Ala-ud-Din's son and captured the throne of Delhi. The fort, built between 1321-5, is situated to the south-east of the present city of Delhi. The fort's massive protective walls and bastions (15-30 metres high, built of enormous blocks of stone, the wall in places 10 metres thick) are perched on a natural rocky outcrop on the south side that once overlooked a large lake. It is a wonderful place to have a picnic and one can wander through the ruined palace rooms, the citadel, the tunnels, and clamber along the ancient fort walls.

On the south side is a causeway that takes you across the (now) dry bed of the lake to the perfect little tomb of the founder of the Tughluq dynasty. **Ghiyas-ud-Din Tughluq's Tomb**, designed by the ruler himself, is enclosed in a private courtyard with fortified walls. It is square in plan but the walls lean inwards to uphold a great marble dome. The simplicity of the lines and the tomb's robust, august presence served to inspire the architecture of the future. The tomb contains three graves: the largest is Ghiyas-ud-Din's, the other is said to be of his wife, and the third of his son and successor, Muhammed bin Tughluq. One story describes how Muhammed bin Tughluq killed his father by building a false, capsizeable wooden balcony on the fort. The murderous son then ascended the throne of Delhi and built an adjoining fort called Adilabad on the neighbouring southern hill and the fourth city of Delhi called Jahanapanah, of which little survives. After conquering part of the Deccan he moved his capital with all its citizens to his new capital at Daulatabad over 1000 kilometres to the south. When this hair-brained plan failed he marched his people back again to Delhi, with unimaginable loss of human life and suffering.

Hauz Khas

One of the most elegant structures with minimal ornamentation is **Hauz Khas**. A complex surrounding a water reservoir constructed by Ala-ud-Din, lined on one side by a triple-storeyed building with arched corridors and quiet corners that was once a madrassa for religious education. The simple but majestic **Tomb of Firoz Shah Tughluq** is a special monument for a great ruler of Delhi who in his time (1351-88) carefully repaired and preserved many older buildings of his capital. The tomb can be entered from the south side through a magnificent gateway or through a concealed secret entrance from the main building. Thus hidden from one side it loses its resemblance to Ghiyas-ud-Din's Tomb in Tughluqabad. This complex deserves a visit on a winter evening to enjoy the skyline of the madrassa and the surrounding gardens. The area is now being encroached upon by the Haus Khas village where boutiques and ethnic shops have colonised and cannibalised what was once a simple old Delhi village. The site is on the Delhi Mehrauli road that leads to the Qutub area and nearby are the remains of **Siri Fort**, the second medieval city of Delhi constructed around 1303 by Ala-ud-Din Khalji. Apart from extending the Tughluq empire, Firoz Shah built in Delhi the fifth fortified city called Firuzabad or **Firoz Shah Kotla** where he installed an inscribed Ashokan pillar (third century BC) as a curiosity. The pillar can still be seen protruding like a flag-pole above the fort, from the Ring road on the way to the Red Fort.

After the death of Firoz Shah Tughluq the dynasty began to wane and was succeeded by the Sayyids and the Lodis. It was a period of great unrest and no palaces were built in Delhi, only tombs for the kings. The most significant ones are now enclosed in the **Lodi Gardens,** one of the most beautiful and once well kept greenhouses of Delhi. It is a pleasant walk (and jogger's paradise) through the undulating lawns amidst the bamboo, palm groves, and flower-beds which are visited by some of Delhi's rarest birds. The Lodi tombs are significant for the art historian tracing the evolution of tomb structures in India. They are elegantly proportioned square or octagonal structures built out of severe grey granite, embellished with touches of brilliant tile-work and coloured sandstone. The **Bara-Gumbad Mosque** (1484) and **Sikandar Lodi's Tomb** (1489-1517) are significant landmarks of the evolution of architecture in this period.

Purana Qila

For almost two hundred years the armies of the Mongols plundered the territories of north-western India. Finally, factions within the Lahore Lodi house invited the Timurid prince Babur to defeat Ibrahim Lodi of Delhi. In 1526, Mughal rule was established in India after a series of battles. Babur died in Agra in 1530, having consolidated a small empire and constructed a few buildings and gardens in the vicinity of Delhi and Agra. His royal diaries claim that he was tired of the heat and dust of the plains of Hindustan and yearned for his home in Ferghana and Samarkand. He was finally laid to rest in Kabul. Babur's son Humayun began by building a new fort in Delhi on the banks of the Yamuna near **Nizam-ud-Din's Tomb**, one of city's holiest pilgrim centres. Within a short period Humayun was driven out of India by the ambitious zeal of Sher Shah Suri, an Afghan chieftain in the service of the sultans of eastern India. Sher Shah ruled Delhi for

Lodi Gardens. Below: Qal'a-i-Kuhna Masjid, Purana Qila.

fourteen years and completed what is now called Purana Qila, the old fort. The fort is constructed on a historical mound that covers the remains of several centuries of habitation, the earliest dating to 1000 BC. There are three grand gateways to this massive fort (perimeter of 3 kilometres) and, like Tughluqabad, it is a monument of bold design, sturdy, straightforward, and every inch a fortress unlike the manicured, carefully dressed, and ornate palatial forts of the later Mughals. Within the fort are two buildings constructed by Sher Shah, the **Qal'a-i-Kuhna Masjid** which is a superb spartan building with sparse, sophisticated ornamentation in sandstone and a little marble. To the south of the masjid is an octagonal two-storeyed building called **Sher Mandal**, Sher Shah's pavilion with tile and inlay work on red sandstone. The exiled Humayun took refuge with his young son Akbar (born in 1542) and wife in the Persian court. His host helped him reconquer his kingdom. In 1556, barely six months after returning to Delhi and re-establishing himself in this fort, Humayun died. He is said to have heard the call of the priest for daily prayer and slipped while hurriedly descending the stairs of the Sher Mandal, which he used as a library.

Humayun's Tomb

Humayun left the Mughal throne to his son Akbar who was just fourteen years old, but proved himself over a reign of fifty years by conquering vast territories of northern India and Pakistan. Humayun's senior wife Bega Begum began the construction of a permanent and monumental tomb for her husband some years after his death. This fabulous tomb stands south of Purana Qila within a walled enclosure (east of Mathura Road).

The tomb is set in the centre of a charbagh garden plan which is divided into smaller geometric sections by a network of water channels and fountains. The tomb rises out of a high platform of arches and is approached by some very steep stairs. On top of the platform, the sense of space is breathtaking and the colossal size of the octagonal tomb defuses into details of inlay and the

Humayun's Tomb, Delhi and Taj Mahal, Agra.

playful dance of light on the faceted body of the building. Within the tomb are chambers that occupy the angles of the octagonal structure while the central hall contains the (false) tomb of the emperor Humayun laid to rest beneath a lofty, heavenly, bulbous dome. Carved lattice stone windows placed in all directions and on all three floors allows light to stream into the central hall throughout the day. This tomb is the model on which the famous **Taj Mahal** of **Agra** was built three generations later. But Humayun's tomb is in many ways more exciting than the Taj. It is bold and unpretentious, smartly dressed in greys, reds, and whites. There is a mature air of experimentation and discovery about it, and though there are some minor faults and warts these just add to the charm of this tomb, and are absent in the flawless construction of the Taj Mahal.

Humayun's tomb is usually a quiet place in which to reflect and wander, and its stoic silence records in many ways the beginning and the end of the Mughal empire. The building evokes many memories of Humayun who never really enjoyed Delhi, and all the others buried in the premises: Bega Begum his courageous widow, Hamida Begum who gave birth to the royal son Akbar while they were in exile, Dara Shikoh, the beloved son and heir apparent of Shah Jahan who was brutally beheaded by his own brother Aurangzeb. Finally, the last Mughal emperor Bahadur Shah II who was captured and dethroned here at Humayun's Tomb while Delhi was drenched in blood after Indian soldiers rose in mutiny against the British in 1857.

Red Fort with marble palaces, Delhi.

Red Fort

Akbar, busy with expansion of his territories, preferred to live in Agra and Lahore while his son Jahangir loved the beautiful hills of Kashmir. Shah Jahan (1628-58), Akbar's grandson, decided to move his capital to Delhi in 1638, and once again a new fortified royal city was designed. This time the ruler chose a site further north of Purana Qila, though still on the west bank of the river Yamuna, and called it **Shahjahanabad**. It was quite clearly his city. This huge fortified area with a perimeter of 2.41 kilometres has a moat around it that was once connected to the river. Beyond the walls of the fort on the west side is the sprawling maze of old Delhi, residential quarters, congested bazaars with lanes specialising in particular goods like jewellery and clothing, recalling the days of the caravan and market serais which served and supported the grand style of the Mughals and their courtiers.

One enters the fort, affectionately called the **Red Fort** (Lal Qila), through the Lahori Gate which forms part of the massive stone fortification covered completely in a veneer of dressed dull pink sandstone. On 15 August, India's Independence Day, the Prime Minister addresses the nation from the ramparts of the Red Fort. Behind it is an arcade of shops which leads to an open quadrangle where once visiting royalty dismounted from their elephants and horses. The Naubat Khana, where you buy your entrance ticket, was the drum house where musicians played and announced the ceremonial arrival of dignitaries. Only the rich and famous were allowed into the courtyard of the **Diwan-e-Am**, the hall of public audience. It was in this flat-roofed hall with several rows of splendid cusped arches that the emperor sat, at the appointed time, on a lavish throne set within an inlaid and painted alcove built into the back wall of the hall. Below the throne stands a platform where the announcer read out the gifts given by each visitor, their titles, and purpose. The emperor would then view his gifts of horses, elephants, rare gems, and jewels and decide whether he wished to meet the visitor. All along the hall the attendants stood according to rank and file, for Mughal paintings rarely portray the presence of the poor and the hungry in the emperor's durbar.

N

Hayat-Bakhshi Bagh

Moti Masjid
Hammams

Lahori Gate

Diwan-e-Khas

Khas Mahal

Naubat Khana
Diwan-e-Am

Rang Mahal

Mumtaz Mahal

0   100   200   300 m
0   400   800 ft.

Delhi Gate

© The Guidebook Company Ltd

Plan of Red Fort, Delhi.

With the Diwan-e-Am as a screen are the private quarters and gardens of the king and his family. At the southern end is **Mumtaz Mahal**, now converted into a little museum. To the north is the **Rang Mahal** which, as the name suggests, is a palace of colours, with rooms connected by archways, trellisses, channels and fountains that brought cool fragrant water murmuring gently through the building. One of the favourite buildings of Mughal India was the **Shish** (mirror) **Mahal** (palace). An apartment with ceilings and walls studded with tiny mirrors embedded in them which reflect the light of lamps and candles, creating the perfect atmosphere for the emperor to relax and entertain his special friends.

The **Khas Mahal** and the **Diwan-e-Khas** beside it are halls of splendid cusped arches set in white marble and inlay-work, and it is here that the emperor met his close relatives and family. The apartments also had windows that looked out on to the river-front (though in the interven-

Translucent marble screen and decorated door, Red Fort, Delhi.

ing period the river has moved far away), catching the river breeze and enabling the emperor to look out at his citizens below and the boats that sailed down to Agra, where the emperor Shah Jahan's wife lay buried in the Taj Mahal. The painted, decorated ceiling, screens made of single slabs of marble cut and carved to look like lace, are the only remainders of the original splendour. These rooms were once filled with plush carpets, luxuriant cushions, silver and jade objects and ornaments, curtains of the finest fabrics. The rooms were filled with music, the gentle recitation of the Quran, and the lounging figures of royalty dressed in their silks and priceless jewels.

Beside the private palace are the **Hammam**s, lavish bathing rooms with marble floors, walls, and sunken tubs inlaid with precious gems. To the west of the Hammams and aligned to face Mecca is the little **Moti Masjid** built by Aurangzeb for the emperor's private use. You have to remove or cover your shoes both because it is a sacred place and to protect the inlaid floor. The miniature masjid has a tiny pool for ritual cleansing, and an arched façade with small onion-shaped domes clothed in pure white marble. The air of simplicity is deceptive: it is truly an emperor's gem. A spectacular public **Jama Masjid** was built outside the fort and remains one

of the most elegant mosques in India, perfectly proportioned with touches of restrained decoration.

Beyond the mosque is the best part of the palace, the formal garden called **Hayat-Bakhshi Bagh**, the 'life-bestowing' garden, which give you some idea of how the emperors and their beautiful wives really lived. The Mughal garden is divided by channels and the water was disciplined so as to flow over carved stone that created uniform ripples and a steady babbling sound. The water cascaded in front of pigeon-holed screens filled with

lamps so that on summer evenings, when the emperor sat in his marble garden pavilion listening to music and poetry, he could see the effervescent water sparkling in the gentle moonlight.

Much of the open, spatial attractiveness of the Red Fort has been marred by British army barracks and administrative buildings, but it is still a splendid monument. Perhaps it is a little effete in places, designed as if war and death were a thing of the past.

But war and the hunger for wealth and power never seem to end. At the beginning of this century Delhi, the favoured capital of so many rulers, was chosen once again to be the imperial capital of the British Raj. The foundation stone was laid at the royal durbar in 1911 by King George and Queen Mary. Colonial architecture in the early cities of Madras, Bombay, and Calcutta were elegant and modest structures, capturing a nostalgic fragrance of Britain. The site selected for the new imperial capital

Rastrapathi Bhavan, New Delhi.

was a hill called Raisina that rose at some distance away from the river and directly west of the Purana Qila. The entire modern capital was designed on a complex geometric grid with squares and circles radiating from the central axis of **Raj Path** (the King's Way). The chief architects were Sir Edwin Lutyens and Sir Herbert Baker. Their concept of an imperial building for the Viceroy's residence (now **Rastrapathi Bhavan** or the President's house), the processional King's Way (now Raj Path), and the stately colonnade and buildings of the north and south blocks

(Government administrative buildings) were all conceived in a composite style with features of Indian architecture mixed with imperial traditions from Greek, Roman, and European cultures. Along with these stately monuments came the laying of roads and residential areas, commercial centres like Connaught Place, and parks and churches. Today Delhi's master plan incorporates the old and the new, the ugly and the beautiful, the palaces and the slums, and contemporary architects appear to have learnt nothing from their glorious architectural past.

WHAT'S IN THE NEIGHBOURHOOD

Most people use Delhi as a base from which to visit Agra and Jaipur, the golden tourist triangle. It is a convenient base to branch out to the other cities of northern India, the forts of Rajasthan, or the temple cities of Khajuraho and Varanasi.

HOW TO GET THERE

There is an international and domestic airport. Trains branch out from Delhi to almost every city in India. Cars, taxis, and three-wheeler transport is available on hire. There is a wide range of hotels and guest-houses in New Delhi. North India can be excessively hot in summer so the best time to visit is in winter between October and March.

Red sandstone detail from Qutub Area and Red Fort, Delhi.

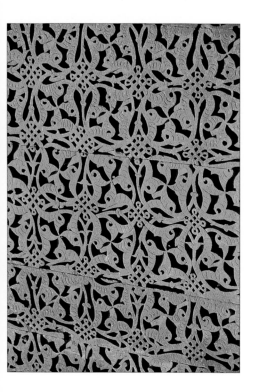

Agra

Delhi, Agra, and Lahore are bound together by centuries of history, but of the three, Agra is undoubtedly the ugliest modern city with the most sensational buildings. Agra lies downstream from Delhi (204 kilometres by road) on a sweeping curve of the Yamuna river and, like Delhi, the fort and the old city were built on the west bank of the river.

Agra Fort

According to legend Agra is very ancient site. In the 1500s Sikandar Lodi, the Delhi Sultan, established a fort of which nothing remains. This Lodi ruler died in Agra in 1517 and was buried in Delhi, in an area called **Lodi Gardens**. It was his son Ibrahim Lodi whose defeat at the hands of Babur led to the beginning of Mughal rule in 1526 and the glorious rise of Agra as a favoured city. Sikandar Lodi built a small fort at Agra and some buildings situated 9 kilometres away (on the Mathura Road, north-west of Agra) at **Sikandra,** which was named after him. It is here that the third Mughal emperor, Akbar, was buried in a spectacular tomb. When Akbar came to rule he was just 14 years old, but at the age of 23 (1565) he launched his first major architectural venture by knocking down the Lodi fort and beginning the construction of Akbarabad Fort in Agra. The fort has an irregular triangular shape with a perimeter of 2.5 kilometres. Its longest side is placed parallel to the river to afford all the major palace rooms a magnificent view of the bend of the river, the great expanse of water and the gentle sunrise.

The fort walls are made of roughly hewn blocks of stone and rubble masked completely with slabs of carefully cut pale pink sandstone. The continuous fort wall is punctuated with bastions and monumental gateways: Amar Singh Gate, Delhi Gate to the west, and the Water Gate on the riverside (now closed) which enabled the royals to alight from their boats on the Yamuna. The Amar Singh Gate has a passageway of many parts and a clever line of defence. The gateway leads to the line of palace rooms and halls set behind massive protective walls.

The **Jahangiri Mahal** was built in 1570 by Akbar and is one of the few structures in the fort (apart from the fort walls) that survives from his reign and was not reconstructed nor clothed in marble by his grandson Shah Jahan. It is a stately building with rows of ornate pillars with elaborate hanging brackets set around an open courtyard. The predominance of columns and

(opposite) : Taj Mahal, Agra.

flat roofs is regarded by many scholars as yet another testimony to Akbar's eclectic taste: his preference for Hindu architectural schemes, his many Hindu wives, his desire to establish a world religion, Din-i-Ilahi. Yet this palace of Akbar is more indicative of the fashion of the times exemplified in the forts of **Gwalior**, **Orchha** (Madhya Pradesh), and Rajasthan. It is reminiscent of an older tradition that had been mastered by indigenous artisans and which found experimental perfection in the fortified palace of **Fatehpur Sikri** that Akbar constructed in the 1570s.

North of the Jahangiri Mahal is an open courtyard and the formal garden called **Anguri Bagh** (the Grape Garden) designed like a jigsaw puzzle with interlocking bordered flower-beds. Perhaps flowers in each segment were colour coordinated to create the intricate designs of a persian carpet. Behind Anguri Bagh, on the river front, is one of the loveliest enclosed complexes of the fort called **Khas Mahal**, constructed by Shah Jahan in 1636. The middle area has a marble courtyard, a rectangular pool with frilled edges, and a fountain. The building behind it, as in the Delhi fort, is a flat-roofed pavilion with many rows of cusped arches and lattice marble screens that look out on to the river. On either side of this pavilion are smaller enclosed courtyards named after the emperor's daughters. These elegant pavilions built in marble have roofs that are covered with copper tiles and are referred to as the golden pavilions. The cen-

Plan of Red Fort, Agra.

1 Jama Masjid	6 Royal Hammams	10 Macchi Bhavan
2 Amar Singh Gate	and Shish Mahal	11 Nagina Masjid
3 Jahangiri Mahal	7 Mussaman Burj	12 Diwan-e-Am
4 Khas Mahal	8 Mina Masjid	13 Delhi Gate
5 Anguri Bagh	9 Diwan-e-Khas	14 Hathi Pol
		15 Meena Bazaar
		16 Moti Masjid

© The Guidebook Company Ltd

tral one is larger with a quaint curved ceiling; the design is said to have been derived from the thatched bamboo huts of Bengal. The graceful curved roof motif was reproduced in stone and became a popular feature in later Mughal and Rajasthan palaces after eastern India was conquered by Akbar in 1574-6.

The **Shish Mahal** lies on the north-east corner of the Anguri Bagh and is a palace apartment decorated with small mirrors embedded in the walls and roof. A quiet area, that would glow when lamps were lit, like the night sky with a million twinkling stars. Beyond, in the same corner, is **Mussaman Burj** (the octagonal tower) also called Samman Burj or Jessamine Burj, the jasmine tower. The protruding octagonal bastion of the fort afforded a lovely uninterrupted view of the river and allowed gentle breeze to waft through the marble screens. Utilising this ideal location, the rooms have been decorated with fine stonework and inlaid designs, niches for lamps and books, and quiet alcoves. In 1658, Shah Jahan was deposed by his youngest son Aurangzeb and, to add a touch of tragedy to this romantic setting, it is said that here he spent his last seven ailing years until his death in 1666 under the care of his daughter Jahanara. It was here that Shah Jahan, the once great emperor, used to sit and gaze at the Taj Mahal, the monument he erected in memory of his beloved wife Mumtaz Mahal. From the fort there is a commanding view of the Taj Mahal further downstream.

From the Burj, a few steps northward lead to the **Diwan-e-Khas**, the hall of private audience, which was completed by Shah Jahan in 1637. Like the palace apartments in the Delhi fort, these structures carry the stamp of his evolved and mature style, a trademark partiality for expensive marble veneers. In front of the Diwan-e-Khas is a large courtyard which (presumably) once had a fish pond as it is called **Macchi Bhavan** or fish building. To the north-west of the Bhavan is a tiny mosque specifically designed by Shah Jahan for the royal women of the

Mussaman Burj,
Red Fort, Agra.

fort and is called **Nagina Masjid**, the gem mosque. There are two other mosques in this fort, one called **Mina Masjid**, for the private use of the emperor (near the Mussaman Burj) and the **Moti Masjid**, the pearl mosque (north of the apartments) which is a grand architectural accomplishment with an arched mirhab and domes that can be seen rising above the enclosed courtyard. A large congregational Friday mosque, **Jama Masjid**, stands outside the fort walls and was built by Shah Jahan's eldest and favourite daughter Jahanara.

In front of the Macchi Bhavan, on the western side approached by a staircase, is the hall of public audience, the **Diwan-e-Am**. Here Shah Jahan is said to have sat on his famous peacock throne supported by pillars embedded with emeralds, and figures of peacocks studded with the rarest and finest gems (which was stolen by Nadir Shah in the eighteenth century and what remains of the throne is now in Iran).

Similar to the one in the Delhi Red fort, the Diwan-e-Am is a hall of rows of cusped arches. From whichever angle you look at the wavy arches, they seem to replicate themselves, their branches echoing the exuberance of their form.

Itimad-ud-Daulah's Tomb

This is one of the most attractive structures in Agra, built across the Yamuna river, and is approached by road over a crowded bridge. The tomb, set within a garden, resembles a jewel box and is completely dressed in marble and intricate inlaid stonework. The history of the man who is buried here is as romantic as the tomb. Mirza Ghiyas-ud-Din or Ghiyas Beg (later to be called Itimad-ud-Daulah) was a poor merchant in Persia who travelled to India in search of work. On the way his wife gave birth to a baby girl. Since they had nothing to eat the desperate parents decided to abandon the new-born child. Her wails carried by the desert air forced the parents to return and pick her up. The fortunes of Ghiyas Beg seemed to have turned with the arrival of this little girl, for soon he found a caravan which brought him to the court of emperor Akbar. Ghiyas Beg quickly rose to become Akbar's trusted Treasurer and Minister, and later served in the court of Jahangir and was honoured with the title of Itimad-ud-Daulah, the Pillar of the State.

His lucky daughter was called Mehr-un-Nissa, the sun of womankind. She grew to be a fabled beauty but became a young widow when her husband died (or was murdered) in Bengal. She returned to the court of Jahangir where her father was employed. The young amorous Emperor Jahangir saw her, fell in love, and eventually married her. She came to be called Nur-Mahal, the light of the palace, and Nur Jahan, light of the world. Nur Jahan, whose fate prevented her from being abandoned in the desert, became one of the most powerful personalities in Jahangir's court. It was she who had this lovely tomb built in Agra for her father Itimad-ud-Daulah (who died in 1622) and later constructed her husband's tomb (in much the same style) in **Lahore**. Nur Jahan had a brother whose daughter was given in marriage to Jahangir's son and heir to be, Shah Jahan. It was for her, Mumtaz Mahal, the chosen one of the palace, that Shah Jahan built the tomb called the Taj Mahal.

Itimad-ud-Daulah, the poor Persian merchant, father and grandfather of two of the greatest Mughal queens, was buried in this tranquil little enclosed garden set against the open skyline beside the river, an idea that was used later in the Taj Mahal. The tomb stands on a low platform and is rectangular, with four minars or domed towers growing out of its four corners. The roof is flat and at the centre is a small roofed pavilion (a sort of single-storey version of Akbar's Tomb in **Sikandra**). What makes this building so special and a landmark in Mughal architecture is that it is completely encased in white marble and inlaid with precious gems, with some of the most intricate and beautiful marble screen-work—an undeniable forerunner to the design of the Taj Mahal. The marble casing was a magnificent departure from previous tomb structures: **Humayun's Tomb** in **Delhi** is dressed in pink sandstone with highlights in coloured marble, which replaced an even older tradition. In Pakistan and Persia the practice was to cover brick and stone structure with mosaics of coloured tiles. There is a ruined tomb of Afzal Khan, a Minister of Shah Jahan (just 800 metres from Itimad-ud-Daulah's Tomb in Agra), referred to as **Chini-ka-Rauza**, the tomb with china tiles. Here too, following the Persian tradition, brilliantly coloured tiles of blues, yellows, and greens were cut and assembled to create wonderful geometric designs and patterns over the surface of the walls. The pietra dura, stone-inlay work in the tomb of Itimad-ud-Daulah is the best of its kind, created in hues of warm reds and browns and soft greens and greys (with agates, jasper, and other semi-precious stones) embedded in a white marble surface. The entire wall has been divided into sections and decorated with bold geometric, arabesque patterns, floral motifs and still life scenes. The gentle play of colours and forms is most intriguing.

Itimad-ud-Daulah's Tomb, Agra.

Taj Mahal

Nothing, neither photographs nor descriptions, can prepare you for the experience of this monument, the tomb of Mumtaz Mahal, where the cherished companion of Emperor Shah Jahan was laid to rest. It is an acclaimed architectural masterpiece and every individual sees in it many and often different wonders. The tomb building stands with one side to the Yamuna river, against a curtain of sky that changes from blues to oranges and midnight black. A walled enclosure of red sandstone protects the tomb, and while emperors used the northern river-front entrance when sailing in from the fort, at the other end of the garden is a mighty red gateway that leads into the tomb complex from the south. This gateway is an accomplishment in itself, in red sandstone with flamboyant inlaid patterns. It has a huge recessed arched doorway which screens the view. On entrance it frames the tomb within like a gem.

The garden is enormous (300 metres in width) and was once filled with fruit and flowering trees, and shrubs. It is designed in the charbagh pattern and the large garden is cut into four smaller segments by water channels. Down the centre is a water channel which reflects the perfect symmetry of the Taj Mahal. At the centre of the garden complex (where the tomb could have been placed) is a raised platform with a fountain. At the northern end of the garden, the tomb stands between two similar looking smaller sandstone structures. The one to the west is the mosque attached to the tomb and the other was built for purposes of balance and visual harmony.

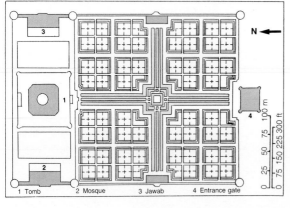

1 Tomb   2 Mosque   3 Jawab   4 Entrance gate

Nineteenth century engraving of the Taj Mahal.

Below: Plan of Taj Mahal, Agra.

As one walks towards the northern end of the garden along the central path, the tomb building grows bigger with every advancing step. The Taj Mahal is truly a colossal structure, over 73 metres high, and it is as wide as it is high; taller than the Qutub Minar and Humayun's Tomb in Delhi. Yet, despite its obvious height and size, the Taj Mahal looks like a white weightless cloud rising out of the earth. More so because the entire building is clothed with a veneer of fine quality marble from Makrana in

Rajasthan, chosen specifically for the manner in which it reflects light. At sunrise or sunset the cool white marble captures the red glow of the sun, and turns from pinks to fiery orange; in the day the marble is a shimmering cold white and at night the building appears luminous, glowing in the darkness.

From afar one is struck only by the harmonious plan of the tomb and one is quite oblivious of the detailed inlay work and decorative yet restrained splendour of the monument. The tomb is raised above ground level by a high platform with arches along the sides with no other apparent purpose than to create a sense of drama; four tall minars sprout from its four corners. A concealed staircase leads up to an unimaginably wide open platform, where the perspective of the building is completely lost and attention is drawn to the carvings and decorations of the outer walls. Walking in the shadow of the Taj Mahal one feels dwarfed by the sheer size of structure, the magnificent stone decoration, and the riverside view.

Royal Tombs, Taj Mahal, Agra.

Looking from the platform back on to the garden one can see a magnificent display of geometric designs in the layout of the complex, mosaic patterns on the footpaths.

The building has eight sides, an unusual octagonal with four broad sides alternating with four narrower corner ones. The major arched doorways, facing the cardinal directions, are flanked by slim walls divided into two storeys with two arched windows that together match the size of the central opening. All the doorways and lattice windows are bordered by rectangular frames decorated with inlaid calligraphic designs and patterns in subtle colours and hues. Each design was corrected to prevent any visual distortion that might occur at such great heights and distances. The faceted walls of the building avert the monotony of a square structure and create a play of light and shadows, hence its semblance to a jewel. The massive walls of the tomb hold aloft a huge dome supported on a tall neck, which is surrounded by domed kiosks. The base of the dome has a necklace of inlay, while its bulbous form is pristine and unadorned, just outlined by the sky. As the dome narrows to its peak it is crowned by an upturned carved marble lotus and a long pole with brass finials, shaped like the pot or kalash of a Hindu temple. The tomb is made up of proportionate parts and relative ratios in which the height of the building is also its breadth, the sum of two arches making up the size of a large one.

The Taj Mahal, is a tomb, a temporary resting place awaitng the great Day of Judgment. As a tomb building it evokes a sense of peaceful equilibrium which has been achieved by the pure geometry of the structure.

The main archway on the south side leads into the tomb chamber, a sensational white hall, lit up by diffused daylight that filters in through lattice windows. Above the hall is the exalted dome that creates a sense of hallowed space. The dome is not the one seen from the outside, for that would have been too high, but is a false ceiling proportionality adjusted to the dimensions of the hall. The ceiling was acoustically designed so that when professional readers of the Quran sat and chanted the sacred verses their voices rose, spiralled up the dome, and came echoing back again like the chorus of a million angels of paradise. The walls of both storeys are lavishly ornamented with decorated panels. Marble flowers emerging out of marble backgrounds, petals fluttering in the breeze, and young flowers molested by bees and butterflies. Tiny buds beside flowers in full bloom and fading blossoms, reminding us of the theme of the tomb, that even the fairest rose must die. These walls with their silent message look towards the centre of the hall and the exquisite screen that encloses the tomb of Mumtaz Mahal. The screen is made up of single marble slabs, each one so delicately carved that they no longer look like stone but fine lace held together by marble frames exquisitely designed with borders of flowers. Within is the false tomb of Mumtaz Mahal, for the real tomb is below in a secret, protected chamber. The tomb of the great empress stands in the centre, and on one side is that of her husband Shah Jahan. The tomb of the emperor and empress have the finest examples of inlay work anywhere in the monument. The theme of the tomb decoration is the flower, the symbol of hope in the garden of Paradise. One inlaid flower, though less than an inch long, may be composed of over sixty individually cut gems, that follow the turn and twist of each delicate petal, the stamen, and the leaves.

Shah Jahan married Mumtaz Mahal in 1612 and ascended to the throne of the great Mughal empire in 1628. Unfortunately Mumtaz Mahal died soon after, in 1631 in childbirth, having borne him thirteen children. It is said that she was his constant companion, accompanying the emperor on all his journeys. Shah Jahan died in 1666 and was buried beside his beloved wife in the Taj Mahal, perhaps unable to build a tomb of his own. Some say he was keen to build a replica of the Taj Mahal on the opposite side of the river and dress it in black marble. Perhaps it was a question of time and expense, for Mumtaz Mahal died in 1631 and the construction of the Taj Mahal took more than twenty years to complete; by 1658 Aurangzeb had overthrown his father, claimed the throne, and imprisoned the frail, ailing Shah Jahan in the fort at Agra.

It had taken years to design and construct the Taj Mahal and the garden that surrounds it. Hundreds of thousands of workers, craftsmen, and artists worked to create this memorial legacy. Precious stones were brought from India and abroad, and the rest were gifts from neighbouring rulers. The rich pure quality of marble used to face the entire Taj Mahal was brought from Makrana in Rajasthan.

Some implicate foreign artists for the design and plan, but seen in the context of the monuments in Delhi and Agra there is no doubt that the Taj Mahal is the direct descendent of a rich artistic tradition sustained by the Mughal emperors, derived from the ethos in which they lived and died.

For those long years Mumtaz Mahal lay in a temporary grave. Contemporary accounts relate that the installation of the body of the empress and the annual death anniversary were celebrated with great pomp, witnessed by the royal family in private. The doors of the Taj Mahal were not opened to outsiders as they are now, much less for the commoner, until the British period several hundred years later. It is our privilege to share the beauty of the Taj; this monumental tomb for an empress is now the heritage of the world and needs to be preserved.

Map of Agra.

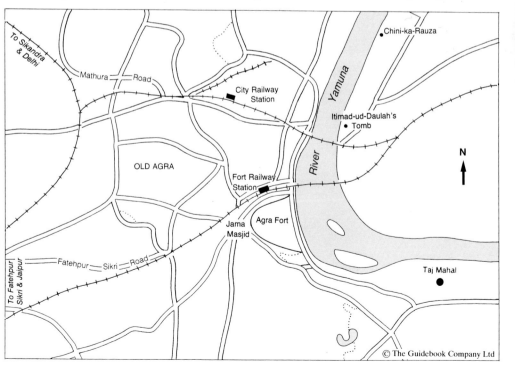

© The Guidebook Company Ltd

A trip to Agra should be planned for at least two full days to see the monuments, the museum, the tomb of Akbar in **Sikandra**, to do a little shopping or take in the atmosphere, and to visit the deserted royal palace of **Fatehpur Sikri** 37 kilometres away.

Sikandra

From Agra (eight kilometres on the road to Mathura and Delhi) is Sikandra, a small town named after the Lodi king of derivative name who ruled between 1489 and 1517. There are a few monuments of this period but the town is famed because it was here that the Mughal Emperor Akbar was buried. It is a very special mausoleum, not only because it commemorates a great emperor but for its unusual style and form. Akbar died in 1605, and according to legend, had not constructed his tomb during his lifetime though he had approved of a plan. Work on the tomb started the year of his death and his son Jahangir, the reigning emperor, saw to its completion, though he was not over-pleased with its rather unconventional design. The tomb at Sikandra carries the characteristic flavour of those airy tiered pavilions of Akbar's fort and Fatehpur Sikri.

The tomb is entered through an elegant southern gateway which leads into a huge enclosed garden. At the centre of the formal garden stands the tomb, a predominately bright red

Akbar's Tomb, Sikandra.

tiered structure, stacked like a castle of playing cards. A complete departure from domed square and octagonal single unit structures of previous Islamic rulers, the building has five levels. The first is a podium of arches. In the centre of each face is a high inlaid *iwan* or framed doorway. The next three levels are in red sandstone and have no arches but the flat roof is held up by rows of pillars. Right on top, as if perched there by accident, is a white marble wall with arches. At the corners of each level are small kiosks with domed roofs. The real tomb of Akbar is situated below, in a protected region, while the false tomb is placed at the centre of the fifth and final storey in a courtyard open to the sky. The tombstone, chiselled out of a single block of marble, is finely carved with floral motifs and inscribed with the ninety-nine names of Allah. The open air courtyard is surrounded by arched marble walls with perforated lattice windows, jalis, and are very special because each section has a different design.

HOW TO GET THERE

Agra has been a tourist spot for a long time. There are old hotels of every description and new ones are always being built. The town is well linked to other metropolitan cities by road, air, and rail. The golden triangle tourist route has Delhi as the entry and departure point, with the star attractions, Agra and Jaipur, at the

Detail of inlay, Akbar's Tomb, Sikandra.

other corners. (Agra is 204 kilometres from Delhi and Jaipur 237 kilometres from Agra).

The people of Agra know a tourist when they see one and associate them with dollars and generosity. So beware if neither apply! There are shops selling artefacts, inlaid plates, and souvenirs of good quality, a little reminder of Agra's great craft tradition. The best time to visit is just after the rainy season in August–September when the buildings are washed clean of pollution and dust, and in winter (October through to March) when the gardens are in bloom and walking through the vast forts and palaces is not so arduous. A great way to see the Taj Mahal used to be on moonlit nights but the complex is now usually closed for security reasons after sunset.

Fatehpur Sikri

South-west of Agra is the deserted imperial city Fatehpur Sikri, one of India's most alluring and breathtaking monuments. Built by the Mughal Emperor Akbar, this royal city is one of a kind. Every building, pavement, and courtyard in the complex is completely covered in red sandstone. It has a wonderful sense of space and freedom, a perfect combination of intricate workmanship and architecture on a monumental scale.

The royal road from Agra to Fatehpur Sikri (37 kilometres) linking the two imperial cities was once lined with shops and stalls selling merchandise to Mughal courtiers. As one approaches (from Agra or Bharatpur) a high long stony ridge rises out of the plains aligned from south-west to north-east. The fort wall runs an 11 kilometre circuit around the ridge while on the north-western side there was a huge lake (now dry) that supplied water and served the fortress as a natural line of defence. This hillock was once the retreat of a celebrated Chisti saint called Shaikh Salim. By the end of the fifteenth century there were several Sufi orders in northern India. The most popular was the Chisti order with its network of saints, such as Khwaja Moin-ud-Din Chisti who settled in Ajmer (thirteenth century), and Nizam-ud-Din Auliya in Delhi. These Sufi teachers attracted thousands who came to hear their teachings of love and devotion. Later their tombs became places of pilgrimage where vast numbers would gather to revere their master.

In 1569 the Mughal Emperor Akbar, after the capture of the fort of Ranthambhor, came to the hamlet of Sikri to see Shaikh Salim. The young emperor was 27 years old, but still childless as three children had died in infancy. Shaikh Salim prophesied that he would have not one but three sons. The following year a son was born and called Salim in deference to the saint. In gratitude emperor Akbar began to construct a great mosque at this site. The saint died in 1572 and a tomb for Shaikh Salim (or Salim Chisti) was built within the mosque complex. It is still a venerated place of pilgrimage, especially for childless women who come and tie a thread on the lattice windows of the tomb chamber as a reminder of an unfulfilled desire; untying it when their wish is granted, believing that like Akbar's wish, theirs too will be granted. When the royal Salim (later Jahangir, the next Mughal emperor) was a year old, construction of the fort and palaces began in earnest, and continued until 1585. Emperor Jahangir describes the beauty of the site in his memoirs:[3]

(opposite) : Shrine of Shaikh Salim, Fatehpur Sikri.

My revered father, regarding the village of Sikri, my birthplace, as fortunate to himself, made it his capital, and in the course of fourteen or fifteen years the hills and deserts, which abounded in beasts of prey, were converted into a magnificent city, comprising numerous gardens, elegant edifices, and pavilions of great beauty. After the conquest of Gujarat, the village was named Fatehpur: the town of victory.

Emperor Akbar occupied this fort for fifteen years and then moved his court to Lahore when trouble and instability threatened his north-western frontier. For Akbar, Fatehpur Sikri proved to be extremely lucky and the fortunes of the mighty emperor are woven into every building of this beautiful city. It was during this period that he expanded his empire, till it was so large that it virtually covered the entire Indian subcontinent. In 1572 Akbar conquered the fertile cotton and indigo plains of Gujarat and its famous ports which had links with Persia, Egypt, and Arabia. To celebrate his triumph and the addition of this enormous wealth to his treasury he built **Buland Darwaza**, a royal southern entrance to the mosque and named his new capital Fatehpur Sikri, the City of Victory. The gateway is approached by a steep flight of steps that add height and majesty to the entire structure (which is 54 metres high). The Buland Darwaza is designed in coloured sandstone and marble. On one side is a deep well where children today make a quick buck from the tourists with their exhibitionist dives.

Nineteenth century engraving of Buland Darwaza.

The Buland Darwaza leads into the grand **Jama Masjid** of Fatehpur Sikri which stands at the south-western end of the royal city complex. A high wall with gateways on three sides opens into a huge courtyard, 111 by 139 metres, making it one of the largest of its kind in the Mughal kingdom. The inner walls are lined with colonnades and cloisters (unfortunately partly inhabited by persistent shopkeepers) and the western façade has a massive arched doorway behind which are three (stunted) domes. A row of little kiosks stand like domed sentries along the boundary wall, guarding the pearl tomb of Salim Chisti within the courtyard.

The **Tomb of Shaikh Salim** was originally built in red sandstone but is now entirely faced with marble, a later addition. The tombstone within is covered by cloth and lies under a canopy of ebony, mother of pearl, and brass. The square

tomb chamber is surrounded by a corridor (for circumambulation) with lattice marble jalis of a quality unmatched anywhere in the world. The jalis are linked together by a series of
ornate marble pillars with branching brackets. The tomb has a
low dome and heavy protruding eaves that hang over the edge
of the roof like a decorative canopy. Its design and ornamentation is traced to contemporary tombs of Gujarat, the region that
Akbar had annexed. The tomb of Salim Chisti is a beautiful
monument to the Sufi saint who, amongst other things, greatly
influenced the life of Akbar, one of
the greatest Mughal emperors.

On the periphery, and as you
enter the fort area of the royal city,
there are service apartments and
stables along with palaces constructed by courtiers invited to build
at the site. The royal complex is
entered through the **Diwan-e-Am**
on the north-eastern side, at the
opposite end of city from the
mosque. There is also an entrance
to the private quarters from the
Jama Masjid. The Diwan-e-Am
(Hall of Public Audience) is an
enclosed space surrounded by
colonnades, and on the western
face is the pavilion where the
emperor sat in honour surrounded
by his courtiers. (The mirhab marks
the western side, the direction of
prayer in a mosque. What was
Akbar trying to say by seating
himself at the western side of this
hall?) From the throne room side
an entrance leads to the protected
private domain of the imperial
palace which contains mansions
for the royal harem and the ladies-

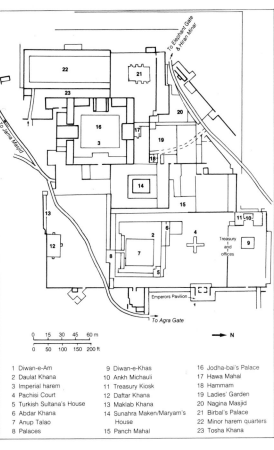

1 Diwan-e-Am	9 Diwan-e-Khas	16 Jodha-bai's Palace
2 Daulat Khana	10 Ankh Michauli	17 Hawa Mahal
3 Imperial harem	11 Treasury Kiosk	18 Hammam
4 Pachisi Court	12 Maklab Khana	19 Ladies' Garden
5 Turkish Sultana's House	13 Daftar Khana	20 Nagina Masjid
6 Abdar Khana	14 Sunahra Maken/Maryam's	21 Birbal's Palace
7 Anup Talao	House	22 Minor harem quarters
8 Palaces	15 Panch Mahal	23 Tosha Khana

in-waiting, residences for the ruler and living quarters. The
private courtyards are magnificent open spaces paved in red
sandstone, and the palace buildings are aligned like a string of
rectangular blocks to one another. Contemporary architecture
dictated that these palace buildings were themselves independent units encased within high walls and designed around an
open courtyard. The rooms and verandahs all look out on to the
courtyard, offering the residents a comfortable assortment of
warm areas that received direct sunlight, and cool chambers
shrouded in shadows and shade.

Plan of Palaces,
Fatehpur Sikri.

The spacious *mardana* or courtyard behind the Diwan-e-Am is surrounded by several interesting structures, though the function and purpose of some of them remain an enigma. To the north is a square red sandstone building standing by itself a little aloof and self-composed, referred to as the **Diwan-e-Khas**. The building from the exterior has two storeys, the upper one with a deep hanging eave around it like a hood and the lower floor is demarcated externally by a balcony supported by decorative brackets. The flat roof has a tall kiosk at each of the four corners. Inside, it appears that the building is not two-storeyed but one high-ceilinged room. At the centre is a single faceted pillar with long tapering brackets clustered around it supporting a walkway with branching catwalks connected to corners of the room. Was the emperor meant to sit at the centre and command proceedings from above or was this a conference room for Akbar's philosophers discussing the religions of the world? What was the purpose of this peculiar building? Perhaps we will never know.

As you walk southward along the paved sandstone courtyard there are designs that appear on the floor like a giant game of ludo, which the guides will tell you was used by the emperor who played the game using live human counters.

Central decorated pillar, Diwan-e-Khas, Fatehpur Sikri.

At the opposite end is a lovely architectural composition of a tank called **Anup Talao** with embellished edges and a platform at the centre that can be reached (like the catwalks of the Diwan-e-Khas) by narrow bridges. It is said that music performances were held here and acclaimed musicians of Akbar's court, like Tansen, sat on the central platform entertaining the emperor.

At the north-eastern corner of the Anup Talao is another elegant miniature building of Fatehpur Sikri. It is called for some reason the **Turkish Sultana's House**. It is an amazing tiny little unit because it seems to have been built, like many structures here, on the model of a wooden house, with pillars and brackets, joints and sockets, though, in actuality it is constructed entirely out of sandstone. The inner face of the eaves, the brackets and pillars, and the entire expanse of the interior stone walls are decorated with carved arabesque patterns and panels of flowering trees, birds, and animals that look today like a very sophisticated monochrome wallpaper.

Surrounding the courtyard are other storeyed buildings and apartment rooms, but the most intriguing is the **Panch Mahal**, the five (tiered) palace. The first two floors are of equal size while the next two are graded, and on top is a single kiosk or open pavilion. The building perhaps once had sandstone jalis around the outer row of pillars. Now the pillared halls of each floor are open to the breeze and it is understood to have been used by the royal ladies as a garden pavilion where they could enjoy a magnificent view of the fort and the palace below in the glowing light of an Indian sunset. From the top of the Panch Mahal one can appreciate the layout of the imperial city, the private areas and the public ones, and the courtyards that link them together. Directly behind, on the south-western side, is the huge well-protected harem mansion known as **Jodha-bai's Palace**. Near the entrance is the little **Kitchenette** (though it does not look like one) and further west another apartment and stables referred to as the **Palace of Birbal**, Akbar's minister notable for his wit. Each palace is full of sculptural detail and one has only to imagine (not furniture) but silken carpets, brocade bolsters, pillows, silver, jade, gold vessels, and lamps spread out around the room so that its aristocratic inhabitants could use the space in any way they liked.

Jodha-bai's Palace is entered from the east side. The entrance to the palace is cleverly conceived so that the inmates are not seen directly on admission and we are told, by contemporary accounts, that it was guarded by formidable eunuchs. It is

Royal Apartments, Fatehpur Sikiri.

possible that this was the zenana or harem for Akbar's wives (some put the number at 500, others at 3000 courtesans) and their ladies-in-waiting. Some of these beautiful princesses and queens were from royal Hindu families of Rajasthan, a clever political move by Akbar to win over neighbouring princes and forge alliances. There is no doubt that the decoration and motifs used to adorn the sandstone walls of this building are similar to ones that the indigenous artist used when constructing temples. At the centre is a courtyard and around it are the living rooms. The rounded roofs above are covered with turquoise tiles that contrast dramatically with the red of the sandstone. The use of ceramic tiles in this building in Fatehpur Sikri is interesting, for it compares with architectural decorations often found in Persia and Pakistan. Perhaps one can suggest other structures at Fatehpur Sikri, now bare: the kiosks of the Diwan-e-Khas and the domes of the mosque were once adorned with similar tile-work.

The city of Fatehpur Sikri is a complicated complex of palaces and courtyards, full of light and air, unlike any of the palaces of Europe where the climate necessitated closed cloisters. But, here, like everything Mughal, care was taken to see that every detail was designed to cultivate the senses: the warm red texture of the stone, elegant visual forms and shapes beside shimmering ponds filled with fragrant perfumes and flowers, while the sound of music forever echoed through the spaces.

Hiran Minar, Fatehpur Sikri.

WHAT'S IN THE NEIGHBOURHOOD

Not far (18 kilometres away) from Fatehpur Sikri (50 kilometres from Agra) is the **Keoladeo Ghana National Park**. Here at Bharatpur (Rajasthan) a small man-made reservoir from the mid-eighteenth century has developed into a fascinating bird sanctuary where one may view many species of Indian water birds (painted storks, egrets, herons, and cranes) and in the winter months (October to March) migratory species, like the rare Siberian Crane, Falcated Teel, and several birds of prey that fly in from Siberia, China, and Mongolia. The wetlands, lakes and bunds (artificial ridges containing water) offer a home to some wild animals like the *nilgai* (the blue bull), *sambar*, jungle cat, and the mongoose.

HOW TO GET THERE

The imperial fort of Fatehpur Sikri may be approached from Agra 37 kilometres away or 18 kilometres from Bharatpur. Most visitors prefer to make a day trip to the fort *en route* from Agra or from Bharatpur, as it requires at least half a day to explore. There are now a few rest-houses and hotels enabling you to see the fort at sunrise and sunset.

The best time to visit the fort is during the winter months when the long walk through its labyrinths is not hot and wearying. The Fatehpur Sikri complex is open to the public from sunset to sunrise. There is a minimal entrance fee at the gate. You are advised to wear a pair of good walking shoes and carry some drinking water for your trip. If you would like to conserve your energy, walk through the fort without climbing up the stairs of the Panch Mahal (though it affords a good view) and the other palaces. Small stalls and shops sell items used for worship at the mosque but there are no adequate facilities for food.

Marble jali or screen, Fatehpur Sikri.

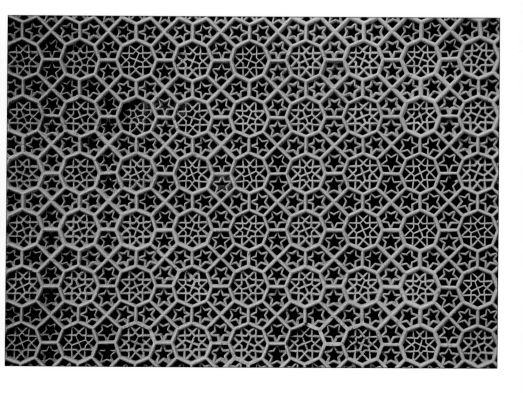

Jaipur

The story of Jaipur city begins with the magnificent medieval fort of Amber, just outside its city limits. Amber and the royal city of Jaipur built in the eighteenth century are a wonderful introduction to the desert kingdoms of Rajasthan. Lured by the romance and charm of these cities, many will yearn to see the more distant castles and palaces of Bundi, Bikaner, and Jaisalmer. They all have a special beauty concealed within their landscape (for they have been created out of local stone) and majestically embrace the hillside, jealously protecting their sand-dunes and barren dominion. The forts are so well camouflaged that their tall towers are barely visible from afar and their serene appearance gives no hint of the splendour and wealth to be found within the palace walls.

Amber Fort
A lovely wooded road runs north of Jaipur (11 kilometres away) winding around the low hills and suddenly, quite unexpectedly, the fortified palace of Amber looms into view. It stands on a high terraced plateau at the foot of the south-west face of the Jaigarh fort hill overlooking the Maota lake. The location is superb, surrounded as it is by low hills covered only with scrub and bushes, their ragged crests silhouetted against a never-ending line of fort walls and watch-towers. The history of this site goes back several centuries. It was inhabited by the Susawat Minas and then in AD 1106 the Kachhwaha clan occupied this territory when they moved away from central India.

The Kachhwaha claim their descent from Kush, the second son of Ram, the hero king of the epic poem Ramayana. Their divine descent is traced from the solar race or *surya vamsha*, and its fiery insignia appears on their banners and royal decrees.

The clan grew in strength and increased their territorial control and when Babur, the first of the Mughal rulers, staked his claim to the throne of Delhi the fortunes of the Kachhwahas changed dramatically. Bihari Mal, or Bihar Mal, made an alliance with Babur in 1527 and was appointed a *mansabdar* (a title which denoted a feudal relationship in which he could govern the territory and in turn offer a specified number of horses and horsemen for the emperors service whenever required). His daughter, Jodha-bai, was given to Akbar in marriage, and after the birth of an heir, Jahangir, the Hindu wife exercised great influence over the emperor. His son Bhagwan Das (Bhagwant

(opposite) :
Jal Mahal, Jaipur.

Das) was selected as a high ranking commander in Akbar's imperial army. Bhagwan Das's adopted son Man Singh I became Akbar's most trusted friend and general in the army (with successful campaigns in Bihar and Bengal), and was also given the premier title of Raja or King. It was this powerful Man Singh I and his successors (like Jai Singh I) who built the palace and fort of Amber.

Amber (pronounced ambear) is derived from the name of the goddess Amba and was at one time called Ambavati. It remained the seat of power for the Kachhwaha family from the twelfth century till 1728 when the city of Jaipur was built. At the foot of the fort, on the northern side, is the **Maota Lake** with a garden (best seen from the palace windows from above) called **Dil-e-Aram** (which brings restful tranquillity to the heart), which has two pretty pavilions, and the **Archaeological Museum**. Beside it is a car park where elephants can be hired to take you up a serpentine road to the palace apartments the royal way.

At the top an arched gateway, **Suraj Pol**, the sun gate, leads into the **Jaleb Chowk**. On all sides of the square are shops selling colourful moundfuls of snacks and (tacky) souvenirs. On the west side, opposite the Suraj Pol, is the **Chand Pol** or the moon gate which leads to a number of ancient temples and palaces. On the south-western side is a steep flight of stairs that leads to the **Shri Shila Devi Temple** or **Kali Mata Mandir**, containing an idol of the goddess brought to Amber from Bengal by Man Singh I after his campaign there in 1604. The shrine is still a popular place of worship.

The temple is looked after by a family of priests from Bengal and it is from this illustrious family that the architect of the city of Jaipur was born centuries later. The temple is in worship and the deity is still held in great esteem by the royal family of Jaipur. There are several accounts of worship in the temple. The most intriguing one comes to us from Bishop Heber who visited Amber palace in 1825 and saw a goat sacrifice in the temple:[4]

Plan of palaces, Amber Fort.

1. Elephant steps (Chand Pol)
2. Balcony and back exit
3. Jaleb Chowk
4. Suraj Pol
5. Singh Pol
6. Kali Mata Mandir
7. Diwan-e-Am
8. Rooftop terrace
9. Ganesh Pol
10. Sukh Niwas
11. Sunken Garden
12. Jai Mandir
   (Diwan-e-Khas, Shish Mahal and Jas Mandir)
13. Zenana
14. Man Singh's buildings

© The Guidebook Company Ltd

The guide told us on our way back that the tradition was that, in ancient times, a man was sacrificed here every day; that the custom was laid aside till Jye Singh had a frightful dream, in which the destroying power appeared to him and asked him why her image was suffered to be dry? The Raja, afraid to disobey, was reluctant to fulfill the tradition to its ancient extent of horror, took council and substituted a goat for the human victim...

Beside the temple staircase is the **Singh Pol** or the lion gateway (the direct entrance is cleverly staggered) which leads to the first courtyard. At the north-eastern end of the open courtyard is the beautiful **Diwan-e-Am** built in a style (dangerously) similar to the halls of public audience of the Mughal forts at Agra and Delhi. This rectangular hall, built by Jai Singh I has a vaulted roof supported by a row of marble pillars and is enclosed on all sides by verandahs of sandstone pillars with elephant brackets.

The elegance of the Diwan-e-Am structure is said to have evoked a jealous reaction from Emperor Jahangir, and to appease him the pillars were later covered with coats of stucco plaster. In 1637, a decree was issued by Shah Jahan ordering Jai Singh to halt his marble palace constructions at Amber because marble-cutters were required urgently for work at the tomb (now called the Taj Mahal) and at the imperial fort at Agra!

The flat open roof of the Diwan-e-Am was called Sharad Punam-ki-Chandni (the light of the autumn full moon) and it is said that the king with his royal companions spent their evenings

Garden courtyard and Shish Mahal, Amber Fort.

(here and in other areas of the palace) under a sky, swept clean after the monsoon rains, bathed in autumn moonlight which is more brilliant and luminous than at any other time of year.

To the south side of the courtyard is the impressive **Ganesh Pol** (with a painted image of Ganesh, the elephant-headed Hindu deity). This arched and playfully decorated gateway was built by Jai Singh II and leads to the private royal apartments. A long passageway opens on to a lovely walled-in private garden with fountains and pretty water channels (get the guard to demonstrate how the water trickles delicately over the carved waterways). On the eastern side is the **Jai Mandir** (not to be called the Diwan-e-Khas for fear of directly competing with their Mughal overlords). The main hall is in white marble (obviously built before the imperial decree) with decorative ceilings, alabaster and glass-work. To the side is the delightful **Shish Mahal**, the palace of mirrors. A well-hidden narrow staircase leads up to the top floor. The finely carved stone windows provide a splendid view of the lake and the ornamental garden below (also based on the Mughal tradition. One must believe that the Rajputs of Amber/Jaipur were not merely Mughal clones but that mutual imitation was the best form of flattery!) One of the many pleasures of wandering through this palace are the many unexpected views of the surrounding hillside, the Jaigarh Fort, and the peaceful valley below.

Amber Fort with Jaigarh Fort above.

Jaigarh Fort is accessible by a road leading a few kilometres off the main highway to Jaipur. It is an enjoyable place to visit. There are cannons (in working condition ?) and a little museum of artifacts that tell the story of the fort and its vast, well-protected treasury.

Jaipur

This capital of the present state of Rajasthan gets its name from its illustrious founder Jai Singh II, a direct descendent of Jai Singh I and Man Singh I of Amber. It is said that the Mughal emperor gave him the title of Sawai Maharaja, meaning literally one and a quarter, or more poetically a term used to denote that he was more (valuable) than one. The new city was founded in November 1726 by Sawai Jai Singh II. It was designed as a spacious residential and commercial centre, a model of its time, by a brilliant Bengali architect Vidhya Bhattacharaya.

The city was designed on a system of grids and even today the squares and market complexes are lined with jewellery shops and wholesale stores, each one often confined to specific areas determined by their trade and produce. Important local families were invited to the new city to build their city palaces there. Jaipur boasts of hundreds of lovely *haveli*s and palace apartments that line the broad avenues and tiny side streets, each one constructed in a blend of Rajasthani and Mughal style.

Hawa Mahal, Jaipur City.

The most photographed building in Jaipur must be the **Hawa Mahal** (the palace of the wind) which is a tall, oddly-shaped structure. It is designed one room deep but raised on five storeys so that the angled and lacy lattice windows may capture the slightest wisp of breeze. The building was added to the palace complex in 1799 by Pratap Singh for the ladies of the royal family to watch processions and festivities on the street below without being seen themselves.

The colour pink which now appears on most of the façades of the mains streets of Jaipur was added to welcome the Prince of Wales in 1876. Today it is still the Pink City and the customary coat of 'welcoming pink' paint is enforced by law.

The city has a geometric grid plan divided into nine sections, of which the royal quarters occupy two sections on the western side. The intersecting streets are broad, and from early photographs it is clear that, at the time it was built, there was enough room for the buggy carts and horse-drawn carriages but not for the pell-mell of the motley traffic of today, where the camel cart competes for space with the outsized limousine.

Plan of City Palace, Jaipur.

The city is located in a cradle (431 metres above sea level) of hills and aligned to two hill-top shrines. Along the hill ranges one can see the protective fortification walls and forts, while the immediate city is secured by seven monumental gateways.

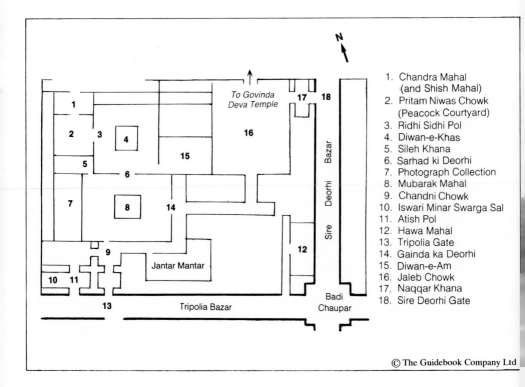

To Govinda Deva Temple

1. Chandra Mahal (and Shish Mahal)
2. Pritam Niwas Chowk (Peacock Courtyard)
3. Ridhi Sidhi Pol
4. Diwan-e-Khas
5. Sileh Khana
6. Sarhad ki Deorhi
7. Photograph Collection
8. Mubarak Mahal
9. Chandni Chowk
10. Iswari Minar Swarga Sal
11. Atish Pol
12. Hawa Mahal
13. Tripolia Gate
14. Gainda ka Deorhi
15. Diwan-e-Am
16. Jaleb Chowk
17. Naqqar Khana
18. Sire Deorhi Gate

Jantar Mantar

Tripolia Bazar

Badi Chaupar

Sire Deorhi Bazar

© The Guidebook Company Ltd

City Palace

A series of gateways and courtyards bring you to a complex of office buildings and temporary stalls. The first apartment encountered is the **Mubarak Mahal**, the welcome home which stands at the centre of a courtyard. It is a two-storey building in marble inspired by the Diwan-e-Khas of Akbar's Fatehpur Sikri. This little show-piece gem was constructed by Madho Singh II in 1900 as a guest-house and is now the **Royal Wardrobe Museum**. The collection is well worth seeing to capture a glimpse of the fine muslins, prints, and silk brocades that once were produced in this region, and even though the exhibits are a bit dusty it does suggest that matching contrasting colours was the fashion of the time. Amidst the clothes and textiles on display are some rare and beautiful pieces of glassware and an assortment of huqqa stands.

Diwan-e-Khas, City Palace, Jaipur.

To the north-western corner of the courtyard is the **Sileh Khana** which now contains an extraordinary display of traditional armoury. The highly decorated halls on the first floor (with pretty painted ceilings), once for dance or music, now display some deadly weapons: daggers, swords, and other mean contraptions. There are some very ornate ceremonial daggers with carved jade handles and some very imaginative ammunition cases.

From the Mubarak Mahal courtyard you can see the flag of the Jaipur royal family flying if the (former) Maharaja is at home. A large gateway to the north of this courtyard, with huge wooden and brass doors, leads into another court with the elevated pillared **Diwan-e-Khas**. The open arched plan of the hall of private audience is yet another example of how the styles patronised by the royalty of Rajasthan and by the Mughal emperors was a synthesis created by borrowed elements from both. While the Diwan-e-Khas here is similar to the ones in the Mughal capitals of Delhi and Agra, the design has its roots in the flat-roofed pavilions of a period that predates the Mughals. Within the hall are two large silver water jars (earning their entry in the *Guinness Book of Records* by virtue of being the largest single silver objects in the world). They were used to carry holy *ganga jal* (water from the river Ganga) for daily prayers and purification when the Madho Singh II went to Britain to attend the coronation of Edward VII in 1902.

To the right of this courtyard and in a very different style is the **Diwan-e-Am** which has been converted into a museum that displays carpets from the royal household, priceless manuscripts, paintings, portraits of the family of Jaipur, and an assortment of howdahs and carriages for elephant and camel-back rides.

On the opposite side of the courtyard is a passage which leads to the ladies quarter and further. The surviving Maharaja of the royal Jaipur family still resides in a portion of the palace and has been estimated to be one of the wealthiest men in India.

Though the architecture of the city palace is not of an exceptionally high standard, it is the **Jantar Mantar**, the observatory built by the founder of Jaipur, that is truly remarkable and unusual. Jai Singh II had a passion for astronomy and scientific inventions. Dissatisfied with contemporary metal astrolabes he worked out a way of making permanent structures to measure time, the position of the stars and planets. He built four other open-air observatories in sacred centres of learning: Varanasi, Ujjain, Mathura, and for the imperial city of Delhi. The **Samrat Yantra** (supreme instrument) is a gigantic sundial that measures the shadowy path of the sun. The **Jai Prakash Yantra**s bear the name of their inventor who devised the concept of two huge hemispherical sunken bowls across which wires were attached to record the sun's journey through the sky. In a sense this observatory reflects the ideals of Jai Singh II and are the essence of the city of Jaipur that he built. A novel idea, of something that was in many ways ahead of its time, with an air

Jantar Mantar, Jaipur.

of innovative charm and experimentation. Some of the results are satisfying while others now appear whimsical or quaint.

WHAT'S IN THE NEIGHBOURHOOD
The golden triangle trip encompasses Delhi, Agra, and Jaipur. From Jaipur there are some interesting short trips that you can take. **Samode** is 42 kilometres from Jaipur and has recently been introduced on the tourist map to popularise the fort built by Jai Singh's minister. Nestled between the hills, part of the old fort has been converted into a hotel and there are some lovely rooms decorated with murals and mirror-work. **Sanganer** is a (dirty) little village (16 kilometres from Jaipur) which is the centre of the block printing industry of the region. Here cotton cloth is still printed by hand using wooden blocks, a different block for each colour, making the craft both exacting and very beautiful. While much of the wide variety of Rajasthani textiles are available from shops in Jaipur, the block printing process is worth seeing for those interested in such crafts and ancient techniques. Most of the artists in the village are used to visitors and their questions. Jaipur has streets full of shops which sell textiles, jewellery (silver, gold, and stonework, for it was an ancient gem-cutting centre), and handicrafts (leather shoes, toys, puppets and enamelware).

HOW TO GET THERE
Jaipur is connected by road and rail, and is just a half hour flight from Delhi. There are regular flights to and from Calcutta, Varanasi, Delhi, Jodhpur, Udaipur, and Bombay. Jaipur is 261 kilometres from Delhi and 237 from Agra by road. There are conducted tours by bus and car around the city and to Amber (11 kilometres away). Amber can be visited on a day trip from Jaipur. Lots of hotels and a few palaces converted into guesthouses or expensive hotels are available in Jaipur.

Udaipur

The city of Udaipur, surrounded by pale fawn-brown rambling hills, is like a water-colour painting. A quiet romantic air is cast over the city by the play of light on its buildings and lakes. At sunrise the palaces of Udaipur emerge and stand majestically against their background of shimmering water. Udaipur, the 'Sunrise city', derives its name from the founder Maharana Udai Singh, and the title also hints at the solar descent of its rulers. By moonlight the city acquires a fairy-land quality. Today, like all cities in India, it has its share of noise and bustling traffic, filth and squalor, but it remains in many ways one of the most picturesque royal cities of the state of Rajasthan.

The city of Udaipur was built when the Mewar Rajput family were forced to leave their traditional home and fort of **Chittor** or **Chittorgarh** in 1567. Choosing a strategic site between their other forts at **Kumbhalgarh** and **Chittor**, a new royal city was built that has grown and developed over several generations. The Mewar family, unlike the Jaipur Rajputs, initially resisted the comfortable temptation of allying with the Mughal emperors. They refused to give their daughters in marriage or to allow their sons to join the emperor's forces. This brought the Mewars enormous trouble and their kingdom was under attack for much of the medieval period, and there are innumerable stories, romantic ballads, legendary songs, and love poems composed to extol their bravery and valour.

The city of Udaipur is situated between two major lakes, the Pichola and the Fateh Sagar to the north. **Pichola Lake** takes its name from a small village nearby which was enlarged by Udai Singh when he planned his new capital on its banks. Overlooking the lake, on the eastern bank, was a natural hillock which was incorporated into the protective fortification of the **City Palace**. The royal palace walls stretch over a mile on the eastern side of the lake and within the palace are a maze of inner courtyards, apartments, and decorated halls.

Legend has it that Maharana Udai Singh was out hunting one day when he came upon a holy sage seated beside the Pichola Lake. The sage prophesied that should the king build his palace at this site the fortunes of his troubled family would soon change. The Maharana built a small shrine to mark the spot and this sanctuary is the oldest part of the City Palace.

Much of the palace is now open to the public and one can wander through the halls and see some of the royal possessions

(opposite) : City Palace, Udaipur.

on display. There are rooms covered with frescoes (like **Krishna Vilas**), stone and glass mosaics (**Shish Mahal, Manak Mahal,** and **Moti Mahal**), and ornamental doors and painted windows. Unlike the Mughal forts of Agra and Delhi where figurative art was taboo, there was no such restriction here and charming portraits of the kings and their courtiers were painted on the walls. Windows with wooden shutters were painted with lovely maidens standing beside flowering trees, evoking a lush landscape that Rajasthan rarely saw. Each painting was a happy blend of bright mineral colours, vibrant earth reds, yellows with highlights in white and green.

The marble throne in the coronation room was last used in the time of Maharana Sangram Singh II (1710-34). One courtyard has large peacock motifs decorated with coloured mosaics. Nearby is the Sun Window installed by Bhim Singh (1778-1828). This is the divine symbol of the royal Mewar family which traces its lineage to the *surya vamsha*, the descendants of the sun.

The **Zenana Mahal** is situated south of the city palace museum and was built for the women of the royal harem of Maharana Karan Singh in 1620. The fortified private living quarters of the ladies of the royal family is entered through a well-guarded doorway. Within the walls are the temples of the royal household, and each of the apartments are referred to by

Pichola Lake and the city of Udaipur.

romantic names, e.g. the **Rang Mahal,** the hall of colours, and **Badal Mahal**, the palace of the clouds. The **Museum** has halls filled with miniature paintings, which provide glimpses of the royal lifestyle of the Maharanas of Mewar. There are paintings of the royal hunt, where the king is seen crouched dramatically on one side as the fleeing tiger or deer is shown well within shooting range. There are other portraits and scenes of court life which give a classic view of the way the royal kings and queens of Udaipur dressed themselves. Yards of the finest cotton, muslin, and silken brocade, over which were displayed the most spectacular jewel necklaces, belts, bracelets, rings and anklets.

Glass inlay, Crystal Room, Shiv Nivas, Udaipur.

Towards the southern end of Pichola lake is **Jag Mandir**, an island palace built by Maharana Karan Singh. It was here that the Mughal prince Khurram took refuge from his father, Emperor Jahangir. Prince Khurram, later to be named Shah Jahan (and to build the Taj Mahal in Agra), revolted against his father in 1623 in a bid for succession. He inherited the throne on the death of Jahangir in 1627 and some say that this beautiful sandstone palace amidst the lake at Udaipur, with its fine inlaid designs using onyx, jasper, and agate, had great influence on the the young prince and became his inspiration when building his palaces in Delhi and Agra.

Another lovely structure built amidst the Pichola Lake is **Jag Niwas** now the **Lake Palace Hotel**. It was built on a four acre natural bed of granite and marble, and originates from the time of Maharana Jagat Singh I (1628-52). One can only imagine the tremendous effort that went into building this wonder palace set in a sea of water. The palace is designed with a series of interconnecting gardens and courtyards filled with fountains and trees, while the royal apartment rooms look out on the glittering lake encircling it.

The palace was converted into a hotel in 1963 and, with the addition of a few more rooms and facilities, it has become a romantic place in which to stay. For a price one can live in tastefully decorated rooms in the lap of luxury of a forgotten world, marooned in the midst of a lovely lake with twentieth century comforts, of which the Maharanas of Udaipur could never have dreamt.

North of Pichola Lake is **Fateh Sagar** built in 1678 with an embankment added by Fateh Singh in 1889. A lovely walk along this lake and in the **Saheliyon-ki-Bari** (the garden for the lady companions) offers an opportunity to appreciate Udaipur in the way it was meant to be enjoyed. The old city has a charm of its own. The narrow and undulating roads are lined with shops and stores in which the wares are as colourful as the customers. Beside the shops there are workshops and cottage industries tucked away on roof-tops and in side lanes, like any traditional market-place of old. It is well worth a visit to see how the celebrated tie-and-dye and textile block-printing is done.

Of architectural interest are the elegant chattris of **Ahar** 3.2 kilometres from Udaipur. At this royal cremation ground there are several artistic open pavilions with hybrid Islamic domes built to commemorate the death of the Ranas.

Maharana Bhupal
Singh of Udaipur.

WHAT'S IN THE NEIGHBOURHOOD
Apart from local sightseeing and shopping for beautiful Rajasthani printed and embroidered textiles, enamelwork jewellery and handicrafts there are lovely gardens and lakes in and around Udaipur. A number of interesting day trips can be made out of Udaipur to see the romantic fort of Chittor, Kumbhalgarh, and the extraordinary Hindu and Jain temples nearby.

Eklingji
The road from Udaipur to Eklingji is very beautiful. The undulating countryside, gentle hills and valleys carry the charm of the miniature paintings of this region. About thirty kilometres north of Udaipur is an ancient temple called Eklingji dedicated to Shiva. The temple was originally built by the founder of the Mewar family who came upon this site one day when he was herding his cattle. A holy sage he met there advised him to build this temple and the stone image, a *linga* of Shiva with four faces, became the patron deity of the royal family. Even today the Maharana worships here and he is considered the representative of Eklingji. The temple was rebuilt in the fourteenth century in granite and marble, and is still a celebrated pilgrimage site in Rajasthan (open alas to Hindus only).

Nagada Temples

About four kilometres to the west of Eklingji are some interesting ruined eleventh century temples called Sas-Bahu (for some reason, the mother-in-law and the daughter-in-law temples) with exquisite stone carvings.

Nathdwara

Sixty kilometres north of Udaipur is one of the most popular pilgrim sites of Rajasthan built around a temple dedicated to Shri Nathji or Krishna. Within the temple (open only to Hindus) is an idol of Krishna in jet black stone and in his dimple is a huge sparkling diamond. It is said that when the Mughal Emperor Aurangzeb banned worship at Mathura, the home of Shri Nathji, the Mewar Maharana offered the image a home. While transporting the idol the Maharana received an omen. At one point the wheel of his chariot refused to move, as though the deity wished to remain there. A temple was built and a small but interesting township grew around the shrine, serving the needs of thousands of pilgrims. The temple is always crowded. Nathdwara is also an artists' colony. Well-known musicians who play and sing for their lord live and study here. *Pitchwais*, painted cloth curtains to screen the sanctum of the temple, are also made here by skilled artists. There are interesting musical instrument shops and other cottage industries, and the life on the streets of Nathdwara offers an ephemeral glimpse into the past.

Carved marble ceiling, Ranakpur.

Ranakpur

North-west of Udaipur is a collection of beautiful Jain temples which are still a popular pilgrimage site for the Jain community. The temples were built in the fifteenth century by a wealthy Jain merchant. The delicate, profusely carved Adhinatha temple with a thousand elaborate marble pillars is a masterpiece of Jain architecture of this period and region.

Kumbhalgarh

Another spectacular fort of the Mewar family, named after Kumbha who ruled the territory from Chittor and founded the site in 1458. It stands 1087 metres above sea level (two hours drive north from Udaipur) and is strategically placed on the northern spur of the Aravalli hills. On the crest of the highest mountain ridge is the fort, and below it run the winding serpentine protective walls which then get lost in the surrounding jungles and ravines. The fort's impressive location is enhanced by the extensive forest which surrounds it. Seven massive gateways guard the entrance to the fort. The main wall, at some places is eight metres thick. Much of the area is forest and forms part of the nearby wildlife sanctuary. Within the fort walls were once 365 temples and shrines, a self-sufficent village, tanks, and the remains of the garrison, numerous chattris commemorating the dead, and the palaces of the Ranas. The appartments of the palace were rebuilt during the nineteenth century and many of the now deserted rooms were decorated with elaborate plaster-work. From the top-most building, the Badal Mahal or Cloud Palace (the palaces amidst the clouds), is a spectacular view over the forest, hills to the south and west while to the north stretch the flat desert plains of the Thar desert.

Kumbhalgarh.

HOW TO GET THERE

Udaipur is linked by rail, road, and air to Delhi, Jaipur, Ahmadabad, and Bombay. There are a number of reasonably priced hotels and there is also converted palace accommodation. The best season to visit the region is during winter when it is cool and if there has been a good monsoon then the lakes of Udaipur will be particularly lovely and the hills draped in lush green.

Chittor

Perhaps there is no other place on earth like Chittor. A fort whose name is synonymous with honour, especially with what today appears like a very strange form of feminine loyalty. A very Indian, or more correctly Asian, social value is the notion of 'losing face', when a person would rather sacrifice his/her life than bring shame to the family name. This added to the soldier's motto 'never give in' became the theme song of Chittor.

This fort, also called Chittorgarh (or Chittaurgarh, *garh* means fort), was the traditional home of the Rajput rulers of Mewar. The hill on which the fort is built is 152 metres above the plains and the almost impregnable fortification walls encompass a tableland (five and a half kilometres long but in width less than a kilometre at the widest point).

This long plateau is studded with buildings that cover the seven hundred years of occupation from the ninth century to 1567 when Udai Singh moved his capital to Udaipur. During this long period the Mewars and the fort of Chittor occupied an important political place in the history of the subcontinent. But a fort cannot survive without the economic means to do so. Not far from the fort are some ancient mines which yielded a large supply of silver, copper, lead, and antimony. These Zawar mines may well have added to the coffers of the Maharanas of Chittor in the fourteenth century and their wealth provided the much needed funds to build the palaces and temples.

The hill-top plateau of Chittor offered a commanding strategic position and there were several sources of water like the **Gaumukh Kund**, a reservoir at the centre of the western side of the fort. Gaumukh means cow mouth and the lake is so called because that is what the shape of its entrance resembles. The name is also an indirect reference to the source of the Ganga (Ganges), the heavenly river believed to have appeared here to feed the fort and to sustain its heroic occupants during battles and sieges. Over its long period of occupation the fort was laid under siege a number of times and held out, but eventually three events proved fatal.

The first tragedy struck in 1303 when Ala-ud-Din Khalji, the Sultan of Delhi (who had built the lovely **Alai Darwaza** at the Qutub complex in **Delhi**), sent his army to the Deccan, Gujarat, and Rajputana to extend the boundaries of his kingdom. Ala-ud-Din came himself to the foothills of Chittor because, we are told, he had heard of the beauty of Padmini, the wife of Ratan

Singh of Chittor. Ala-ud-Din was granted permission to see this legendary beauty from the reflection of a mirror on the water below. Ratan Singh, a true gentleman, then accompanied his guest to the foot of the fort where he was treacherously captured. Padmini was ordered to surrender to the Sultan with a promise that her husband would be released. Aware that Ala-ud-Din was not one to keep his word, she worked out a counterplot. A caravan of palanquins carrying the royal beauty descended, and when they entered the camp of the enemy it was the Rana's

General view, Chittorgarh.

soldiers who jumped out of them. A fierce fight ensued, and in the confusion the brave warriors ensured that their king Ratan Singh escaped. Finally, defeating the Rajput soldiers, Ala-ud-Din entered and captured the fort of Chittor but found no lady Padmini. All that was left was a huge fire, the *johar*, into whose flames thousands of royal ladies and their companions had leaped rather than face capture and dishonour. The flames had offered them a death more honourable than surrender to the Sultan of Delhi.

To the southern end of Chittor fort lies a building called **Padmini's Palace**. It is here that they say that Ala-ud-Din Khalji gazed in wonderment at the reflection of the queen's face. The present building is a replica of the original structure reconstructed by Maharana Sajjan Singh in 1880. Near Gaumukh reservoir is an open court known as the **Mahasati**, the royal cremation ground, where the women were said to have joined the funeral pyre in a grand procession.

The second tragic event occurred in 1535 when Chittor was besieged by the Sultan of Gujarat, a leading figure who had been a power to reckon with in western India for some time. At the time the Rana was a minor and the army of Chittor was led by Jawahir Bai, the Queen Mother. She was slain in battle and the young prince went into hiding. The traditions of the land of Chittor prohibited anyone but the royal family from leading the army so the Prince of Deolia was crowned as the sovereign head. Realising that their army was incapable of combating the might of the Sultan's, a huge sacrificial johar was organised and another generation of brave women, daughters and mothers of Chittor, jumped to their deaths.

The great palace within the fort is that of Maharana Kumbha (AD 1433-68), possibly rebuilt several times but providing an idea of early Rajputana royal architecture. The **Palace of Rana**

Kumbha is built of finely cut stone covered with coats of stucco
and possibly painted. At the southern end it is entered through
a gate called Tripolia (three *pols*, gates) which leads to an open
courtyard. To the north is the **Sabha**, the council chamber where
the Rajput heads of family met. A three-storeyed building to the
west is the **Pade ka Mahal** or the Kanwar ka Mahal, the palace
apartments for the heir apparent.

Also built by Rana Kumbha is the Victory Tower called
Vijaya Stambha built (1457-68) to commemorate the victory
over Mahmud Khalji of Malwa in
1440. The tower is an interesting
architectural structure located in
the central area of the fort south of
the Ram Pol (the last of the seven
gateways, of which more will be
said later). A similar tower, though
of somewhat earlier origin, is the
(22.8 metre high) seven storey
Tower of Fame, the **Kirtti Stambha**,
near Rana Kumbha's palace. It was
probably built in the twelfth century
and stood in front of a temple. The
design of the Vijaya Stambha or
Victory Tower is an amalgamation
of religious (square ground floor
converted into a form with many
angles, niches with images, and a
quantity of decoration) and secular
architecture (elaborate brackets and
lattice windows). It has nine storeys
and rises 37.2 metres above the
ground, with a steep stairway that
winds up to the top, offering a
wonderful view of the fort and its
environs. The tower is constructed
out of a pale yellowish limestone
and is covered with elaborate
carving and decorative panels.

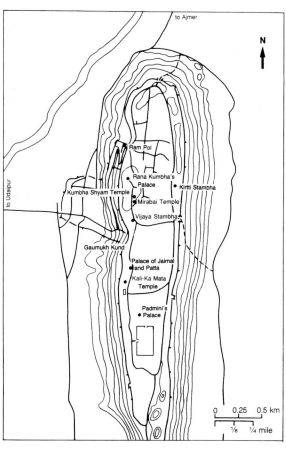

Plan of Chittorgarh

Although the tower has no ostensible function apart from a
commemorative one, it has come to symbolize Chittorgarh, a
place of honour and valour.

South of the Kumbha Palace is a compound housing two
temples. The larger one was built by Rana Kumbha in 1450. The
temple is dedicated to Vishnu and the images now placed in the
sanctum are of Vishnu's incarnation Krishna and his consort
Radha. The temple is called **Kumbha Shyam Temple** after its
founder, *Shyam* refering affectionately to Krishna, the dark one.

The smaller temple in the same courtyard is the **Temple to Mirabai**, a poetess and a saint born in 1504. But before she was married she had, as the legend tells us, fallen in love with Shyam, the dark Lord Krishna. In 1516, hardly 14 years old, she was engaged to the heir-apparent of Chittorgarh, but defied all conventions and continued to love, praise, and even talk to her heavenly Krishna (Hari). This infuriated the Rana, her father-in-law, who suspected that her lover was human. A sample poem of Mirabai's runs thus:[5]

> Life without Hari is no life, friend,
> And though my mother-in-law fights,
> My sister-in-law teases, the Rana is angered,
> A guard is stationed outside,
> A lock is mounted on the door,
> How can I abandon the love I have loved in life after life?
> Mira's Lord is the Giridhara: Why would I want anyone else?

Mirabai became a widow within ten years and was forced to leave Chittor because the royal family could not accept her unconventional behaviour. She wondered through India and made pilgrimages to places associated with Krishna, like Dwarka and Brindavan, and devoted her life to prayer and worship. At this temple in Chittor her picture and an image of Krishna have been placed to commemorate this daughter (in-law) of the for whose popular devotional songs are still sung throughout India

The third and final blow came when Akbar led his army to the foothills of Chittor in 1567. There are several heroes of this battle and, as the legend would have us believe, even Emperor Akbar was impressed by the bravery and allegiance of the men and women of Mewar. Two princes, Jaimal and Patta (from vassal states of Chittor), came to the defence of the fort for Maharana Udai Singh (who later founded the city of Udaipur, had gone elsewhere for strategic reasons. Jaimal was hit on the thigh by a shot from Akbar's matchlock. Unable to walk, but refusing to give in, he was carried to battle on the shoulders of his courageous cousin Kalla. The two of them, linked together in this manner, posed a formidable threat and fought their way down the fort. Near the **Bhairon Pol**, the second gateway of the fort, are the *chattri*s that mark the place where this brave pair finally died. In Jahangir's diary there is an entry that notes:[6]

> Akbar named the matchlock with which he shot Jaimal 'Sangram' being one of great superiority and choice, and with which he had also slain three or four thousand birds and beasts.

The account of the other hero, Patta's death is recorded by Tod the nineteenth-century British historian:[7]

> He was only sixteen and recently married: his father had fallen in the last shock and his mother survived but to rear this sole heir to their

house. Like a Spartan mother of old, she commanded him to put on the 'saffron robes', the colour of sacrifice, and to die for Cheetore ; but surpassing the Grecian dame, she illustrated her precept by example. She armed the young bride with a lance, with her descended the rock, and the defenders of Cheetore saw her fall, fighting by the side of her Amazonian mother. The young Patta of Kailwa fought bravely and, himself on foot attacked the war elephants of Akbar. The names of Jaimal and Patta are as household words inseparable in Mewar, and will be honoured while the Rajputs retain a shred of his inheritance.

The battle continued, and by the time Akbar's forces entered Chittor more than eight thousand Rajputs had died defending their traditional home and the fires of the johar had devoured the lives of several thousand women.

The entrance to the fort of Chittor is well-preserved and gives a perfect idea of how difficult it was to capture the fort without trickery and deception. The road zig-zags up to the fort which had seven gateways making it exceedingly difficult for the enemy to get past the several lines of defence. The last and final entrance gateway (pol) called the **Ram Pol**, is one of the most elegant structures of Chittor and gives some idea of Hindu fortification techniques. Near the gate stands a memorial to the young Patta of Kailwa. The ruined **Palaces of Jaimal and Patta** are within the fort just south of the Gaumukh reservoir.

Apart from other ruined palaces, there are a few historical temples in the fort complex like the **Kali-ka Mata Temple** (further south from the palace of Jaimal and Patta). It was first built in the eighth century and dedicated to the Sun god Surya, the heavenly ancestor of the Mewar family. The temple is raised on a high platform and is embellished by some very fine sculptures. The original image was said to have been destroyed by Ala-ud-Din Khalji when he captured Chittor in 1303 and was replaced by the present one of Kalika, the patron goddess of Chittorgarh, in the middle of the fourteenth century.

WHAT'S IN THE NEIGHBOURHOOD
The palace and lake city of Udaipur is 110 kilometres from Chittor. There are numerous Hindu and Jain temples and medieval forts to be seen in and around Udaipur.

HOW TO GET THERE
Chittor or Chittorgarh (the fort of Chittor) can be reached by train, car, and bus from Udaipur (110 kilometres away). There is a small guest-house and tourist bungalow near the base of the fort. Most people like to travel from Udaipur on a day trip, with an early start and a strenuous but wonderful day spent walking through the ruined fort. Shops and facilities inside the fort tend to be minimal so go stocked with adequate supplies of water, snacks, and a light, generous, romantic heart.

Gwalior Fort

The great fortress of Gwalior is situated on a flat-topped isolated rocky sandstone and basalt hill 100 metres above the plains, commanding a spectacular view. The hill plateau is aligned north to south and is about three kilometres long, but extremely narrow and never wider than 500 metres. In some places the cliff overhangs and at others it is scarped, the eastern side being the more vulnerable. The western side is protected by a deep gorge called the Urwahi Valley. Ringing the entire plateau of the hill is the fortress that witnessed the drama and changing fortunes of this historic town.

The township of Gwalior that lies in the shadow of the fort has several historic buildings and museums. These include the **Tomb of Mohammed Ghaus** (a favoured saint of Babur and the Mughal family) and the **Tomb of Tansen** (a celebrated musician at the court of the Mughal Emperor Akbar) where a grand classical music festival is held each year.

Gwalior, as a line of defence, is superior to most of the other fortresses of northern India and for this reason was the bone of contention for generations of Delhi rulers. Standing almost directly south of Agra and Delhi, Gwalior Fort was one of the gateways to central and southern India: an important stronghold and political temptation throughout the medieval period.

The beginnings of the story are partly shrouded in mythology and recorded in local ballads. They narrate that a Kachhwaha chief while hunting on this hill called Gopagiri (the hill for cattle grazing) met with a sage called Gwalipa who cured him of leprosy with the sacred mountain waters. The present name of the fort is derived from the saint and the hill. The sage then asked the chief to assume the title of Pal.

This line of Pals was followed by the Prathiharas who ruled here till they were defeated by Iltutmish, the Sultan of Delhi, in 1232 after a twelve month siege. Fortunately the fort, unlike most others, has an efficient water supply system of tanks, *baolis*, and cisterns, and many of these impressive waterways can still be seen within it. Then for a period the Gwalior Fort remained with the Delhi Sultans and they used it as a prison safe-house for their unwanted citizens and family. Mubarak Khalji put his three brothers to death here; Muhammed bin Tughluq imprisoned all 'those of whom he entertains any fear'. Around 1399, when Timur's (Tamerlane) attacks intensified political confusion in northern India, the fort of Gwalior fell into

(opposite) : Tile-work, Gwalior Fort.

the hands of a Tomar chief. The fort, and many of the well-known beautiful buildings within, were built by his family who ruled over the region till 1516 and the accession of the Mughals.

The fort is entered through a series of no less than six gates, built over many centuries. The lowest one on the north-east side is called **Alamgir**, erected (around 1660) by a Governor of Gwalior in the reign of the Mughal Emperor Aurangzeb Alamgir. The next, **Hindola Pol** (meaning gate with a swing, which it once is believed to have had), is a fine specimen of stately Hindu secular architecture with bold details, balconied windows, and a broad arch. Close-by is the **Gujari Mahal** built by Raja Man Singh for his Gujar queen. It now houses the **Archaeological Museum** which has a collection of ancient Hindu and Jain sculpture excavated in the vicinity of Gwalior. The existence of Jainism in this region, just prior to Mughal conquest, is further corroborated by the appearance of gigantic larger than life-size images (one more than 19 metres high) of Jain Tirthankaras carved on the stone cliffs of Gwalior Fort. These incredible specimens can be seen on the sides of the fort. Emperor Babur visiting the fort in 1527 and, though not an idol worshipper himself, makes special mention of them in his diary:[8]

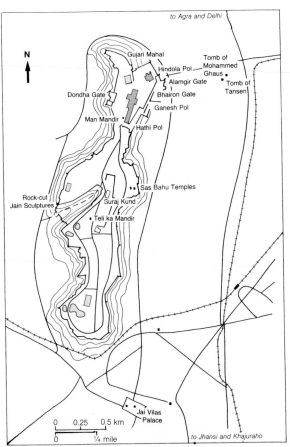

Plan of Gwalior Fort.

> They have hewn the solid rock and sculpted out of it idols, which may be about 20 gaz [13 metres]. These figures are perfectly naked without even a rag to cover the parts of generation.

After the Hindola Pol come the two monumental **Bhairon** and **Ganesh** gateways. Past these last gates on the right hand side is a small masjid and a little Hindu shrine marking the site where the sage Gwalipa once lived and where the story of Gwalior Fort began. Then comes the **Lakshmana Gate**.

The monumental **Hathi Pol** which follows, is one of the most beautiful structures in the fort. It is called Hathi Pol or elephant gate because it was once guarded by two life-like stone elephants. This elegant gateway with balconies, stone screen-

work and brilliant tiled details was constructed by Raja Man
Singh who reigned from Gwalior Fort between the years 1486
and 1516. This gateway leads to the highest point on the
northern end of the hill and forms part of the fabulous **Man
Mandir**, the palace of Man Singh. From the gateway, the vista
of this sophisticated fortress wall bordering the cliff, though
built to defend the palace, has an artistic vitality that echoes the
beauty of the building it protects. No wonder then that the later
Mughal emperors were impressed by the structural design of
the Gwalior Fort and incorporated several of its features in their
forts at **Lahore**, **Delhi**, and **Agra**.

From the Hathi Pol one enters the most sensational portion
of the fort, the **Man Mandir**, also called the Chit Mandir, the
painted palace. It is like a jewel-box, with stunning decorations,
large and small rooms, and many exciting narrow secret passageways and secluded spaces. The entire solid stone palace is
profusely adorned with tile-work patterns: ducks in a row,
branching trees, and arabesque motifs.

Babur, the first Mughal emperor, who visited the palace
about twenty years after it was built, described it at length,
claiming that its stone walls were entirely whitewashed with
lime, the domes covered with plates of copper gilt, and the outer
walls inlaid with painted tiles. The traditional craft of preparing
ceramic tiles for architectural ornamentation was, in Babur's

Jain Tirthankaras and
Teli ka Mandir,
Gwalior Fort.

time, more popular in West Asia than in India. Obviously impressed by the workmanship of Man Singh's palace, the founder of the Mughal empire hastily quips:[9]

Though they [the palaces] have all the ingenuity of Hindustan bestowed on them, yet they are but uncomfortable places.

Inside the palace there are courtyards (Man Mandir and Vikram Mandir) with an arrangement of small rooms around them, some two, others four storeyed (basement and dungeon). The charming character of the palace is achieved by a profusion of ornamentation on the walls, pillars, and brackets. The stone slabs have been carved with several intricate bands of geometric and arabesque designs that run along the walls, twirl around the pillars, and then drop like flower pendants from brackets and ceilings. Though the sandstone is naked now, without Babur's whitewash, the surviving colourful tile-work still glows with brilliant intensity as if created yesterday.

Tile-work, Gwalior Fort.

South of the palace (200 metres) on a projection of the cliff is another historical area with two important temples dating to the eleventh century. The **Sas–Bahu Temples** are for some unknown reason called the Mother-in-law and Daughter-in-law temples: obviously the original names have been forgotten. The Sas (mother-in-law) Temple is the larger one with a triple-storeyed mandap and projecting porches on three sides (unfortunately the spire is missing). The smaller one has a pretty porch with a pyramidal roof. Both the temples are dedicated to Vishnu and have elaborately decorated interiors.

To the western side of the fort is a lofty building, now called **Teli ka Mandir** (the Oilman's temple). The temple dates to the Prathihara occupation of the fort around the ninth century. It is peculiar in design and conception, with massive walls and discreet carved decorations. The sanctuary doorway is elaborate, adorned with the customary auspicious figures of the river goddesses, amorous couples, and serpents. The central position on the doorway lintel is occupied by the figure of a flying Garuda, the vehicle of Vishnu to whom this temple was originally dedicated. The temple tower is distinctly vaulted, with a rounded barrel-like form on top rather than a pinnacle. In some ways this temple roof appears similar to the experiments in shikhara roof-tops and *gopurams* (gateways) carried out in southern India. While records and legend claim that there were several temples within the fort, one cannot but admire the catholicism of the Islamic rulers who from the time of Iltutmish lived in the fort for two hundred years and permitted these and many other shrines to be preserved for posterity.

While Gwalior city is quite crowded and ugly, it has a few interesting buildings and museums mentioned above. To this list one must add **Jai Vilas Palace** built in 1872-4 by Sir Michael Filose for the royal family of Gwalior. The former Maharaja still lives in part of this pseudo-Italian palazzo, while another portion has been opened to the public as a museum for the royal treasures.

Durbar Hall, Jai Vilas Palace, Gwalior.

After the fall of the Mughal empire the British took possession of the fort of Gwalior and the Scindia family promised abiding loyalty to the British crown. In their climb toward European respectability and power they acquired what must be the most absurd collection of kitsch, mixing a cocktail of poor western taste and hybrid Indian craftsmanship that made an utter mockery of both. The museum has to be seen to be believed: grotesque (three ton) chandeliers, opulent bedroom furniture (in glass), a marble Leda sexing a swan fashioned as a night-light, a huge dining table equipped with a silver toy train that chugged along serving drinks and condiments to the guests seated around it.

From Gwalior the historic towns of **Datia** and **Orchha** can also be approached. This south-bound road also leads to Jhansi and then to **Khajuraho**. Gwalior is about 271 kilometres from Khajuraho, and an interesting historical excursion of some of the wonderful monuments of Madhya Pradesh can be planned with Gwalior as the entry point.

Gwalior is on the main rail, road, and air link to all the important cities of northern India and there are reasonably priced and five star hotels. There are buses and taxis to take you up to the fort for a leisurely day excursion. In the evenings a colourful *son et lumiere* programme is organised, narrating the history of the fort to the play of lights and exotic music.

Sanchi

Sanchi is a perfect site, located nearly 70 kilometres from Bhopal (the capital of Madhya Pradesh) amidst beautiful natural surroundings, far from the madding crowd, with well-preserved monuments and exquisite sculptures that are two thousand years old. No photograph seems able to capture the splendour of this rural landscape. Quite unexpectedly a round hill, an earth mound, protrudes gently above the plains, like a natural stupa on which an ancient Buddhist community built their venerated religious building. There are structures and sculptures here that date from the third century BC to the seventh century AD, confirming that Sanchi flourished as a centre of pilgrimage and as a monastic home for several hundred Buddhists for almost a thousand years.

It is not known why this site was chosen as a religious centre. It is not connected directly with the life of the Buddha in any way. The reason Sanchi remained active for more than ten centuries may have been because it was situated near Vidisha (a thriving town seven kilometres away, and Sanchi's ancient name was Vidishagiri, the hill of Vidisha).

It was a strategic trade centre beside the confluence of the Beas and Betwa rivers. We are told that rich merchants and patrons from Vidisha sustained the religious life and building activity at Sanchi. Buddhism appealed to the mercantile classes because it was a way of life that was not hindered by caste restrictions and gave to everyone the respectability which comes with wealth and social mobility. For the Buddhist monks the location was most convenient. They could reside in the peaceful sanctuary of Sanchi (also called Chaitya-giri, the hill of Chaitya prayer halls) and walk to Vidisha (according to their prescribed custom) to beg for alms and their daily food. We are also told that it was to Vidisha that the Mauryan Emperor Ashoka's wife belonged and that he had wished to honour the area by establishing an important Buddhist centre. It was her son, Mahindra, who led the royal embassy to the island of Shri Lanka and carried the message of the Buddha there.

The Sanchi hillock is a mere 91 metres high, no more than a swelling on the earth's surface. At the base is an entrance gate, a ticket counter and an **Archaeological Museum** (that houses sculptures and artifacts excavated at the site, including a wonderful lion capital of the Mauryan period and beautiful images of the Buddha of the Mahayana period) which can be

(opposite):
General view with
Stupa No. 3, Sanchi

best appreciated after seeing the site. A road has been built to the summit where most of the monuments stand; there are later buildings, principally monasteries, on the eastern and southern sides. Stupa No 2 is to the west and Sanchi village lies to the north-east on the road to Vidisha.

At the summit of the hillock is a large enclosed area that contains several ruined and excavated structures, but most dramatic is the hemispherical mound (16.46 metres high and 36.6 metres in diameter) of **Stupa No. 1**. This stupa is completely

solid, with a smaller, older brick structure enclosed within (constructed at the orders of Emperor Ashoka, who converted to Buddhism). Over this ancient brick formation (belonging to the second to third centuries BC) an outer layer was added, faced entirely with stone. Right on top is the *harmika* of the stupa, the stone-tiered umbrella representing the levels of heaven, a symbolic Bodhi tree and the way to enlightenment. This umbrella is protected, as a sacred sign, with a square railing from which spreads the immense expanding form of the stupa body or *anda* (referring to the egg, the promise of Life).

At the lower level is another railing, an elevated pradakshina patha or circumambulatory passage which is approached by a flight of stairs. At ground level is a similar (but deceptively) high stone railing (3.2 metres) that encircles the stupa, with lozenge-like horizontal bars that fit into the pillar

Details of toran, Stupa No. 1, Sanchi.

sockets of the upright posts. If one looks closely at the railing one cannot but marvel at the labour involved in making a rather simple wooden railing design out of stone.

A number of inscriptions appear engraved on such railing posts which register gifts made by patrons and suggest that such widespread artistic activity was sponsored by a variety of patrons rather than by a single donor.

Facing the four cardinal directions, encompassing all humankind within the radius of Buddha's philosophy, are four gateways. These *toran*s are the unchallenged, unsurpassed artistic achievement of Buddhist art at Sanchi. The gateway is staggered like a cattle gate, and consists of two upright pillars (8.5 metres high). Above and across the pillars are three separate horizontal, slightly bowed beams all minutely carved on the front and reverse sides. The crowning emblems of the toran are symbols of the ceaseless motion of the wheel of dharma, the law of life. The pillars of the gateway are divided into smaller panels, each carrying a story relating to the life of Buddha, while the horizontal beams have longer depictions of well-known Buddhist tales.

The **north gateway** depicts several scenes of the Buddha teaching: at Shravasti, in a grove, at Kapilavastu, and so on. Since much of the work at Sanchi was done during the height of the Hinayana period, many of the sculptured panels do not actually show the Buddha in human form but refer to his divine presence with symbols like the umbrella, the empty throne, and the Bodhi Tree. There is a delightful scene of a monkey bringing a bowl of honey to worship the Buddha, represented by a decorated Bodhi Tree (on the second panel of the left post of the northern gateway). There are four elephants with swaying trunks and robust figures which hold up the beams of the toran. Beside the elephants are two bracket figures, the most sensuous depictions of *salabhanjikas* or *yakshis*, sacred tree spirits. John Marshall, who was responsible for the conservation of Sanchi in 1912, says of these lovely forms:[10]

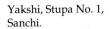

Yakshi, Stupa No. 1, Sanchi.

> Holding with both hands to the arching bough of a mango tree, the shalabhanjikas curves the woodbine of her body in an attitude which brings out her breasts like urns of gold.

These figures bend with natural grace and their curvaceous forms bedecked with jewels reiterate the symbols of abundance and fertility. The architraves or horizontal beams also tell suggestive stories. The lower panel (back and front) expound a Jataka tale about a generous prince called Vessantara who never refused anyone who asked for a gift. Having given away the state elephant who was believed to bring rain, he and his family were banished from the palace. On the lower front beam panel of the northern gateway one can see the scene of the giving of the elephant and the magnanimous prince being forced to leave the palace. On the reverse side (seen best from the railing at the first level) the story unfolds, with the royal family living a humble life in the forest when a crafty man

asks Vessantara for his children and he gives them away as well. Having passed this ultimate test of pure, selfless generosity, the prince receives his family and kingdom back again.

On the west gateway (top panel on the right post) there is another very charming Jataka tale about Mahakapi, a kind and compassionate monkey, a previous incarnation of the Buddha. This monkey lived in the forest amongst his friends and relatives. One day a prince out hunting spotted the monkeys frolicking amidst the branches. The Buddha, to help his family escape from the arrows of the hunter, swung himself across the river clasping the branches of trees and formed a live bridge. His companions were all able to flee but one jealous monkey jumped so hard that he broke the Buddha's back. The brave and altruistic monkey collapsed, but the sequence of events had been witnessed by the princely hunter who came to his aid. The scene shows the monkey bridge, the fleeing monkeys, the hunter seated beside the Buddha listening to his teachings and his philosophy of life.

These panels with shallow carved friezes are full of vitality and playful energy. Sanchi encapsulates an early phase of Buddhism on Indian soil and the sculptures found here bear the stamp of a beguiling innocence and charm.

To the north-east of Stupa No.1 is another smaller one numbered **Stupa No. 3**, built around the second to first century BC, which has only one gateway. The sculptures here are more naive with delightful medallions of elephants bathing and peacocks with fanned tails performing their mating dance. This stupa has a special significance because, enshrined within it, is a casket containing the earthly remains of Sariputra and Maudgalyayana, two loyal disciples of the Buddha who predeceased their master. It is the sage Sariputra who is connected with the great Buddhist university site of **Nalanda** (Bihar, India).

There are several other types of structures and ruins at Sanchi. The monasteries on the east side follow a regular plan

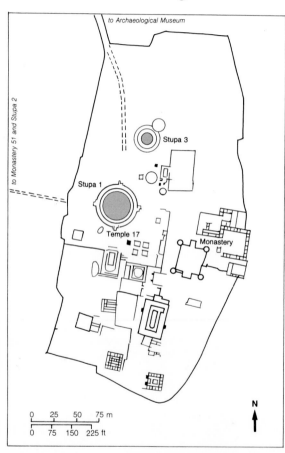

Plan of Sanchi.

with a central courtyard surrounded by a continuous pillared verandah, behind which are a line of monastic cells. The most impressive example is the ruined **Monastery No. 51** on the lower western terrace of the hill.

To the south of Stupa No 1 is an interesting structure, **Temple No. 17**, belonging to the fifth century, the Gupta period. This small building is accredited as being the first representative Hindu temple to have been built in stone. It is a flat-roofed, one roomed structure, which has a small porch with carved pillars leading into the sanctum where the idol would have been kept. From the humble form of Temple No 17, the Hindu temple design grew in size, with the addition of a number of rooms. Its flat roof was replaced in later centuries with towering shikharas of grand dimensions.

WHAT'S IN THE NEIGHBOURHOOD

Near Sanchi (6 kilometres west of Vidisha) is **Udaigiri** with fifth century rock-cut caves carved into the hillside. This series of rock-cut (Hindu) monuments of the Gupta period have some very interesting sculptured panels which foreshadow the dramatic carving of Ellora and Elephanta in subsequent centuries. Cave No. 5 has on its back wall a huge image of Varaha, the boar incarnation of Vishnu who rescued the Earth from primordial floods. Here the massive (4 metres high) sculpture depicts the august form of the Varaha standing at ease (for the gods do everything with graceful ease), lifting up in his arms the tiny earth goddess high above the swirling waters, while below all of nature (fish, sea serpents, and nagas) come to witness this cataclysmic moment in the history of the universe.

To get to Sanchi the best way is to stay at Bhopal, the capital of Madhya Pradesh. From here a number of interesting day trips can be made. **Bhimbetka** is a beautiful site with natural caves and rocky hillsides where you can visit some of the oldest human habitations of the Indian subcontinent. These huge rock caves have paintings made by Stone Age communities some ten thousand years ago. Another day trip from Bhopal can be to **Bhojpur**, situated across a small stream amidst the rocky plains, which has an amazing (unfinished) eleventh century Shiva temple. Through the high doorway can be seen the massive form of the linga on a platform that is over 8 metres high.

HOW TO GET THERE

Bhopal is linked by air, rail, and road to every major town in northern and western India. There are several museums (like Kala Bhavan) that can be visited and a stay of two to three days at Bhopal would be necessary to visit Sanchi (70 kilometres away), Udaigiri, Bhimbetka, and other places of interest.

Khajuraho

This pretty little village in the state of Madhya Pradesh has over twenty temples belonging to the tenth to eleventh centuries. A number of historical stone inscriptions found at Khajuraho proclaim that these magnificent temples were built by the Chandella rulers, a branch of the Rajput clan that claimed its lineage from the Moon. The site, overgrown by jungle and apparently abandoned, was rediscovered in 1838 by a young British officer, Captain T.S. Burt of the Royal Bengal Engineers. From that time on Khajuraho has attracted enormous attention since the temples represent the culmination and exalted reaches of the central Indian style of temple architecture and are adorned with candidly sensuous and erotic sculptures. As Captain Burt records in 1839:[11]

> I found in the ruins of Khajrao seven large Diwallas, or Hindoo temples, most beautifully and exquisitely carved as to workmanship, but the sculptor had at times allowed his subject to grow rather warmer than there was any absolute necessity for his doing; indeed, some of the sculptures here were extremely indecent and offensive...

There are twenty temples at Khajuraho and each of them is distinct in plan and design, yet they all share several common features that constitute the personality of this style of central Indian architecture. The temples are all built on high platforms several metres off the ground. The structures comprise an entrance porch, hall, or mandap, and the sanctum or garbha griha. The roofs of these various sections of the building have a decisive shape; the porch and hall have pyramidal roofs made up of several horizontal layers, while the roof over the sanctum is a conical tower, a colossal pile of stone (often 30 metres high) made up of an arrangement of miniature towers or shikharas. No inch of outer wall space appears to have escaped the artistic hand of the sculptor and there are bold basement mouldings, bands of figurative sculptures on the main body of the temple, while the shikhara or roof penetrates the sky with an abstract design of *chaitya* windows and lattice-work.

The village of Khajuraho has been divided, for purposes of convenience, into two directional areas in which the major groups of temples stand. The **Western Group** of temples is entirely Hindu and boasts of some of the finest examples of high Chandella art. This group of temples is enclosed in a protected area on the main road beside the **Shiv Sagar** lake. A kilometre to the east is the **Eastern Group** which comprises two historic

(opposite): Sculptured wall, Duladeo Temple, Khajuraho

Jain temples along with other rebuilt shrines maintained by the Jain community. There is one small temple located to the south-east, near the airport, called **Chaturbhuj**, with a wonderful 2.7 metres image within the sanctum. To the south-west of the Western Group (along a not very congenial pathway) is the **Chausat Yogini Shrine** dedicated to the sixty-four *yogini*s or manifestations of the Mother goddess. Raised on a mammoth platform is an open courtyard surrounded by miniature shrines for the 64 manifestations of the goddess, and it is considered to be the oldest (ninth century) monument at Khajuraho.

Western Group

A compound wall encircles this group of temples and near the entrance is a ticket counter. Within the enclosure there are several large and small shrines, and each can be seen individually. To the left of the entrance is a path that takes you up to the **Lakshmana Temple**, a grand edifice that stands, like all the other temples of the group, on a high platform. In front of it are two open pavilions or mandaps. The one furthest to the south is the **Varaha Mandap** with a gigantic monolithic image of a standing Varaha , the boar incarnation of Vishnu, the preserver who rescued the earth from the primeval floods. The entire body of the divine creature is carved in low relief with the figures of more than 600 or more gods and goddess of the Hindu pantheon.

Plan of Khajuraho.

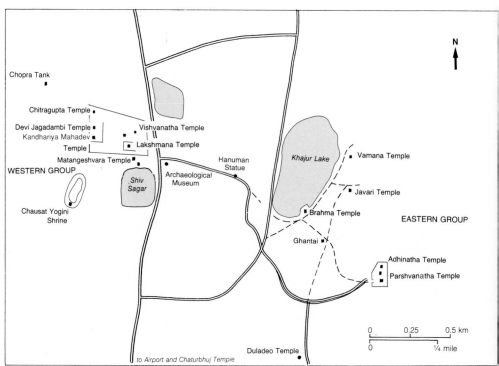

Beside the Varaha Mandap is a reconstructed Devi Mandap which once contained an image.

The **Lakshmana Temple** stands on a platform which has a charming sculptural frieze of elephants and horsemen in procession. On the southern side are a few of the more explicit erotic panels. Climbing the stairs one reaches the broad platform of the temple, meant for ritual pradakshina or circumambulation, which is noteworthy in having a boundary railing and subsidiary shrines on the four corners. Walking in a clockwise direction, keeping ones right shoulder parallel to the main temple, one can view the bands of sculptural decoration that form the most delectable section of the temple scheme. There are figures of the guardians of the directions, divine creatures, and celestial ladies. Erotic panels take a central position on the southern and northern side between the two balconies of the temple. On the western side are a few outstanding sculptures, one of a woman bathing and the other of a woman who has raised her foot for inspection. The voluptuous curvaceous form of the women, attired in skimpy clothing and bedecked with ornate jewellery, is the remarkable achievement of this school of art.

The temple faces east and a steep flight of stairs leads up to the inner sanctum placed high above ground level. There is an entrance porch, a hall of pillars, and interesting sculptural motifs on the side walls. The inner ritual passage winds around

Chitragupta Temple, Khajuraho

the sanctum and is dressed with bands of sculpture in imitation of the temple's external wall. The deity's alcove is further raised above floor level and contains within its dark interiors a large image of Vaikuntha Vishnu, bearing three heads representing his various incarnations.

Walking westward along the garden path one comes to the largest and most handsome monument at Khajuraho, the **Kandariya Mahadev Temple**. This sandstone structure (like all the other temples built entirely without the use of cement and mortar) stands almost 30 metres above ground level and is as long as it is tall. The temple is dedicated to Shiva, with a linga at the centre of the garbha griha. The temple stairs lead to the platform where one may enjoy the rich sculptural decoration of female figures in a variety of poses. There are ladies playing with a ball, some engaged in writing a letter, others applying make-up, and absorbed in a multitude of other activities. On the southern and northern sides, between the balconies are the large-scale erotic panels, and in this temple they are distinctly acrobatic in nature. Below the bands of the main body of the temple are smaller, narrower friezes depicting court life, the army, processions of elephants and horses. The temple is approached by the eastern stairway which has the most beautiful ornate toran, or entrance decoration of the entire group of temples. The floral toran is carved out of a single block of stone.

Nineteenth century drawing of Kandariya Mahadev Temple, Khajuraho.

The **Devi Jagadambi Temple** stands on the same platform as the Kandariya Mahadev Temple and is smaller and more delicately proportioned, decorated with some of the finest examples of sculpture at Khajuraho. The temple has an entrance porch, a mandap, and the sanctum or garbha griha now houses a huge image of the goddess (Devi) of the Universe (Jagadambi). Since it is on a smaller scale than the Kandariya Mahadev Temple it is possible to see each individual sculpture. The *dikpalas*, or guardians of the directions, are characteristically portrayed: Indra with his elephant guards the east, Yama the lord of death, protector of the south, bears a skull and rod. Within the niches on the external wall are figures of the Gods with their consorts. The southern side has a lovely depiction of the Varaha, the boar incarnation of Vishnu. Similar in design and execution of fine sculpture is the **Chitragupta Temple** dedicated to the sun god, Surya. The well-proportioned temple stands on a high platform a short distance north of the Devi Jagadambi Temple.

Moving back in the entrance gate, to the north-eastern corner of the Western Group complex, is the magnificent form of the **Vishvanatha Temple**, similar in plan to the Kandariya Mahadev Temple. It has, however, many unique features; the mandap for the vahana is incorporated in the plan. It is approached from the southern side and is guarded by two stone ceremonial elephants wearing ankle bells and ornamental chains.

On top of the wide platform is the small dainty **Nandi Mandap** with an elegant pyramidal roof. Within the open mandap is a large single stone image of Nandi, the devoted companion and mount of Shiva. He stares longingly out at the temple before him, the house of his lord and master. The mandap is a lovely place in which to sit and rest a while and offers a good view of the street below, the distant Dantla hills, and the Western Group complex.

The Vishvanatha Temple has some exquisite sculptural details and within the shrine is a marble linga of Shiva. The inner passage around the sanctum and the mandap are also adorned with images of the gods and celestial ladies in characteristic poses. The mandap pillars in front of the sanctum bear the last remains of exquisitely carved bracket figures that have escaped the cruel hand of the thief and art dealer.

Erotic panel, Khajuraho.

A short kilometre walk or ride away takes you on a meandering route past the village and the smaller shrines near the **Khajur Sagar** (where you will always see some interesting birds like the tall Sarus crane and egrets). The **Brahma Temple** is one of the smallest shrines in Khajuraho and has only a single room with a Shiv-linga in the centre protected by a huge pyramidal roof. The **Vamana** and **Javari Temples** are set against a rural landscape amidst fields and cattle pastures, and are miniature versions in plan and design of the large Western Group temples. Each temple has an entrance porch, a small mandap, (no inner circumabulatory passage) and the shrine.

Eastern Group

This group of temples is enclosed within a high compound wall, and of them several Jain temples are still in worship and contain sculptures and carved doorways from older ruined temples of the area. Within the protected zone is the **Parshvanatha Temple**, a medium-sized building with an image of the Jain Tirthankara in the sanctum. The temple has been heavily renovated in this century. Along the outer wall are two bands of sculptures depicting various gods and goddesses of the Hindu pantheon. There is a lovely figure of a woman feeding her baby, a woman putting kohl around her eye and another putting on her ankle bells (on the northern side). While the figures depicted at this

Kandariya Mahadev Temple, Khajuraho.

temple are full and heavy, the sculptured figures of the neighbouring **Adhinatha Temple** are winsome and lithe.

Returning from the Jain temples is a small side road leading south to the **Duladeo Temple**. The temple is set amidst the fields beside the meagre Khodar stream where the local buffaloes bathe. This temple, believed to have been built in the twelfth century, forms the last phase of building at Khajuraho, and this is apparent from the profusely ornate wall decoration in which each figure is adorned with heavy, intricately carved jewels. The temple follows a similar plan to the other medium-sized temples of Khajuraho but has an exaggerated star-shaped ground and wall design. The projections of the star are so angular that the play of light (especially at sunset) is extremely dramatic. The inner hall has unusual proportions and very striking sculptures on the side pillars.

WHAT'S IN THE NEIGHBOURHOOD

Khajuraho has one temple that is still in worship and this is located right next to the Western Group of temples. It belongs to the Chandella period but is different from any other shrine for it lacks ornamentation so characteristic of this school. The **Matangeshvara Temple** has a gigantic (2.5 metres) linga which is the centre of worship for the community and draws large crowds during the festival of Mahashivratri (Feburary–March). At the festival of Mahashivratri the village of Khajuraho celebrates the divine wedding of Shiva and Parvati. The ritual enactment of the wedding is also the theme of the sculptures of the temples. The sculptures of Khajuraho also tell the story of Shiva's wedding; the celestial guests who attended the marriage, the wonder and amazement of the ladies of the city who interrupted their work (feeding the baby, applying make-up, dressing up) to see the divine procession go by and finally the consumation of the cosmic union of Shiva and Parvati, in the erotic panels.

Monuments of Orchha on the Betwa river.

Khajuraho has a small but very well-kept **Archaeological Museum** which stands near the Western Group of temples. The temple entrance ticket affords access to the museum. In the central hall is an impressive and very endearing figure of the Dancing Ganesh, the elephant-headed son of Shiva. The museum galleries have some Vishnu and Shiva masterpieces, and a few samples of the Jain and Buddhist legacy of the village.

Beyond the confines of Khajuraho are a number of interesting picnic spots like the Raneh Waterfalls (17 kilometres north-east of Khajuraho) and the Pandav Falls (32 kilometres away). An early morning jeep ride through the Panna National Park (45 kilometres from Khajuraho) is an exhilarating diversion for the nature lover, with a short break beside the Ken river, one of the most beautiful rivers in India. Other contemporary monuments of the Chandella period can be seen at the striking hill fort of Ajaygarh (80 kilometres away). Another pleasant day excursion can be made to Rajgarh palace (25 kilometres away).

HOW TO GET THERE

Khajuraho now has an airport that is linked with daily services to Delhi, Agra, Varanasi, and also Bombay. There is no direct rail connection to Khajuraho and the most convenient station would be Jhansi which is linked to Delhi and other major northern cities. From Jhansi station a number of buses and taxis ply to Khajuraho and the journey takes over three hours. If you are taking the Jhansi route it is well worth your while stopping for a short break at **Orchha**, a deserted sixteenth century city. Here, on the banks of the lovely Betwa river, stand the painted palaces, temples, and cenotaphs of a provincial kingdom.

The best time of year to visit Khajuraho is between October and March when it is cool and one can sit on the lush lawns and admire the temples. The Department of Tourism organises a dance festival at Khajuraho in the first week of March each year at which artists from different parts of India are invited to perform to a large enthusiatic audience.

The accommodation ranges from well-managed five star hotels to friendly guest-houses and budget hotels. To enjoy the beauty and peace of Khajuraho and to see the temples at leisure it is worth staying at least two days. Bicycles can be hired, and this is an ideal way to see the temples and the countryside.

Sarnath

Sarnath is one of the most beautiful sites in the world, marking the place where the Buddha delivered his first sermon, taught his first disciples and introduced the world to his doctrine of peace. The site lies 10 kilometres north of the city of Varanasi, and it is said that the Buddha came here to a tranquil shady forest teeming with deer and was persuaded by his followers to speak of his experiences after his enlightenment at **Bodh Gaya** (Bihar) and to set up the first Buddhist sangha or order. Its religious significance and association with the Buddha made Sarnath a popular pilgrim spot for more than a thousand years (third century BC to the thirteenth century). Today the site consists of commemorative stupas, remains of monasteries of different historical periods, some new Buddhist institutions, and a museum with a wonderful collection of Buddhist art.

The main area has been enclosed and consists of a labyrinth of half-ruined monasteries and votive stupas. It is fascinating to walk amidst these relics of the past. The building that dominates ones attention is the **Dhamek Stupa** (fifth to sixth century) that commemorates the spot where the Buddha gave his first sermon. It is a cylindrical tower (30 metres high) and, like all other stupas, is a solid structure. The trunk of the stupa is decorated with panels carved with geometric and floral designs. Several attempts to excavate the stupa have revealed that the structure was enlarged no less than twelve times, with each successive patron adding and embellishing the original shrine. Another ruined stupa, the **Dharmarajika Stupa**, lies to the west of Dhamek Stupa (third century BC) and is believed to have been built by Emperor Ashoka. Within its solid hemispherical mound a casket of funerary relics was found.

The **Archaeological Museum of Sarnath** is a splendid building built early this century and stands adjacent to the historical ruins. The museum contains a large collection of sculptures which stands testimony to the fervent artistic and religious activity at Sarnath for more than a thousand years. The first sculpture to be encountered in the entrance hall is a huge capital (2.31 metres in height) that once crowned a free-standing pillar amidst the Sarnath ruins. The **Lion capital** is made of pale yellowish-grey speckled sandstone, and has been burnished so well that its polished surface still shines. This style of highly polished stone sculpture is associated with the times of the Mauryan Emperor Ashoka (third century BC) when pillars carrying Buddhist symbols were erected throughout the kingdom to mark places of special religious significance. The capital has four lions seated back to back and their snarling (smiling?) faces gaze towards the four cardinal directions which they protect. Below, on the abacus, are four wheels, the emblems of the law of dharma (spiritual movement and progress). The Dharmachakra wheel is also the sign of Sarnath, for it is here that the Buddha set the spiritual wheel in motion by showing people the way to truth and enlightened living. Separating the wheels on the capital base are symbolic attributes which the devotee should acquire: the patient devotion of the bull, the trustworthy strength of an elephant, the fearless power of the lion, king of the jungle, matched by the swiftness of the horse. This lion capital with its message of peace and dedication was chosen as the emblem of the Indian Republic and is to be found on all government documents and on all Indian currency.

Within the same hall is another sculpture called **Buddha Preaching the Law** which sums up the events at Sarnath. The Buddha is shown seated with his hands indicative of 'turning the wheel of dharma', and below are his disciples, the deer of the jungle, and at the centre is the dharmachakra. Other sculptures of the museum are of the Bodhisattva, the potential Buddhas who, out of compassion for the world, remain on earth to lead people to the path of truth, *ahimsa* or non-violence. The later

Plan of Sarnath

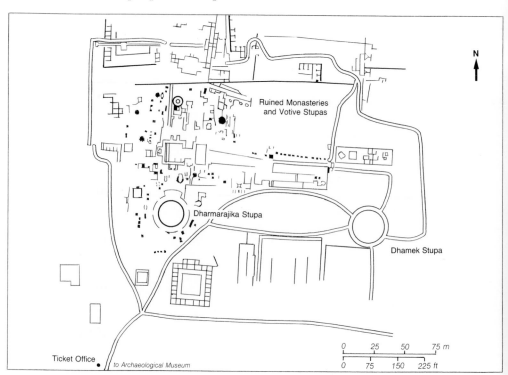

Kushan period (second century AD) statues depict the Bodhisattva in flowing togas and striking jewellery. There are any number of statues of the Buddha, as if there had been a sculpture factory at Sarnath in the Gupta period (fourth to fifth century AD).

In these images the essence of the Buddha's philosophy is portrayed. The half-closed meditative eyes directing self-reflection to one's inner strengths. His face is shown without any expression or emotion for the Buddha has these under control. The halo around the head denotes that wisdom is the only means to true liberation. His plain flowing robes symbolise the importance of simplicity. The Buddha taught that the conquest of material desire is the only way of attaining true happiness. He is often shown with one outstretched hand in the gesture of peaceful reassurance (*abhaya*) blessing all devotees. There are many such objects that add to the splendour and beauty of the ruins of Sarnath. One often wishes that one could see the buildings and their sculptural decoration together with the hum of the monks chanting their prayers to capture once more the authentic spirit of the site.

There are several Buddhist monasteries and viharas in the Sarnath area. Buddhist monks from all parts of India and abroad come here to continue their studies and to visit one the most important Buddhist sites in the region. During Buddhist festivals Sarnath is full of pilgrims and visitors.

Panel with the story of the Buddha's life. Statue of the Buddha, Sarnath, National Museum, New Delhi.

WHAT'S IN THE NEIGHBOURHOOD

For Hindus, **Varanasi** is the holiest city in the world but it is not representative of India, just as Rome is not typical of Italy. Varanasi's special beauty and sanctity is derived from the location of the city along a bend of the Ganga. The river Ganga is considered holy and the most sacred in the land, believed to have descended from heaven. Rising in the northern Himalaya, the river cuts across the expanse of the northern Indian plains till it finally mingles with the sea in the Bay of Bengal. There are many places along the course of the Ganga that are considered sacred to Hindus, and the continuous cleansing and rejuvenating powers of the river are also symbolically worshipped. Since the river moves constantly towards the sea where all the waters of its various tributaries mingle, it is believed that it will also carry the ashes of the dead to their final resting place, re-integrating them once again with the creator, the ocean from which all life began. To die at Varanasi or to immerse the ashes of a loved one in the Ganga is believed to ensure liberation from the cycle of mundane life and the attainment of eternal life. It is, quite simply, a great place to die.

The holy Ganga or Ganges flows in a south-eastern direction, and by the time the mighty river reaches Varanasi it has lost its furious speed and meanders leisurely along the level plains of northern India. The river, as it approaches Varanasi, takes a

Bathing at the ghats of Varanasi.

wide curve, turning back towards the north, as if reversing its flow. It is around this bend of the holy river that many myths and legends have grown. It is believed that the omnipotent god Shiva was washed clean of his sins while bathing in the holy Ganga at Varanasi and therefore the city is associated with him and spiritual cleansing. The entire city is orientated towards the river, with *ghat*s (stepped platforms) that line the banks to enable pilgrims to descend to the river to bathe, collect holy **Ganga jal** (water from the Ganga), and to pray beside the sacred waters.

The best way to see this vital aspect of the city is to take a boat-ride downstream, preferably at dawn. **Rajghat Plateau** is the oldest historical part of the city. Excavations here have brought to light evidence of occupation of this region from the first centuries of the Christian era. For hundreds of years Varanasi was ruled by many Hindu kings. In 1033, the city was raided by Mahmud of Ghazni and again by Ala-ud-Din Khalji. After that it remained under Muslim rule till in 1775 when the city was ceded by the Nawab of Oudh to the British. Many temples were destroyed and replaced by mosques. The Great Mosque of Aurangzeb, beside the Gyan Kup (Well of Knowledge) was constructed over the ruins of several temples in the late seventeenth century. Its minarets (70.7 metres high) tower over the landscape and can be seen dominating the horizon of Varanasi.

Over the past three hundred years some of the shrines have been rebuilt and the skyline of Varanasi, from the riverside, reveals this amalgamation of different cultures and traditions. As the boat moves away from Malaviya Bridge, the city and ghats rise out of the western river bank. The **Panchaganga Ghat** is dominated by a view of Aurangzeb's mosque, the **Ram** and beside it the **Lakshmana Ghats**, a popular bathing area with temples associated with the heroes of the epic poem Ramayana. The **Manikarnika Ghat** and the adjacent cremation ghat are perhaps the most revered places along the river front. They are associated with Vishnu, the lord of preservation, who dug a well (previously a lake) when he began the process of creation. From the steps of the ghats there are narrow lanes and passages that lead to the temples and residential quarters of the city. From these ghats one can approach the most famous temple, the **Vishvanatha**, which marks the presence of Shiva, the presiding deity of the city. The temple, as it stands today, was rebuilt by the Rani Ahilya Bai Holkar of Indore in 1776. A cluster of spires rise above the congested area and below a multitude of pilgrims gather to enter the temple. (The shrine is open only to Hindus.) It is considered an act of great religious merit to make donations for the construction of ghats and temples, or even rest-houses for pilgrims at Varanasi. Many royal families, like the Holkars of Madhya Pradesh and others, have immortalised their name by building ghats and temples here. Above the **Lalita Ghat** is the Nepalese temple, characterised by its wooden architecture, sloping roofs, and ornamental woodwork. It was built early this century by Rajendra Bir Vikram Shah, King of Nepal, the only surviving Hindu kingdom in the world. After the Mir Ghat, with its popular Vishalakshi temple dedicated to the goddess, is the **Dashashvamedha Ghat**, where the lord of creation, Brahma, is said to have conducted his ten (*das*) ritual sacrifices. Further south is the **Asi Ghat** which marks the confluence of the Asi river with the Ganga. It is believed that the name of the city, Varanasi, is derived from two rivers: the Varana, that marks the northern boundary of the city, and Asi to the south. At the southern boundary of the new city and on the opposite bank rises the **Ramnagar Fort** and palace of the ex-Maharaja of Varanasi. This seventeenth century fort has massive bastions and walls protecting the palace and courtyards within. The palace can be reached by road and by boat, and some areas within are open for public viewing.

Varanasi is traditionally called **Kashi**, the city of light and spiritual wisdom. Kashi is of considerable religious significance to the Hindus, for it is also a place of learning and education. Throughout history we hear of pilgrims, scholars, and teachers coming to her sacred banks from every corner of the country. It still remains a city of learning and there are several *gurukuls* or traditional schools of Hindu philosophy and education. The **Benaras Hindu University** lies to the south of the city and was built in this century to enhance and promote traditional Indian studies. The campus buildings have been built on an interesting semi-circular plan. Within the campus is one of the finest museums in India, the **Bharat Kala Bhavan**, which houses an excellent collection of early Indian stone and terracotta sculpture. Priceless seventeenth and eighteenth century paintings, textiles, and other artifacts are also on display.

HOW TO GET THERE

Sarnath lies ten kilometres north of Varanasi city which is linked by road, rail, and air to all the major towns of northern India and by air to Kathmandu. A large number of hotels and guest-houses have sprung up over the years to meet the needs of tourists, who pour in to see one of the most important historical and religious towns of India. There are buses and cars available from Varanasi for a half-day trip to Sarnath. The best time to visit Varanasi is in winter, for summer temperatures can soar.

In October and November each year fabulous festivities for Dussehra, Divali, and Kartik Purnima are held. The Dussehra festival is spread over ten days and there are fairs, processions, and spectacular nightly theatre performances of the *Ram Lila*, the epic story of the the hero-god Rama. In the Buddhist calendar it is believed that the Buddha was born (in Lumbini in Nepal) on a full moon night in the month of Baishakha/Vaishakha (April–May), and a similar full moon occurred years later when he attained enlightenment (at Bodh Gaya, Bihar) and also on the day of his final salvation (at Kusinagar, Uttar Pradesh, India).

Mount Abu

On the boundary separating Gujarat from Rajasthan stands a hill with some of the most outstanding (eleventh to thirteenth century) Jain temples. The somewhat drab exterior of these temples, like oyster shells, do not even hint at the profusion of delicate pure white marble sculptures within. The arid, near desert region of the state of Gujarat held a crucial position on the western projection of the Indian subcontinent that juts into the Arabian sea. Along its coastline were ancient trading posts that brought enormous wealth to the territory. In the tenth century the Solanki kings (a branch of the Rajput clan) inherited this vast and prosperous land from the Prathiharas. Their reign also coincided with the period when Islamic forces were vying for power over the identical trade routes. The great and opulent Somnath temple had been destroyed by the armies of Mahmud of Ghazni in 1025, and although the Solanki rulers were having to ward off the armies of the Sultans of Delhi for some time, and despite the threat of iconoclastic destruction, they continued to patronise and sponsor great building activity. During this time the lavishly decorated Hindu Sun temple was built at **Modhera** (see **Ahmadabad**) and profusely ornate Jain fortress-temples were constructed on hill-tops at Satrunjaya, Mount Girnar, and Mount Abu, and later in the fifteenth century at **Ranakpur** near **Udaipur** in Rajasthan.

During a very brief period, between the fall of the Somnath temple (1025) and the invasion of Gujarat by Ala-ud-Din Khalji in 1297, a group of Jain temples were constructed on the Abu plateau. Mount Abu rises 1000 metres above the plains and its highest point is called Guru Shikar (1772 metres) where there is a small shrine. The hillock derives its name from mythology:[12]

In eons gone by it was a favourite resort of the Hindu gods. A wide abyss mysteriously formed there and the sons of the Himalaya (Lord of the snow-clad mountains) were called to help fill it up. The youngest son, called Nandivardhana (Giver of increasing happiness), was lame and he came riding on the back of his friend Arbuda, a snake. Nandivardhana and the wriggling snake plunged into the hole and filled the great abyss and only his nose poked out on the surface of the earth and became a hill that trembled with the movement of Arbuda. This hill which contains Nandi (happiness) was called Arbuda (swelling tumour) or Abu after the friendly snake.

On this beautiful hill-top (built on increasing happiness) are a number of lovely lakes and houses, and strategic points from where the magnificent scenery of the plains may be viewed. Obviously a place of great religious significance, a site on the hill called **Dilwara** (*deval-vara*, province of temples) was chosen for the construction of Jain temples. The Solanki rulers gave their patronage to several rich Jain ministers and merchants who contributed to the construction of these magnificent shrines. There are four principle temples at Dilwara. The earliest is the **Adhinatha (Vimala Vasahi) Temple** founded by Vimala Shah, a minister under the Solanki ruler Bhima I, in 1032 and reno-

vated many years later. To the south and east of this great temple are the Parshvanatha and a second Adhinatha Temple built between the fourteenth and fifteenth centuries. The northernmost temple of this complex is the **Neminatha (Luna Vasahi) Temple** constructed around 1230 by two merchants, Vastupala and Tejapala, and extended in subsequent years. There is a wonderful story about how these two merchants had accumulated so much wealth that they did not know what to do, and they came up with this novel idea:[13]

General view,
Mount Abu

Together they spent many hours discussing where they could hide their wealth and ensure that it would never get stolen. The discussions so concerned them that one day they forgot to eat their lunch. Tejapala's wife, Anupama, came to see what was the matter. She advised them to put their treasure on the summit of a hill so that it would always be visible and so safe that thieves would not dare to steal it. When she was asked what was meant she replied that Tejapala and Vastupala should build a temple on Mount Abu, Satrunjaya and Girnar, a treasure that would last forever.

The plans of the temples are quite similar and follow the Hindu temple model evolved much earlier (and similar to the ornate interiors of the Sun Temple at **Modhera**). The temples are aligned east to west with the entrance facing the rising sun. A wall surrounds the main shrine, providing it with a protective, rather unattractive, sheath. As you enter the gateway, the courtyard opens out into a pool of light and the inward-facing enclosure wall is studded with miniature shrines garlanding the temple in the centre.

The concept of the bland outer enclosure wall and the jewel-like interior is consistent with Jain philosophy, based on the belief that all entities on earth, whatever their colour or shape, are in varying degrees imperfect, yet they all carry the seed of potential perfection. All beings, though they dwell in sorrow, greed, and hate, are intended to be omnipotent, unlimited, unfettered, and free. Potential perfection and unlimited beauty lies within us all. As you step into the halls bathed in light and advance into the inner chambers the essence of the belief becomes clear, for beauty of this kind lies deep within the soul of the good and the kind.

Each temple is aligned on an axis and all the halls lead to the sanctum where the central image is placed. In the **Adhinatha (Vimala Vasahi) Temple** the central aisle leads into the mandap or hall adorned with the most beautiful carved pillars and walls. Above the mandap are domed ceilings (not true domes but corbelled ones), made up of concentric rings each level projecting slightly and completely covered with sculptured panels of dancers, musicians, horses, and elephants. At the top of the dome the design closes in and descends in the form of an upturned lotus suspended from the heavens, as though showering blessings on all who pass beneath it.

The interior is covered in a pale white marble, and every inch of it appears to have been carved into intricate forms of female goddesses of learning and wisdom, animals, creepers, and floral motifs. The marble was quarried in the plains below and hauled up the 1000 metre hillside for the construction of these temples. The marble work inside is exquisite, for the hardness of the stone allowed for very detailed and intricate

Plan of the Dilwara temples.

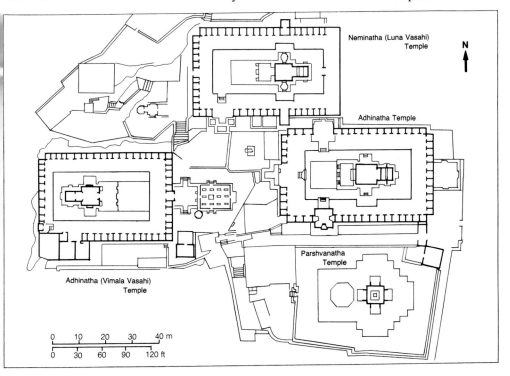

Neminatha (Luna Vasahi) Temple

N

Adhinatha Temple

Adhinatha (Vimala Vasahi) Temple

Parshvanatha Temple

| 0 | 10 | 20 | 30 | 40 m |
| 0 | 30 | 60 | 90 | 120 ft |

workmanship. It is said that the sculptors did not merely chisel out the marble statues from blocks of stone but spent hours rubbing the sculptures down to create a satin smoothness and a cream-like softness in stone. The workers, we are told, were paid not by the amount of work they did but by the quantity of marble dust they produced.

There have been many critics of the Jain temples of Mount Abu, with widely divergent views. Some have felt that the craft exhibited here 'was on the brink of smothering, exhausting itself and degenerating', others that the sculptural decoration is 'crisp, thin, translucent, shell-like treatment of marble [that] surpasses anything seen elsewhere, and some of the designs are veritable dreams of beauty'. There is something unreal about the whiteness of the halls, the play of light on the sculptures, and the abundant profusion of decorative work. It is perhaps appropriate to return to Jain philosophy to understand the meaning of the whiteness and the profusion of 'frozen lifeless beauty' that characterise the interiors of these Jain temples. For in fact, form and idea are perfectly synthesised.

Marble interior of Jain Temple.

In Jain thought there is a symbolic concept of the crystal of the life monad, which through a series of actions, ideas, and deeds gets stained and darkened. Ahimsa, non injury, is central to this way of life and should a person harm, even think of hurting or killing another, the crystal will grow dark and clouded. For himsa, violence, goes against karmic laws, adversely affecting the possibilities of reunion with the Almighty in future lives. From the darker shades of life and materialistic obsessions one can move like a buoyant balloon up to the realms of pure uncontaminated whiteness and purity. Rising through a succession of honourable reincarnations one can shed the colours of one's hatred and fear and become self-luminous, transparent, whiter than milk and pearls, resplendent like crystal. With incessant introspection, cleansing wisdom, mental and physical discipline, ahimsa, one can move upward from selfish existence to the pure realm of the selfless and the 'stainless' sphere of the gods. Jain temples, adorned in the purest white marble, reflect this very idea.

Marble then was the perfect material. Its cool, superior, stainfree whiteness becomes the symbol of the shining light of wisdom and divine life. A constant reminder that everyone can attain pure wisdom. That all who follow the path of ahimsa will rise and mingle with those elevated self-illuminated souls that cluster on the ceiling of the temple.

A typical Jain image of a Tirthankara is then a perfect saint, completely detached from worldly bondage, selfish self-perpetuating desires, calm and unmoved by negative emotions that contaminate and dehumanize us. To call the figures rigid or lifeless would actually be complimenting the artist whose chief endeavour was to portray that undisturbed calm of the saint and his complete disinterest in all that diverts and amuses us. For health, prosperity, and life-sustaining values the Jain pantheon incorporated several Hindu deities to pray to, but the Tirthankaras are always honoured for having risen above the mundane world of needs and wants.

WHAT'S IN THE NEIGHBOURHOOD

There are several beautiful temples to be seen at Mount Abu. The site has been developed as a tourist resort with hotels and walks along the lake and hills. Mount Abu is 165 kilometres from **Udaipur** where there are several lakes and palaces to see.

HOW TO GET THERE

Today there are buses and cars that can take you up to the summit of Mount Abu. It is 250 kilometres from **Ahmadabad** and 165 kilometres from **Udaipur**. The nearest railway station is at Abu Road, 27 kilometres from Mount Abu on the Delhi–Ahmadabad line. There are small hotels and guest-houses for a comfortable stay. The major holidays of the Jain calendar fall on important days related to the life of the Tirthankaras. At Mount Abu a grand procession is taken in the month of Chaitra (March–April) to celebrate the birth of Risabhanatha, the first Tirthankara. The birth of Mahavir Jain, Mahavir Jayanthi, or Vaisali (the place where he was said to have been born) Mahotsav is also celebrated in Chaitra.

Sculptured pillar, Mount Abu.

Ahmadabad

It is a pity that few tourists go to Ahmadabad. It is a lovely city with beautiful fifteenth and sixteenth century monuments, and some fascinating museums. From this city one can visit **Lothal**, one of the oldest cities in India built almost 5,000 years ago, and the Sun Temple of **Modhera**. Visits can also be made to Kutch, the desert peninsula and its communities, with an artistic tradition of weaving, embroidery, and other crafts. In the Gir forests, now a beautiful nature reserve, one can see (if one is lucky) the last surviving Asiatic lion in the wild.

Gujarat derives its name from Gurjara Rastra, the land of the Gurjaras, a migrant tribe that was responsible for the development and preservation of an ancient and exotic cultural heritage. The state of Gujarat lies on the westernmost part of the Indian subcontinent that projects into the Arabian Sea. Since time immemorial the land and its people have been associated with maritime trade, industry, and wealth. Today Ahmadabad is a bustling industrial city, with huge textile mills and trading houses run by some of the wealthiest families in India. The state of Gujarat is also associated with Mahatma Gandhi, born in this region, who became India's premier ideologue and freedom fighter for independence from British colonial rule. A chain of Sevagrams (villages of charity), like Sabarmati in Gujarat, was set up by Gandhi as experimental villages where caste, colour, and creed had no part, where people from all walks of life could work together to rebuild a self-sufficient economy and the secular fabric of India.

Ala-ud-Din Khalji, the Sultan of Delhi, had conquered this region in 1300 (a few years before taking the Mewar stronghold at **Chittor** and laying the foundations for the second Islamic city of **Siri** in Delhi). For nearly one hundred years Gujarat became a provincial state of the Sultans of Delhi and then in 1407 Ahmad Shah's grandfather broke away and formed an independent Sultanate of Gujarat which lasted from 1298 to 1573. Ahmad Shah succeeded his grandfather and moved his capital from Patan to the new city of Ahmadabad.

The city was founded in 1411 by Ahmad Shah at the site of an ancient town. Ahmadabad, named after its founder, was built beside the mighty Sabarmati river which flows from north to south. Today the old and new city spill over the left and right banks, and four large bridges link these two parts of the city. The river and its vista is an intrinsic part of the landscape of urban

(opposite) : Sidi Bashir's Minars, Ahmadabad.

Ahmadabad, a feature that once lent it so much charm. Between his rule (1411-42) and that of his grandson, Mahmud Begada (1458-1510), nearly fifty mosques and tombs were added to the city. Ahmad Shah spent much of his reign warring with his Rajput neighbours, but with the foundation of his new capital in 1411 he secured a kingdom that his descendants ruled for nearly two hundred years until Emperor Akbar in 1573 conquered Gujarat (in commemoration of this victory Akbar built the great Buland Darwaza, the gateway of the mosque at **Fatehpur Sikri**).

The old city of Ahmadabad once had huge fortification walls with magnificent gateways, in accordance with the norms of most medieval towns in northern India. Within the walls, the city was divided into residential areas, markets, and squares. Characteristic of Ahmadabad are the blocks or pols that divide the city. When two or more roads meet, the junction becomes a mini meeting place where you will often see ornately carved pigeon-rests erected on long slender poles. Gujarat has a wonderful heritage of intricately carved wooden domestic architecture with elaborate façades with shuttered windows, carved pillars, and overhanging brackets.

A short distance from the triple-arched gate, **Tripolia** or **Teen Darwaza**, which marks the entrance to the busy market area and the Bhadra or royal citadel of the city, is the **Jami Masjid**, the huge Friday mosque. This mosque must be one of the most elegant mid-fifteenth century monuments to be built in India and was completed in 1424. From the busy street one walks into a walled enclosure which opens out into an immense and breathtaking open courtyard. The entire complex, the western façade facing Mecca, the arcaded corridors around the courtyard, and the floor of the courtyard itself is covered with a pale, yellowish sandstone. The western façade has a prominent central portion consisting of three arches, the one in the middle being the largest, once framed by two tall minarets. These, now broken, were very slim and elongated (as can be seen

Plan of old city of Ahamdabad.

n the minarets of the Rani Sipri Mosque), serving an ornamental rather than an architectural function so characteristic of this school in Gujarat. Though arches, an invention introduced into India with Islamic architecture, have been used throughout the building, the dominant feature is still the stone beams and overhanging eaves. Pillars and beams of this type (that are reminiscent of the temples of Gujarat and Rajasthan) and the interplay of arch, dome, and flat-roofed buildings became the signature of this period and region.

Lattice window, Sidi Sayyid Mosque.

Akbar, who was born exactly a hundred years after Ahmad Shah died, was obviously impressed by what he heard and saw of the wonders of this region. Many features of his city palace of **Fatehpur Sikri** show a marked influence of the artistic genius of these regions. A wonderful play of light of varying intensity is created by the dark shadows cast by the interior prayer halls and corridors, and the delicacy of the stone carving. The beauty of Jami Masjid lies not in its size and plan, which are common to other mosques in India, but in the refinement of its decorative details. In this mosque one sees a great example of a regional style of Islamic art, one of so many in the Indian subcontinent. Gujarat, with its ancient tradition of temple architecture and fine sculptures, provided the Islamic rulers with artists who had generations of experience. Using their traditional skills to meet new demands and needs they created a style that was truly innovative; a hybrid not to be found anywhere else.

To the east of the mosque is the magnificent **Tomb of Ahmad Shah I**, the founder of Ahmadabad, who died in 1442. It is a square building topped by a dome with latticed windows that allow light and air to enter the building. Nearby are the tombs of the wives of Ahmad Shah I in a very similar style.

Belonging to the next important phase of building in Ahmadabad, i.e. in the sixteenth century, are two lovely structures: the **Rani Sipri Mosque and Tomb** (*c.* 1514) and the **Mosque of Sidi Sayyid** (1572-3). The tomb stands in front of the Rani Sipri Mosque and the grave of the queen is in the centre of the room, under the dome surrounded by columns. The mosque is small in proportion to the Jami Masjid and very elegant, with a characteristic blend of Islamic and Hindu motifs.

The **Sidi Sayyid Mosque** is perhaps the best known monument in Ahmadabad, famed for its perforated windows and stone screen-work. It is unclear who Sidi Sayyid was, or even whether there was a person of that name. Was he a slave of Ahmad Shah or a nobleman of a later court?

The mosque is exquisite because it is small and elegant in proportion and scale. The courtyard has a pretty tank for ritual cleansing before prayers. The sides of the western façade have delicate motifs, as in the Jami Masjid. In the western prayer hall the back wall is decorated with ten semi-circular skylight windows. Some of them are filled with square carved stone screens, of which the most beautiful is the one with the tree of life motif (which should also be seen in silhouette with the sun on the west side streaming through). The semi-circular window is fitted with one large piece of stone that has been so finely cut that it resembles lace. The design is of a central tree with twirling branches full of blossoms, that loop and swirl with abandon, their movements restricted by the window-frame and the restraining example of straight rigid palm trees that grow beside them. It is a perfect play of straight lines and curves, evergreens and transient blossoms, symbolic of all that is permanent and ever-changing in life.

WHAT'S IN THE NEIGHBOURHOOD

The streets of old Ahmadabad are fascinating if you enjoy wandering through narrow streets looking at old shops and houses. There are also a number of old mosques and beautiful tombs to see. Two museums, the **Calico Museum of Textiles** and the **Utensil Museum** must be on every visitor's agenda. The Calico Museum has been accommodated in a large residential house and garden (of botanical interest) where you can see one of the richest collections of Indian textiles, both ancient and modern, in their context and setting and study their history and development. Textiles used for religious purposes, as in clothes for the gods, hand painted curtains to screen the gods when they are resting, are among of the treasures on display.

Even if you are not a museum buff a visit must be made to the **Utensil Museum** where a one-man collection (as the textile museum is largely a one-woman collection) is on display. The utensils range from tiny perfume vases and huge water and grain storage jars to patterned ornate metal boxes and plain, elegant cooking pots. A wonderful restaurant complex run by the same management, is next door and offers a taste of authentic Gujarati food in a very pleasant, simulated rural setting where traditional aritists entertain with their music and dance.

Sarkhej is 9 kilometres south-west of Ahmadabad and was once a retreat for the Gujarat Sultans replete with palaces, gardens and beautiful tombs of saints and rulers. The **Tomb of Makhdum Shaikh Ahmad Khattu** (1336-1445) is the largest of its kind in Gujarat and was built in honour of the saint who exercised great influence over the local sultans. The tomb of Sultan Mahmud Begada is also a lovely structure and is built near an artificial lake.

To understand how important water is in the life of Gujarat one has to see the architecturally beautiful and ornate stone step-wells built to conserve water. These are, even today, considered the most efficient designs for water management and conservation in arid areas. The **Adalaj Baoli** (13 kilometres from the city) and **Mata Bhavani's** step well (1.2 kilometres northeast of Daryapur Gate) are built at many levels with steps, landing platforms, and pillared halls that reach down underground to water level. Within the step well it is cool and only dappled light enters, lighting up the carved decorated pillars and walls of the huge well complex.

Lothal

In the 1920s two major ancient sites called Harappa and **Mohenjodaro** (now in Pakistan) were discovered in the Indian subcontinent. What shook the world was that these huge cities had been built over 5,000 years ago and proved that a very sophisticated civilisation had grown and matured here, as it had done in China and the Middle East. After, Partition, Indians seeking to prove that their culture was as old as that of their brothers, set out to find sites of Harappan civilisation within Indian territory. Many sites were discovered and one of the most important of them is at Lothal, excavated in the early 1950s at a distance of 85 kilometres from Ahmadabad. Located in the Sabarmati Valley, on an inlet stream connected with the Gulf of Cambay, Archaeologist S.R. Rao surmised that Lothal was a port and an essential dockyard for the prosperous trade links between the Harappan civilisation and Sumeria.

Lothal (Mound of the Dead), like Mohenjodaro suffered several floods but continued to be occupied from 2400 to 1900 BC when the last devastation drove the inhabitants away from their city. It shares many features with the twin cities of Harappa and Mohenjodaro (now in Pakistan) and is a well laid out township with residential and work areas clearly demarcated. Just beyond the city, in a special area, are the remains of the graveyard. Bones of one and even two people have been found buried in urns at Lothal. It is however estimated that some 50,000 people lived in Lothal at the height of its power and the remains in the graveyard do not add up. This may have been because cremation was also practised as a safe and hygienic way of disposing of the dead.

The buildings were built in neat rows with wide streets and service lanes. The ruins, unlike the remains to be seen at

Mohenjodaro, are very shallow and hardly a few feet above the foundations of the buildings, are now visible above the ground or their platforms. The houses were all made of brick, sometimes unfired, which meant that they were wrecked by weathering over time and by the elements. What is truly remarkable is the well-designed sewage system, with pottery drain-pipes that lead into a very competent underground drainage network, that excavations have brought to light. The homes are made of a standard size brick, following the norms of the bricks of Harappa and Mohenjodaro, with a ratio of three sides of 1:0.50:0.25. This astounding conformity to mathematically-determined standards across an expanse of territory thousands of kilometres in diameter is a feature that has fascinated historians and visitors. There are standard weights and measures, scales, and seals at all the Harappan sites which raises the question of who ruled the city and who imposed these uniform, exacting standards on all its far-flung cities.

Nothing is known of the rulers or the ruled, beyond the evidence provided by these deserted remains of a sophisticated urban culture. Terracotta toys and images that may or may not have religious significance were also found, along with incredibly elegant pottery, storage jars, seals, and painted household items. A large quantity of stone and clay beads was found at Lothal, and in one building, called the bead factory, several hundred beads were discovered in a jar. This and other clues have led scholars to believe that Lothal was a manufacturing centre as well as a port. That Cambay, a modern town nearby, is still a major crafts centre for stone cutting and bead-work further supports the notion.

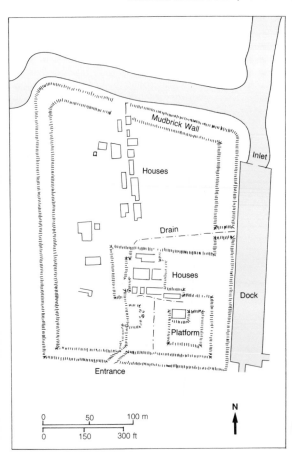

Plan of Lothal.

Supervision of the Lothal site is the responsibility of the Archaeological Survey of India who run a small but interesting **Site Museum** here with objects collected from the excavations, such as painted pottery, terracotta and shell bangles, clay figurines, toys and seals.

Modhera

To appreciate the high level of artistic sophistication that Gujarat had reached prior to its conquest by the Delhi Sultanate, and to understand how the artists here were able to construct such perfect monuments in the Sultanate period, one has to see one of the few remaining eleventh century temples of the region. There is no better example than the **Sun Temple** at Modhera. The temple was built during the reign of the Solanki ruler Bhima I in or around the period 1025 (*see* Jain temples of this period at **Mount Abu**, that share a marked cultural heritage in style and detail).

The temple, as it stands today, has been renovated and restored a great deal. The entire complex is aligned to the east, to the rising sun whose movements and moods are reflected in one of the most beautiful tanks to be seen in India. A patterned flight of stairs with niches for images of the presiding deities and platforms for rituals in geometric order descend down to the water level from all sides, and the sunlight casts brilliant shadows over the entirety. The tank was used for ablutions and ritual cleansing. Leading to the temple from the tank is a huge ornamental gate or toran. From the toran one enters the highly ornate and decorated, detached mandap or hall of the temple dedicated to Surya the sun god. Within the main hall the pillars, ceilings, and walls of the temple are finely carved and the

Plan of Sun Temple, Modhera.

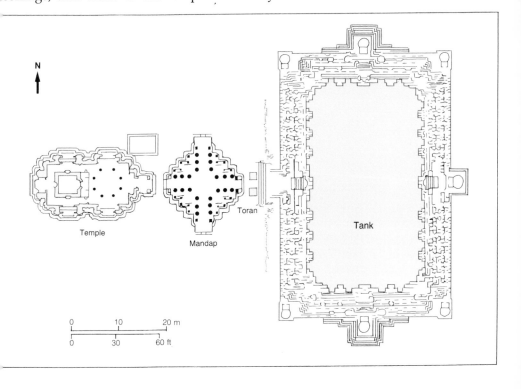

N

Temple

Mandap

Toran

Tank

0   10   20 m

0   30   60 ft

monochrome yellowish sandstone glows in the light of its celestial deity. There are graceful figures of women, couples in embrace, animals, camel riders, and the entire gamut of life that prospers and grows in the care of the sun. The garbha griha roof has collapsed but the shell has been reconstructed to give some idea of the dimensions of the structure. The outer wall of the temple carries numerous sculptures in bands around the surface of the wall, and some of the pieces are excellent examples of the high level of refinement this school of art had reached in the early eleventh century. There are several images of Surya standing astride his chariot as it makes its way across the sky each day, drawn by seven horses representing the seven colours of light and the days of the week.

Sun Temple, Modhera

Champaner

The ruined, deserted city of Champaner lies 125 kilometres south-east of Ahmadabad and 43 kilometres north-east from Baroda (Vadodara). The site was once the stronghold of Rajput rulers. During the reign of Mahmud Begada, a war and siege forced the inmates to surrender and the region was incorporated into the territory of the Gujarat sultanate. Here the new victorious Sultan built a new city and made it his capital. It only survived for a short time, for after the death of Mahmud Begada it fell to ruin and was only rediscovered by the Mughal Emperor Humayun and was then occupied by the Marathas. The fort, built on the hill-top, has many lovely structures, tombs, and mosques, and because it stands deserted today is filled with an air of nostalgic romantic charm.

HOW TO GET THERE

Ahmadabad is well-connected to Bombay, Delhi, and Bangalore by air, rail, and road. The city has several budget and star hotels. It is possible to hire a car or join a tour to Lothal, Champaner, and Modhera. There are buses, trains, and cars that can take you near or to Lothal. A day trip to Lothal from Ahmadabad can be made, for it is less than 90 kilometres away. Champaner is 125 kilometres away while Modhera is 110 kilometres away from Ahmadabad.

Elephanta

India has greater variety and quantity of rock-cut architecture than any other country in the world. Rock-cut architecture is technically not really architecture but monumental sculpture through which entire temples and buildings are carved out of solid rock. The skill in large-scale carving lies in accurately chiselling the side of a hill to create a temple, not brick by brick from foundation upwards, but cutting the rock from roof downwards. One wrong move, one broken bit would mean the failure of the entire scheme. The best examples of Indian rock-cut architecture are to be found in Maharashtra at **Ajanta**, **Ellora**, and **Elephanta**, in Orissa at **Udayagiri** and **Khandagiri**, and in the southern state of Karnataka at **Badami** and **Aihole**. But these are not isolated monuments and many other sites in Maharashtra, (for instance Karle, Kanheri, and Bedsa) trace the development of this unique form of architecture.

One of the many pleasures of visiting the island of Elephanta is the hour-long boat ride off Bombay harbour across the waters to the tiny patch of greenery surrounded by the sea. Why this sea-locked emerald island was chosen for a seventh century shrine to Shiva we may never know. There is very little inscriptional evidence to inform us of the intent and purpose of the temple. Was it was built by royal patrons, or a religious community, or even by those who inhabited the island more than a thousand years ago? The name Elephanta is from the Portuguese, for the island once had a huge stone elephant sculpture (now in the Bhau Daji Lad Museum or Victoria Gardens in Bombay). The original name of the island appears to have been Gharapuri from the ancient Agrahara-puri.

The boat takes you across the six mile expanse of sea separating Elephanta from Bombay and drops you off on the island. From the jetty there is a long but pleasant (half kilometre) uphill walk to the sculpted grotto. At the clearing a huge carved pillared opening (facing north) becomes visible and it is through this that you enter the enclosed secret of the hill.

The shrine is nearly 40 metres square and is planned like a cross with four projecting sides and an inner hall of pillars. Like the rest of the grotto the pillars too have been carved out of solid rock (top downwards) to hold up the roof as they would have done in a structural shrine. The dark interior of the hill is lit, very subtly, by sunlight that streams obliquely through the three openings in the shrine. You enter through the northern doorway, the eastern one is the traditional entrance, and there is a complimentary approach on the western side.

At the western end of the shrine is the sanctum, a room carved out with high walls guarded by gigantic figures of *dvarapalas* or guardians of the doorway. Within the shrine, which has no doors, is the linga of Shiva, a phallic-like form representative of the potent energy of Shiva the Creator. Along the walls of the cross-shaped pillared hall are huge images depicting scenes from the mythology of Shiva. It is as if the linga was a candle in a room whose flickering portraits flash momentarily on its reflecting walls. This perhaps was the intention of the sculptures of this shrine that holds the formless image of Shiva in the sanctum while all around are the ever-changing, apparently contradictory, manifestations of the Creator–Destroyer of the Universe.

Moving from the north side entrance, in a clockwise direction around the shrine to look at the sculptures, the first image one encounters (on the left hand side) is of **Natraj**. Here Shiva is portrayed as the king of dance, in the cosmic dance of creation. With eight swirling arms he holds up emblems of his potential energies. While Shiva dances the entire universe and divine hosts of gods and goddesses look on in awe—there is Parvati his wife on the right, above her is figure of Vishnu the Preserver, and Brahma the Creator flying past on his *hansa* or swan; there is

Plan of Elephanta caves.

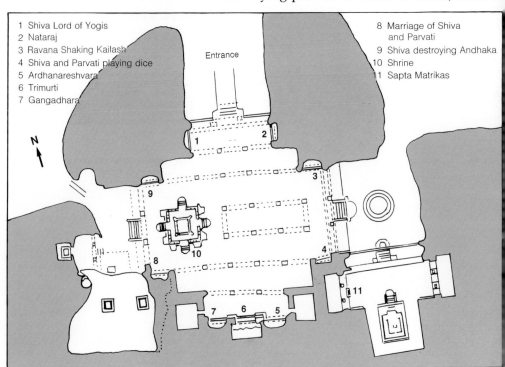

1 Shiva Lord of Yogis
2 Nataraj
3 Ravana Shaking Kailash
4 Shiva and Parvati playing dice
5 Ardhanareshvara
6 Trimurti
7 Gangadhara
8 Marriage of Shiva and Parvati
9 Shiva destroying Andhaka
10 Shrine
11 Sapta Matrikas

Entrance

N

Indra, the lord of the skies, floating on his cloud-like elephant, to the left are Kartikkeya and Ganesh (the elephant-headed god), both sons of Shiva.

These scenes set the stage for a wonderful story in which the chief protagonist is Ravana. Gifted with ten heads Ravana, full of (false) pride, decides that he is as mighty as Shiva. He attempts to overthrow Shiva's omnipotent position by shaking Mount Kailash, where Shiva and Parvati are said to reside. Parvati, feels the rumblings of the mountain as it quakes, and stretches out to find comfort in Shiva seated beside her. The invincible Shiva is portrayed in this sculpture completely unperturbed, despite the hysteria of his companions who fly to all corners in search of safety. Shiva continues with his game of dice, apparently oblivious of the confusion, but with his toe effortlessly presses the mountain below him and crushes Ravana's ego. Ultimately Ravana acknowledges Shiva's supremacy and becomes his ardent devotee.

On the left hand side of the eastern entrance is a favourite depiction of Shiva and his wife Parvati playing dice; together resting on Mount Kailash.

On the south side are three very powerful images, the first on the eastern side is **Ardhanareshvara**. It is a composite symbol of a half-male, half-female figure which represents the coming together of all the opposites of the universe, the divine union of two forces of the world, spirit and matter, that makes all creation possible. It is one of the most concentrated and intense symbols of Shiva with part of his body attired as a woman and the other as a man. The figure with its lyrical lines, the curvaceous female form and the strong contours of the male, stands leaning gracefully against Nandi (Joy). As if to indicate that true lasting joy can only be attained when we reconcile the contradictions of life and comprehend that we are not different but intimately related to all living creatures; to other human beings and to the divine.

The central image on the south side is the most celebrated sculpture of Elephanta: a huge 5.45 metres (triple-headed) **Trimurti** bust of Shiva Mahadev, the great god. This too is a symbolic representation of Shiva the creator, revealing only three of his many faces. The one facing east has a wild, angry expression with a grim moustache and emblems of death, the skull ornament and snakes in his matted locks. The opposite face is feminine and graceful, adorned with beautiful jewellery like the **Ardhanareshvara** figure. The central face is calm and meditative, and the composite character of the image carries a pivotal message and philosophy. Shiva is the creator of the universe, which implies that he is also the destroyer (for everything born will ultimately die, such is the rule of nature).

Neither birth nor decay, beauty nor horror, perturb Shiva who upholds the entire world and is its maker. He remains calm and aloof for he knows that everything created from him will return to him and the oneness of the universe will be preserved. The sheer size of the image, the impact of its form cast in shadows and the power of the meaning underlying it, makes this one of the most dramatic sculptures ever created by the Indian artist and was never attempted again.

Linga in the shrine.

Beside the triple-headed or Trimurti image (on the western side) is the graceful figure of **Gangadhara**, of Shiva receiving the river Ganga. The myth tells of a great king, Bhagiratha, who prayed to Shiva to bring down the celestial river Ganga to earth to wash away the ashes of the dead. The haughty goddess Ganga warned that should she come to earth the entire universe would vanish beneath her waters. Then Shiva consented to take the force of her waters on his head and also teach the arrogant lady a lesson or two. All the divine beings of heaven assembled in the sky to see this cosmic event. As her titanic waves descended on Shiva's head, the river lost its way in his matted curls and it was a thousand years before a trickle fell and formed the great Ganga of India.

The story has many levels of meaning but also explains why the Ganga is considered to be the most sacred river in India. It also explains why it is on her banks that cities like **Varanasi** were built so that the ashes of the dead could be taken by its holy waters and returned to Shiva where we all belong. In this sculpture Shiva is depicted as a tall elegant man, above whose head is the small three-headed female goddess Ganga, at his feet the image of the praying king Bhagiratha, and beside him the lovely figure of Parvati. We are told in poetry that Parvati was none too happy with this relationship and was a little jealous that the beautiful Ganga, lost in Shiva's hair, would remain so close to her husband for all eternity. The sky, as indeed in all other panels at Elephanta, is crowded with divine spectators witnessing a cosmic event. Most of them can be identified by their symbols and vehicles: Vishnu flying on Garuda the celestial bird, Brahma riding on Hansa the swan, Indra on his elephant, and many others.

The next panel on the south-western side portrays the **Marriage of Shiva and Parvati**. The central figures are of Shiva, the divine bridegroom, holding the right hand of Parvati. As daughter of the mountains, she symbolises the earth and stands demure and a little shy as she weds her divine partner. The portrait of Shiva is wonderful. His strong masculine figure adorned with handsome jewels and wearing a dhoti with a knotted sash presents a powerful contrast to the delicate form of Parvati exquisitely attired in her bridal finery. Brahma, the creator, is seated (to our right) and plays the part of the holy priest who joins these two together in matrimony, while Vishnu stands behind him as the best man wearing a elongated crown. On the other side is Chand, the moon god, framed by a crescent halo, while the sky above is packed with hosts of heavenly beings who have gathered to celebrate the cosmic marriage of Shiva and Parvati.

Marriage of Shiva and Parvati.

Opposite the marriage scene is another panel completely different in mood and execution. It depicts Shiva destroying Andhaka, the blind one. Being (spiritually) blind, the demon knows no better than to try and imitate Shiva. For this transgression Andhaka is forced into combat and the mighty Shiva spikes him with his trident and hauls him up, leaving him suspended there to meditate on his misdemeanours and repent. The virulent figure of Shiva swinging the diminutive Andhaka off the ground and giving him real 'insight' is another Elephanta masterpiece.

Returning to the northern entrance, facing the **Natraj** figure, is a very peaceful image of **Shiva, Lord of Yogis**. He is seated on a lotus which springs from the primeval waters held up by two genii, snakes of the underworld. Unfortunately the figure is badly damaged. The entire composition of the Elephanta cave is based on the theme of how opposites and apparent contrasts can be reconciled in the philosophy and mythology of Shiva. As the cosmic dancer (opposite), Shiva is full of potential energy creating the everchanging universe, but he is also the meditative, calm, unmoved symbol of all that is constant, permenant and unchanging in the world.

On either side of the main shrine are smaller ancillary cells with sculptured panels. In the eastern one there is a panel of the seven Mother goddesses (**Sapta Matrikas**) and Ganesh, and in the western shrine is the image of **Shiva as a Yogi**.

WHAT'S IN THE NEIGHBOURHOOD

Bombay was once just a chain of islands linked together by creeks and marshes, but the entire stretch has been reclaimed or linked by bridges and turned into India's most important industrial and commercial centre. Bombay is also India's Bollywood, producing more films each year than any other city in the world. In 1534 the local nawab handed the islands over to the Portuguese in exchange for assistance against the Mughals. The Marathi name Mumbai comes from Mumba devi, a local deity. The Portuguese called it Bom Bain or the good harbour, which it was. In 1662, Charles II of England married Catherine of Braganza of Portugal and was given the islands as part of the dowry. Then the British crown rented out the islands to the British East India Company for a paltry sum of ten dollars per annum.

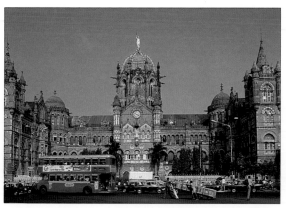

Victoria Terminus
Railway Station,
Bombay

It was only after 1668 that Bombay really started to flourish as a port and trading centre, attracting people from all walks of life and from all faiths. There are several Jewish synagogues, Zoroastrian fire temples, mosques, and temples for worship in this cosmopolitan city. In 1858 the East India Company returned the islands to the British crown and when trade in Indian goods reached new heights (with the opening of the Suez canal) the new Governor of Bombay began to develop the city with renewed zeal. The **Afghan Memorial Church** (to commemorate those who fell in the first Afghan war) in Colaba was consecrated in 1847. This church, dedicated to John the Evangelist, is a lovely building with gothic arches and beautiful stained glass windows. The **University Hall** and **Elphinstone College** funded by Sir Cowasjee Jehangir Readymoney was completed in 1878. The **School of Art** (where Rudyard Kipling's father was principal) was also built at that time and is still well known as the nursery of many significant contemporary Indian artists. The programme to develop schools and colleges for Indian students based on the British educational system, culture, and language had many far-reaching advantages and disadvantages in the years to come.

A striking example of high Victorian Gothic structures (the likes of which can only be seen in Britain) is the **Victoria Terminus Railway Station** (affectionately called VT). This structure, built for the great Indian Peninsular Railway, looks more like a grand cathedral than one of the greatest railway stations and commuter centres in India. It was with particular reference to VT that Jan Morris wrote (*Stones of Empire*) that the British in India often built railway stations like palaces and palaces like railway stations! The building was designed by architect Fredrick William Stevens in 1878 and built out of yellow sandstone and gray granite. The highlights on the magnificent arched doorways and windows have been introduced with an assortment of coloured stones.

The **Gateway of India** was built to commemorate the visit of George V and Queen Mary to the Delhi Durbar in 1911, when Delhi was chosen as the capital of the British empire in India. Subsequently, colonial architecture in Delhi set new trends in the imperial style while Bombay preserved the best examples of the earlier period. The imitative Roman triumphal arch stands facing the sea and it was through it that the last of the British troops were flagged off, leaving India an independent country. The **Prince of Wales Museum** nearby was designed by George Wittet and is a curious mixture of European and Indo-Islamic details, domes and colonnades, and a touch of India. The museum has one of the finest collections of Indian art, from artifacts from prehistoric times, sculptures from almost every major period of Indian history (especially from Gandhara) exquisite miniature paintings (many from the Mughal period), textiles, jade, and chinaware.

Gateway of India, Bombay.

HOW TO GET THERE

Bombay is connected with just about every country in the world by air and sea. As a major commercial centre it is also an important entry point into India and is well-connected to other parts of the country. There are hotels and good shopping facilities. For Elephanta a host of (motorised) boats are parked by the jetty beside the Gateway of India. The trip to the island takes about an hour and the visit takes between one to two hours. Boats leaving for Bombay leave the island every hour and a half so you can time your trip accordingly. The island has a few shops vending curios, soft drinks, beer, mineral water, snacks and a well-appointed Maharashtra Tourism Development Corporation cafeteria. A half-day trip, leaving by 8 am in the morning, would see you back in Bombay in time for a good lunch.

Ajanta

The ancient Buddhist caves of Ajanta bequeath to us a threefold artistic heritage. Havell, a leading art historian early in this century, had this to say about them:[14]

> Very rarely in the world's history has there come together that true symphony of the three arts: painting, sculpture and architectonic design, creating the most perfect architecture, which are so beautifully harmonised at Ajanta.

The story of Ajanta is fascinating. Sometime in the second century BC this rugged horseshoe-shaped cliff, carved out by the Waghora river, was chosen to be the site of a great Buddhist establishment. Buddhist monks or artisans sculpted out shrines for prayer (chaitya halls) and monasteries for their stay (viharas). The next phase began around the fifth century AD with chaitya halls and viharas for monks of the Mahayana sect who portrayed in their paintings and sculptures images of the Buddha, their spiritual teacher and guide. The Buddhist order lived and worked here, worshipping and sustaining themselves on the fruits of the forest and donations made by wealthy patrons. The caves once had steps and pathways that led to the meandering river shimmering below, and it is from here that the monks obtained their supply of water.

The volcanic rock of the Deccan plateau, rich in minerals, provided the colours for the paintings: ochre reds and yellows, lamp black, lime for white, and lapis lazuli from distant lands for touches of brilliant blue. The rooms, after they had been roughly hewn, were coated with layers of plaster mixed with hay and husks to bind the mud to the ceilings, pillars, and walls. Then paint was applied on the entire expanse, not on wet plaster, as in the technique of fresco painting, but on a semi-dry surface. The caves were carved out of the solid face of the hillside, sculpted with pillars, rooms and images, and painted almost simultaneously. Then for no apparent reason the caves were abandoned for several hundred years.

On 28 April 1818, while out boar hunting, John Smith of the 28th Madras Cavalry noticed the carved openings to the deserted Buddhist retreat. The years that followed saw a number of visitors, some who wrenched out fragments of paintings as souvenirs and others who came to study this 'wonder of the east'. James Fergusson visited in 1839 and documented the treasures in each cave and listed them, not in chronological

(opposite) : Painting of a dancer, No. 2 Vihara, Ajanta.

sequence, but 'numbered them like houses in a street', and since then they are referred to as Cave No. 1, 2,.... For nearly twenty-seven years a young artist worked assiduously to copy the paintings of Ajanta, but his work was sadly burned in a fire at a London exhibition in 1866. Another artist named Griffiths prepared a similar set of copies and strangely these too perished in a fire in England. Fortunately these had already been photographed. Inspired by these works of art the great Russian ballerina Pavlova performed a piece called 'Ajanta Ballet' in Covent Garden, London, in 1923.

Today, after much trial and (major) error, little can be done to save these incredible paintings from fading and crumbling with time. Ajanta has been listed by Unesco as a World Heritage site and it is up to us to preserve this window into the past, which presents such a beautiful and vivid picture of life and fashions fifteen hundred years ago.

The caves (erroneously so called, for they are not natural formations in the hill but each is a hand carved vihara or a prayer hall), belong to different historical periods. Nos. 8, 9, 10, 11, 12, and 13 belong to the Hinayana early phase and the rest were for the later Mahayana order of Buddhists. Of the total, there are five chaitya grihas or prayer halls (Nos. 9 and 10 of the early phase, 19, 26 and 29 of the later); the other twenty-four are viharas (monasteries). Each cave is separate and has been cut

Plan of Ajanta.

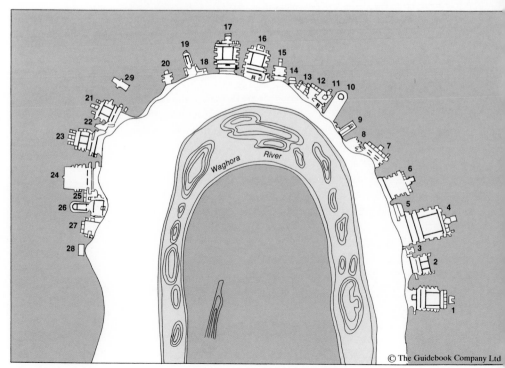

© The Guidebook Company Ltd

into the solid rock, presenting only its entrance on the face of the hillside. If your time is limited, try and see Nos. 1,2, 9,10, 16,17,19, and 26 for the best examples of rock-cut architecture, sculpture, and painting.

No. 1-Vihara This is one of the most beautiful monasteries of Ajanta and has been dated stylistically to the end of the fifth century. It consists of a verandah with attractive carved entrance pillars, which once had a little entrance portico. Within is a large hall with twenty decorated pillars and fourteen residential cells for the monks. At the extreme end of the hall is a prayer room or antechamber with a very large image of the seated Buddha flanked by a Bodhisattva. The Buddha's hands are arranged in the *Dharmachakra pravartana mudra,* or the hand gesture that sets the wheel of dharma in motion. This attitude of the Buddha recalls his historic visit to the Deer Park at **Sarnath** where he delivered his first sermon and 'set the wheel of dharma in motion', inaugurating the Buddhist order or Sangha. Below the Buddha, the sculpted panel has the wheel, some kneeling disciples, and seated deer who have lost their natural shyness in the presence of the Buddha and listen to his sermon which is to benefit all living beings.

While most of the hall was once painted, the excellent and superior quality of the workmanship can be gauged from the two figures of the Bodhisattva that flank the antechamber. In the

Rock-cut shrines at Ajanta.

painting, the group of divine beings are obviously paying their respects to the Buddha with offerings of flowers. On the right is **Avalokiteshvara** and on the left **Padmapani** wearing elaborate headgear and elegant jewellery, holding in his hand a water lily. The downward glance and the shy humble expression in the eyes of these saints are the benign expressions of those who, out of compassion for their fellow beings, reside on earth as teachers. This group of paintings is one of Ajanta's most endearing. The sides of the chamber are also profusely decorated, and on the right is the celebrated depiction of the **Miracle of Shravasti** where the Buddha performed a number of miracles to convince a group of doubting spectators of the truth of his word. He is seen here multiplying himself into innumerable Buddhas. The hall and ceiling was once adorned with paintings of which only a few fragmentary traces remain. The mural paintings relate the Jataka tales of the previous lives of the Buddha.

No. 2-Vihara This monastery follows the plan of No. 1, though it is smaller in size. In the verandah alcove is a beautifully carved seated Naga (snake) king and his attendants. The pillars of the hall differ in this vihara from those in No. 1, but the remains of the decoration of the ceiling are its principal excellence. Parts of the ceiling are decorated with a pattern of regular compartments, each with an exuberant arrangement of flowers, fruits, birds and creatures, and the most amazing geometric

No. 1-Vihara with painting of Avalokiteshvara and Padmapani

arrangements. There are concentric circle designs with rows of flowers, flying figures, and one with a magnificent march of geese. At the rear end of the hall there is a similar antechamber with a large figure of the Buddha. The side walls of the prayer room, and part of the hall are painted with countless Buddhas in a variety of attitudes, reminiscent once again of the great miracle of Shravasti.

No. 9-Chaitya griha This is one of the earliest prayer halls with a very interesting façade and entrance, dating to the first century BC. Following tradition it has many elements that derive strictly from contemporary wooden architecture, such as the rafters, the rounded window openings with lattice screens, railings, and pillars with brackets. In stone these emblems have acquired a new decorative and symbolic meaning, and the rounded window, called a chaitya arch, becomes a subsidiary motif that was to be used profusely in later Buddhist and Hindu architecture as a decorative pattern.

The images of the Buddha carved on the outer façade are believed to have been added at a later period when the new order of Mahayana priests and monks continued to use the older shrines (perhaps while waiting for their own halls to be completed) and made these additions according to their own religious requirements. Within the Chaitya griha is a hall divided into a central nave and bordering aisles by a row of wonderfully

No. 2-Vihara paintings on the ceiling and the Buddha's image in the shrine.

ornate pillars. At the rear end of the prayer hall is a huge dome-like stupa. It once had finer wooden details attached to it, as in the crowning umbrella. On the walls there is evidence of several layers of painting and careful restoration has revealed an older layer of paintings dating to perhaps the same century as the hall itself. The very special atmosphere of this prayer hall stems from its high vaulted roof, the ribbed cage effect from the stone imitation rafters, and the soft defused light that streams in through the chaitya arch of the entrance.

No. 10-Chaitya griha This is perhaps the oldest excavated site at Ajanta and has an inscription that dates it to the second century BC. In plan it is larger than the chaitya hall of No. 9 but it follows the same scheme with a central nave and aisle divided by thirty-nine octagonal pillars. It is believed that many details, like the roof rafter, were once covered with wooden beams. The stupa, at the semicircular apsidal end of the hall, is tall and carved out with a two-tiered drum base. Some fragments of older levels of painting are visible on the left, behind pillars 11 and 12, depicting the Buddha's life in previous incarnations. In the Sama Jataka he was born to blind parents and was accidentally shot. Though dying, his only concern was for his ageing handicapped parents.

No. 16-Vihara This is one of the most beautiful viharas of Ajanta and belongs to the latter half of the fifth century. The central hall has twenty pillars and some of the border and bracket sculptured designs are quite extraordinary. At one end of the hall is a shrine with front pillars and a gigantic image of the Buddha. Though much of the painting is lost there are some excellent examples, such as that of the beautiful princess, the wife of Nanda, who mourns the conversion of her husband to the way of the Buddha.

No. 17-Vihara An elaborately carved and decorated vihara, exquisite in every detail. On the back wall of the verandah, to the left of the doorway, is a highly acclaimed mural painting of divine figures in flight. They are seen amidst clouds accompanied through the heavens by celestial musicians (look for the flute player with her beautiful back to the audience).

No. 9-Chaitya griha façade.
No. 19-images of the Buddha on the façade.

The doorway, full of sunlight, leads to the hall cast in shadows and dark corners. The doorway, carved with motifs, frames the image of the praying, meditating Buddha within.

This hall also has some exemplary paintings, like the one to the left of the entrance, which depicts scenes from the **Chhaddanta Jataka**. Here the Buddha, as an elephant, had two wives, one jealous of the other. In her next birth she takes revenge on her beloved husband and asks for Chhaddanta's magnificent tusks. When they are cut and brought to her dripping in her husband's blood she realises the aweful consequences of her pathetic jealousy and falls into a faint.

The story of **Vessantara Jataka** on the left wall between two pilasters is also well known. It narrates how a kind prince gave his state elephant, believed to be the harbinger of rain, to people suffering the consequences of severe drought. Banished from his palace we see the prince leaving, accompanied by his wife and children. Then in the forest the prince is further tested and gives his wife and children to a brahmin who asked for them. The detail of the nasty expression of the brahmin can only be seen at close quarters. Numerous other notable paintings and sculptures are also to be seen in this vihara.

No. 19–Chaitya griha This belongs to the later phase of development. Here one can see how the art of rock-cut architecture has been perfected over the years. It follows the essential details of the earlier prayer halls though separated from them by some five hundred years. The façade is beautifully conceived with a chaitya window, carved figures, and side

Painting of lady on a swing.

chapels. Most comely are the relaxed seated figure of the Naga king and his wife framed by the hoods of a many-headed snake. The interior hall has a nave and aisles divided by a line of pillars. The stupa at the rear of the hall is now a mere backdrop for the standing Buddha who is framed by a bower of leaves springing from the mouths of auspicious crocodile-like creatures. The capitals of the pillars also have images of the seated Buddha and figures of elephants with their riders. There are no provisions for details in wood to be added to the framework of the hall and it would appear that the artists had outgrown the need to imitate earlier architecture. Of the paintings, one of the most touching images is of the Buddha begging for alms. Sadly faded, it is set by the sixth pillar on the left wall of the hall. The Buddha is shown standing unaware that he is actually begging at the door of his old palace where his son Rahul and wife look up at him, waiting for some sign of recognition. From the heavens flowers rain down on the Buddha who, having surmounted the most difficult of all tasks, no longer suffers egotistical desires and has, therefore, found the path to eternal happiness. The figure of Buddha is drawn to almost the same size as the palace building, as if to convey his greatness, extraordinary life, and sacrifice.

No. 26–Chaitya griha This prayer hall is larger than No. 19 and is embellished with much more decorative work than any other shrine at Ajanta. Following the same plan, it had a pillared verandah outside and within it is a hall with pillars. The stupa that once dominated the interior view of the chaitya griha has now almost disappeared and has become a shrine alcove for the image of the seated Buddha. The elaborate bands of sculptures around the stupa and above the carved pillars are very distinct and form an effective mode of decoration. From this ornate lower portion, the rafters of the vaulted roof spring with simplicity and grace.

No. 26 - Chaitya griha with seated Buddha.

On the left wall of the aisle, near the side doorway, are two profound sculptured panels. The first is the Mahaparinirvana with a gigantic (7 metre long) figure of the Buddha reclining on his side on a couch, as though preparing to die, to gain everlasting release from the cycle of life. Below the couch are figures of his disciples mourning the departure of their teacher and guide. The sheer scale of the composition makes it one of the most unusual images at Ajanta. The next panel is also on the same wall and depicts the great scene of the Temptation of the Buddha or Bhumisparsha, when the Buddha calls on the earth to be his witness. The Buddha is seen seated under a huge tree, the Bodhi Tree beneath which he was to attain enlightenment. While meditating, Mara the temptress riding on an elephant, appears on the right, to try and disturb the Buddha's concentration. In the foreground are Mara's beautiful daughters tempting the Buddha to the ways of the world and sensual pleasure. The Buddha continues to pray in silence, stretches out his right hand

and gently touches the earth, calling upon her to be his sole witness. She appeared, we are told, and watched his conquest over Mara, the physical world of transient sensations and insatiable desires. With this spiritual victory and the Buddha's ultimate enlightenment, Mara is defeated and is seen leaving on the right hand side. This temptation episode (like a similar one of Jesus Christ) is one of the greatest moments in the story of Buddha and subsequently became a favourite theme in paintings and sculptures.

WHAT'S IN THE NEIGHBOURHOOD
Most visitors find it convenient to stay at the historical city of **Aurangabad** and make a day trip to the rock-cut caves of **Ellora** and another to **Ajanta**.

HOW TO GET THERE
Ajanta is linked by road to Aurangabad (106 kilometres away) and can be visited on a long one day trip. Special bus trips and tours are available from other cities in Maharashtra. There are a few small medium-grade rest-houses in Fardapur a few kilometres away. The best season is just after the monsoon rains, between August and March when the landscape is lush and green, or in the winter months when it is relatively cooler.

Ellora

At Ellora one finds the mature final expression of rock-cut art in the Indian subcontinent. If you found **Elephanta** captivating then Ellora is truly breathtaking. The awesome size of the shrines and viharas here are on a much grander scale than at Ajanta and other earlier sites at Bhaja, Bedsa, and Kanheri. What is extraordinary is that at one site, along a two kilometre stretch of hillside (aligned north to south), three major religions chose to create fascinating retreats and temples. There are altogether 34 of them, of which twelve are of the Buddhist Mahayana sect (belonging to the sixth to the eighth centuries AD), located at the southern side, and seventeen Hindu shrines in the central area (belonging to the overlapping period of the sixth to the ninth centuries), and towards the northern end are five Jain ones (belonging to the later period of activity here in the ninth century). If you have limited time to see these great works of art then try not to miss the real masterpieces, Nos. 5, 6, 10 (of the Buddhist section), Nos. 14, 15, 16, 21, and 29 (the Hindu section), and Nos. 30 and 32 (Jain shrines).

The Buddhist viharas and chaitya grihas

Nos. 1-12 belong to the Buddhist section and are dated over a long period ranging from the sixth to the early eighth centuries. Of these Nos. 1 to 4 belong to the early phase and the rest to the second phase of building. **No. 5** is a large vihara in which the central community hall is divided into three aisles by a low row of benches carved out of the floor, believed to be the area where the monks sat and partook of their communal meals. There is the usual shrine at the rear end of the hall carved with Buddhist images. Some of the columns are decorated with elegant medallions and other motifs.

No. 6 A vihara with an original plan that has a central pillared hall with adjacent smaller halls, each with two cells for the monks to live in. At the end of the central hall is a columned antechamber leading into the shrine. The walls of the antechamber have figures of several Buddhist Bodhisattvas and goddesses. Within the shrine is a huge figure of the seated Buddha surrounded by myriads images of smaller ones.

No. 10 The most beautiful chaitya hall of this group. When John Seely of the Bombay Native Infantry visited the site in 1810 he first saw the Hindu shrines at Ellora. Believing that all the caves were of similar origin he tried to find a name for the large

(opposite) :
No. 10 Chaitya griha interior.

image of the Buddha within the chaitya hall of No. 10. He named it Vishvakarma, after the divine artist-architect of the Hindu pantheon, and explained that it was a place where the carpenter community came to pay respects to their patron deity. It is however a chaitya hall and similar in plan to those found at Ajanta belonging to the Mahayana phase. The entrance to the prayer hall has been made by cutting the projecting hillside to form an open courtyard. The façade of the chaitya hall is very interesting with several innovations. Firstly it is designed with

No. 10 Chaitya griha.

two storeys (linked by a connecting staircase). The lower one has a verandah, with a series of pillars decorated with the motif of the overflowing 'pot of plenty', divided from the next level by a (damaged) parapet wall. The façade of the second storey has, at the centre, a shrunken form of the chaitya window held up by pillars. This diminished circular opening bears only a faint resemblance to the exuberant, wide, curvaceous chaitya windows of Ajanta, which are quite evidently offspring of a wooden prototype. The window, now a symbolic motif, is framed by decorative borders and figures of flying sky nymphs. Above, just beneath the line of the hillside, is another carved parapet-like projection divided into compartments, with amorous couples cavorting within each. The central nave of the chaitya hall has two parallel rows of ornate pillars that form aisles on either side. At the top end of the shrine is the stupa carved out of the womb of the rock. A larger-than-life image of the serene Buddha in teaching attitude is seated below a protective canopy of leaves with two Bodhisattvas beside him.

No. 12 Also called **Teen Thal** or three-storeyed vihara and **No. 11 Do Thal**, a two-storeyed vihara (plus one basement level). Both were huge monastic establishments. The courtyard carved out of the hill opens out onto the plain, very arresting façade where all three floors with pillared halls are to be seen. The ground floor has a long pillared hall with small cells, some with high stone bed-like platforms carved out of the rock. The antechamber leads to the shrine, which houses an image of the Buddha. The second floor is reached by way of a staircase from the south-western corner of the lower hall and has a similar arrangement to the plan below. The top, third floor, is far more spacious and has four rows of plain pillars with a shrine at the back. Carved on the side walls are five huge figures of the compassionate Bodhisattvas. On either side of the shrine entrance are rows of images of the Buddha, each in a different pose, depicting the various episodes in his life and symbolic attitudes.

The Hindu section

No. 14 For some reason called **Ravan ki khai**, it belongs to the early part of the seventh century. It is single-storeyed with a small shrine, a pillared hall or mandap, and an entrance porch. Within the shrine is a (broken) image of Durga, the invincible goddess, and she is flanked by guardian figures and river goddesses. The columns of this hall, following the design prevalent in many Buddhist shrines, have the 'pot of plenty' motif. On the side wall are figures of deities of the pantheon. On the left is Durga, then Lakshmi, the goddess of good fortune emerging from the ocean at the time of creation, being honoured by elephants who bathe her with purifying waters. Varaha, an incarnation of Vishnu, the gigantic boar who rescued the earth from drowning in the primeval floods, is next. This image is followed by the human manifestation of Vishnu, the preserver and sustainer of life, seated with his two consorts Shri and Bhu Devi. On the right wall is Durga (at the top end); the next panel is of Shiva playing dice with his wife Parvati, then there is Shiva as Natraj dancing the dance of creation, followed by Ravana, the ten-headed one (the villian of the Ramayana), who tried to unseat Shiva on Mount Kailash. The last panel in the series is the dramatic scene of Shiva spearing Andhaka, the blind demon, to teach him (as he did Ravana) that pride and petty egos come before a fall.

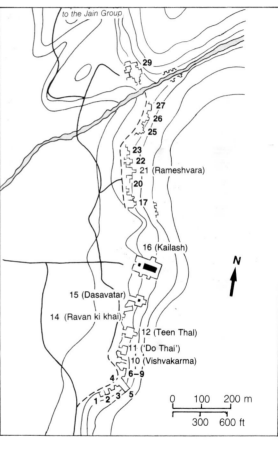

Plan of Ellora.

No. 15 Also known as **Dasavatar**, a term which refers to the ten (*das*) incarnations (*avatars*) of Vishnu, and among these are many representational images of Shiva. It is believed that No. 15 started out as a Buddhist vihara and was subsequently converted into a Hindu establishment. There is an open courtyard, a free-standing hall or mandap (what purpose could it have served in a Buddhist vihara?), and a two-storey temple at the back. The shrine is dated by an inscription recording a donation made by Dantidurga, a Rastrakuta king (*c*. AD 730-55). The upper

No. 15 Pillared hall with sculptured panels, Ellora.

floor of the central hall has rows of pillars between which one can see the panoramic arrangement of deep recesses on the three back walls. Perhaps the original Buddhist images on these walls were first erased and the rock scooped out to a deeper level to accommodate huge panels of Hindu gods enacting popular scenes from mythology. The drama of the hall, the angles of the pillars, the sharp contrast of the sculptured panels of intense movement and quiet repose, is quite extraordinary and cannot but be one of the highlights of a visit to Ellora.

From the front of the hall on the left wall is the action-packed image of Shiva spearing Andhaka, the blind demon, who stupidly tried to imitate Shiva. There is a beautiful rendering of Shiva as Natraj, as king with his arms unfolding in the dance of the creation of the universe. Similar to the scene depicted in No. 14 is Shiva playing dice with his consort and companion, Parvati, while the next panel depicts the marriage of these two cosmic forces. At the rear end of the hall, on the left, the stage is set for Ravana to shake Mount Kailash with Shiva steadying the great mountain and crushing Ravana's ego with the mere pressure of his toe.

This is followed by a theatrical scene of Markandeya, a young devotee of Shiva (his father had chosen a wise, intelligent son who would live only till his sixteenth year rather than a foolish son with a long life). In this sculpture Death has came to snatch Markandeya away. The young teenager is seen clinging to the linga image. Shiva emerges from the linga and saves him from the grip of Yama, the god of death and decay. The sculpture is full of movement and drama.

On the wall of the antechamber is the scene of Shiva receiving the holy river Ganga as she descended to earth from the heavens, his beautiful wife Parvati standing beside him. This is followed by the image of Ganesh, the elephant-headed son of Shiva,

Parvati, and some musicians, Lakshmi being bathed by elephants, and Kartikkeya, the warrior son of Shiva and Parvati.

On the right wall is Shiva establishing his omnipotent power, Shiva emerging from the linga, and Shiva riding on a divine chariot proceeding to destroy the triple palace (underworld, earth, and the skies) belonging to the demons. After these great Shiva panels are a few depicting Vishnu's incarnations: Krishna the human incarnation of Vishnu brought up by a humble family of cowherds; Vishnu resting on the celestial serpent of endless time on the ocean of eternity; Vishnu flying on his faithful mount, the celestial bird called Garuda; Vishnu in his incarnation as Varaha, the gigantic boar that saved the earth from floods; Trivikrama (*tri*, three; *vikrama*, victor of) when Vishnu came to earth as a dwarf and demanded from a powerful but proud king a small plot of land covered by three strides. Granted just three strides, Vishnu resumed his cosmic proportions and with one step crossed the sky, then strode over the earth. When the proud king realised his stupidity he offered his head so that Vishnu, the all powerful sustainer of the universe, could take his final third stride as 'victor over the region covered by three strides'. The series ends with the destruction of Evil (a king called Hiranyakashipu) by Vishnu as Narasimha, half-lion, half-human.

No. 16 Kailash Temple.

No. 16 This is **Kailash Temple**, the abode of Shiva (Kailash). It looks like an ordinary temple within a courtyard, a mandap, free-standing temple pillars, and a stone shrine with a tiered roof. It is only once you look carefully that it becomes clear that this is no ordinary temple but has been cut out of the living rock. Work began 30 metres above the present ground level when three great trenches (90 metres long and 53 metres wide) were cut into the hill to create a courtyard with a solid block at the centre that would eventually be carved into the mandap and temple. Beginning from the top, the artists worked to prepare the pyramidal roof of many tiers, moving down to the body of the temple, then cutting the stone to make doorways, then chiselling out the stone within it to create the space for the hall of the temple (which you can enter), and the inner sanctum with the Shiva linga. Chipping the stone away towards the ground level, the basement for the temple was made, not a plain platform

but with a row of majestic mythical elephants who bear the weight of Mount Kailash, the entire universe, on their backs. At the western end a causeway was cut to lead to the mandap where the image of Shiva's mount, the faithful bull called Nandi (Joy) would gaze upon his master. As more stone was hacked away a double-storey gateway was carved out of the rock, releasing from its stone womb free-standing pillars and gigantic images of elephants that guard and protect the temple of Shiva.

The architectural style of the temple is also extremely interesting in its resemblance to the **Kailashnatha** of **Kanchipuram** in Tamil Nadu and the **Virupaksha Temple** of **Pattadakal** in Karnataka state, both of which are several hundred kilometres away. The story is a historical one and begins when the Chalukyas of Aihole and Pattadakal made inroads into the Pallava empire. They were impressed by the architecture found in this southern most part of India. Political rivalry expressed itself in turn when they copied the Kanchipuram temple style at Pattadakal. Then not long after Pattadakal was brought under Rastrakuta rule by Krishna I (AD 756-73), the Dravida temple style was reproduced in the Kailash temple at Ellora, carrying the Kanchipuram model across to the other side of the Indian peninsula from south-east to north-west, all in a matter of years.

Apart from the great, overall beauty of the temple, its sculptural decoration is worthy of particular praise. Along the three sides of the trench other rooms and shrines were created. The shrine on the northern side has beautiful images of the sacred river goddesses, Ganga, Yamuna, and Sarasvati. The temple and its walls were also decorated with sculptured panels and auspicious motifs. There are bands of sculpture depicting episodes from the epic poems: Ramayana (southern side front of temple) and Mahabharata (opposite side northern front wall), and Puranic myths about Shiva (Ravana disturbing Shiva and Parvati on the southern side wall); and a few amorous couples on the temple walls. The gateway is

1 Ganga
2 Yamuna
3 Ramayana
4 Mahabharata
5 Entrance
6 Nandi Pavillion
7 Elephants
8 Columns
9 Mandap
10 Shrine
11 Shrine of the
   River Goddesses
12 Lankeshvara Shrine

N ◄—

0   10   20   30 m
0   30   60   90 ft

© The Guidebook Company Ltd

Plan of No. 16 Kailash Temple.

adorned with a lovely pair of river goddesses; the entrance nandap has a figure of Lakshmi, and within and around the temple the walls abound with sculptural details that dance and spring out of its dark surface. When the sculptures were finished, painted, and fine details completed the temple had no additional structures joined to it. This implies that in the process of carving out the temple from the rock no error whatsoever had been made anywhere in the course of the entire project! Today the Kailash temple stands testimony to the devotion and faith of the artists who converted mountains into shrines and will remain one of the most spectacular rock-cut monuments in the world.

No. 21 Also called **Rameshvara**, it belongs to the late sixth century and has an interesting plan. The courtyard has a Nandi carved out of the rock on a platform at the centre, with side shrines leading to the verandah entrance of a sanctum with a linga within. Along the columns of the verandah are very sensuously portrayed female bracket figures. There are panels with a variety of scenes: Kartikkeya, the Marriage of Shiva and Parvati, Ravana shaking Mount Kailash, the dancing Natraj, the seven Matrikas with Ganesh, and finally, the wonderful (almost endearing) rendering of the skeletal form of Kala or Kali (of Time which causes all things to decay).

No. 29 This is a temple which resembles Elephanta both in plan and conception. Three sides have entrances to the pillared interior hall which contains a shrine for the linga guarded by guardian *dvarapalas*. Large panels adorn the side walls and there are again depictions of Shiva spearing Andakha, Ravana attempting to shake Mount Kailash, the scene of the marriage of Shiva and Parvati.

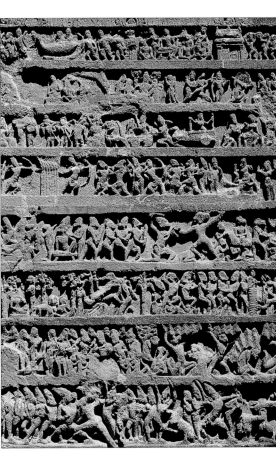

Ramayana frieze, No. 16, Kailash Temple.

The Jain group

Once again the mood of the excavated shrines changes to meet the needs of a different religion and philosophic outlook. **No. 30** is called **Chhota Kailash** for it is a small (though incomplete) replica of the temple of Kailash (No. 16). This monolithic temple has an entrance porch, pillared hall, and a sanctum at one end with a seated figure of Mahavir, the 24th Tirthankara. **No. 32 is** the most beautifully decorated shrine of the Jain group and has been dated to the early part of the ninth century. The gateway leads into an open courtyard in which the temple stands. The temple has a pyramidal roof like the Kailash Temple, and free-standing pillars and elephants. The entire temple is decorated with figures of the Tirthankaras and other deities of the Jain pantheon. Nearby, there are several other caves, some unfinished others recently excavated.

WHAT'S IN THE NEIGHBOURHOOD

While most people use **Aurangabad** city as a base from which to see Ajanta and Ellora, there are some interesting sites in and around this historic place. About 3 kilometres from the city is a range of hills which harbour the remains of rock-cut architecture of the Buddhist period (first to fifth centuries), similar in style to those found at Ajanta. North-east from the caves (2 kilometres away) is **Dil Ras Banu Begum's Tomb**, a Mughal tomb built around 1660, in memory of Aurangzeb's wife. The tomb is modelled after the **Taj Mahal** and is set at the centre of a huge garden surrounded by a high wall. The square tomb building with a tall dome was constructed on a high platform with four

Dil Ras Banu Begum's Tomb, Aurangabad.

minarets at the corners. Aurangzeb was the third son of Shah Jahan (who built the Taj Mahal as a tomb for his wife). We are told that Aurangzeb was not the favourite son and despite his valour and conquests in the Deccan (in this area) his father, Shah Jahan, preferred to shower favours on his elder son. The embittered and unloved Aurangzeb was driven eventually to revolt against his father, imprisoned Shah Jahan in the Red Fort at Agra, and murdered his rival brothers to ascend the Mughal throne. Yet here in the garden of the **Bibi-Ka-Maqbara** (Dil Ras Banu Begum's Tomb) one can see how keen poor Aurangzeb was to emulate and impress his father by building a replica of the Taj Mahal for his wife, and the city of Aurangabad derives its name from him.

The fort of **Daulatabad** (city of Wealth/Fortune) preserves the tragic story of much earlier rulers of Delhi. The fort was built on a steep hill 180 metres above the plains. Nearby stands Chand Minar, a 61 metre tower built by a Bahamani king to commemorate his victory over the fort of Daulatabad. This fort has many structures belonging to different historical periods. In 1294, Ala-ud-Din Khalji laid siege to it and the local ruler had to pay a heavy ransom. Muhammad bin Tughluq who ruled from **Delhi** chose to move his entire capital and its citizens to Daulatabad in 1326. The plan failed miserably and the (mad?) king marched his people back to Delhi at awesome cost in human life and misery.

HOW TO GET THERE

Aurangabad can be reached by plane, overnight train, or a very long trip by road from Bombay. Ajanta is 106 kilometres away from Aurangabad which has a few rest-houses providing reasonable accomodation. Most visitors prefer to make a day visit to Ajanta from Aurangabad. Ellora is 29 kilometres from Aurangabad and can be reached by road and tourist bus. Daulatabad is on the road to Ellora. The best times to visit Ellora and Ajanta are just after the monsoons, or in the winter months.

Velha Goa

For most people Goa is paradise. The south-western coast of India has the lushest and most exuberant landscape in the subcontinent. Its undulating terrain is covered with areas of rich red earth, coconut palms, elegant whitewashed houses with sloping tiled roofs, golden beaches, and sparkling waters. Goa's deep waters and calm beaches once provided some of the most accessible harbours on India's western coast. Historic evidence proclaims that this region was prosperous from the time of the Mauryan empire. After the third century BC many kingdoms sought to control its tranquil waters. At the cost of untold barbarous bloodshed, east–west trade brought enormous revenue and power.

In the medieval period the Khaljis and later the Tughluqs captured portions of Goa and the Konkan. In the fourteenth century it became yet another target of rivalry between the Hindu Vijayanagar rulers of the Karnataka area and the Muslim Bahamani kings of Bijapur, Gulbarga, and Bidar. In the fifteenth century what happened in Goa was linked to the history of the Mediterranean world when Portugal, led by its well-known explorers, established a long-lasting overseas empire. Trade in gold and spices (especially pepper, indispensable for food-preservation in Europe), and other natural resources, were exchanged for the much-coveted Arabian horse that furnished the armies of the Indian subcontinent (where the humble Kathiawar pony was the only indigenous breed).

The traditional controllers of these trade routes were the Arabs. The Portuguese, like many other foreign colonisers, played the inevitable game of power politics, supporting one side against the other till they virtually controlled the region and paved the way for Mediterranean merchants to make their appearance on Indian soil.

It was also from the Arabs that the Portuguese inherited their maps and navigational information. In 1497, Vasco da Gama sailed from Portugal along the African coast, across the Indian Ocean (for twenty-three days), and eventually landed at Calicut in Kerala. Along the west coast of India in Calicut, Cochin, and Canannore the Portuguese began to establish their sovereignty, upturning old trade alliances and forging new ones. When Vasco da Gama returned home in 1502 he left behind a fleet of patrol ships under the command of Alfonso de Albuquerque to guard the coast. In 1510 Albuquerque captured

(opposite) : Basilica of Bom Jesus, Velha Goa.

Goa from the Sultan of Bijapur and made it the capital of the Portuguese eastern empire. The new rulers were quick in establishing their distinctive culture in the region. Homes, administrative units, and churches were built and, in a unique attempt to assemble a corpus of loyal subjects, the Portuguese were encouraged to marry girls from aristocratic Goan families. The experiment proved successful and the colony remained for 450 years under Portugese rule, outlasting all other colonial powers in the region.

As a memorial and in thanksgiving for the significant victory won on 25 November 1510, St. Catherine's day, Albuquerque laid the foundations of a church (dedicated to St. Catherine) which became the nucleus of a Christian centre, now referred to as Velha (old) Goa.

Just ten kilometres from Panjim, the modern capital of Goa, lies **Velha Goa**. A new Christian township (where in 1565 200,000 people lived) was built over the remains of the second capital of Adil Shah (the Sultan of Bijapur) beside the Mandovi river. The road from Panjim enters the complex from the west and leads to a central square from which you can visit the historical buildings at a leisurely pace. At the north-western tip of the complex is the **Chapel of St. Catherine** erected by Albuquerque after his defeat of the Bijapur forces in 1510. The original construction has undergone numerous changes and

Plan of
Velha Goa.

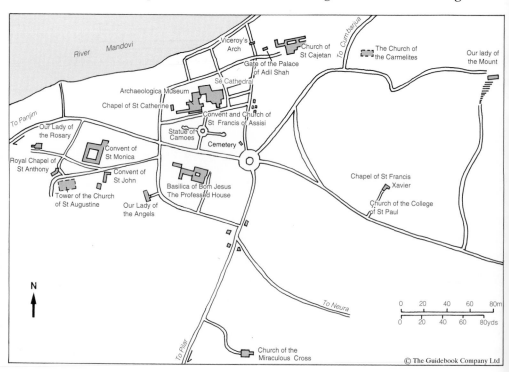

has been rebuilt several times. Beside it is the **Convent and Church of St. Francis of Assisi** built of local laterite stone and clothed in white plaster to protect the porous stone from the heavy tropical monsoons rains. The convent is entered through a narrow passage which leads into a beautiful enclosed court-yard and internal garden surrounded by cloisters. Part of the convent has been converted into the **Archaeological Museum** and has an interesting collection: there are statues (sati stones to commemorate the heroic dead) and idols of the Hindu period, portraits of Vasco da Gama, Alfonso de Albuquerque, and other gover-nors of the province. Paintings, coats of arms, sculptures, armoury, coins, maps and medals capture some of the drama of the events that make up the history of Goa.

The **Church of St. Francis of Assisi** was built around 1661 and is a classic example of contem-porary architectural styles. The church faces west and has an im-pressive façade of three storeys. The building is rectangular in shape with a central nave and ancillary chapels on either side. Part of the barrel roof is adorned by wooden panels profusely painted with flower patterns that appear to be the work of Indian artists under Portuguese direction. The high altar, on the eastern side, is richly decorated with gilded wooden pillars, ornamental motifs, and at the centre is the crucifix with the kneeling figure of St. Francis below worshipping Jesus. On the altar appear the words Poverty, Humility, and Obedience which spell out the three vows taken by monks who join the Franciscan order founded by St. Francis of Assisi.

Sé Cathedral, Velha Goa.

The **Sé Cathedral** is the largest of this group (76.2 metres long, 55.16 metres wide) and was designed to be the most imposing cathedral of the Portuguese empire in the East. Building construction (by the Portuguese government for the Dominican monks) began around 1562 and took nearly a century to complete, with funds coming in from native sources. The cathedral is roughly cruciform in shape with a central nave, side aisles with eight chapels and six side altars along the transept, and the supreme altar at the centre. The façade and profile of the cathedral are dramatic, painted white with a series of arches and windows that introduce a shadowy play of light. Two towers were built to frame the cathedral entrance but one fell, struck down by lighting in 1776, and was never rebuilt. The interior of the cathedral is as dramatic as the external proportions. The cool, pure white walls are adorned with elaborate paintings, wooden screens and carvings on the chapels, altars, and ornamental pulpits. The cathedral is dedicated to St. Catherine of Alexandria and the principal altar in three storeys has opulent panels depicting her life and martyrdom.

The **Basilica of Bom Jesus** (literally Good Jesus), where the imperishable body of St. Francis Xavier is laid in state, was built in 1560 though rebuilt in the eighteenth century after an accidental fire. The building has one of the nicest façades in Velha Goa made of red laterite stone from which the protective plaster has been removed. It consists of three storeys, the lowest one with three entrances into the nave and aisles of the church, the middle one with rectangular windows, and the top one with circular port windows. To crown the Basilica are arabesque designs culminating on a central halo carried by a circle of angels inscribed with IHS (one translation is *Iaeus Hominum Salvator*, Jesus, Saviour of Mankind). The interior of the basilica is plain with commemorative plaques and statues. On the left is a sensitively carved wooden figure of St. Francis Xavier adoring the crucifix of Jesus. Completely overpowering the silent interiors is the exuberant baroque altar at the centre of the eastern side. The altar rises up to the vaulted roof from the sacred table on magnificent twisted gilt columns. Between them is framed the figure of St. Ignatius Loyola who looks up in adoration at the

St. Francis Xavier, Basilica of Bom Jesus.

sun-like halo inscribed with IHS and to the scene above, the line of angels singing in praise of God Almighty, his son Jesus Christ, and the Holy Spirit.

On the southern side of the transept is the glorious sarcophagi and tomb room of St. Francis Xavier. Born to a noble family of the castle of Xavier, on 7 April 1506 in Spain, St. Francis became a pupil of St. Ignatius Loyola, founder of the Jesuit order (that has since earned great respect for its well-run educational institutions established throughout India). In 1542, St. Francis Xavier was granted permission to work in the East and came to Goa where he spent years tending to the sick and the suffering. He went further east to Malacca, Japan, and in 1552, while returning from there, fell ill and died at the age of forty-six. His body was buried in Sancian, off the coast of China, but when the tomb was opened it was noticed that it had not decomposed in any way.

In 1613, St. Francis Xavier's body was transferred to Goa; after his canonisation in 1622 it was kept in state in the Basilica of Bom Jesus. The tomb was a gift of the Grand Duke Cosmos III of Tuscany and was erected in 1698. The rectangular red jasper base is surmounted with marble and bronze plaques narrating the life of service of St. Francis Xavier. The silver reliquary casket is elaborately carved and, after several mutilations, the body of the saint is only exposed to the public once every ten years.

On the hill west of **Bom Jesus** is another cluster of monuments. **The Church and Convent of St. Monica** is one of the oldest and largest convents for nuns in Asia and was completed in 1627. It still serves as the Mater Dei Institute for Nuns. Next to it is the **Convent of St. John** founded for the order who care for the sick. The **Church of St. Augustine**, now in ruins, was once the largest edifice in Velha Goa, built in Gothic style, but only a portion of its dramatic 46 metre tower remains. At the edge of the holy hill commanding a wonderful view is the **Church of Our Lady of the Rosary**. The cenotaph to the right of the main altar belongs to Dona Catarina who was married to Viceroy Gracia De Sa at a ceremony performed by St. Francis Xavier. This votive chapel was built as an act of thanksgiving by Alfonso de Albuquerque who had watched from this very spot his forces battling triumphantly against the Sultan of Bijapur.

Church interior, Velha Goa.

To the north-east of the **Sé Cathedral** are several other monuments, the oldest being the **Gate of the Palace of Adil Shah**, near the magnificent façade of the **Church of St. Cajetan**. The ruined gateway is made of beautiful hardy basalt brought all the way from Bassein. As part of the entrance to the palace of Adil Shah, which can only be reconstructed from literary references left by early travellers, one can assume that it must have been an imposing structure of grand dimensions. The main northward road, in front of the Church of St. Cajetan, leads to the Mandovi river and marks the ceremonial gateway to the old township from the waterfront. The arch is built out of laterite and granite, and has suffered many attempts at reconstruction. A figure of Vasco da Gama stands in the central niche announcing the foundation of a great Portuguese province, where once ships from the far corners of the world brought thousands of merchants and luxurious goods to the shores of Goa.

WHAT'S IN THE NEIGHBOURHOOD

Traditional Goan architecture is very charming and anywhere you go you will see the bright tiled houses, mica windows, and delightful little gardens. Panjim is a lovely town, where the sea meets the Mandovi river. The harbour, hill-top view of the river, gardens, and the Church of Our Lady of the Immaculate Conception are the highlights of this capital city of Goa. From Panjim a number of day trips can be made, besides routine visits to the beaches. **Aguada**, 18 kilometres from Panjim, has one of the oldest forts in Goa, a beautiful whitewashed turret lighthouse, and a wonderful (though crowded) beach. **Velha Goa** or Old Goa, described above, is approximately 10 kilometres away and well-connected by road and bus links, and conducted tours. **Goa Velha** or **Pilar**, about 11 kilometres south-east of Panjim, is another Christian settlement built over the ruins of the ancient city of Gopakkapattana. Pilar Monastery, St. Andrew's Church, and the scenic view of the harbour and Zuari river are all worth a visit. The singular influence of Portuguese art on Hindu architecture can be seen at the famous sites of Shri Mahalsa at **Mardol** (7 kilometres from Ponda, 30 kilometres from Panjim), the Shri Mangesh Temple at **Priol** (22 kilometres from Panjim), where the temples have slanting tiled roofs like the houses of old, European ornamentation, and tall unusual towers that mark the entrance of the temples.

HOW TO GET THERE

The main airport is at Dabolim, 30 kilometres from Panjim, the capital of Goa. There are a number of medium-priced, and four and five star hotels. Rail travel to Panjim is best through Margao (33 kilometres away), which is connected to other major Indian cities. It is a lovely colonial town with architecture typical of the region, gardens, and churches. Bus connections from Mangalore, Bombay, and Bangalore are regular and efficient. A steamer service was available between Panjim and Bombay, (travel time approximately twenty hours) requiring advanced booking and organisation. It is currently (temporarily?) suspended.

Bodh Gaya

There is no other place more venerated by Buddhists than Bodh Gaya, where Gautam Siddhartha attained enlightenment and came to be called the Buddha, the Awakened one. A visit to Bodh Gaya is to commune with that sparkling illumination, that perceptive light of wisdom which removes unhappiness. This is why each year on the full-moon night in the month of May one can still see pilgrims (from India, Nepal, Burma, Thailand, China, Japan, and other countries) thronging here to celebrate the sublime event of the Buddha's Nirvana.

The story begins with Siddhartha, born in Nepal, who renounced his royal household, young son, and wife, and wandered through the foothills of the Himalaya to the plains to visit religious centres such as **Varanasi** on the banks of the Ganga. Searching for the meaning of life and unconvinced by current philosophic discourse he visited **Rajgir** (65 kilometres away) and finally came to Gaya, an ancient religious centre (blessed by Vishnu as the site where all human sins could be washed away). Siddhartha retreated for some years to the outskirts of Gaya (13 kilometres away) beside the Falgu stream. There, seated beneath a pipal tree (*Ficus religiosa*), he spent forty-nine continuous days and nights in deep meditation. Several important events took place during this period, all of which find popular expression in later Buddhist sculpture and painting. In one tale, a great storm broke, as if to deliberately drown the fasting Buddha. From the depths of the waters an enormous serpent, Mucalinda emerged and, 'enveloping the body of the blessed One seven times within his folds, spread his great hood above his head and protected the Buddha'. This scene of Mucalinda protecting the Buddha became a favourite theme not only in the Indian subcontinent but throughout East Asia.

Then comes the story of the temptation of the Buddha by Mara. Seated cross-legged under the Bo tree, on the immoveable spot, the thirty-five year old princely-ascetic was deep in meditation and completely engrossed in his search for truth. Mara appeared before him, in the form of the eternal temptress, to distract him from his meditation and lure him to sensual earthly (transient) pleasures. Throughout the period of temptation offered by Mara, her lovely daughters, and frightening followers, the future Buddha remained unmoved. He merely lowered his hand to the ground and touched the Earth, who witnessed his ultimate victory over desire, the source of all human suffering. That night, under the light of the full moon as the heavens rained flowers, the whole universe celebrated the conquest of wisdom over all else. The young man became the Buddha, the Awakened One, full of Buddhi or wisdom. The tree which sheltered him through this trial and victory was named the (Bo) **Bodhi Tree**, and the site **Bodh Gaya**.

At the pilgrimage centre of Bodh Gaya there is one main road and one focus of attention, the grand **Mahabodhi Temple** and situated behind it (to the west) the **Bodhi Tree**. Although Bodh Gaya has structural and sculptural remains from the Mauryan–Shunga period (third to first centuries BC), the Mahabodhi Temple was presumably built up to its present dimensions by the seventh century because it was described by Hiuen Tsang, the Chinese scholar who visited this holy site. Continuous renovation and rebuilding have resulted in the present form of the temple, which actually dates only to the nineteenth century but is believed to be a reasonably accurate copy of the original shrine. The Mahabodhi Temple was built of brick and lime with plaster-work niches with sculptures. It consists of an inner sanctum above which stands a large looming tower (over 55 metres) that rises in several horizontal planes, each one portioned into a series of niches and chaitya windows. Architecturally it has an interesting design, for though built in brick, the tower has many features that were to be found later in Hindu temple shikhara constructions in stone. The niche at the main entrance holds a sixth century figure of the standing Buddha. Within the inner shrine is a colossal image of the cross-legged seated Buddha, in the earth-touching posture, a reminder of the triumphant event so closely connected with the site.

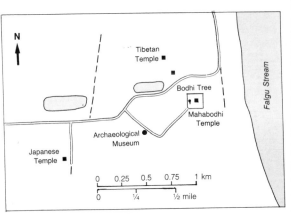

Plan of Bodh Gaya.

After the ritual pradakshina procession around the main temple and a visit to the shrine one must see the great **Bodhi Tree**. It has an elevated platform built around it and the area is enclosed with a railing (the original belongs to the second century and is kept in the **Archaeological Museum** at Bodh Gaya). The way to honour the Bodhi Tree is to perform a ritual pradakshina, walking around it slowly once, thrice, or seven times. The holy tree is always festooned with offerings of flowers and banners. It is no longer the original one under which the Buddha sat (almost two thousand five hundred years ago) but is believed to be a close relative and the *vajrasana* is the seat marking the hallowed spot. There is a story about Emperor Ashoka who, when he converted to Buddhism, earned the zealous wrath of his wife. She destroyed the Bodhi Tree in a fit of mindless anger. The tree or a shoot was saved and a sapling from the original Bodhi Tree was sent as a message of peace by Ashoka with his son Mahendra to Shri Lanka, to enable a Buddhist order to be established on the island.

Several other shrines, votive stupas, and newer temples (the Tibetan, Chinese, and the Japanese ones built early this century) form the rest of the complex. To the north of the temple is **Lotus Lake** with an image of the Buddha shielded by the serpent Mucalinda. Beyond is the **Jewel Walk** where the Buddha is said to have walked and pondered on what to do with his great gift of enlightenment that had been bestowed on him. There is another site further away where a stone sculpture of the Buddha's feet or footprints are worshipped.

The **Archaeological Museum** has a very interesting collection (the Japanese temple nearby also has some lovely things brought from Japan). The remains of the second to first century BC railing of the main temple is displayed here. There are a number of images belonging to the Pala period (eighth to twelfth centuries), several of them beautiful bronze cast figures of the Buddha made at a celebrated craft centre nearby. There are a few sculptured panels and medallions that formed the railings of other buildings constructed over the long period of occupation (from the third century BC to the twelfth century AD before the Muslim invasions). Bodh Gaya's fame reached far-flung corners of the world, which brought donors and visitors to see the original site where the Buddha attained his spiritual awakening, or Nirvana.

Mahabodhi Temple, Bodh Gaya.

Nalanda

Hiuen Tsang describes the famous University city (to which he came all the way from China to study, in the seventh century), and says it was 7 *yojana*s (80 kilometres) from the holy pipal tree at Bodh Gaya. It is an amazing site, both in scale and for what it represents. The site was known during Mauryan times as the birthplace of the Buddha's right-hand disciple Sariputra (whose commemorative stupa No. 3 is at **Sanchi**). Excavations and layers of successive habitation have proved the antiquity of the site. No building dates from before the Gupta period.

It is conceivable that in the early days students lived in humble *gurukul*s or abodes with their gurus and over a period of time the place grew into one of the most prosperous and well reputed centres of learning. We are told that Emperor Harshvardhana (AD 606-47) made generous gifts to Nalanda university with grants of rice, butter, and milk from a hundred villages to enable students to devote themselves exclusively to their studies. From all accounts this site was famous throughout the ancient Buddhist world as the greatest university where students from distant lands could come to study the various branches of Buddhist logic, sciences, medicine, and philosophy. Hiuen Tsang tells us that:[15]

The priests to the number of several thousands are men of the highest ability and talent. Their distinction is very great at the present time, and there are many hundreds whose fame has rapidly spread through distant lands ... If men of other quarters desire to enter and take part in the discussions, the keeper of the gate proposes some hard questions; many are unable to answer, and retire.

At prayer,
Bodh Gaya.

The dimensions of the site are incredible: there were several 'noble tanks' which surrounded the ruins, a line of monasteries (numbered from 1-10) on the eastern side, with religious buildings assembled along the west (facing the monasteries). The only really irregular part of this scheme is **Temple No. 2** which housed several very beautiful Hindu images with carved panels of Rama and Sita. A typical monastery consisted of an entrance gateway which opened on to a large rectangular courtyard for communal work. On all four sides of the court were verandahs which led into a line of small cells or cloisters for the religious order to live in. A small shrine, usually placed at the rear, housed an image and served as a prayer room for the monastery.

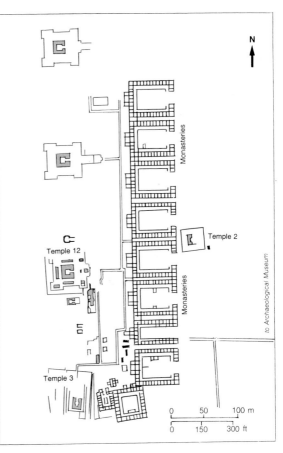

Plan of Nalanda.

As you enter the Nalanda complex you walk down a passage between monasteries 1 and 4–5, moving westward to approach the domineering presence of the **Main Temple, Site No. 3**. It is a huge brick structure (31 metres high) with an imposing stairway that offers a splendid, breathtaking view of the entire area and the layout of the university city. The Main Temple stands in a central courtyard surrounded by several brick and plaster-coated stupas and octagonal based votive shrines which were once adorned with beautiful images of the Buddha, his loyal followers, and the Bodhisattvas.

Nalanda reigned supreme as a centre for education for over five hundred years, and it was only in the twelfth and thirteenth centuries, when Muslim invasions in the region threatened the establishment, that the monks fled to Himalayan retreats, establishing Buddhist centres in these secluded places. We are told that the great library of Nalanda (or what remained of it) was burned down.

The **Archaeological Museum** of Nalanda is also well worth a short visit for it holds a representative collection of artifacts, establishing the idea that Nalanda was once also a prolific art centre. There are beautiful clay, plaster, and bronze images of Buddhist orientation in the museum collection.

WHAT'S IN THE NEIGHBOURHOOD

The best way to approach Bodh Gaya and Nalanda is to arrive through **Patna**, the capital city of the state of Bihar. It is not a particularly pleasant city, but the **Patna Museum** has one of the finest collections of early Indian sculpture in the region. Priceless terracotta images, early Mauryan statues like the grand Didarganj Yakshi, and several bronze icons of the regions are housed in this (dusty, dismal) museum.

Near Nalanda, at a distance of 15 kilometres, is **Rajgir** or the Mauryan township of Rajgriha, the abode of kings. Surrounded by a ring of hillocks, this once ancient city was visited by the Buddha who, we are told, loved to stay on Grihrakuta Hill. Old Rajgir is also where Mahavir, the last Jain Tirthankara, enjoyed spending the monsoon season. It was here, after the Buddha's death, that the first Buddhist council was held (*see* Introduction) at the Vaihara hill caves near the hot springs.

HOW TO GET THERE

Bodh Gaya is 13 kilometres from Gaya which is connected by road and rail to Patna, Varanasi, Calcutta, and other cities. From Gaya it is 65 kilometres to Rajgir and another 15 kilometres to Nalanda. Nalanda or Baragaon is 90 kilometres south-east of Patna and is linked by road and rail. A variety of accommodation is available at Bodh Gaya; and there are also several *ashrams* and *dharamshalas*. Both Patna and Gaya have adequate accommodation and regular bus links to these celebrated Buddhist sites. You should plan your stay with a one day visit to Bodh Gaya, another to Rajgir and Nalanda, and some time to see Patna Museum. There are discourses and religious studies conducted at these sites which may tempt you to stay longer, to listen and learn about one of the greatest religions of the world.

Vishnupur

There are two principal reasons for choosing to write about Vishnupur. Firstly, it is a wonderful site at which to see terracotta temples, a style unique to this region of the subcontinent. Secondly, the recommended entry point to Vishnupur is through Calcutta, India's most resilient city.

Vishnupur (or Bishnupur, as it sounds in Bengali) was once a flourishing town and served as the capital of the Malla rulers of Bengal from the seventeenth to eighteenth centuries. As to its origin, as with most stories about local chieftains wishing to add respectability to their name, there are several myths that explain how the Malla family became rulers. One variation of the myth recalls how a high caste prince from the north was travelling with his pregnant wife on his way to Puri for a pilgrimage. His wife gave birth to a son, and finding it difficult to travel, he left them behind, hoping to pick up his wife and young baby on the return journey. The queen died soon after, but left her young boy in the care of a local tribal family with enough jewels to ensure his well-being. When the child was seven years old he went to a tribal funeral feast that was being celebrated to honour their leader. There, before a large community gathering, the elephant of the departed king picked up the boy and placed him on the throne and a new dynasty of rulers was established, as it were, by divine intervention.

The young ruler was given the title Adi Malla (the first ruler of the forest of Mallabhum), and forty generations ruled after him. The most prosperous period of recorded Malla history begins with Veer Hambir, a contemporary of Akbar. Veer was an ardent devotee of Vishnu and hence the name of his capital Vishnupur, meaning the city of Vishnu. It was in his reign that the first of the surviving temples was built at Vishnupur. Today there are as many as thirty brick and stone temples, each with a different design and scheme, scattered over a large area. The city was once known for its beautiful lakes and ponds, and its lush vegetation. A fortification wall once encircled the capital, its lakes, palaces, and temples, but little of it remains.

There are a few general characteristic features of these varied temples at Vishnupur, which should be described first. Most of the temples are placed against an expansive background and are built on raised platforms. A well-established local tradition of brick construction (found throughout the eastern part of the subcontinent in Bengal and Bangladesh) served as the basis for the creation of a distinct style of architecture. The brick built temple structure was usually covered, by way of protection against the humid climate, with a layer of burnt brick tiles. These tiles, only a few centimetres in size and very slim in width, were produced to fit the shape and design of the temple. The tiled veneer soon became a surface for decoration. In time the entire façade of the temple was covered with terracotta tiles embellished with intricate sculptured motifs and patterns.

The tiles were produced, apparently, in two ways. The first, an easier technique, was used to make segments of a repetitive pattern, while a more time-consuming method was reserved for special tiles carrying thematic sculptures. For the repetitive pattern the design was first worked out on a wooden mould, which had segments of the design carved on its surface, in reverse or intaglio. Wet clay, when pressed into the mould, took the impression of the design so that parts of it stood in relief, raised above the background. The tiles were then fired in a kiln till they were a nice toasted brick red. They were then assembled along the base of the temple, around the doorway, windows, or to create borders along the temple wall scheme. In the temples of Vishnupur one can see yards of wall space covered with recurrent panels of flower motifs, lotus petals, and creepers.

The other technique required much more skill and time. Each clay tile was individually carved with figures and narrative

Stories of Krishna, Keshta Raya or Jor Bangla Temple, Vishnupur.

panels. The artist worked with an array of pliable knives to carve out on the soft clay tile individual details of the figure: costume, hairstyle, and facial expression. Several such tiles fixed in sequence would be used to relate a particular episode of a story. There are temples at Vishnupur which illustrate entire scenes from epic poems: the Ramayana, the Mahabharata, and the amorous escapades of the romantic Krishna, the human avatar of Vishnu.

Not merely in decoration but in architectural temple style, Vishnupur is very interesting. Throughout the region, with its once dense tropical forests, locally available bamboo and wood was used for rural house construction. One of the joys of working with bamboo is that it is extremely flexible. Bamboo beam roofs attained a sweeping bow-like curve, a sort of graceful arched appearance, when used in house construction. This bamboo hut roof façade was adapted to the stone and brick construction in the temples at

Vishnupur and many of them have expansive curvilinear façades, often repeated on all four sides of the building. The graceful shape of the Bengal bamboo roof so impressed the Mughal Emperor Akbar (during his campaigns in the region in 1574-6) that he reproduced these forms in his palaces and later emperors continued the tradition in their royal forts.

The earliest temple at Vishnupur is **Ras Mancha**, built during the reign of Veer Hambir (1587-1600). It is a peculiar structure with a huge, stepped masonry pyramid-shaped roof. Around the base, like a gentle wave, run a series of Bengal hut roofs. The vaulted, pillared verandah, with shapely pillars, draws light into the dark interiors and casts deep shadows on the external façade. This temple is located near the **Archaeological Museum,** which also has an interesting collection of carved tiles from the region.

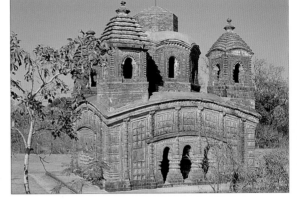

Due north is the **Shyama Raya Temple** built around 1643. Growing out of the base, the square temple body is framed by an artistically curved roof. The side walls of the temple are broken into details with three curvaceous arches of the entrance on each side and elaborate tile-work.

Shyama Raya Temple, Vishnupur.

Above, the roof is formed in several layers. Over each corner is a turret with a peaked roof and from the centre a taller single tower emerges, also with a pyramid-like roof. The interior and exterior of the temple is adorned with wonderful terracotta tile-work decorations. Near the entrance are huge medallions with Krishna, the divine cowherd, playing his flute, with the *gopis*, his cowherdess companions, forming a lively circle around him as they dance in celebration.

Near the Shyama Raya Temple is the **Keshta Raya Temple** built around 1655. This brick temple imitates the indigenous double hut (*jorbangla*) design, in which two huts with sweeping curved façades are built, back to back, as one unit. Above the vaulted chambers is the protrusion of the central tower with a peaked roof. The front of the temple has a triple-arched entrance and the entire wall is alive with miniature sculptures and decorative motifs. There are scenes from the Ramayana: the great battle scene between Rama, assisted by Hanuman and his monkey army battling to rescue Sita (Rama's wife) kidnapped by Ravana, the lord of Lanka. In these scenes chariots clash, arrows fly menacingly, and hordes of hapless victims fall to their death in the most theatrical poses. A whole universe of ideas have been captured by a diminutive set of tiles.

Further north of the Shyama Raya Temple is the lovely form of the **Madan Mohana Temple** (constructed around 1694). It is less complex in design and consists of a square building with deep bow-like curved cornices framing the edges of the roof on all four sides. From the centre a tall many-sided tower is capped with a rounded roof. Rows of tiles line the wall surface of the temple, each portraying a theme. Most playful and original are the rows of (plump) ducks waddling around in single file imitating the life-like gestures of a noisy flock.

One can spend hours enjoying the world of terracotta tiles, the humorous details the sensitive rendering of a face, the folds of a garment, the subtle compositions of the miniature tiles, because their impact is both aesthetic and pleasing.

WHAT'S IN THE NEIGHBOURHOOD

Vishnupur is accessible by road and rail from **Calcutta** (201 kilometres away) and is a city which has to be seen to be believed. In the seventeenth century foreign (Portuguese, Armenian, etc.) traders had already selected sites along the Hooghly river to set up trading posts. In 1690 an Englishman, Job Charnock, selected three villages (one was Kalighat or Kalikata, from which the present name is derived), and this constituted the nucleus of present-day Calcutta. The city was designed beside the Hooghly river. **Fort William** (named after

Plan of Vishnupur.

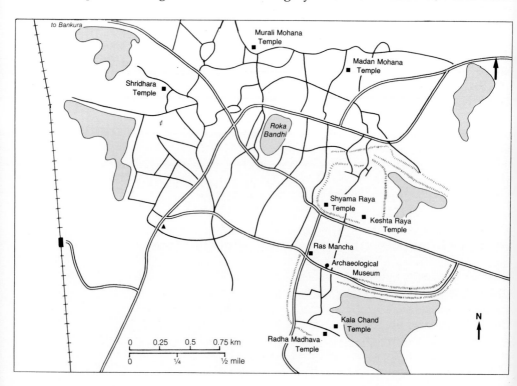

King William) was rebuilt in 1773. Around it is the open expanse of the **Maidan**. At the southern end is the shapely white form of the **Victoria Memorial Hall** (built in 1921), housing an interesting collection of artifacts, sculptures, and paintings of the Raj, much of which commemorates the declaration of Queen Victoria as Empress of India. At the south-eastern corner of the Maidan is **St Paul's Cathedral**, a wonderful example of Indo-Gothic architecture. Along Chowringhee, the road that borders the Maidan, is the **Indian Museum** with an outstanding collection of early Buddhist and Hindu sculptures, textiles, and paintings. Further north of the Maidan are **Eden Gardens**, the hallowed cricket stadium of Calcutta which draws crowds of over 50,000. North of the Maidan stand the stately government buildings: the **Town Hall** (1813), **High Court** (1872), **Metcalf Hall** (1840), the striking **Writer's Building** (1880), and a few old churches (**St John's**, 1787 with Job Charnock's tomb and **St Andrew Kirk**, 1818). At the end of Park Lane, off Chowringhee, is the old **British Cemetery** (sadly, very poorly maintained) with lovely tombstones recording the tragic plight of these early traders and administrators who died, most of them very young, from the devastating heat, fatal illnesses, and the floods of tropical India.

But these romantic buildings and places do not adequately represent Calcutta or capture its spirit, which is always lively and full of fun. There are street stalls, shops, and bazaars, excessively crowded roads where you can catch glimpses of some amazing architecture—a bit of Art Nouveau here and Indo-baroque there—trams, horse carriages, and rickshaws drawn by half-starved human beings. The rich, the famous, the poor and the jobless, all take a keen interest in politics, a game of cricket or football and, because of their lovely women, are lovers of all things beautiful.

North of Vishnupur is **Shantiniketan**, the haven of peace, the renowned university, developed by Rabindranath Tagore the Nobel Laureate poet of India. Set in a rural landscape, like the ancient gurukul or traditional school, the university still attracts great teachers and has been (for the last ninety years) the nursery of some of India's finest artists and scholars.

HOW TO GET THERE

Calcutta has an international airport with connections from Europe and East Asia. There are air, road, and railway links to all major towns in India. Calcutta has a whole range of hotels and small motels to suit the budget of every traveller. From Calcutta it takes 8 hours by train to Vishnupur and this is the best way to visit, though there is a 'motorable road'. Trains from Calcutta also can be taken to visit **Shantiniketan**, and there is an overnight train journey to the state of Orissa to see **Puri**, **Bhubaneshwar**, and the Sun Temple at **Konarak**.

Bhubaneshwar

The best thing to do, were it possible, would be to take a low balloon flight over Bhubaneshwar to view the magnitude and concentration of temples in this town. It literally abounds with hundreds of exquisite temples spread around a central lake called **Bindu Sarovar**, the nucleus of the universe. The earliest temple dates to the seventh century, but the history of this region extends far further back than the Christian era.

The present state of Orissa was renowned in ancient times for its seaports facing the Bay of Bengal on the east coast of India, looking out at the distant islands of Java, Bali, and Indonesia. We hear of its strategic significance in the account of a terrible battle of conquest in the third century BC when the Mauryan Emperor Ashoka, with his capital at Pataliputra (Patna, Bihar) waged war on Kalinga (the ancient name of Orissa). The contents of his rock edict (No. 13) can only be described as one of the most dramatic and epoch-making religious conversions in history:[16]

When the king, Beloved of the gods [*Priyadarshini*] and of gracious men, had been consecrated eight years Kalinga was conquered, 15,000 people were deported, 100,000 were killed, and many times that number died. But after the conquest of Kalinga, the Beloved of the gods began to follow righteousness (the Buddhist dharma), to love righteousness and to give instruction in righteousness.

When Emperor Ashoka surveyed the carnage and bloodshed that his armies had caused he decided to follow the middle path expounded by the Buddha, here at the battlefields of Kalinga. To mark the historic event the hillock site called **Dhauli** (8 kilometres south of Bhubaneshwar) was honoured by Emperor Ashoka by a sculpture depicting a huge standing elephant cut out of the rock. On a large rock surface carved with a set of edicts Emperor Ashoka records his policy on non-violence, his desire to give up military conquest for spiritual victory (or political gain!), and to pacify the newly-conquered people of Kalinga. Dhauli is a sort of two thousand year old version of Hiroshima. It stands testimony to the senseless cruelty and inane violence of human nature and the need for non-violence or ahimsa. Today Japanese Buddhists have marked the site by building the **Shanti** (Peace) **Stupa** at Dhauli, a reminder that wisdom is the only hope of ushering in an era of lasting peace and happiness.

At **Udayagiri** and **Khandagiri** (6 kilometres south of Bhubaneshwar) is a series of rock-cut monasteries and shrines. These first century rock-cut caves in the eastern region are

(opposite) :
Lingaraja Temple,
Bhubaneshwar.

extremely interesting early samples of architecture in a style that reached its climax of development at **Ajanta**, **Ellora**, and **Elephanta** in Maharashtra in western India. Honeycombing the entire face of a hillside of sandstone are over thirty-five caves of the Jain community. The most beautiful at Udayagiri are the **Hathi Gumpha** (the elephant cave), which has carved stone elephants at the entrance and the **Rani Gumpha** (the Queen's cave), which is a double-storey residential apartment scooped out of the living rock, with pillared verandahs, and beautiful sculptured panels on the side walls of the entrance courtyard.

Musicians, Parashurameshvara Temple, Bhubaneshwar.

From the seventh to the thirteenth centuries the focus of architecture in the region was on the construction of temples to the gods and goddesses of the Hindu pantheon. The Bhauma Kara dynasties in the seventh to eighth centuries built temples in their capital and the tradition was carried on by the Gangas through their reign beginning from the twelfth century. One can almost trace the development of this distinct school of architecture from its inception, with the phase of early experimentation, given expression in the monuments of Bhubaneshwar and its most mature, perfected phase in the magnificent temples of **Puri** and **Konarak**.

The **Parashurameshvara Temple** is a small, decorative example of the best-preserved earliest temple form at Bhubaneshwar. It dates back to the seventh century and is built within an enclosure. The temple consists of a main garbha griha or sanctum with a tower-like roof, referred to in local terminology as the *rekha deul*. This tower (only 12.80 metres high, and yet to rival that of the Lingaraja temple at 36.5 metres) is conical in shape and is made up of discrete horizontal levels which curve inwards as they meet the pinnacle, surmounted by a cushion-shaped *amalaka* and a *kalash* or pot of ambrosia. The front face of the tower has prominent arched windows and sculpted motifs. The hall in front of the tower is rectangular with a two-tiered flat roof which, as the style progressed, was to give way to more dramatic many-tiered pyramidal roofs. The walls of the mandap (locally called *jagamohan* or *pida deul*) are elaborately carved with sculptured panels and lattice windows. The west facing windows have a lively band of musicians and dancers carved on them. As you perform a pradakshina of the temple you will see several beautiful sculptures, such as that of the pot-bellied Ganesh, the lord of good fortune, on the southern side and of Karttikeya, the chief of the army and son of Shiva. Below the figure of Karttikeya is his animal emblem, the peacock (who seems busy guzzling grain at his master's feet).

Though not in practical sight-seeing order, to maintain chronological sequence one needs to describe the eighth century **Vaital Deul Temple** (at some distance from the Parashurameshvara Temple, to the west of the Bindu Sarovara). It is quite distinct from any other and also has some of the finest sculpture. The temple has a sanctum but instead of the usual conical roof above, the tower here slopes like a pyramid surmounted by a long vaulted cap (a little like the gopurams of southern India). The front face of the temple tower has a wonderful ornate design and in the sculptured windows are the figures of the Cosmic dancer Shiva and below, Surya the sun god, riding on his seven-horsed chariot. On the main body of the temple are some dramatic works of sculpture. Mahishasuramardini depicts the goddess Durga spearing the demon Mahisha and ending his reign of terror (she, in her more awesome manifestation as Chamunda, is also the deity worshipped within the sanctum of this temple). There is a figure of Parvati on the south side and Ardhanareshvara (half man and half woman, symbolising the concept of singularness in Hindu philosophy) on the west wall.

Near the Parashurameshvara Temple is the most perfect 'gem of Orissan architecture', the **Mukteshvara Temple** (late tenth century). Stylistically it is *petite*, and a landmark in Orissan temple development. It stands at one end of a large enclosure, which boasts several other temples, and has its own small ornamental enclosure wall around it. The Mukteshvara Temple faces west and on the eastern side, behind it, is a holy water pond where pilgrims can still be seen bathing. In front of the temple is a beautiful opulent gateway. It has two sculpted pillars that hold up an arched lintel with reclining women whose sensuous forms follow the curve of the gateway. From a distance one is able to appreciate its overall design and plan. The temple consists of a sanctum with a conical rekha deul above it. The tower is made up of horizontal levels, and a series of amalaka and cushion-like motifs have been added along the entire outline of the rekha deul as if to outline and highlight its elegant form. In front is a square mandap or jagamohan with a low pyramidal tiered roof that was

Mukteshvara Temple, Bhubaneshwar.

to become the hallmark of the mature Orissan temple style. The outer temple wall is profusely adorned with pure, decorative sculpture and figurative art. There are figures of celestial females standing beside half open doorways and elfish dwarf characters up to all kinds of tricks. Around the temple, in the niches, are Ganesh, Kartikkeya, Parvati, and the strange figure of Lakulisha, the Shaivite teacher and guru.

Not far from the Mukteshvara temple is the **Rajarani Temple** built in a lovely reddish-gold sandstone (a superior stone and

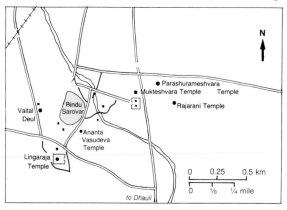

Plan of
Bhubaneshwar.

perhaps the origin of its strange name which literally means the king-queen temple). Surrounded by empty space the temple stands serene and majestic, glowing in any light of day. Here the temple has reached a new stage of development. The tower is elongated and consists of many miniature towers clambering up its conical surface (like the temples of Khajuraho). The mandap or jagamohan has a square body and a many-tiered pyramidal roof above. The treatment of the wall surface around the deul (the mandap is quite plain) is especially beautiful, with long rows of projecting wall spaces, like faceted pilasters, adorned with rows of images of the guardians of the cardinal directions and graceful female figures: one fondling her baby, another clasping a branch of a tree, a third applying her make-up or merely admiring her beauty in the mirror, wearing her ankle bells, or talking to her pet parrot. There are also lady musicians and dancers, all of whom seem to be celebrating life and all that is beautiful.

The **Lingaraja Temple** represents in its magnificence and grace the mature and highly developed temple form of the Orissan style. Enlosed within a compound wall is the towering vitality of the Lingaraja's rekha deul rising to a height of 36.5 metres. The Lingaraja temple is still used for worship and is open to Hindus only. A viewing platform outside the compound provides the best view of the temple and its plan. Surrounding the main temple are a number of smaller shrines, cluttering up the compound slightly; yet this plan is extremely interesting in that it provides an insight into how the temple grew. With popular favour, and with additional donations, buildings sprang up within the complex, making it a heavenly mini-universe marked by the presence of many gods and goddesses. An inscription within the complex records the donation of a village, the income from which would provide oil for a lamp to be continually burning at the temple (referred to as *Krittivasa*). The inscription dates to AD 1114-15, in the reign of the Ganga King Anantavarman Chodaganga.

The temple consists of four parts (not just the two, as in the earlier examples), the sanctum with the high tower, the mandap or jagamohan, the *nat mandap* (dance hall), and the *bhoga mandap*. In latter years, as temple functions were expanded, a dance tradition grew as a form of worship of the gods. The dance, performed by special devotees in the temple, was based on devotional poetry and music which described the wonders and magnificence of the deity of the temple. Today Odissi, which was born in the temples of Orissa, is performed not in temples, but on the stage as a classical dance form. The outer walls of the temple are embellished by superb sculptures that cover every inch of wall space, sometimes hidden by a protecting pillar or lost in the shadows of the towering superstructure. In these sculptures one can see the inspiration of dance, music, and poetry for which Orissa is famous.

WHAT'S IN THE NEIGHBOURHOOD
There are several other temples that can be seen in the Mukteshvara complex, in the Lingaraja temple complex, and around the city. There is a fine **State Museum** which has a special collection of early Orissan sculptures and exquisite palm leaf manuscripts. Orissa is also the home of many beautiful handicrafts, appliqué work from Pipli (*en route* to Puri), *ikat* textiles, palm leaf paintings, *patta-chitras* prepared on stiffened cloth with bright colours and intricate filigree silver jewellery.

Dhauli is 8 kilometres south of Bhubaneshwar and the rock-cut caves of **Udayagiri** and **Khandagiri** are 6 kilometres away. Bhubaneshwar is a good starting point for day or longer trips to the holy pilgrimage centre of **Puri** (65 kilometres away) and its pretty beach (though the temple is only open to Hindus). From the capital city of **Bhubaneshwar** one can travel by road (64 kilometres away or 33 kilometres from Puri) for a day trip to the fabulous Sun Temple at **Konarak**.

HOW TO GET THERE
Bhubaneshwar is well-connected by road, air, and rail links to Calcutta and other major cities of India. There are daily tours to both Konarak and Puri organised by the State Tourism Department. There is a reasonable range of hotels both at Bhubaneshwar and Puri to stay in when visiting this land with a rich and ancient cultural heritage.

Konarak

What could be more spectacular than an entire monument built in honour of the Sun, whose great chariot travels through the sky measuring out Time and driving away darkness and ignorance? According to sacred literature of the Rig Veda, the sun or Surya is described as:[17]

Filling heaven, earth and the space between; the sun is the inner self of both the moving and the motionless. The splendid bay horses of the sun, bright and swift, celebrated and revered, mount the back of the heavens and encompass earth and heaven in a day.

Dawn, the beautiful goddess, awakens the people, making their path easy, high on her lofty chariot arousing every creature, Dawn spreads out her light at the beginning of days ...

In Hindu mythology the great sun travels through the sky on a seven horse chariot, its arrival heralded by the beauty of the Dawn. As the sun moves through the heavens in each season, it is accompanied by a set of hermits, *gandharva*s or flying musicians, celestial maidens, serpents, and giants who sit as envoys on the chariot. The sun, in mythology, is given two wives from whom many children are born: the senior one is Samjyna and the other Chaya (shadow) who always remains (at a safe distance) behind her fiery husband.

This is the concept underlying the Sun Temple at Konarak. It is a huge stone chariot designed like a mighty temple cart being pulled across the sky. As the sun measures time, the temple's symbolism incorportates the same theme and is fashioned with twelve wheels, the months of the year, and each wheel has sixteen spokes (that are said to work as a giant sundial, with the shadow falling at a particular angle each hour of the day). The chariot is drawn by seven horses, the number of days in the week and the seven colours constituting light.

Sun worship has ancient roots in India and West Asia, and there are many sun temples to be found in the Indian subcontinent. Nowhere else, however, was the scale and magnificence of this temple ever attempted again.

Like the sun, in whose light all creatures grow and in whose warmth all life blossoms, Surya is poetically attributed with powers of healing. An ancient custom, that survives to this day, is performed at the beach near Konarak (the coastline has moved over three kilometres away from the temple in the intervening 700 years). In a myth we are told of a son of Krishna afflicted with leprosy, of which he was cured by his unceasing

(opposite) : Surya Mandir, Konarak.

worship of the sun. Others too bathed by the temple beach and were cleansed of their afflictions. Even today people believe in the curative powers of the sun and thousands throng to the beach (on the seventh bright day of the waxing moon in the Hindu month of *Magha* (January–February) near Konarak to absorb the touch of the sun. It is said that an earlier temple to the sun marked the site. It was in this hallowed area that Narasimha the Ganga ruler, chose to build in the thirteenth century this monument in homage to the preserver of life on earth.

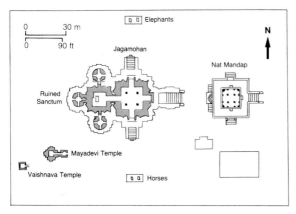

Plan of Konarak.

The Surya Mandir or sun temple complex is a huge open rectangular enclosure which once must have had some beautiful gateways. The entire temple is aligned east to west to follow the path of the heavenly sphere. Standing in front, detached from the main temple, is the square **Nat Mandap** or dance hall. Like the principal shrine, this mandap is also built on a high platform profusely decorated with dancing figures, musicians, and lovers celebrating the glory of the sun. There are steps on all four sides that lead up to a pillared hall which no longer has a roof. The eastern steps of the Nat mandap are flanked by wonderful (rather fierce looking, or are they smiling?) rampant lions that pounce on the backs of kneeling elephants.

The main temple entrance stands directly behind the nat mandap. In front of the eastern entrance was erected a free standing chlorite pillar or *dhvaja stambha* of the temple. This pillar carried Aruna, the charioteer of Surya, on its crown. The dvaja stambha was moved from this location and placed in front of the main gate of the temple at **Puri**.

To enter the temple there are three stairways, each guarded by animals, like the crouching elephant and lion on the eastern side, well caparisoned elephants to the north, and lovely richly decorated horses on the southern side. Positioned along the side of the stairway are the caparisoned, prancing horses of the sun chariot, their reins held firmly by great attendants who control the horses so that they move only at the measured pace that we call time. One of the most beautiful extant examples of the energetic sun horse is installed on a platform on the southern side of the complex.

The temple is built on an elevated platform which has bands of sculptures on it. Walking around the temple one cannot but admire the creative energy of the artists who displayed, on the walls of this temple, almost every conceivable thing that prospers under the light of the sun: animals and plants, fish and fowl, men and women. The lowest panel of the temple has a row of elephants gambolling in the forest. This must be the most superb example of animated, humorous, and highly sensitive Indian art bubbling with an effervescent love for nature and all that is natural. There are sculpted friezes of all the activities that are witnessed by the sun each day: warfare and love-making, music and dance, hunters, courtiers, sages, saints, and animals frolicking peacefully in the forest.

Along the platform of the temple are positioned at regular intervals the twelve great wheels of the sun chariot. Each spoke, hub, and rim of the wheel is minutely carved with auspicious figures of deities, amorous couples, and floral wreaths and scrolls. Like a gigantic wheel of time that relentlessly moves on, the images on the wheel urge one to be happy and joyful, to be at one with life and all of nature.

Nat Mandap and jagamohan, Surya Mandir, Konarak.

The entrance stairway leads to the gigantic mandap or jagamohan of the temple. This structure, which is intact, rises to a height of 38.4 metres above the ground. The jagamohan is square in shape with three stairways leading up to it on three sides (east, north, and south). The main eastern doorway of the mandap is breathtaking. The door-frame is made of chlorite and consists of eight facets, each on a different plane and with elaborate carvings. While the doorways are made of cholrite, a hard stone, the rest of the temple structure is built of laterite and khodalite blocks. This somewhat inferior stone has weathered badly, sustaining pits and crevices. The colour of the stone is a wonderful motley yellowish-pink that changes its hue with the moods of the sun to whom it is dedicated. At early dawn the temple is pale, at high noon it is an almost wheatish-white colour, and in the flaming colours of the setting sun it turns to a glowing pinkish-orange.

Above the main body of the jagamohan rises an enormous tiered pyramidal roof. It is divided into three segments by the alignment of its tiers. In these intervals are placed huge larger-than-life stone figures of musicians: female drummers, cymbal players, and flautists. These gigantic musicians appear small and proportionate in the perspective of the overall scale of the temple. They symbolise the heavenly sky nymphs who herald with joyful divine music the arrival of dawn, the beginning of a new day, and the journey of the sun. Above the musicians are a row of powerful lions who hold up the massive finial and amalaka (the kalash and finial are now missing).

Behind the jagamohan is a jagged platform that marks all that remains of the sanctum and the towering roof of the temple. Until 1848, a fragment of this tower was still standing and it was estimated that its original height would have been around 60 metres when it was intact. Much of the tower apparently collapsed through disuse of the temple, the inferior quality of stone used, fierce sea gales, and lightning.

There are several large images kept in the niche of the outer temple wall. The image of Surya (one that stands 1.88 metres high at the entrance of the National Museum, New Delhi) contains all the classical symbols of identification. The tall, handsome sun deity stands erect on a base, which represents the seven-horse chariot, with his charioteer, the lame Aruna, seated in front of him. Aruna is always shown in action, with lifted reins and whip in hand, for his journey never ends. Surya is draped in a *dhoti*, or loincloth, and his torso is shielded by chain-mail. Surya wears high boots and is the only deity in the Hindu pantheon to do so, for shoes are for walking and hence unclean, but some leniency had to be given to Surya given the nature of his occupation and his fiery hot chariot. (The boots led many historians to surmise that Surya was originally a god imported into India from West Asia and the fire-worshipping communities who once lived there.)

Erotic sculpture, Nat Mandap, Konarak.

One can only imagine the splendour, pomp, and colour that must have enveloped the temple when it was first built: the temple complex and subsidiary structures built for various rituals, stalls and shops clustered around selling items for worship, and thousands of people from every walk of life thronging to worship Surya, the light of their lives. Today the temple stands shorn of its noble tower, with only the pyramidal roof of the jagamohan to give some idea of the scale of the grand concept and design of the chariot of the sun.

WHAT'S IN THE NEIGHBOURHOOD

There is a small but fine **Site Museum** at Konarak with some beautiful sculptures and carved friezes from the sun temple.

The temple and beach town of **Puri** is only 33 kilometres away from Konarak. Though non-Hindus are not allowed into the temple compound, Puri is a typical religious centre with streets lined with shops and handicrafts, rest-houses and ashrams. One major road leads to the mighty temple dedicated to Jagannath (Krishna), the lord of the Universe, and this is one of the greatest pilgrimage centres in India. The temple was built in the late twelfth century with additions over the years. Its great towering rekha deul rises to a height of 57.7 metres and belongs to a mature phase of Orissan temple architecture bearing an affinity to the Lingaraja Temple at **Bhubaneshwar**. Each year, in the month of June-July, a great festival called the *Rath Yatra* (or *jatra*), the chariot procession festival, is held here. Over a hundred thousand people assemble to help haul the mighty wooden temple chariots of the gods on their annual procession. There are three chariots for Jagannath (Krishna), his brother Balabhadra, and sister Subhadra. One needs to witness this grand occasion to understand the Surya Temple at Konarak, for here it comes alive. Temple chariots, some 14 metres high on sixteen

Puri.

wooden wheels, with conical cloth-canopied roofs that reflect the temple tower and decorated with colourful banners flying in the breeze, are hauled by thousands of human devotees. These chariots of the gods moving through the streets, like the Sun Temple, have ancient roots in the psyche of the people.

HOW TO GET THERE

Konarak and Puri are linked by road to **Bhubaneshwar**. At **Puri** there are lovely places to stay in, some located by the beach where fishing boats and a long winding sandy shore provide a restful environment. Most people prefer to visit Konarak for a day and stay in Puri or Bhubaneshwar. The road to Puri from Bhubaneshwar runs through two lovely villages: one called **Pipli**, which is well-known for its appliqué cloth hangings and the other **Raghurajpur** (16 kilometres from Puri) is a crafts village where you can see artists (who worked once in the service of the temples and pilgrims) producing beautiful *patta-chitra*s, scroll paintings, and other traditional crafts.

Golconda Fort

Geographically the Deccan forms part of the oldest land mass on the Indian subcontinent, and within its plateau and folding hills are rich deposits of minerals and precious stones so vital to trade and building empires. The present state of Andhra Pradesh (in the Deccan, India) is bordered on the north-east by Orissa, the southern tip almost touching Madras (the capital of Tamil Nadu), the western fringe bordering Maharashtra and Karnataka. The history of Andhra Pradesh is intimately associated with its geographical position and its heritage is interwined with the cultural development of these neighbouring states. The story begins far back into the second century AD when two large Buddhist establishments were founded at Amaravati and Nagarjunakonda (166 kilometres from Hyderabad). Excavations here have revealed enormous religious settlements with monasteries and shrines that mark the greatest centres of learning and pilgrimage in the Deccan.

From northern India inroads into the Deccan came at regular intervals from the time of the Tughluqs. The mad sultan Muhammad bin Tughluq forced the citizens of Delhi to move *en masse* to his new capital at Daulatabad in 1326 and, when the venture failed brought them (i.e. those who survived) back.

It was during this time that Islamic architectural styles took root, and in 1347 the Bahamani kingdom was founded in the Deccan. Their first capital was Gulbarga (Karnataka) where the earliest Deccani experiments in architecture are to be found. In 1425, the Bahamani ruler moved the capital to the beautiful location of Bidar (in the present state of Karnataka, 130 kilometres west of Hyderabad). The fort here is one of the most glorious examples of secular art in the Deccan, it has massive fortification walls, palaces decorated with tile-work (some imported from Persia), and tombs for the Islamic rulers with large bulbous domes. The style developed (whether it be of glazed tiles and arabesque sculptures or the manneristic paintings) was unique, for it was based on ideas that evolved from interaction with Persia rather than those from local traditions.

Trade across the Arabian sea was well-established, and by the fourteenth to fifteenth centuries there was a steady flow of traffic in luxury goods, exchange of ideas, innovations, and artists. From Iran, Arabia, and Turkey artists flocked to the Mughal courts of Delhi and Agra, and to the Deccan where the royal patrons were renowned for their generosity and apprecia-

(opposite) : View of Golconda Fort,

tion of artistic accomplishments. Painters, poets, and architects trained in Persia sought the patronage of the Deccani rulers. From the fifteenth century onwards Decanni paintings and illustrated manuscripts reached superior heights of creativity. Samples of the paintings and crafts can be seen in the **Salar Jung Museum** in Hyderabad, and these give one an authentic flavour of the forts in their heyday.

In 1489 the Bahamani kingdom split into five independent dynasties with their centres at Ahmadnagar, Berar, Bidar, Bijapur, and **Golconda**. Each state, with autonomous rulers, continued their shared heritage and the tradition of painting, crafts, and architecture reached new heights of excellence. Bidar became famous for its metalware, Bidri, a bell metal with gold or silver inlay-work used for making exquisite huqqa stands, candle stands, ornamental bowls and boxes, and other opulent articles for the royal courts of the Deccan and northern India. Golconda was famous for painted fabrics (*kalamkari*, or hand painted cloth) which furnished the needs of European and Indian nobility. The city was also an acclaimed gem cutting and trading centre for jewels. The early account of Marco Polo's (1254-1324) travels to the East makes an arresting reference to Golconda:[18]

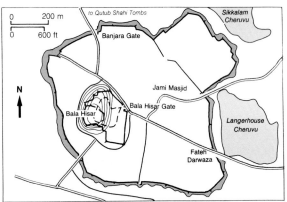

Plan of Golconda Fort.

> This kingdom produces diamonds. Let me tell you how they are got. You must know that in the kingdom there are many mountains in which diamonds are found, as you will hear. When it rains the water rushes down through these mountains, scouring its way through mighty gorges and caverns. When the rain has stopped and the water has drained away, then the men go in search of diamonds through these gorges from which the water has come, and they find plenty. In summer, when there is not a drop of water to be found, then the diamonds can be found in plenty among the mountains.

And in a more whimsical mood he says:

> Another means by which they get diamonds is this. When the eagles eat the flesh, they also eat—that is, they swallow—the diamonds. Then at night, when the eagle comes back, it deposits the diamonds it has swallowed with its droppings. So men come and collect these droppings, and there too they find diamonds in plenty....You must know that in all the world diamonds are found nowhere else except in this kingdom alone.

Golconda, an ancient prosperous land, was ruled for many centuries by the Rajas of Warangal until the Bahamani kings conquered the territory. The breakaway group from the Bahamani kingdom were of Turkoman origin, called Qutub Shahi's after the founder (Sultan Quli) Qutub Shah who made Golconda his capital. Forging a temporary alliance with four other Deccani rulers against their common rival, they defeated the Hindu kingdom of Vijayanagara in 1565 and this victory brought added prestige, extension of boundaries, and commercial activity to Golconda. In 1589, the capital of the Qutub Shahis was moved from their hill-top fort of Golconda to Hyderabad (8.5 kilometres away). In his new capital Muhammad Quli built several structures, including the famous **Charminar**, a massive square (triumphal) gateway decorated with stucco decorations with four (*char*) minarets (*minar*) each 55 metres from the ground. The **Jami Masjid** (the oldest in Hyderabad) and **Makka Masjid** (the largest mosque in southern India) are other examples of the religious architecture of this region and period.

View of Qutub Shahi Tombs, Golconda Fort.

But it is at **Golconda** that one can capture some of the magnificence and splendour of the sixteenth century Deccani world. The fort (8.5 kilometres west of Hyderabad) surrounds a rocky hill that rises over 122 metres. There are three impressive curtain walls of fortification, while huge granite boulders form a formidable landscape, appearing like natural cannons poised to tumble down on the first invader. There are eight entrance gates to the fort, and from Hyderabad one enters through the **Fateh Darwaza** (the victory gate) with its massive doorways of teak studded with (dreadful) spikes placed there as a precaution against enemy elephant charge. Surmounting the crown of the hill is the **Bala Hisar**, the citadel protected by fort walls and approached by a series of winding stairways which provide glimpses of the arched arcades of palaces and court-rooms. Halfway up the hill are the ruins of the royal palace and the **Hall of Justice**. The main street (north-west of Fateh Darwaza) is the magnificent **Jami Masjid**, the Friday mosque built by Quli Qutub Shah in 1518. On the other side (east) of the Bala Hisar are two arches known as the **Habshi Kamaan**, giving way to the **Naubat Khana** where the musicians sat beating out their musical announcements. The Qutub Shahi rulers with their foreign connections (they were Shia Muslims as were the rulers of Persia and Turkey) were said to have employed magnificent Ethiopian guards in their court, and this is where they were placed to protect the palace premises.

Winding down from the acropolis (towards the north) one can catch a splendid view of the royal tombs of the Qutub Shahi rulers set in a vast gardened enclosure.

The **Qutub Shahi Tombs** are remarkable in design and execution. This complex served as a family burial ground, where relatives could visit, pay their respects to the departed, listen to the chanting of the holy Quran, and distribute food and alms to the poor in memory of their loved ones. Many of the tombs are raised above ground level and set upon a huge platform of arches. The square tomb buildings coated with plaster, fringed with small minarets like flower vases (*guldastas*), each supporting an enormous (onion-shaped) dome that springs out of a necklace of lotus petal design, a plan that became the hallmark of the Qutub Shahi architecture of the Deccan. At the centre of the enclosed garden is the **Hammam** where the royal bodies where bathed before ritual burial. West of the Hammam, the earliest building in the complex, the **Tomb of Sultan Quli Qutub Shah,** (1512-43) commemorates the man who founded the dynasty and was responsible for making Golconda his capital. Furthest south of the Hammam is the elegant **Tomb of Ibrahim Qutub Shah**, once beautifully decorated with enamel-work and paint. Directly south, facing the Hammam, is the most impressive structure of the complex, the **Tomb of Mohammed Qutub Shah** (1612-26), the founder of the city of **Hyderabad**.

Qutub Shahi Tomb Complex.

The Deccan continued to be a threatening temptation and, during Mughal rule, many attempts were made to conquer this region. At the time of Shah Jahan and his son Aurangzeb, Mughal troops were found more and more in the Deccan region and mutual influences (in language, music, painting and costumes) were felt in the courts of the Deccan and Mughal India. Aurangzeb finally captured Golconda in 1687 (with a little treacherous help from disloyal subjects) after besieging the fort for almost eight months.

A new wave of artistic activity followed with the changing political structure, and Golconda (and Hyderabad) came under the administrative control of a Mughal Governor. During British rule in India the Asaf Jahis of Hyderabad were faithful allies of the colonial rulers in the nineteenth century, and remained an independent state surrounded by British territory. **Secunderabad**, separated by a huge lake (Himayat Sagar) from Hyderabad, became a British cantonment in 1806 and continued to keep a watchful eye over the independent state. In 1948 Hyderabad was assimilated into Independent India and remains today a city of great character (despite industrialisation and 'modernisation'), with its opulent cultural past reflected in its buildings and museums, and markets where pearls are still sold by the kilo!

WHAT'S IN THE NEIGHBOURHOOD

Bidar is 130 kilometres from Hyderabad and is a magnificent fortified palace of the Bahamani period with resplendent palaces decorated with (hints of) exquisite tile-work.

Hyderabad offers many sites worth seeing: the **Charminar**, a saunter through the crowded bazaars, the **Salar Jung Museum** with its priceless collection of paintings, textiles, and crafts of Andhra Pradesh, and a mass of kitch collected by the family during their sojourns abroad in the last century. The poorly maintained **Archaeological Museum** has a wonderful collection of early sculptures, some from the Buddhist sites of Amaravati and Nagarjunakonda (while the best collection is in the Madras State Museum, Tamil Nadu).

HOW TO GET THERE

Hyderabad is one of India's largest cities and is well-connected by air, road, and rail to other centres. Hotels of all descriptions are available. Conducted tours to Golconda and neighbouring sites, like Bidar, are organised by the State tourist office and private agencies.

Charminar,
Hyderabad.

Vijayanagara

Nothing can quite prepare you for this surreal landscape. As you come in down the road from Hospet (13 kilometres north-east) the prospect is rural and routine. Suddenly the landscape changes dramatically. Great mountains of stone burst out of the earth, gargantuan boulders stand precariously perched on each other as if frozen for centuries in the act of tumbling. From this topsy-turvy protective landscape, the organic forms of the temples and palaces can barely be discerned, playing hide-and-seek behind the boulders, eclipsed by the hillside from which the temple towers seem to grow. It is little wonder then that the gods and the great Vijayanagara rulers chose this site to build one of the greatest empires in southern India. This vast and powerful capital of Vijayanagara stands on the southern bank of the Tungabhadra river. Spread over an area of 26 square kilometres are the temples, many with a glorious view of the river, while the fortification walls enclose magnificent palaces and royal apartments.

The boulders of Vijayanagara, the city of victory, are ingrained with history. Excavations (both by international and Indian teams) have found that the region was under occupation from Mauryan times. It then fell into the territory of successive dynasties: the Kadambas, the Chalukyas of **Badami**, the famed Hoysalas of **Belur**, until the fourteenth century when Ala-ud-Din Khalji and later Muhammad bin Tughluq made inroads into the south. Two officers, Harihara and Bukka, of the presiding ruler fell into the hands of Muhammad bin Tughluq and were taken off to Delhi as prisoners. Legend has it that these two professed to embrace Islam and won the favour of the Sultan of Delhi. When trouble broke out in the newly-conquered southern territories, Harihara and Bukka were sent to quell the rebellions and they did just that, by breaking away from the Sultan and establishing their own independent kingdom, Vijayanagara.

Then came the business of building an empire, extending its borders by conquering lucrative tax-yielding regions, and setting up an efficient administrative system. Under Harihara II, we are told, the kingdom had spread up to the Krishna river in the north to the southern tip of India, with some military forays to Shri Lanka, and that embassies were sent to Burma and China. The new capital, that stood on the opposite bank to Anegondi (the older site), was designed entirely out of the local granite, with magnificent fort walls built out of hewn, dressed blocks

(opposite):
General view of
Tungabhadra river.

and large irrigation projects undertaken to enrich the territory. Temples to honour the gods were built, and artists, scholars, poets, and sculptors flocked to the home of the Vijayanagara rulers. After the forceful reign of Devaraya II (1422-46), the empire fell into the inept hands of weak rulers until Krishnadeva Raya (1505-29) led the Vijayanagara empire to the climax of its power and glory.

As the reputation of Vijayanagara grew, the wheel of history turned again. In northern Deccan, the Muslim Sultanates of **Golconda**, Bijapur, and Ahmadnagar had just gained independence from the Bahamani overlords and established their own small principalities. Rama Raya, Krishnadeva's son-in-law, played one ruler against the other until finally in 1565, an allied army of the Sultans of the Deccan attacked and defeated the Vijayanagara ruler and the glorious city was abandoned. With no ruler to protect it, the magnificent City of Victory began to crumble and the mighty Sultanates of the Deccan grew in eminence.

The ruins of Vijayanagara are vast and spread over 26 square kilometres. There are long walks amidst the palace complexes, breathtaking views from the hilltop shrines. The spectacular temples are in a style reminiscent of Chalukyan art, but which flowered into a style not to be found beyond the Vijayanagara kingdom. The best way to enjoy this site is to walk leisurely over a period of several days around the ruins, absorbing the beauty of the landscape and river, and familiarising oneself with the magnificent palaces and temples.

Any point is a good place to begin an exploration of Vijayanagara. Hampi is the religious centre and **Hemkunta** hill begins with a series of pillared halls. On the eastern face are two huge mandaps with cheerful sculptures on the pillars. The mandap entrance leads into the rock-cut shrine with colossal images of **Ganesh** who presides over every action, and who is the first to be propitiated in every Hindu ritual. Climbing down from the hill on the northern side are several shrines, some with triple shikharas, pyramidal in shape like the temples of **Halebid** and **Somnathpur** though not so ornate in decoration. Wandering through them one can catch a beautiful view of the Tungabhadra river and the layout along it of the sacred complex below. North of Hemkunta hill and beside the Tungabhadra river is the great **Virupaksha temple** with towering gateways or gopurams. In front of the temple is one of the most important high streets of Vijayanagara. This broad avenue (10.6 metres wide) is lined with shops, and even now serves as a bazaar or shopping area where one can buy ritual items for worship in the temple. The temple is an ancient one and predates the Vijayanagara period, but is still in worship because it was considered the most sacred

(opposite) : Map of Vijayanagara.

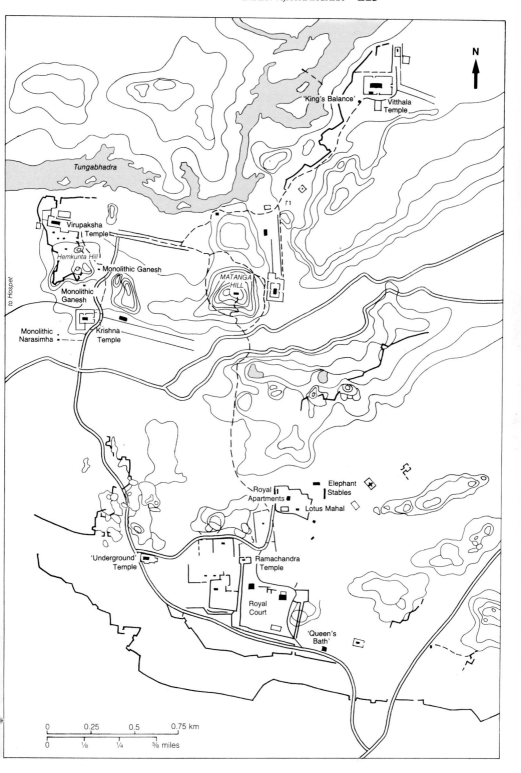

'King's Balance'

Vitthala
Temple

Tungabhadra

Virupaksha
Temple

Hemkunta Hill

Monolithic Ganesh

MATANGA
HILL

Monolithic
Ganesh

Monolithic
Narasimha

Krishna
Temple

to Hospet

Elephant
Stables

Royal
Apartments

Lotus Mahal

'Underground'
Temple

Ramachandra
Temple

Royal
Court

'Queen's
Bath'

N

0   0.25   0.5   0.75 km

0   ⅛   ¼   ⅜ miles

at Hampi. Successive generations of rulers and patrons added and enlarged the shrine complex. The temple, also called Pampapati (husband of Pampa), is associated with Pampa, the daughter of Brahma, the creator of the universe. It is here by the river that she is said to have done her *tapas*, meditating strenuously to win Virupaksha (Shiva, the lord of all) as her husband. The mission was successful and every year in the light of the April full-moon the gods descend to participate in the cosmic wedding. The streets in front of the temple are lined with pilgrims from the neighbourhood who come to this ancient city to celebrate the divine union of of Shiva and Pampa.

Fort walls, Vijayanagara.

The Virupaksha temple follows the standard format of Vijayanagara architecture in that it has (two) large courtyards, the first with an entrance through a tall gopuram (52 metres high). The open space is often crowded with visiting pilgrims, and small stalls laid out on the ground sell (fake) antiques and offerings for the temple. The second gateway was built by Krishnadeva Raya and leads into the main courtyard of the temple. The large mandap has a frieze on the façade proclaiming the wedding of Pampa. The hall is divided by several rows of sculpted columns and the ceiling is painted with scenes from Hindu mythology: Arjuna, the hero of the Mahabharata, shooting at a fish target to win the hand of Draupadi, and Shiva's cosmic marriage attended by all the gods. The garbha griha enshrines the Virupaksha linga and there are smaller side shrines adorned with ancient images of Mahishasuramardini, Parvati, and Bhubanesvari. There is a small complex of temples and a tank to the north of the Virupaksha temple.

South of the river and Hemkunta hill is the **Krishna Temple** built by Krishnadeva Raya to commemorate his victories in eastern India and Orissa. Once again the temple is entered through a gopuram, which leads into a spacious open courtyard at the centre of which are the various temple structures. The entrance mandaps are adorned with low relief sculptures, the outer wall of the temple has a sparse but very characteristic display of themes related to the story of Krishna, to whom this temple is dedicated.

As the road swerves down the hill, amidst lush farmlands is the colossal (6.7 metre) **Statue of Narasimha**. The story of Narasimha is another episode of the gods fighting evil. Here the villain is a demon who was granted a boon that he would not be destroyed by night or day, neither inside nor outside a building, neither by a man nor an animal. Believing himself to be invincible he came up against *Nara*-(man) *simha* (lion). The protagonist, Vishnu in the garb of half-beast half-man, appeared at dusk when it was neither night nor day, and on the threshold of the palace tore the demon to pieces, pulling out his entrails to make sure he was dead. Here the giant half-lion half-man avatar of Vishnu appears like a gentle smiling beast seated cross-legged and on his knee (once sat) his even gentler wife Lakshmi. A huge seven-hooded serpent hovers above, shielding the deity like a canopy.

Nearby is an interesting shrine with a large linga on a high pedestal standing in a garbha griha permanently submerged in water. Following the road southwards one enters the grand citadel area and here too are some extraordinary temples.

The large **Underground Temple** also collects water because it is constructed in a deep rectangular pit. On the road northwards one passes wonderful natural formations; one an arch of boulders called **Akka-tangi gundu** (the big sister-little sister). There are several other structures, like the Queen's bath with an interesting sunken pit and ornate wall decorations and the mint.

Near the royal residential complex is the exquisite **Hazara Rama** or **Ramachandra Temple**. Most spectacular is the decoration of the walled enclosure. This high wall has a series of horizontal panels with marching soldiers, processions of elephants, acrobats, and dancers all celebrating the great festival of the birth of Rama and the subjugation of Ravana of Lanka. Story has it that this region (around Hampi) was the kingdom of the monkeys whom Rama engaged to rescue his wife Sita from her kidnapper, the ten-headed Ravana. The outer wall of the Ramachandra temple has lovely shallow reliefs depicting various episodes of the Ramayana, and they stand like ornaments against the otherwise plain background. The interior hall, in front of the garbha griha, has four heavy black pillars, which carry the images of the ten incarnations of Vishnu: starting from the fish, the tortoise, the human avatars of Krishna, Rama, and finally Kalki, riding on a horse, the one who is yet to come to save the earth.

South of the temple is the **Royal Court**, an area with huge rooms, banquet areas, the grand hall of justice, a beautiful

Lotus Mahal,
Vijayanagara.

ceremonial tank, and the massive platform used by the king to preside over festivities. The platform (like the platform at Persepolis, Iran) is decorated with bands of low relief; groups of people, dancers and musicians, and royal animals participating in the grand court revelry. This is the only site in India where one gets an idea of the grandeur and magnificence of the medieval Hindu court, and though there are several literary accounts one is unprepared for the awe-inspiring scale of everything.

North of the Ramachandra temple is the regal entrance to the **Royal Apartments**. Though some are partly ruined, these buildings give some idea of the magnificence of secular architecture which is matched only by the splendour of the religious buildings in Vijayanagara. The **Lotus Mahal** is a solid structure elegantly designed with multiple-layered arched openings and a tall roof. The Queens court, and further away the so-called **Elephant Stables**, are interesting southern Indian examples of arched and domed architecture. The stable is a long building with eleven chambers topped with domes alternating with vaulted roofs. Beyond the stable are a whole line of excavated sites, temples, and shrines.

Moving back north, along a winding road, towards the riverside are other temples. The enclosure wall of the **Vitthala Temple** protects one of the highlights of Vijayanagara architecture, set as it is in superb natural surroundings. Within the

Vitthala Temple, Vijayanagara.

enclosure wall is an open rectangular courtyard housing the various buildings of the temple. The shrine is modest and has a mandap before it. There is a large open mandap with a series of pillars holding up a very graceful flat roof with turned up corners. The pillars of this mandap are the glory of the temple, each individually fashioned with motifs. The outer ring of clustered pillars are musical: when struck (gently) they ring out in perfect tonal quality the notes of an ancient melodic scale. In front of this mandap, designed as the mandap for Garuda, the vahana of Vishnu is a tiny little stone chariot complete with stone wheels that once rotated. This stone chariot imitates, to the last detail, a rath or cart used in temple processions when the gods were taken out for a grand display of the city and its devotees.

Stone chariot, Vitthala Temple, Vijayanagara.

WHAT'S IN THE NEIGHBOURHOOD

Hospet is a typical town in northern Karnataka. The Tungabhadra river flows past it and a huge dam has been built nearby. The huge reservoir is a regular tourist spot. Visitors walk along the dam and the nearby hill-side to see the sunset on this ocean of water.

HOW TO GET THERE

Hampi, or the site of Vijayanagara, is situated 13 kilometres from Hospet. There are regular buses and taxis that ply to and fro. Hampi is 350 kilometres from Bangalore and linked by a convenient daily overnight train. Hospet is also connected to Goa, Hubli, and Bijapur. There are no luxury hotels at Hampi so stay in Hospet. The best season to visit, when it is not too hot for long walks, is between October and March, and just after the monsoons the river is full and the countryside draped in green.

Badami, Aihole and Pattadakal

This splendid triple-billed site has glorious temples, some of the finest sculptural work in India, all set against a sensational (deserted) landscape. Studying this site one gets a strange impression that somewhere in the seventh century a select group of pre-eminent artists were invited (all expenses paid) for a workshop on 'Temple Design'. The end result (today, one thousand three hundred years later) at Badami, Aihole, and Pattadakal is a group of fifty breathtaking large and small shrines, each with its own individual style of architecture and decorative scheme. Fashions launched here, in the sixth, seventh, and eighth centuries, were to subsequently influence the distinctive temple styles of northern, southern, western, eastern, and Deccan India. Could there have been such a workshop or is the idea all too fanciful?

In the middle of the sixth century, around AD 544, Pulakeshin I instituted the Chalukyan kingdom and his son established Vatapi, identified as Badami, as the capital. The selection of Badami as a capital was a brilliant one for both political and aesthetic reasons. The capital was located on the Malprabha river; following its course (8 kilometres) north-wards is Pattadakal, with a complex of temples built on the banks. Further down (13 kilometres away), where the sand-stone outcrop of the Malprabha valley re-emerges, is Aihole. Badami, Aihole, and Pattadakal lie (in the present Bijapur district) in the lower Deccan region on the the Malprabha that flows into the Krishna river. This large river forms a chain across the country from the western to the eastern ghats. These ghats (hill ranges) run north to south along both sides of the Indian peninsula almost parallel to the sea coast, forging a unifying network of communication over the better part of the southern subcontinent. While trade routes were established along the course of rivers like the Krishna and Godavari, and the line of the ghats, cultural ideas flowed through the region through similar channels. Early Buddhist art from settlements at Amaravati and Nagarjunakonda had a major impact on the construction of temples in the lower Deccan. **Ellora** and **Ajanta** were also encompassed in this network, and mutual exchange of artistic influences are traceable from here all the way to Badami, Aihole, and Pattadakal.

Here is one example. During the course of history, as the Chalukyans grew in power, they pushed their territorial bound-

(opposite) : General view, Badami.

aries to the south, into the Pallava kingdom. Pulakeshin II, and later Vikramaditya II, actually entered the temple city of **Kanchipuram** (Tamil Nadu). Here the Chalukyas saw the best of Pallava art, the great **Kailashnatha Temple** and back home at Pattadakal they built its replica, the **Virupaksha Temple.** But the story does not end here. In the eighth century, when Chalukyan power was on the decline, the Rastrakutas conquered their capital. When doing so they in turn saw the Virupaksha temple and used it as their model to built the mighty rock-cut monumental temple of **Kailash** (No. 16) at **Ellora** (Maharashtra, India). This is but one of many stories of how Badami, Aihole, and Pattadakal, from their central location in the Indian subcontinent, became trend-setters in architecture. It is this 'workshop' of 'experimental model' temple forms that you will see at the site today.

Plan of Badami.

Badami

An imposing sandstone cliff dominates the view of Badami. It formed a natural protective wall for the capital of the Chalukyas. Embraced by the horseshoe-shaped curved cliff is a lake that supplied water. The local pink sandstone was used for building the temples. Badami town, which is relatively small, lies in front of the lake looking out on to this awe-inspiring craggy cliff. At sunset and sunrise you get a wonderful view of the stone wall, the shimmering lake below, and the silhouette of the temples and rock-cut caves on the cliff. These temples are of interest to the art historians as a key to the evolution of different architectural styles. The loveliest is the **Bhutanatha Temple** that stands under the shadow of the cliff, reflecting its beauty on the surface of the lake.

On the southern side of the cliff is a stairway that leads to four exquisite rock-cut shrines carved into the hillside. The first cave is for Shiva, the next two for Vishnu (with superb sculptures), and the furthest is a Jain shrine. The shrines were created deep within the belly of the hill and their façade appears on the overhanging cliff overlooking the lake. Within the shrine is the sanctum, the centre of worship. Like a structural building, the hall in front has rows of carved pillars. The pillar designs in Badami, Aihole, and Pattadakal are very beautiful: some are faceted, octagonal, with rounded cushions and carved medallions, and others have wonderful brackets depicting amorous couples. Carved on the (right) side entrance wall of **Cave No. 1** is the most dramatic sculpture to be found at Badami. It is a rare image of an eighteen-armed dancing Shiva. Here as Natraj, the cosmic creator, Shiva waves his arms in vigorous movement,

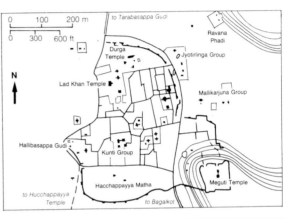

accompanied by his young son Ganesh and musicians on drums. He holds in each hand a symbol of his many varied attributes: the trident of destruction and the *damru* (drum) of creation. One foot is securely on the ground while he is about to raise the other. Shiva, the original parent of the world, who is as old as the earth (is young) is portrayed here as a youthful, ruddy (red from the stone), taut, and very appealing male god.

Aihole

There are several clusters of temples to be seen at Aihole. Of particular interest (to the historian) is Meguti which has an inscription that conclusively dates the shrine to AD 634, the reign of Pulakeshin II. At Aihole too the rock-cut architectural tradition continues in the **Ravana Phadi** cave. On the north-eastern side of the stony outcrop is the entrance to this extraordinary cave which has a linga in the sanctum at the rear end of the hall. Its sculpted

walls and side shrines are peopled with large figures, and lovely motifs adorn the pillars and ceiling. A great dancing Shiva appears here (as in Badami), but in this image the gracefulness of his movements are captured by the swirling forms of two great snakes that he holds and in the lovely images of the Sapta Matrikas or Seven (divine) Mothers.

Plan of Aihole.
Below: Ravana Phadi.

Moving south-west and within a modern enclosure is the domineering form of the so-called **Durga Temple**. It has an entrance porch, a hall, and a sanctum within. The entire structure is then given an open-colonnaded verandah, which swirls around its rounded, apsidal rear. A hint of a turret or shikhara can be seen on top of the temple, a foretaste and worthy experiment of taller, grander things to come. There are some interesting perforated window screens and a noteworthy image of the goddess Durga slaughtering the demon Mahisha, who appeared in the form of a bull. The great goddess with her, Vahana, the cheerful lion as Mahishasuramardini (The One who destroyed Mahisha the demon), is strident and unperturbed. Beside her is the diminutive Mahisha for whom her bell tolls.

Further south is a vast complex of ruined temples, with names that are clearly not the original, perhaps christened after some unknown visitor or ancient resident. The **Lad Khan Temple**, as it is called, is a large squarish building with a projecting porch on whose decorative pillars loving couples are engraved. The temple has some interesting stone screens (whoever thought that jalis were a feature only of Islamic architecture). Above the building is a ribbed stone roof, as if to imitate tiled wooden architecture and a very stunted superstructure, the embryonic form of a shikhara.

Though it is a bit of a walk, the Hacchappayyamatha and the Hucchappayya temples are worth visiting just to see the unusual sculptural decorations and carved animated figures of the gods (Shiva, Vishnu, and Brahma) flying about on the ceilings.

Pattadakal

This is a huge complex of temples attractively located next to the river, which may have been used in rituals. Entering the complex is the **Jambulinga Temple**, its shikhara recalling the temples of **Bhubaneshwar** (Orissa) with a projecting horseshoe arch bearing a figure of dancing Shiva. Next to it is the **Galaganatha Temple** unlike anything else in the region. The conical shikhara is like the (north Indian) *nagara* style with horizontal layers separated by tiny cushion-like motifs. Compare this temple roof with the shikharas of the next two temples, the **Virupaksha** and the **Mallikarjuna**, which are based on the southern Indian temple shikhara format. These two temples (that link

Jambulinga Temple

Galaganatha Temple

Kashivishvanatha Temple

Sangameshvara Temple

Mallikarjuna Temple

Virupaksha Temple

N

0　10　20 m

0　30　60 ft

to Papanatha Temple

Plan of Pattadakal

Kanchipuram and Ellora, though separated by a few hundred kilometres), have tiered pyramidal, not conical, roofs made up of separate levels decorated with an arrangement of miniature temple replicas. A historical inscription here records that the temples were built in the time of Vikramaditya II to commemorate his victory over the Pallavas of Kanchipuram in the eighth century. They may have been built by his two wives, Lokeshvara and Trailokeshvara, whose names these temples originally bore. The Virupaksha Temple has a wonderful Nandi porch in front, a porch leading into a pillared hall, and the garbha griha at the rear end of the building. Around the temple wall are some very high quality sculptures set inside little niches. The sculptures (within and on the exterior wall), as well as the architecture here, mark an obvious advance of ideas and skills from those of some of the earlier shrines.

Sangameshvara Temple, Pattadakal.

WHAT'S IN THE NEIGHBOURHOOD

The Papanatha temple is situated at some distance from the main Pattadakal complex but has very interesting sculptures, friezes from the Ramayana and Mahabharata, and a pillar with a wonderful energetic scene of Ravana shaking Mount Kailash and trying to dislodge Shiva. Three kilometres away from Badami is the magical sacred grove of **Mahakuta** where worship continues. It is arranged around a tank from which flows sweet spring water. There are several temples in this complex, once again each one representing a different school of architecture or shikhara form. There is an **Archaeological Museum** at Badami with some interesting scuptures found at the temple sites.

From Badami one can get to Belgaum and Goa via the beautiful Ghat Road, or to the fifteenth century forts of Bijapur, Gulbarga, and Bidar, all of them deserted and very spectacular (*see* **Golconda**), or move down to Hospet to see the ancient capital of the **Vijayanagara** empire at **Hampi**.

HOW TO GET THERE

Badami is difficult to get to but is worth the effort. There is a railway line to Belgaum, Hubli and Bijapur where buses and cars can be hired. Accommodation is adequate with decent southern Indian fare. There are State tourism run hotels at Badami and Aihole. Badami is 8 kilometres from Pattadakal, which is 13 kilometres from Aihole. The best time to go is during the winter months, when the fields are full of sunflowers that rotate their giant heads all day to follow the direction of the sun.

Somnathpur, Belur and Halebid

A visit to either Somnathpur or Belur-Halebid is an experience, for here you will see a style of architecture unique to the region. The temples were built in the twelfth to thirteenth centuries by Hoysala rulers and their officials. They are comparatively stunted (unlike the temple at **Madurai**, the Lingaraja of **Orissa**, or the large temples of **Khajuraho**). Each small, compact structural temple is lavishly decorated with sculpture and the profusion covers every inch of wall space. This tightly packed sculptural scheme is exclusive to Hoysala art and was never replicated. Part of the reason for such intricate and ornate artwork was the nature of the stone used at these three sites. Chlorite is a dark grey-green stone which offered the sculptor a surface that could be chiselled so finely that it looked like lace. A bangle could be made to rotate on a sculpted hand and stone bells could be made to ring on a statue. While many critics find the rich sculptural decoration too ornate and baroque, no one can question the excellence of each individual statue. The Hoysala artist was a perfectionist: his challenging artistic motto seemed to have been 'make the impossible, possible'.

Somnathpur is 38 kilometres from Mysore (138 kilometres from Bangalore) while the twin sites, Belur and Halebid, are 157 kilometres from Mysore (222 kilometres from Bangalore and 16 kilometres from each other).

Belur
This is the earliest in this group and was built by Vishnuvardhana (in around AD 1117) to commemorate his victory against the Cholas, the belligerent neighbours from Tamil Nadu. It is surprising, but perhaps self-explanatory, that the Hoysalas developed an artistic tradition that was so characteristically distinct from all the dominant traditions that surrounded them in Tamil Nadu and the lower Deccan.

Halebid
Its present name means old (*hale*) capital (*bidu*) but it was once referred to as Dwarasamudra, the gateway to the sea. The main temple here is called **Hoysaleshvara**, believed to have been built around AD 1121 by an officer of Vishnuvardhana. The temple has a joint-double plan. In the Nandi Mandap is a huge image of the bull deity. There are a few remnants of other structures that may have constituted the capital around this temple.

(opposite) : Detail of temple wall, Somnathpur.

Somnathpur

The **Keshava Temple** is the best-preserved most complete monument of Hoysala architecture. The temple is believed to have been built (around AD 1268) under the patronage of Somnatha, a general in the army of Narasimha II.

The Hoysala Temple

The mature Hoysala temple was enclosed within a courtyard, with several sub-shrines, as in Somnathpur. The traditional

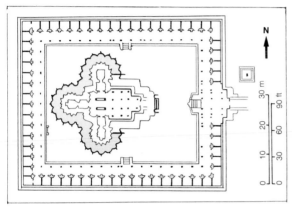

Plan of Keshava Temple, Somnathpur.

Hindu temple consists of a square garbha griha proceeded by a mandap and entrance porch. Elaborating on this, the architects here made a significant innovation by (hypothetically) rotating the square sanctum to form a star with many radiating points. The temple wall, instead of being basically rectangular and plain, acquired, in the Hoysala style, a series of angular projections, which increased (for the sculptor) the surface area of the wall a hundredfold. The star-shaped plan of the shrine is characteristic of this style but such elaboration did not end here—even the shikhara that crowned the building developed a flower-like or star shape. The temples, instead of having merely one sanctum, had three as in Somnathpur, or were built like siamese twins as a joint—double temple, like the one in Halebid. The star-shaped plan was further extended to incorporate these additional shrines, and what resulted was a very flamboyant structure with a minimum of long straight walls.

The entire temple was built on a broad platform to enable devotees to perform a pradakshina of the temple and to view the wonderful world of sculpture that adorns the outer wall surface. Above, the starry temple wall projected a deep cornice that cast strong shadows on the minutely textured surface. At Belur and Halebid the superstructure or shikhara can hardly be seen (if built at all), but at Somnathpur the triple-shrine structure has three shikharas, each a beautiful star-shaped, ornate bell.

Percy Brown, a renowned art historian, noted that these stone temples were like a 'richly carved casket in sandalwood or ivory', and indeed that is what they resemble. From a picture or even from the gate of the temple, it is impossible to imagine how much sculptural work has been added to the temple.

The platform on which the temple stands is moulded, and at Somnathpur it is guarded by seated lions. The actual temple base rises straight out of the platform and is composed of a series of bands that wind around the star form of the building. These bands are estimated to cover a length of over 200 metres and every centimetre is carved. The lowest frieze, just off ground level, has elephants. In Hindu cosmology the universe is carried on the shoulders of powerful celestial guardian elephants. In these temples there are several hundred elephants holding up the temple, which is symbolically a miniature universe. Each elephant is different in stance and poise, and is beautifully bejewelled and decorated with chains and bells. When one thinks of the thousands of artisans who worked on these temples, the uniformity of style of these bands of sculpture is remarkable. Some elephants have their trunks up, others playfully pull the leader's tail, while others appear unconcerned by the weight they carry.

The next band is a line of marching mythological creatures that look like lions with amazing heads and bulging eyes that cast a watchful, protective glance over the temple. The next band is an ornate scroll of creeper tendrils that wind and curl with geometric precision, punctuated by *markara* (mythical crocodiles) heads and dancing figures within the arabesque folds of leaves.

Keshava Temple, Somnathpur.

Above the elephants is a gay procession of little horses and their riders. One must remember that there may be as many as a hundred and fifty horses covering over two hundred metres of wall space of one temple, and in this vast expanse each horse is an individual. The horses are fashionably caparisoned, in the style of the day, with jewelled necklaces, ornate reins, and lovely patterned saddles. Astride the horses, carrying flags and staffs, and galloping forwards are gallant, confident riders.

At the next level is another scroll of arabesque design and above this the miniature world of the gods. This unending band is carved with narrative panels depicting incidents from the Ramayana, Mahabharata, and myths about Krishna. As you walk around the temple (in a clockwise direction) the story unfolds on this band like a cartoon strip, each episode summarising the main events and leading on to the next. At Halebid the story of the great battle of the Mahabharata is told in exacting detail. Minute nuances of the story are included in every scene: chariots going to war with banners flying and horses geared for combat, the dead and wounded lying in theatrical postures on the battlefields. The Krishna stories on the

Somnathpur temple have a charm all their own. A scene from a poem about Krishna near the river would include (though only a few centimetres high) a little river in which tiny fish swim happily, tortoises and frogs sit around, with a few wind-swept trees added to represent the green forest grove where the cowherds frolicked with the young maidens of the village.

Above this lively narrative scroll is a band of *hansa* or mythical birds, with fluffy tails that bunch out in great foamy curls. The next band is another floral creeper scroll, which forms

the base for the next level of sculptural decoration. The entire temple base with bands of animals and heroes is a sort of miniature representation of life on earth.

Every corner and angular projection of the central wall space of the temples is inhabited by familiar deities. They appear in all their glory, adorned with heavy jewels, towering crowns, bangles on every arm, and chunky anklets on their feet. The sculptured deities of Somnathpur, Belur, and Halebid

Keshava Temple interior, Somnathpur.

are unsurpassed by any other sculptures in India for the wealth of jewellery with which each one is decked. Thus adorned, the gods are set beneath a canopy of a curling foliage of branches.

Above this the shikhara is merely an abstract play of geometric temple-like motifs set in deep horizontal levels, representing the region of the mountains where the gods reside and the pure sky which has no form.

Inside the temple, the decorative element is in no way reduced. The shadowy mandap and hallways are pillared with elaborate dark columns. The carved columns in the Hoysala temple are also exceptional for they appear to have been turned on a lathe, with a series of regular, slim horizontal mouldings. The temples of Halebid and Belur have beautiful examples of these lathe-turned pillars.

At Belur an additional example of excellent sculptural decoration is to be found in the bracket figures. These individual pieces of stone are shaped like brackets to support the projecting eaves of the temple. Each bracket design has a canopy of leaves, flowers, and fruit, beneath which is a lovely maiden. This female figure (compared to the fertility symbols of the tree nymphs, Yakshis, or Salabhanjikas), are the hallmark of perfection in Hoysala art. The figures are full-breasted with heavy hips and firm thighs. Each is portrayed in a different stance: gazing into a mirror, playing a flute, drum, or stringed instrument. The intricate inclusion of delicate detail so characteristic of this style is captured in these bracket figures.

WHAT'S IN THE NEIGHBOURHOOD
Somnathpur is only 38 kilometres from Mysore, the grand and very beautiful capital of the royal family of the old Mysore state. One can stay at Mysore and visit a number of sites. The centre of Mysore's sightseeing is the **Amba Vilas Mahal** designed in 1897. It is a strange blend of Hindu, Islamic, and European architecture. Part of the palace is open to the public: the Durbar Hall, the Peacock pavilion, the Armoury, and the **Jagan Mohan Art Gallery** with artifacts from the Maharaja's collection. A **Railway Museum, Zoo, St. Philomena's Church**, and the old **Lalitha Mahal Palace**, once the summer palace, now a hotel, are all worth a visit. Outside Mysore is **Chamundi Hill** with a very popular temple dedicated to the Goddess Chamundi, the patron of the Mysore royal family, and on the way up the hill is a huge (5 metres high) monolithic statue of Nandi.

Srirangapatnam

On the road from Mysore to Bangalore is Srirangapatnam (20 kilometres away). This beautiful river island site was the capital of Hyder Ali and his son, Tipu Sultan, the 'Tiger of Mysore'. In the eighteenth century the Marathas attacked this capital but Hyder Ali was able to push them back. The strong fortification walls (and dungeons) of the capital can still be seen. Tipu Sultan then secured French assistance to ward off the impending conquest by British forces. In 1799, Tipu Sultan was killed fighting for the independence of his territory from colonial forces. A simple tomb marks the spot where this courageous ruler fell defending Srirangapatnam Fort.

At Srirangapatnam a beautiful **Summer Palace** was built within a formal garden. Originally called **Daria Daulat Bagh**, the Summer Palace is situated east of the fort. The elegant building built in wood has richly painted ceilings and wall murals depicting the marching armies of the courageous father and son. A museum in the Summer Palace has some old paintings and engravings done in the last century, which depict the tragic history of the fall of Srirangapatnam, the capture of the fort by the British, and Tipu's young sons being taken into captivity.

Shravenabelagola

Shravenabelagola (53 kilometres from Hassan) is one of the most celebrated Jain sites in southern India. It is not to see a particular monument that one comes here but for the location and the concept. From the early years of the Christian era Jain missionaries moved to southern India in a steady stream, spreading their philosophy of ahimsa or non-violence. Their presence is marked in the Deccan and there are also Jain temples in Tamil Nadu, and in Karnataka at Karkal and Dharmasthal. At **Shravenabelagola** the site is reported to have been well-known from Mauryan times but in the ninth to tenth centuries a large Jain settlement was established. A general of the Ganga ruler Rachamalla, called Chamundaraya, commissioned this statue in AD 981. A hill (143 metres high) called Vindhyagiri stands beside a tank and, along with other hillocks like Chandragiri, all have interesting Jain monasteries and shrines.

Dominating the view from the plains below is the colossal (17.7 metres) monolithic **Statue of Gommateshvara**. This statue, one of the largest in the world, represents Bahubali. Son of the first Tirthankara, Bahubali renounced his kingdom and sought enlightenment. Standing motionless for a year, the naked ascetic meditated on the meaning of life. Creepers and plants grew beside his gentle, calm presence. The idea of creating such a gigantic statue is unusual, but to place it upright on top of a hillock so that Bahubali's naked frame is 'draped by the sky' is an exceptional achievement and idea. The form of Bahubali is also singular. His calm undisturbed expression is framed by elongated ears; his very long arms lie rigid beside him, while creepers have been carved climbing up his colossal legs. Every twelve years (last in 1993) a special celebration takes place and the giant image is bathed (from enormous scaffolds and temporary platforms) with bucketfuls of milk and honey, and other precious condiments.

HOW TO GET THERE

Somnathpur is connected by road to **Mysore**, which is well linked by road and rail to other cities of southern India. It is convenient to stay at Mysore, equipped with a range of reasonable hotels, and visit by day the sites around this lovely city. October to March is the popular season to visit Mysore. During the Dussehra celebrations (October–November) there are special illuminations of the palace.

Belur and **Halebid** lie in the Hassan district of Karnataka. Staying at **Hassan** one can visit the old Hoysala capital and Belur on a day visit. To get to **Hassan** there are regular tourist buses and hired vehicles. The best route is from Bangalore to Hassan (222 kilometres) and from Mysore (157 kilometres). From Hassan it is 40 kilometres to **Belur** and from there it is a mere 16 kilometres to **Halebid**. All year round Bangalore has pleasant weather. It is a lovely city to visit and is served by some wonderful colonial-style hotels. Hassan has minimal accommodation, but Belur and Halebid have none. From Hassan a day trip to **Belur-Halebid**, and another day visit to **Shravenabelagola** (53 kilometres away) can be made at a leisurely pace.

Mahabalipuram

The story of southern Indian stone architecture begins on the
sandy beaches of Mahabalipuram and from here goes on to
reach incredible heights in **Kanchipuram, Thanjavur,** and
Madurai. The location is very lovely: just outside Madras city
amidst swaying palms and Casuarina trees on a long beach
washed by the Bay of Bengal. Along an outcrop of hillocks near
the sea are monumental rock-cut temples, carved out shrines,
and the worlds largest panoramic open-air sculptural relief. All
evidence suggests that Mahabalipuram was an ancient port
even in the time of Ptolemy. It grew to such stature and
importance that by the seventh to eighth centuries the Pallava
rulers of the region invested in large-scale temple construction.
The great Pallava ruler Mamalla (c. 630-68) gave his name to this
historic place and it was called **Mamallapuram** (the city of
Mamalla, which evolved into Mahabalipuram). The beach-side
enviroment is unique and the monuments are aligned north to
south in and around the hillocks and parallel to the sea.

Descent of the Ganga

Sometimes called Arjuna's Penance is an enormous relief (29
metres by 13 metres) sculpted on two huge boulders. A cleft in
the rock enabled rainwater to cascade down between the two
boulders, simulating the descent of the mighty river Ganga.
This cleft is the focus of the entire composition and every image
seems to sway towards it. The river has water serpent deities,
the naga raja and his wife, and people bathing and praying
beside its banks. The water as it fell collected in a pond, which
must have been decorated with real lotus flowers, fish, and
frogs to complete the realism of the relief. The frieze has been
carved on either side of the descending waters. Overhead the
sky is peopled with flying figures of gods and gandharvas, all
celebrating the coming to earth of the celestial river.

Mythology explains that a sage Bhagirath requested the
mighty Ganga (a river appearing as the Milky Way in the
heavens) to fall down to earth to wash away the sins of the dead
and the ashes of thousands of his relatives. In the upper left
hand corner one can see Bhagirath standing in a yogic posture,
meditating and performing (for he is all skin and bones) strenuous
tapas to appeal to the river goddess. Shiva was requested to bear
the brunt of the might of the river on his head for no one else
could support such a burden. He is seen coming up beside

Bhagirath and offering his assistance, accompanied by his *ganas*, followers. As the river descends, all of nature responds to her fertile presence and cleansing spirit. Animals, lions, docile deer, and a delightful family of elephants with their young (on the right) come towards the river to pay their obeisance. A touch of humour, so characteristic of Indian art, is introduced with a cat imitating Bhagirath's tapas, standing on one hind leg meditating. While the cat has gone spiritual, tiny mice frolic in gay abandon. Seated to the right of the relief on a boulder is the celebrated portrait sculpture of a monkey family, busy preening each other and playing with the baby.

Further south is a constructed open mandap, believed to have been added during the Vijayanagar period to protect a huge bas relief on the back wall. Here Krishna, the divine cowherd, shelters his cattle under a hillock (which he lifted with one finger) from the storm sent down by the jealous Indra, the lord of the skies.

Rock-cut Mandaps

Clamber up the hill (the one with the lighthouse) to see, on its southern side, two of the most beautiful rock-cut shrines of Mahabalipuram. The **Adivaraha Mandap** is an elegant shrine that has a simple façade with the famous lion-based Pallava pillars. On either side of the sanctuary are figures identified as

Descent of the Ganga, Mahabalipuram.

royal patrons, kings and queens. A large panel depicts the incarnation of Vishnu as a gigantic boar, and Varaha, rescuing the earth (depicted as a youthful woman) from the depths of a catastrophic flood. The scene is very calm, and especially tender is the careful way Varaha lifts the goddess above the swirling waters below. The **Mahishamardini Mandap** has a long verandah with three sanctums. There are two large friezes at both ends of the verandah, one of Vishnu sleeping on the sea of eternity, on his serpent bed (anant, infinity), while the gods assemble around him to request him to get on with creation. On the opposite side is a huge theatrical panel of the goddess astride her ferocious (smiling) lion Vahana. She is attacking a bull-headed demon called Mahisha. The myth describes how Mahisha had grown to be a terribly powerful force, upsetting the balance of life. The gods, in desperation, pooled their resources together (the sun gave his ever-watchful eyes, the wind his swift feet, etc) and produced a super-goddess, young, beautiful, and invincible. She did what the male gods could not do, and subjugated Mahisha effortlessly. The great battle, witnessed by the gods, is narrated in this superb specimen of monumental Pallava sculpture.

Draupadi and Arjun Rathas, Mahabalipuram.

Pancha Rathas

South of the hill (some 200 metres away) is a complex of rock-cut shrines called the **Pancha** (five) **Rathas** (chariots) named after the heroes of the Mahabharata, which are, possibly, not their original names. It is here that one sees architecture in action and every crucial stage of its evolutionary process. A closer look at the shrines will enable you to see how the artist carved each shrine out of the living rock, beginning from the top and working downwards. Chisel markings and unfinished parts of the shrine add much to our admiration of the herculean task of cutting the hard granite rock, from top to bottom, chip by chip, to fashion an entire temple.

The first Ratha is named after **Draupadi** (the common wife of the five Pandav brothers, the heroes of the Mahabharata). The square shrine has a simple peaked roof, similar to a thatched hut, with decorated corners. This roof design was never used again in southern Indian architecture but was transmuted into a miniature hut motif and placed at every horizontal level of subsequent rathas, and later temples, throughout the region.

The next shrine is the small elegant **Arjuna Rath**, which, like the **Dharmaraja Rath**, is a square building with distinct horizontal levels on its pyramidal roof and small roof motifs along the edges. The finial of the tower or shikhara is dome-shaped with little window-like openings on its faceted sides. This form of tower was to serve as the prototype for all later southern Indian temples. After this successful experiment it was merely a question of increasing the number of levels, and refining and multiplying the miniature roof motifs along its sides. The central shrine of this group is named **Bhima Ratha** and has a huge rock-cut barrel-vaulted roof like a large thatched hut. This experiment was not accepted in subsequent centuries as the appropriate model for the tower above the sanctum, but was used instead for the crown of all the tall gopurams or gateways leading into the walled enclosure of the temples of southern India.

There are some lovely sculptural examples on the Pancha Rathas (walk around the Arjuna Ratha) and three enormous rock-cut sculptures of an elephant, the lion of Durga, and a Nandi. Beside the Elephant, and imitating its rotund backside, is an apsidal-ended shrine, a design found in ancient Buddhist rock-cut caves but not used again in the south. After this phase of rock-cut architecture, the next phase introduces a completely new technique: the structural temple, not built by cutting the rock to make a building but constructed by piling blocks of stone in perfect gravitational equilibrium to create a temple.

Plan of Mahabalipuram.

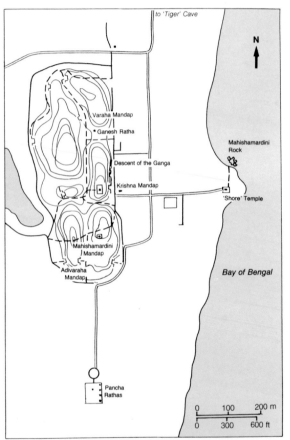

to 'Tiger' Cave

N

Varaha Mandap

Ganesh Ratha

Descent of the Ganga

Krishna Mandap

Mahishamardini Mandap

Adivaraha Mandap

Mahishamardini Rock

'Shore' Temple

Bay of Bengal

Pancha Rathas

0   100   200 m

0   300   600 ft

Shore Temple

North-east of the Rathas and east of the great bas relief of the Descent of the Ganges is the **Shore Temple**. This is a structural temple, built block by block rather than cut out of stone as in the case of the Rathas. The temple was built so close to the shore that its entrance is from the back, i.e. the west. The shrine was possibly built during the reign of the Pallava ruler Rajasimha (the king lion) which is possibly why it (and all Pallava architecture) have a profusion of rampant lions rearing their smiling heads from the base of the pillars. The temple has a compound wall with a charming line of seated Nandis, for this is a monument to Shiva. The temple actually has several shrines. The first has a figure of the lying Vishnu in the garbha griha. The main sanctum is reached by walking along the passage to the east (the correct direction) to the garbha griha and its linga that looks out on to the rising sun each morning.

There are several local legends about six other temples (pagodas), and indeed about the entire city of Mamallapuram, which was said to have been consumed by the waves leaving treasures and beautiful temples at the bottom of the sea. But this seems unlikely, especially since the architects went to such pains to build the Shore Temple at the water's edge and worked the sanctum plans around it to suit the location.

The tower of the Shore Temple breaks free from its bondage with the Pancha Rathas and soars into the sky, its pyramidal shape no longer fat and dumpy, but elongated and elegant, a perfect blend of the parts and the whole. The next step in the evolution of temple architecture is to be found in the beautiful, very special **Kailashnatha Temple** at **Kanchipuram,** built by the Pallavas in their holy capital, and it is here that every experiment worked out at Mahabalipuram finds fruition.

Shore Temple, Mahabalipuram.

In 1924, F.G. Pearce wrote an article in which it was suggested that Mahabalipuram functioned as a school of art:[19]

> Surely there must have been at some times and in some places in India—during the epochs when she gave birth to the many skilled architects, sculptors and artists who planned and built and decorated the mighty monuments for which she is famous even to this day—quiet spots, where the masters in various arts trained their pupils—ashramas, schools of art, in fact.... May not these half-finished monoliths, these bas-reliefs scattered, apparently aimlessly ... here and there ... be the the practice-work of 'prentice-hands, done under the guidance of the teacher or teachers, abandoned when seriously faulty, or when the lesson had been sufficiently mastered, most on miniature scale, of course—which would account for the otherwise meaningless pigmy size doors and windows?

On the main road parallel to the **Descent of the Ganga** is a **School of Traditional Architecture** at Mahabalipuram run by a great scholar and teacher. You can see the young students at work, cutting and carving huge blocks of stone to prepare new temples and sculptures (for India and abroad) using time-tested and perfected techniques.

Madras
The city of Madras is 55 kilometres from Mahabalipuram on a scenic coastal route. It is the capital of Tamil Nadu and the gateway to the rest of southern India. It is a historic city because the British East India company established there one of its earliest factories and seats of power. In the days when black and white communities were segregated, **Fort St. George** was built (in 1640) to protect the British traders from the 'natives'. Today the fort has been converted into the Tamil Nadu Government Secretariat and Legislative Assembly. Within the fort are a number of interesting buildings, including **St. Mary's**, one of the earliest churches in India. There are tombs and church records that read like a 'who's who' of British India. An interesting little **Fort Museum** has a collection of paintings, documents, coins, and medals of this period. Going south from the fort along the 13 kilometres long Marina beach (one of the longest in the world), are the round Ice factory, the nineteenth century **University Buildings**, and at the furthest end is the (much renovated) **San Thomé Church** where the Apostle St. Thomas is said to have been buried. The **State Museum** of Madras is one of the best in India with a collection of early Buddhist sculpture from Amaravati and Nagarjunakonda. There is a separate gallery of priceless tenth to thirteenth century Chola period bronze sculptures and each image is a masterpiece.

Kanchipuram

The temple town of Kanchipuram is 71 kilometres from Madras and well worth a long day trip (at least). It is one of the holiest Hindu cities, second only to **Varanasi**. Kanchipuram (called Conjeevaram, in British days) is still the seat of an ancient gurukul or traditional university, and there are several *maths*, or Hindu religious organisations, here. It is said that there are more than a hundred temples and shrines at Kanchipuram and from a distance one can see a cluster of temple gopurams, looking like beacons to pilgrims who travel here from all parts of southern India. Apart from its fame as temple town it is a great market for neighbouring villages and a major centre for quality hand-woven silk frequently embellished with pure gold thread design. Weaving is a major cottage industry and you can visit homes to see the intricate process of preparing silk brocade.

Of all the great places of worship, **Ekambranatha** (believed to have been built by Krishnadeva Raya, of **Vijayanagara** fame) and the **Kamakshi Temple** are the centres of worship in the city. But these are for devotees and the faithful alone.

At Kanchipuram there are two monuments, both legacies of the Pallava period, the **Kailashnatha** and the **Vaikuntha Perumal**, both natural successors to Mahabalipuram. The Kailashnatha temple is undoubtedly one of the favourite monuments of any art historian and visitor (and if the Chalukyas

Monkey family, Mahabalipuram.

liked it, so will we). It was so attractive that in the middle of the eighth century, when the Chalukyas saw it during their conquest, they imitated the plan in their Virupaksha temple at **Pattadakal**.

Kailashnatha Temple

The temple stands in an uncongested open space. A small Nandi mandap in front of the enclosure identifies the temple as Shiva's. The enclosure wall, to become a distinctive feature of later southern Indian temples, forms a high barrier but the shikhara of the temple is so beautifully proportioned that it rears its statuesque crown above it like a towering mountain of stone. Inside the temple, through a small gateway (a forerunner of the tall gopurams of later temples in the south), the enclosure wall becomes a backdrop for a whole colonnade of tiny shrines. Each one contains an image or manifestation of a deity and on the northern side are some remnants of paintings in original mineral hues of yellow-ochre and reds. The temple was built during the time of Rajasimha (some additions, like the gateway were added by his son), as was the Shore temple at Mahabalipuram, but in the brief period that separates the construction of these two, an amazing maturity and confidence is discernible in the Kailashnatha Temple. The bases of the pillars in Mahabalipuram had sedate seated lions but at Kanchipuram the confident grimacing lions stand on their hind legs, ready to pounce out of the wall at anyone who might cause harm to the temple of god.

Kailashnatha Temple, Kanchipuram.

The tower is much taller, made up of successive diminishing tiers till it reaches its summit crowned by a huge dome-shaped monolithic block of stone. The miniature temple motifs along each tier are also perfectly integrated to create an unrestricted visual movement up to the pinnacle of the temple.

Around the temple the wall space is divided into neat niches and alcoves to house images philosophically associated with the directions. Here too every image serves as an archetype for later temple sculptures. The Cholas who succeeded the Pallavas used a similar formula in their temples at **Thanjavur**, **Gangaikondacholapuram**, and in the mature and very elegant later Chola temple of **Darasuram** near Kumbakonam.

Yet there is something fresh and almost spontaneous about the carvings here. The southern side niche has a wonderful sculpture of Dakshinamurti: Shiva the teacher surrounded by lions and deer who in the presence of the lord have forgotten their natural fears and are at rest. On the western side is the dramatic sculpture of dancing Shiva, engaged in a competition with his talented wife Parvati. He won the contest because he struck a difficult pose, his leg lifted above his shoulder, a posture she felt it was improper to imitate. On the northern side is the Gangadhara figure of Shiva, who has received the descending Ganga river on his head. Inside the temple there is a mandap and the sanctum holds the linga of Shiva. A secret passage or rather a tunnel runs around the sanctum for devotees to crawl through: a virtual rite of passage, rebirth, and a promise of renewed life.

HOW TO GET THERE

Mahabalipuram is accessible (55 kilometres) by road from **Madras** city. There are organised tours, and cars can be hired to take you to Mahabalipuram. A day's visit of the historical temples combined with a beach holiday are possible for there are now a number of beach resorts along the way. Madras, as the capital of Tamil Nadu, has an international airport and internal air, rail, and road links with almost every region of India.

The perfect trip would be to enjoy the beaches of Mahabalipuram (during the winter months of November to February), by the light of the full moon to visit the monuments of Mahabalipuram, representing splendid early experiments in temple building, and then go to Madras for day trips to see the museum and fort, and take a long day tour of **Kanchipuram**. When perfectly acclimatized, set forth to see the rest of southern India, its monuments, great cities, and wonderful wildlife parks.

Thanjavur

In the history of monumental architecture there are two principal stages: the first when experiment and innovation dominate, and the other when the style reaches its full maturity and artistic integrity. In Orissa the temples at **Bhubaneshwar** reached stylistic maturity in the Lingaraja temple. In central India the smaller experimental shrines find their artistic climax in the Kandariya Mahadev Temple, **Khajuraho. Mahabalipuram** of the Pallavas exemplifies the stage of breakthroughs which find fruition and creative perfection in the Chola **Brihadeshvara Temple** at **Thanjavur.**

Thanjavur, also referred to as Tanjore, lies in the heart of Tamil Nadu's rice bowl. Many famous historic cities and temple towns, like **Tiruchchirappalli, Srirangam, Thanjavur, Kumbakonam, Gangaikondacholapuram** grew beside the sacred Kaveri river and its tributaries. This well-watered, fertile land brought enough prosperity in agriculture to support the construction of large towns and a thriving overseas trade, an empire and its enormous army. In the ninth century the Cholas, on an upward swing, expanded their territory to encompass large portions of southern India, and made contacts and alliances with Shri Lanka, Burma, and the Far East.

For the royal family the heart of religious life was the temple at **Chidambaram**, but when a new capital was designed at Thanjavur a grand temple was built to invite Lord Shiva to reside amongst them. The city today has some remains of fortification walls, the old markets, and workshop areas, which signify the growth of a commercial centre which attracted artists and craftsmen to the city. Bronze images were and still are produced by highly skilled artistans, for ever-increasing household requirements and temple worship. In the **Brihadeshvara Temple** there are many large elegant bronzes and lamps donated by Chola kings, their queens, and courtiers. A visit to the market and to the **Thanjavur Art Gallery** will put you in touch with the enormous creative talent that this city harbours to this day. Not only the material arts but music, dance, and literature flourished here under the patronage of the Chola rulers. Amidst this rich, intense cultural milieu one of the greatest temples to Shiva was built.

Brihadeshvara Temple is a monumental architectural achievement. Enclosed within a courtyard dotted with (some later) subsidiary shrines to the directional deities and others, is

(opposite) :
Brihadeshvara
Temple, Thanjavur.

the towering presence of the temple. There is a beautiful large (3.7 metre high) stone Nandi that looks faithfully out of its mandap at the temple where his master resides. Gargantuan statues of the dvarapalas holding clubs guard the entrance into the temple. The mandap, an elegant sixteenth century structure, leads the way into the main building. Inside, one hall leads into another till you reach the sanctum where stands a tall (3.6 metre high) linga of Shiva. The sanctum is in two storeys and is decorated with sculptures and murals. Not so long ago the Archaeological Survey of India found that beneath these murals lay original Chola paintings. Careful restoration has revealed exquisite wall paintings depicting Shiva in his many splendid forms, dancers and attendants.

Walking around the temple one can see the two-storey division of the temple wall. The entire surface is treated with high quality sculpture of myriad manifestations of Shiva. On the southern wall is a figure of Natraj, the Dancing Shiva; on the west wall is the amalgamated symbol of creation and preservation, Shiva and Vishnu, as Harihara; and as one completes the pradakshina on the northern side is the unified figure of Shiva and Parvati or Ardhanareshvara.

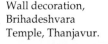
Wall decoration, Brihadeshvara Temple, Thanjavur.

Looking up one cannot but be impressed by the exalted concept and dramatic scale of the structure. The temple tower rises to the incredible height of 66 metres as if it were creating the

great axial mountain of Meru. This temple, actually referred to as the Dakshina Meru, recreates the southern mythical mountain supporting the universe. On a square base (of 29 metres) stands this thirteen-tiered pyramid of stone taking the eye high up into the sky, where an enormous dome-like crown is placed. This solid granite octagonal crown is 7.8 metres high and is estimated to weigh over 81 tonnes. The question that comes to mind is how this monolithic boulder of stone was hauled and placed on the top of this lofty tower. One explanation was that a ramp a few kilometres long was constructed with a gentle slope and the stone rolled up to its position. Another idea suggests that the temple was built stage by stage, and a mountain of earth was packed around the structure every time one level was completed. The mud mountain enabled the artistans to work on each stage without the use of precarious scaffolds, and when the temple was complete it was freed from its womblike mud casing. Then it stood, the loftiest temple tower in southern India, an achievement never to be attempted again on such a scale.

This temple marks a turning point in southern Indian architecture. From the exalted height of this tower, subsequent temple shikharas were made shorter and in converse proportion to the temple gateways or gopurams. Soon a web of concentric enclosure walls, punctuated by gopurams marking the cardinal directions, grew around the temple complex. The tiny sanctum building within the innermost courtyard was protected by the height and powerful form of the gopuram.

We are told through historical accounts that when the **Brihadeshvara Temple** was completed a grand ceremony was conducted. Gifts were made to the temple of villages and produce for its upkeep, and land for the temple servants. An inscription records that in the 26th regnal year (*c.* AD 1010) of the Chola king Rajaraja I, he gifted a golden finial to be placed right on top of the temple, and there it sits to this day.

Gangaikondacholapuram

The name is formed from a string of four words, working backwards, meaning the city (*puram*) of the Cholas to which was brought (*konda*) the Ganga (river). Rajendra I was a mighty Chola ruler and like his predecessor Rajaraja, his overriding concern was to expand the territorial boundaries of his empire. In one expedition he took his army successfully along the east coast of India up to the Ganga. While it is an ancient practice for all pilgrims to return home with a jar of Ganga-jal, it is said that Rajendra Chola brought back with him enough holy water from the Ganga to fill the temple tank.

The temple is similar in many ways to its namesake, the **Brihadeshvara** in Thanjavur, though it is not as large or as tall, perhaps in deference to Rajendra's father. The city and temple fell into disuse, and unlike the Thanjavur temple it suffered from negligence but was spared the enthusiastic renovation and additional construction of successive dynasties.

The temple stands at the centre of a rectangular courtyard. There are smaller sub-shrines and the famous tank with Gangajal on the north-eastern side. The temple building consists of a long pillared mandap that leads to the sanctum housing the linga.

Outside, the temple wall is adorned with sculptures of Shiva. Above the square base rises the tower in nine levels (not thirteen, as in Thanjavur). The horizontal diminishing stages of the tower are clearly emphasised with parapet walls of miniature temple roof designs. The scale and proportion of this temple are dramatic but the total effect lacks the sweeping grace of the one in Thanjavur and is a satisfactory, rather heavy, imitation.

WHAT'S IN THE NEIGHBOURHOOD

If the **Brihadeshvara Temple** of **Thanjavur**, by virtue of its sheer height and monumental grace, is breathtaking, then the bronze collection of the **Thanjavur Art Gallery** reaffirms that small is beautiful and very enchanting. The gallery is located in one of the palace halls and has a stone sculpture collection from nearby temples, paintings on glass of the Maratha period, and the famous bronzes. Bronze-casting in India is a very ancient

Dakshinamurti, Shiva.

technique and dates back at least five thousand years to the lovely dancing girl of the Harappan Civilization. It requires the artist to first create in wax the exact size and shape of the image to be cast in bronze. Then the wax model is enclosed in a mud mould which is then heated and the wax is allowed to run out of an opening at the base of the mud casing. The mould then has a hollow interior with the image set in reverse. Hot molten metal (*panchaloha*, an alloy of five metals) is poured into the mould and allowed to cool. Then the mud casing is removed and the image in bronze is released, chiselled with finer details of hair, jewellery, etc and then polished. The Chola bronze masterpieces in the Art Gallery somehow retain the liquid soft quality of the wax in the cold hardness of the metal. Soft, gentle curves of the stomach or shoulders, the fall of the silken garments of the gods, and the delicacy of the ornamental details are their hallmark. Best among them are images of Shiva and Parvati together at the time of their marriage, with Nandi, or seated with their son Skanda (Somaskanda), or of Shiva as the naked mendicant Bhikshatana-murti, and Vishnu's incarnation as the boy Krishna.

South of Gangaikondacholapuram, on the road to Thanjavur, is **Kumbakonam**, another Chola centre with several temples, some of which have been renovated by later dynasties. Five kilometres from Kumbakonam is **Darasuram** with one of the finest later Chola temples called **Airavateshvara**. This temple, founded by Rajaraja the II (1146-72), has the most elegant stone pillars and decorations on its walls, in a style bordering on mannerism, with an emphasis on elongated limbs and refined features. Best among them are the dark black basalt figures in the temple niches of Dakshinamurti, the image on the southern side of Shiva in a teaching attitude, and to the west, Shiva bursting out of the pillar of light to convince Brahma and Vishnu of his superiority.

Gangaikonda-cholapuram.

Thanjavur is also an hours drive from **Tiruchchirappalli** (abbreviated to Trichy from Trichinopoly, its British corruption), once a Chola stronghold. The great Rock Fort dominates the horizon and there are interesting temples and things to see along the way. **Srirangam**, across the Kaveri, is yet another pleasant temple town.

HOW TO GET THERE

Thanjavur is accessible by road and train from most cities of Tamil Nadu, which includes of course **Madras**. Trichy has an airport with flights from Madras and Colombo (Shri Lanka), and is also an important railhead. **Gangaikondacholapuram** is 71 kilometres from Thanjavur. The city of **Kumbakonam** is 40 kilometres from Thanjavur and a further five kilometres brings you to **Darasuram**.

Both Trichy and Thanjavur are large flourishing cities with hotels, motels, and several eating houses serving southern Indian cuisine. Travel in southern India is best during the winter months when it is relatively cool.

Chidambaram

The **Natraj Temple** at Chidambaram is very special, not merely architecturally, but conceptually. The temple is dedicated to Shiva, the cosmic dancer, who swirls through the universe in his frenetic dance, reabsorbing into himself all that was created by removing ignorance and offering salvation. He is affectionately referred to in this temple as *adavallan*, the one who loves dancing. One Hindu myth, with deep philosophic symbolism, is a story about Shiva and his wife Parvati. We are told that the divine couple spent much of their time sporting in the Himalaya, dallying with and teasing each other. Once, in the course of their jestful banter, a dance competition was set up to see who could outdance the other. The heavenly creatures assembled and while the celestial musicians played divine music, Shiva and Parvati began to dance. As the dance progressed it was clear that the couple were perfectly matched; anything Shiva did Parvati could equal and the other way around, so the competition proceeded virtually without end. Finally, the dance dialogue came to a standstill. Shiva, the strident expert of many yogic practices and tantric norms, stood on one leg and lifted the other high above his shoulder. Standing in this Urdhva-tandava stance, clearly meant for competent male dancers, he waited for Parvati to imitate this difficult position. The celestial audience watched in silence, for this was the ultimate challenge. We are told that Parvati demurely bowed her head, modesty inhibiting her from imitating his posture. It is believed that the grand Chidambaram temple was the venue of this cosmic dance competition between the god and the goddess. A central image of the temple is of Natraj, the cosmic dancer, and there is a shrine in the complex dedicated to his wife Shivakamasundari, the beautiful one desired by Shiva. The gopurams and temple walls are adorned with myriad dancing figures and musicians celebrating this great event of creation.

Throughout southern India you will see images and bronzes of the dancing Shiva. The classical image depicts Shiva with his hands swirling around him, one leg firmly placed on a dwarf called Apasmara (ignorance). In Hindu thought, salvation and release from the eternal cycle of life comes with wisdom, not death. Wisdom is to comprehend the nature of the universe and to understand that everything that one sees on earth has been created out of the very same substance and there are only superficial differences between the divine and man, man and animal or plant. This oneness is the essence of our salvation.

(opposite) :
Natraj Temple,
Chidambaram.

In Puranic literature there are innumerable discussions and arguments framed between Shiva and Parvati. She represents the earth and all matter, the five elements (earth, water, fire, air, and ether) from which everything that exists is created. For this reason, in all Hindu rituals the five elements play a fundamental role with offerings of fire lamps, holy water, fruits, and flowers of the earth. Shiva tauntingly argues with Parvati that the earth would not exist if he, the *akash* or space, did not perpetually embrace the universe. Where would the earth reside if not enfolded in space? This rather abstract philosophical argument of the relationship of the earth and sky, of spirit and matter, are presented in the guise of mythological stories of which this dance competition is one. The temple has therefore a second and far deeper significance, for in the sanctum, the Chit Sabha, as it is called here, is the non-figurative Akash-linga of Shiva. A black curtain (representing ignorance) that veils the garbha griha is removed during pujas to reveal (and remind us of) the Akash linga, the hallowed Space central to our existence and the divine space deep within us all.

Shivaganga Tank, Chidambaram.

Another concept of enormous significance is enshrined in the **Shrine of Govindaraja**, or Vishnu. This sixteenth century shrine houses an image of the recumbent Vishnu. While conventionally Vishnu is the creator-preserver, Shiva symbolises the creator-destroyer. Shiva in his dance waves in his hands a tiny drum, *damru*, symbolic of the nascence of creation, while the flame in the other hand signifies destruction and reabsorption of all that is created into his cosmic presence. Vishnu too carries similar symbols, the conch from the life-giving waters and the disc of destruction. Placed together, the reclining one, and the active dancing one, create holistic symbols.

In the words of philosopher-poet Appayya Dikshita when he visited Chidambaram:[19]

> Let him wear yellow silk or the cardinal directions [space],
> Let him go on an eagle mount [Vishnu], the humped bull [Shiva],
> Let him sleep or gaily dance on the stage,
> I see no difference in the Almighty.

This perhaps is the message of Chidambaram, that the myriad images on the temple walls are merely reflections and manifestations of the One from whom emanates all life and to whom all will return. Though God is conceived differently by each individual there is ultimate unity and oneness.

The Natraj Temple at Chidambaram marks another important stage of evolution of southern Indian architecture. Here the original shrine, according to legend, marks a site that exists only in the mythological realm. As the temple grew in popularity, furnished with miraculous stories of healing and blessings, patrons gave financial assistance for its enlargement. The principal shrines, the **Chit Sabha** and the **Kanaka Sabha,** were enclosed within a compound wall with gopurams. The Chola rulers of southern India had great reverence for the deity of Chidambaram and were responsible for building several structures within the complex. Later, when the Vijayanagara rulers, the famous Krishnadeva Raya (of **Hampi**), extended their territory they also extended the complex and ordered gopurams to be built. Today the entire temple complex covers over twenty-two hectares of land right in the centre of the town.

The outer wall of the temple was built by the Nayak rulers in the seventeenth century. Through the passageway one enters the tall gopurams of the next enclosure wall with the beautiful **Shivaganga Tank** (the holy water of the Ganga brought down to earth by Shiva). The tank is surrounded by a bank of stairs and a pillared verandah. To the west of the tank is the large **Shrine of the Goddess Shivakamasundari** with a ritual passageway. The enclosing wall has joyful scenes of dancers in various poses and musicians playing an assortment of musical instruments.

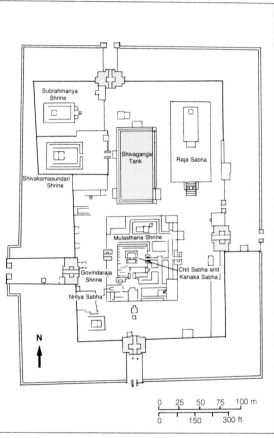

Plan of Natraj Temple, Chidambaram.

Next to the goddess's temple (to the north) is the **Shrine of Subrahmanya**, the chief of Shiva's army, the son of Shiva and Parvati, and a great favourite in southern India. Following the pattern of the early rock-cut rathas of **Mahabalipuram** designed with bases that look like miniature chariots drawn by horses and elephants, the mandaps of several temples here have a ratha-like stairway entrance to the hall.

On the opposite side of the tank is the **Raja Sabha**, the hall of the kings. A magnificent thousand-pillared mandap (mandapam in southern India), it is used for rituals and festivals, and many Chola kings and later rulers were anointed and crowned here in the presence of the deity.

Southward, facing the main temple enclosure, is the Nandi pavilion. It is within this enclosure on the western side that one finds the entrance to the **Govindaraja Temple**.

The splendid gateways lead into the main temple complex extensively renovated over the years. The gopurams of southern India were usually built with stone bases, one or two storeys high. Above this cubical building rose the tall inspiring gopuram, in diminishing tiers made of brick and mortar with stucco decorations. The base and each level of the temple gopuram were adorned with sculptures derived from mythical tales.

Within the main temple enclosure is the **Chit Sabha** or **Chit-ambalam**, from which the temple town has derived its name, Chidambaram. Many structures fill this area, some used for rituals, others for storage and as community kitchens. The main buildings include the **Deva Sabha**, the hall of god, the **Mulasthana** with its Devi shrine. The **Nritya Sabha**, the hall of dance is a beautiful building of the Chola period and is elevated on a basement decorated with lively figures of musicians and dancers. In front of the garbha griha is the **Kanaka Sabha**, and here devotees assemble to focus their prayer on the akash, the inner and outer space in which we all reside.

The temple of Chidambaram had received patronage from many rulers through the ages. The gilding of the shrine was done during the time of the Cholas, and additional buildings were added in later years. Today a traditional family of brahmins serve and maintain the temple. It is a wonderful place which propels you physically through corridors and verandahs, open and closed areas, sculpted halls, and richly ornamented gateways to the dark peaceful space within.

WHAT'S IN THE NEIGHBOURHOOD

Chidambaram is about 50 kilometres north of **Gangaikonda-cholapuram** with a vast temple similar to the famous Brihadeshvara temple of **Thanjavur**. Staying at Chidambaram or Thanjavur one can make day trips into the area. It is possible to see **Thanjavur, Gangaikondacholapuram, Kumbakonam**, and **Darasuram**, all fabulous Chola sites with magnificent temples, on a week-long trip. Shopping, for there is always something to buy in well-known pilgrim centres, would include locally crafted items, bronze statues, and cotton textiles.

HOW TO GET THERE

The temple city is connected by road and rail to Tiruchchirappalli and Madras, and to neighbouring sites. Tamil Nadu is always warm, and very hot in summer. The best time to tour south Indian temples is in winter between November and March.

Madurai

For ten days in the month of Chaitra (March-April), Madurai is a riot of colour and festivity. This historic city is built on the banks of the Vagai river, whose sacred presence is celebrated in the annual Vagai River Festival. On the tenth day of the Vagai River Festival the climax is reached when the goddess Meenakshi's wedding is celebrated. Great processions with gilded chariots proceed through the streets carrying the richly ornamented images of Meenakshi, a local goddess (sister of a southern Indian manifestation of Vishnu) and Sundareshvara (Shiva). Thousands of devotees come to attend this divine wedding, and it is then that the *raison d'être* of the temple at Madurai can be fully appreciated. The great temple at Madurai is dedicated to this couple and is called the **Meenakshi Sundareshvara Temple**.

This city was the capital of the Pandyan rulers between the seventh and thirteenth centuries, after which it fell into the hands of the Vijayanagara dynasty. The Vijayanagara rulers (from **Hampi**, northern Karnataka) divided their kingdom into various administrative units under the control of appointed governors. The local governor of Madurai soon broke loose from his overlords and established the Nayaka dynasty. Their greatest king was Tirumala (1623-60), responsible for building a large portion of the town and the Meenakshi Sundareshvara Temple. Every year, on full moon day in January (Magha) on the birth anniversary of Tirumala Nayak, the seventeenth ruler of Madurai, another great festival is held. The temple deities are richly dressed and adorned with jewellery and taken in a long procession to a water tank 5 kilometres east of the city. This reservoir, called **Mariamman Teppakulam**, is rectangular with steps leading down to the water's edge. The procession meanders from the Meenakshi Temple down the broad streets of Madurai till it reaches the Teppakulam tank. There, with much ceremony, the deities are placed on rafts, gaily bedecked with oil lamps and set afloat to the accompaniment of devotional music. Right at the centre of the tank is a beautiful square island with a whitewashed pavilion lavishly decorated with flowers and lamps for the festival.

The **Meenakshi Sundareshvara Temple** is one of southern India's most celebrated temples. It is an enormous complex with two principal shrines, one for Meenakshi the other for Shiva, a tank, several other subsidiary shrines, corridors, and long colonnades of carved pillars. The entire complex is enclosed within high walls with huge gateways or gopurams in the middle on each side. From great distances one can see these multicoloured gopurams with unrestrained decorations of plaster-work figures. To add to the profusion of forms, recent renovations of the towers were undertaken and the figures were coated in outlandish colours in enamel chemical paints! These gopurams, virtual mountains of figures with not an inch of space to spare, depict scenes and characters from Hindu mythology. The tallest gopuram of the Meenakshi Temple is the southern one which reaches an awe-inspiring height of 60 metres.

The temple complex is aligned west to east, with the main entrance on the eastern side. The **Nandi Mandap**, called **Viravasantaraya**, stands before the eastern gate. In front of this is the **Pudu Mandap**, the new mandap with rows of massive pillars lavishly carved with mythical creatures and portraits of the Nayakas, the chief patrons of the temple. An unfinished gopuram lies before the Pudu mandap and consists of a basement storey of a gopuram, said to have been be built by Tirumala Nayaka. The dimensions of the foundation suggest that this eastern gopuram was intended to be higher than all the others.

Entrance to the temple is from the eastern gate or the Shrine of the Eight goddesses. Once within the temple compound it is a maze, a kaleidoscope of patterns, colours, and structures. Shops and temporary stalls selling items for worship are the first to come into view, because one does not enter the abode of god empty-handed. Flowers, fruit, coconut, camphor, and agarbatti sticks are for sale, along with trinkets and souvenirs of the temple.

Golden Lotus Tank, Madurai.

Continuing westward, within the temple complex, one comes to the lovely **Golden Lotus Tank**. A rectangular tank with stepped banks that lead to the water's edge. In the middle is a tall brass lamp column. The tank is surrounded by a colonnade, for which this temple is also famous. The walls are decorated with vividly painted murals depicting the various exploits of Shiva, the bridegroom of Meenakshi. The ceiling of the colonnade is richly decorated with huge circular floral medallions. Unfortunately, since the recent renovation, the temple has assumed a garish appearance for, instead of using natural subtle shades, a most outrageous colour scheme was chosen. Yet standing near the tank and looking out at the open patch of sky, with glimpses of the towering gopuram, one gets one of the nicest views of the temple from within.

To the western end of the tank is the enclosure wall of the **Meenakshi Shrine**. Within it are many subsidiary shrines and a 'bedroom' where the image of Meenakshi's husband is brought each night to rest.

North of the Golden Lotus Tank is the entrance gopuram (not as tall as the outer gates) that leads to the **Sundareshvara Temple**. Hundreds of columned halls and verandahs are clustered around this area, like the Kambittari mandap of the late nineteenth century.

South of the tank is the **Kalyana Mandap** (marriage hall) where the divine wedding takes place each year. Under the roof, and surrounded by floral decorations, the images of Meenakshi and Sundareshvara are ceremoniously married by the temple priests. It is a glorious affair and one is considered doubly blessed to be a witness and a guest at the celestial marriage ceremony.

Mandap, Meenakshi Sundareshvara Temple

Right in the north-west corner of the enclosure is the **Airakkal Mandap**, a magnificent thousand-pillared hall. It has been converted into the temple museum and has an interesting collection of stone and bronze sculptures. It was common practice in such temples to have several bronze images, which were movable (unlike the image in the sanctum which was not), and could be used during festival processions. These images were dressed in fine clothes, covered with jewels, decorated with flowers, and then taken in their gilded chariots through the streets so that devotees could receive a *darshan* of the divine.

Plan of Meenakshi Sundareshvara Temple.

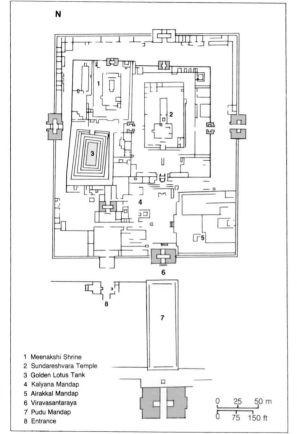

N

1 Meenakshi Shrine
2 Sundareshvara Temple
3 Golden Lotus Tank
4 Kalyana Mandap
5 Airakkal Mandap
6 Viravasantaraya
7 Pudu Mandap
8 Entrance

0   25   50 m
0   75   150 ft

WHAT'S IN THE NEIGHBOURHOOD

Apart from the great Meenakshi Temple, there are a few other remains of the Nayaka period, including the impressive palace constructed nearby (1.2 kilometres south-east). The building has been substantially renovated and reconstructed with throne rooms and grand courtyards.

HOW TO GET THERE

Madurai has a domestic airport as well as an efficient rail and bus system. There are a number of hotels and guest-houses, and since it is a pilgrimage centre there are a wide range of services for visitors. The best time to visit is in the cooler winter months. Following the cycle of the moon special celebrations of the marriage of the goddess Meenakshi are held in the month of Chaitra (March-April).

Palace at Padmanabhapuram

Though technically in the state of Tamil Nadu, this palace is the traditional home of the Travancore royal family of Kerala. The palace is one of India's best specimens of secular building and of the distinctive wooden architecture of the west coast. Kerala is a state with lush green paddy fields stretching to the horizon, watered by a network of backwaters and dotted with lovely small villages. Local laterite pink stone is used for village huts and sloping tiled roofs offer the best protection against the heavy monsoon rains that come cascading down from the heavens in the months of May, June, and July. It is today one of India's most densely populated states and one where literacy levels have reached almost a hundred percent.

On the road from Trivandrum (Thiruvanathapuram), the state capital, down to Kanyakumari, the tip of the Indian subcontinent, is Padmanabhapuram. The meaning of the name goes back to the great Anant-padma-nabha-swamy temple in Trivandrum. In the sanctum of the temple lies a long stone image of a reclining Vishnu. According to mythology, Vishnu lies on the sea of eternity resting on the coils of a gigantic serpent called Anant, the endless one. This symbolic bed refers to a region of quietitude and divine grace where Vishnu reclines and rests in the intervals between creation. From Vishnu's navel (*nabha*) grows a lotus flower (*padma*) on which is seated Brahma. This deity meditated for many god-years and ultimately was granted a boon to begin creating the universe. So while Brahma creates, Vishnu rests, preserving and sustaining the world. It is Anant who upheld the entire universe on his multi-headed hood 'as if it were a mere mustard seed', and the region where Anant reigns is associated with Kerala. This is why Vishnu is called the lord (*swamy*) who lies on Anant, from whose navel (*nabha*) the lotus (*padma*) creation is born: Anant-padma-nabha-swamy. The royal family of Travancore were considered to be the consecrated appointed regents of the **Anant-padmanabhaswamy** deity of the temple at Trivandrum. To this day they perform their ritual obligations to the deity and their palace home is called **Padmanabhapuram**.

The fort walls surround **Padmanabhapuram** by and nearby there is a little village from which a long driveway leads up to the ornamental wooden gateway of the palace. The building created over many generations in the seventeeth and eighteenth centuries has richly carved doorways and windows, sculpted brackets, and lovely sloping tiled roofs. There is a certain delicacy and richness in wooden architecture that can never be attained when working with any other material.

From the entrance gate a path leads to a steep stairway up to a large hall, completely covered from ceiling to floor with dark warm wood. This hall, which used to receive important visitors and to hold ministerial meetings, is a perfect example of classic Kerala secular architecture. Huge seasoned wooden beams form a chequered patterned ceiling, the central squares studded with wooden floral motifs and rosettes placed on every cross beam. The sloping roof is incorporated into the design of the interior walls of the hall that slant dramatically downwards. The slanting wall blocks out the brilliant sunshine and heat, preventing the glare from entering the room. At the base of the slant is a line of windows with wooden shutters that filter the light and diffuse its intensity. Around the room are regal benches and wooden thrones for the distinguished family and visitors. Where bare feet is a climatic necessity, not a fashion, the highly polished floor of the council room is soft to the touch and smooth under the royal feet.

From this relatively public area, where important visitors were entertained, one comes into the private royal living quarters. It is a maze of lovely open corridors and pillared verandahs leading into rooms and chambers. Open courtyards and little

Entrance to
Padmanabhapuram
Palace.

garden areas are incorporated into the plan of the buildings to offer areas of warmth and sunshine, since the living areas and rooms are always cool and dark. The kitchen, the dining hall, the royal bedrooms with minimal furniture are part of the traditional Kerala domestic style. In wooden architecture it is the beams and pillars, joints and brackets that receive special attention, and in this palace every minute detail is carefully designed and beautiful carved.

Central to the plan of the palace are the four-storeyed **Royal Apartments** with the kings bedroom (on the second floor) with a medicinal bed of 64 different types of wood and a beautiful prayer-room right on top. This room is decorated with murals with a lovely one of Vishnu as Padmanabha Swamy.

At one end of the palace is a large stone **Natakshala** or performance hall for dance, music, and theatre. This relatively new structure in quasi-religious style has a mandap with carved stone pillars. It was built by Maharaja Swathithirunal, a great music composer and patron of the performing arts. South of the dance hall is a little granite temple (similar to the style found in Tamil Nadu) appropriately dedicated to Saraswati, the goddess of learning, music, and the arts.

From this beautiful royal home the Travancore family shifted their capital to Trivandrum in 1934 and the Padmanabhapuram Palace was restored and opened to the public.

Anantpadma-nabhaswamy Temple, Trivandrum.

WHAT'S IN THE NEIGHBOURHOOD

From Padmanabapuram one can travel south to see **Kanyakumari**, the very tip of the Indian subcontinent, where the three waters meet: of the Indian Ocean, the Bay of Bengal, and the Arabian Sea.

Padmanabhapuram is 55 kilometres south of **Trivandrum**, the capital of the state of Kerala. Trivandrum is also called **Thiruvanathapuram**, the abode of the sacred serpent Anant, the endless one. It is a great religious, cultural, and administrative centre. The religious centre is the great **Anantpadmanabhaswamy Temple**. This temple, unfortunately open only to Hindus, attracts thousands of pilgrims and is one of the finest examples of religious architecture in Kerala on a grand scale. The temple has a tank in front for rituals, a pathway lined with shops selling ritual items and flowers, souvenirs for pilgrims, and a place where the local people can meet and chat. Once inside the temple there are great halls with ornamental pillars and carved wooden beams that support typical tiled sloping roofs. Within the sanctum (never seen completely, only partially), viewed through three doorways, is the reclining figure of Vishnu supporting creation from the lotus that emerges from his navel.

There are several European-style colonial buildings in Trivandrum. The **Napier Museum** was constructed in 1880 and is set amidst a huge formal garden with an Art Gallery and the

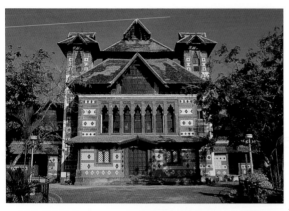

Zoological Gardens at one end. The building is a cheerful pink and yellow structure, and the wooden beams that support it are incorporated in the overall exterior design. The interior of the museum building is equally impressive and houses a wonderful collection of bronzes, wood, and stone sculptures, and musical instruments.

Not far from the Zoo is the **Maharaja's Palace**, now converted into government buildings. Other buildings like **Parliament House**

Napier Museum, Trivandrum.

with its European stylistic features were built in the mid-1930s.

The tourist department is making a great effort to provide visitors with an interesting agenda sprinkled with cultural programmes of dance and music. Kerala has a rich and very ancient tradition of music, dance (dance drama like Kathakali and the lyrical Mohiniattam), and the martial arts (Kalairipettu).

Most attractive and certainly one of the loveliest beaches on the west coast of India is **Kovalam**. The calm aquamarine sea waters of the small cove of Kovalam is a safe and lovely place in which to swim. To the south is a rugged hill with boulders gently lapped by the sea from where you can watch the little fishing catamarans (from the the local word Kattu-maram) bobbing up and down with the waves.

HOW TO GET THERE

Trivandrum has an international and domestic airport. Road and railways connect this southern city with most parts of India. Large and small, expensive and inexpensive hotels are available in Trivandrum and at Kovalam from which a day trip to the palace of Padmanabhapuram can be made. The winter months between October and March are a pleasant time to travel in Kerala and the beaches are then calm and serene, after the turbulence of the monsoons.

Cochin

Kerala is one of the most beautiful states of India. Situated on the south-western coast with several harbours like Cochin, its story is as ancient as the history of trade, merchants, pirates, settlers, and conquerors. The geography and history of Cochin distinguishes it from any other city in India.

The mainland is marked by Ernakulam, the modern commercial centre, shielded by two arms of the peninsula that protect the quiet harbour. The northern arm is Vypin, the southern one **Fort Cochin**, where the city's early history is recorded in its buildings and monuments. Into the enclosed Vembanad Lake harbour-friendly dolphins accompany the large ships that come to dock right in the centre of the city. Flowing into this sea lake are the freshwater streams of the backwaters which meander through a countryside rich in agricultural produce. Safe and reliable water travel by sail and rowing boat bring to the harbour the bounty of spices and timber that enticed early western sea-merchants to battle the great oceans in search of wealth.

Along the water's edge of Fort Cochin, on the narrow passageway to the harbour, are a line of **Chinese fishing nets**, the first visual symbol of ancient trade and age-old shared influences. Trade with the Far East was well-established in the early years of the Christian era. Southern Indian princes sponsored a huge fleet of ships to the coast of China in search of trade and wealth. The Chinese fishing nets still work (except in the monsoons), their fine nets being lowered into the water at sunrise. At sunset the nets, full of fish, are hauled up by a pulley weighed down by enormous rocks and boulders. They rise like giant butterflies, their wings painted with the vibrant colours of the setting sun.

Wandering past the line of Chinese fishing nets through the streets of Fort Cochin is a wonderful experience. This little Dutch colony has some lovely timber and masonry houses painted white, which have steep sloping roofs as a protection against the heavy monsoon rains which descend non-stop for days from May to July.

Cochin was the earliest European settlement in India. In 1500 the Portuguese, in search of trade contracts in pepper, landed in the harbour. Pedro Alvarez Cabral, the Portuguese adventurer-explorer brought with him some Portuguese Franciscan friars who established a church and began their missionary work. **St. Francis Church** was originally built of wood, which was, later replaced by stone in 1546. It is the oldest European church in India. Vasco da Gama, who travelled here in the mid sixteenth century, received permission to trade from the local ruler. Unfortunately he died on Christmas Eve in 1524 and was buried in this church. His body was later taken to Lisbon, but a railing and tombstone still remain in the memory of this brave adventurer who opened the route to the Indies and became its governor. The church, originally Roman Catholic,

was converted into an Anglican one during the British period. It is now under the Church of South India and looks a little uncared for. But its modest proportions, simple lines and form are suggestive of an elegance of those pioneering days when this little church offered refuge and comfort to those who chose to live in a strange land.

Moving a kilometre south into the Fort Cochin area is the **Dutch Palace**, now called **Mattancherry Palace**. This large, but modest-looking building is set in a grand, spacious compound. The palace was built by the Portuguese in 1557 and presented to the local Raja of Cochin who had granted to them several favours and trading rights. In 1663, the town fell into Dutch hands and the palace was renovated. It stands today a pale painted building with sloping roofs. The structure has two storeys and part of it is open to the public as a museum. There is a collection of the palanquins, costumes, and portraits of the Cochin royal family.

St. Francis Church, Cochin.

Along the walls of the bedroom chamber and other areas are the mural paintings for which the palace is famous. The paintings belong to the seventeenth century and are large in scale and concept. The murals congested with figures inhabit the empty space of the museum. Enormous figures of Hindu deities, with exaggerated large breasts and thighs, peer out of the wall with lovely sensuous eyes. Painted in hues of yellow ochre, red, and green are scenes of Krishna, the divine lover surrounded by his female devotees, and of Vishnu and Shiva in dramatic poses.

On the eastern side of Fort Cochin, south of the main Mattancherry street, is an ancient area called **Jew Town**. According to local legend, trade flourished between the Middle East and Kerala even in the time of King Solomon of the Old Testament. Western trade was established five thousand years ago, as is evident from the remains of the Indus civilisation excavated in ancient Mesopotamian cities. Following the great ocean winds, the seafaring boats from Arabia found their way to the west coast of India by the first century AD and from there proceeded to the Far East. These trading ships brought men of different faiths to the Indian shore, amongst them Jewish settlers. The Jewish quarter in Fort Cochin has charming old cobbled streets and rows of residential houses. There are still enormous stores and warehouses in this area bursting with spices: pepper, cardamon, and cloves. It was this trade that first brought these early travellers. Later, in the sixteenth century, when the Inquisition drove the Jewish community away from Europe, some of them with their brethren from central Europe settled in Cochin. A large, white Jewish community inhabited the harbour region, established their trade, and received the protection of the local rulers. Today only a small aging community of 'White Jews' continue to live here, many of the young having migrated to Israel. They marry within their community, mixing little with 'black jew' converts of Cochin. They now speak the local language and eat local Malayali food, but have succeeded in preserving their customs and cultural identity after so many centuries of living in isolation.

Painting from Mattancherry Palace.

A **Jewish Synagogue** was built at one corner of **Jew Town** in 1568 (though renovated in subsequent centuries), and is the oldest in the Commonwealth. The building is so positioned that it is difficult to appreciate the external design except to see the clocktower that peeps over the surrounding wall. Inside, the synagogue has a large hall lit with magnificent chandeliers and lamps, while daylight streams in through large open windows.

The entire flooring is paved with white and blue willow-patterned Chinese ceramic tiles (each one said to be of different design). These were donated by Ezekiel Rahabi who brought them all the way from Canton in the mid-nineteenth century. A pulpit stands in the centre of the room and at one end is the holy tabernacle, with gilded doors. Within are kept the great scrolls of the old Torah capped with golden crowns given by the Maharaja of Travancore and Cochin. Amongst the prize possessions of the synagogue is a copper plate recording a grant made to the Jewish trading community by Raja Ravi Varman (962-1020). The community has dwindled greatly in numbers, apparently to a mere twenty-five families (many have returned to Israel), and only when the obligatory quorum of ten male members is assembled can the service be properly conducted in this historic and very lovely synagogue.

WHAT'S IN THE NEIGHBOURHOOD

Across the bridge from Fort Cochin is **Willingdon Island**. This man-made island was made in the twentieth century and serves as the Naval headquarters, airport, and railhead serving the multiple needs of the commercial port of Cochin. From the tip of Willingdon Island one can see fishing boats and steamers. A lovely (motorised) boat ride around the Vembanad Lake will take you to see the little fishing colonies on the northern side and

Synagogue interior, Cochin.

the lovely **Bolghatty Island** and the old **British Residency**. The building was built by the Dutch in their colonial style with deep-set verandahs, grand columns, porches, and sloping roofs, set in a garden that once was used as a small golf course. The Bolghatty Palace is now run as a Government Tourist Bungalow and, sadly, is not very well-maintained.

Longer boat rides (by motor or row boats) through the backwaters bring you in touch with the 'real Kerala', lush green, with wonderful bird life and a glimpse at the villages of the interior with its smiling, hard-working, intelligent people.

HOW TO GET THERE

Cochin is connected by air, road, and rail to almost every part of India. There are several modest and expensive hotels in which to stay. Cochin is a good place to start a tour of Kerala and continue on to **Trichur** and **Guruvayyur** (with celebrated temples, unfortunately open only to Hindus), the beaches of **Alleppey**, the temples of **Kottayam**, the tiger/elephant reserve beside the **Periyar Lake** and south to the capital **Trivandrum** or **Thiruvanathapuram**. The best time of year in southern India is between October and March, before summer and the torrential monsoon rains set in.

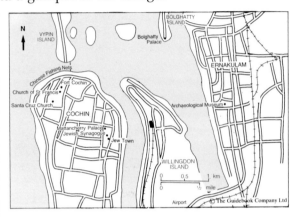

Plan of Cochin.

Bhutan

The royal kingdom of Bhutan lies hidden in the eastern Himalaya, with India to the south and south-west, and Tibet to the north and north-west. For centuries inaccessible, surrounded by mountains and dense jungle to the south, Bhutan remained in isolation from the rest of the world. Unlike India or Pakistan it was never reduced to the status of a colony, and both its geographical seclusion and history have preserved a pristine cultural heritage deeply influenced by Buddhism and the spartan physical environment.

By road one leaves the Indian plains at Phuntsholing for a long, winding, uphill ride, the scenery changes with every twist and turn. From thick tropical bamboo jungles with orchids clustering around old tree-trunks, moving up to the cool regions of evergreen coniferous forests until, far in the distance, you glimpse the bleak grey peaks of the arid cold desert and snowy pinnacles that pierce the bright blue sky.

Against this bleak background, the vibrant hues of sacred Buddhist colours—saffrons and orange, deep maroons and yellows—stand out in striking contrast. It is almost as if the inhabitants were seeking to brighten up their world of greys and browns with the promise of eternal summer and spiritual warmth. Great strings of prayer-flags flutter in the breeze as the wind carries these earthly messages up to the region of great clouds rolling and curling around barren mountains where the gods are said to reside. It is a region haunted by strange images, weird sounds, and the fortress-like monasteries and temples are always protected by huge guardian figures of deities who assume terrifying forms to keep the forces of evil at bay. Great watchful eyes and brightly coloured faces stare out at the vast expanse of space, snarling silently at the invisible demons of ignorance and darkness.

Nestled in a cradle of mountains are green river valleys, a patchwork of bright paddy-fields that follow the course of the meandering streams. In the fertile valleys of western Bhutan lie **Paro** (2250 metres above sea level) on the banks of the Paro river and **Thimphu** (2300 metres) on the Wangchu river. Dotting the low hills of the valley are houses, severe white or mud-brown blocks that rise out of the ground with straight walls that tilt slightly inwards, their shallow sloping roofs covered with shingles (of wood or slate). The houses look in rather than out, and like mini-fortresses have tiny windows (more on the top

(opposite) : Monks preparing a thanka, Bhutan.

floor than at the lower level). The mud and stone walls are painted with a coat of protective white limewash which shimmers in the pure, unpolluted light. Against this austere surface, details, such as window-frames and wooden beams, are cheerfully painted and shine like gems. Monasteries, palaces, and administration buildings all exude an air of sacred art. Even the local petrol pump in **Thimphu** bears the stamp of the traditional style, with brightly painted rafters and window frames highlighting the straight, chaste lines of these elegant buildings.

Bhutan is the only country in the world that practises Tantric Mahayana Buddhism as a state religion. It is this, more than anything else, that has influenced the architectural styles of the region. Buddhism came, mainly by way of Tibet, over successive centuries, and religious leaders rather than political rulers governed the land. In the eighth century Padmasambhava, known as Guru Rinpoche, founded the Nyingmapa school in Bhutan. His influence still pervades in religious practices and the ritual arts. Drukpa Kunley in the fifteenth century, and his later followers, set up several monasteries in various parts of central and eastern Bhutan, unifying it with their philosophy and lifestyle. Another distinguished saint was Pema Lingpa who founded several monasteries and religious establishments in northern and central Bhutan. In the seventeenth century, under the religious leadership of Shabdrung Nagawang Namgyel

Dzong, Paro.

(of the Drukpa school), Bhutan was unified under the Drukpa philosophic umbrella. In the local language Dzongkha, the name for this beautiful land, is appropriately, Druk yul, Land of the Thunder Dragon.

Shabdrung (to whose feet one submits) instituted an administrative system and divided the land into units under local authorities called Penlops. It was these local governors who eventually tussled for political power and in 1907 the Penlop of Tongsa, Ugyen Wangchuk became the first King of Bhutan. Jigme Singhye Wangchuk, the fourth in this direct line of descendants, ascended the Bhutanese throne in 1972, when he was merely seventeen years old. Like his father and grandfather before him, his mission too has been to integrate Bhutan with the international community (UN membership was granted in 1971). His endeavour at the same time has been in preserving the natural and cultural heritage of this unique, beautiful little kingdom.

Paro

The view of Paro valley is delightful, lined with whitewashed houses along the riverside, dotted with wispy willow trees, and farmers working on their little fields. Several pilgrim centres and great monasteries are perched precariously on the hilltops around Paro valley, like **Taktsang Lhakhang** (Taktsang means Tiger's lair, where Guru Rinpoche meditated and prayed), and **Drukyel Dzong** (built by Shabdrung Nagawang Namghyel). Right beside the river is the magnificent genteel form of the **Paro Dzong** (both a monastery and administrative building). Its sloping walls stand on a high embankment, and the central tower with a low tiled roof peers above the surrounding courtyard. Inside are administrative offices and quarters for the religious community. Every inch of wall space is covered with wonderful bright mural paintings depicting themes of religious significance: the Buddha, Bodhisattvas, great prayer mandalas that evoke the heavens and the sacred elements from which all life on earth has been created. Circles of yellow represent the air on which we all exist, flaming red the heat and warmth in which we grow, blue the life-giving waters and the dark earth which supports all life.

Just above the Paro Dzong is the **National Museum**, reached by a lovely walk with a view of the valley. The collection is representative of the arts and handicrafts of Bhutan and since many of the objects are of religious significance and not easy to see elsewhere, it is worth spending some time in this temple of art. The galleries have a display of costumes, traditional Bhutanese textiles that are still woven and worn by people. There are wonderful wooden masks and hats used by ritual dance performers, that depict the forces of evil and good in the eternal struggle of life that leads all to Buddhahood. Great painted cloth hangings, called *thanka*s are also on display. These ritual paintings are usually displayed in temples on ceremonial occasions and are worshipped, not as art, but as religious images. The central theme of the painting may be of Bodhisattvas or mandalas, with many other sacred symbols along its brocade borders and corners. Each colour has a philosophical meaning: flowers like the lotus suggest all that is pure and divine, the wide eyed fish is always watchful against evil, the conch sounds the message of the Buddhist doctrine, the royal umbrella protects those seeking refuge in the Buddhist faith, the fluttering flag heralds the victory of righteousness, and the vase over-flowing with flowers and treasures is like a spiritual cornucopia. Curling (Chinese) clouds mark the endless passage of time, reminding all that it is time to follow the flaming dharma-chakra, the wheel of faith, that unceasingly moves toward the path of Dharma and Buddhahood, the conquest of desire, release from suffering, and to Nirvana (true liberation) and Shanti (all-pervading peace).

Dzong, Thimphu.

The National Museum also houses silver objects, ritual items, armour. It has a small collection of stamps for which Bhutan is famous, some three-dimensional, others with brilliant colours depicting the exotic flora, fauna, and cultural life in this Himalayan kingdom.

Thimphu

The road from Paro (the airport) to the capital of Bhutan is particularly charming, as all along the way you go weaving through the lovely river valley landscape, which is punctuated by glimpses of deserted houses, the gentle Bhutanese at work, the lovely smiling faces of young children, and the time-worn wrinkled face of old age.

Thimphu must be the world's most extraordinary capital city with a population of less than 200,000, no traffic lights, no flyovers and no high-rise buildings. It resembles a calm monastic settlement, serene, composed, and very clean; where even the petrol pump and the post office are painted, and the police boxes are protected by mythical dragons. It was established as the capital in 1953 and takes pride in preserving its unique cultural and architectural traditions.

Past the market and along the meandering course of the river is the domineering presence of the **Tashichoedzong**. It is an ancient building that has been reconstructed many times, and its massive fortification walls serve to protect the administrative buildings of the capital. Within, even the National Assembly Hall and Administrative Chambers have guardian statues, murals, mandalas, and scenes depicting the Buddha and the way of righteousness.

WHAT'S IN THE NEIGHBOURHOOD

There are many other interesting places to visit and short treks to nearby sites like the **Changangkha** area and the **Simtokha Dzong**. Even within Thimphu there are many pleasant strolls along the river, through the market selling traditional handicrafts, fruit and vegetables. The memorial **Chorten area** is a relatively new construction of the 1970s and was built in memory of the former ruler (the father of the present King of Bhutan). The chorten or funerary commemorative stupa is a religious structure with images and paintings that portray the essence of the Buddhist creed. The **National Library** preserves a much-loved collection of manuscripts and the tradition of bookmaking. The Hospital uses herbal medicines, following a tradition that is Buddhist and holistic in its approach, and which derives from the ancient practices of Tibet and India.

HOW TO GET THERE

According to Bhutanese government policy only maximum of 2500 tourists are accorded entry each year, a sound approach to preserve Bhutan's natural and cultural environment and to protect the religious sentiments of the people from the ill-effects of commercialisation. Groups of six or more people with prior permission and visas are permitted to enter this land of the Thunder Dragon. There are bus services from Phuntsholing and air services from Delhi, Calcutta (India), Kathmandu (Nepal), or Bangkok (Thailand). Travel within the country is possible by bus and hired vehicles. Most of the religious monasteries and temples are not open to tourists as they are highly venerated places of worship.

The best season in which to visit Bhutan is between April and September when it is relatively warm, though it also rains at this time. Festivals are calculated by the lunar calendar and one would be fortunate to see a spectacular Dzong festival, or even to see the young men of Thimphu out in the open fields practising archery, their national sport.

Kathmandu Valley

Nepal, the only Hindu kingdom in the world, holds a unique place in the artistic heritage of the subcontinent. Its great contribution is the preservation of a continuous tradition of sacred, royal, and domestic architecture. Cradled in the lap of the Himalayan mountains, the highest in the world, the spectacular brick-timber temples and secular buildings are picturesque creations. Each city and building is modest, demurely proportioned, and unpretentious against the grand mountainous backdrop; an attitude rare amongst arrogant plains people who easily forget the scale of mother earth.

According to mythology (now partially substantiated by geological evidence), the Kathmandu Valley was once a holy lake encircled by mountains. To this body of sacred water, inhabited by giant serpents and nagas, came the first Buddha who tossed a lotus seed into the lake. The seed took root and grew into a magnificent thousand-petalled lotus flower. On the dark waters it shone brilliantly with the pure light of self-born (*swayambhu*) wisdom. Then Buddha Manjushri (honoured here by both Hindus and Buddhists) came to see the divine lotus and, taking his sword of wisdom, struck the mountainside and drained the lake, so that the lotus would be protected always by a rim of mountains. Later a Buddhist monk built a stupa with a tall gilded spire, and to this day its pinnacle radiates holy light over the entire Valley. The dramatic **Swayambhu Stupa** stands on a hill just west of Kathmandu city, marking the site of the divine self-born lotus of wisdom, and is considered one of the holiest Buddhist shrines in Nepal. The city of **Kathmandu**, it is said, is in the shape of Manjushri's sword, the city of neighbouring **Patan**, Manjushri's shield (wheel), and a little further away is his conch, incorporated in the plan of **Bhaktapur**, the loveliest city in the Valley.

The cultural distinction of Kathmandu Valley lies in its geographical isolation, situated (1200 to 1500 metres above sea level) in a bowl encircled by mountains, the Himalayan range to the north and the Mahabharata to the south. The Bagmati river, once the artery of the valley, provided it with necessary nourishment and sustained centuries of civilisation in a relatively tiny area (570 square kilometres). It is a self-contained, self-composed culture that has never been disrupted by colonial rule or continual invasions, and was able to grow organically like the mythical lotus. On this huge sacred lotus mandala, the

(opposite) : Surya Dhoka, Bhaktapur.

Valley, there grew several holy pilgrim centres that have attracted Hindu and Buddhist devotees for centuries.

The Buddha was born in the lower foothills of Nepal at a site called Lumbini. For the better part of his life he wandered through the cities and centres of pilgrimage in India, till he attained Buddhahood at **Bodh Gaya** and final Parinirvana at Kusinagar (Uttar Pradesh, India). While Nepal is closely associated with the birth of the Buddha, for two thousand five hundred years his philosophy and religion continued to inspire the country, invigorated by mutual contact with India and Tibet.

The Kathmandu Valley lay on an important trade route between India and Tibet, which explains its historical, political, and economic importance, and its artistic roots. Archaeological evidence points to the habitation of the Valley from prehistoric times, to the establishment of small principalities, tribal republics, and the complex structuring of society into the (abominable) caste system which the Buddha rejected. According to contemporary literature, two thousand years ago (around the time when the Buddha lived), a regular supply of wool, minerals, and gems found their way to India along well-established trade routes. The Mauryan Emperor Ashoka is said it have visited the garden of Lumbini (in the third century BC), and as a mark of respect commemorated the visit with the erection of a (memorial) stambha. Today the site has been further developed.

Map of Kathmandu Valley.

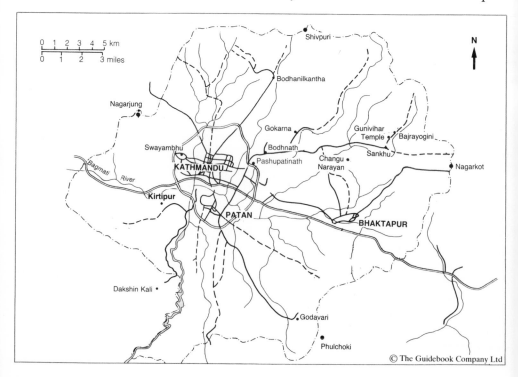

© The Guidebook Company Ltd

Between the fourth and ninth centuries the Licchavi dynasty dominated the Valley, introducing Hinduism, building temples, and sponsoring stone sculptures (beautiful specimens are to be seen in the **National Museum, Kathmandu** and the ancient temple of Changu Narayan to the east). Generous support was also given in this period to the construction of Buddhist viharas and stupas (most important the **Bodhnath Stupa**, seven kilometres from Kathmandu) that sustained the Tibet-bound traders on their hazardous journeys. It was these trade routes that perpetuated the constant flow and reverse flow of Buddhism from India to Tibet through the Valley where it was preserved in a unique synthesised form, blending Hindu and Buddhist deities and rituals in their centres of worship.

The thirteenth century started with stability introduced by Jayasthiti Malla who conquered the area while his son and grandson, Yaksha Malla, expanded the territory. Then the descendent Mallas (between 1482-1767) fell out amongst themselves and the tiny Valley (an oval bowl measuring hardly 24 kilometres east to west and 19 kilometres north to south, which one could traverse in a day) was divided into three independent kingdoms of **Kathmandu** (Kantipur), **Patan** (or Lalitpur, the lovely city), and **Bhaktapur** (the city of devotion, originally called Bhadgaon). Provoked by political rivalry, each city gathered their best local artisans and sponsored architectural ventures that stemmed from the common seed of their heritage.

During the Malla period the three cities acquired their fundamental character and personality. At the heart of all three capitals cities is the **Durbar Square**, the official brick-paved plaza in front of the palace. The **Royal Residence**, in all three cities, consists of a walled enclosure of courtyards, rooms for official and religious purposes, and breezy tall watch-towers or spires of many tiers. The public square on one side of the palace is crowded with temples dominated by a large shrine dedicated to the favoured patron deity and other smaller ones. One temple is built in stone, with large stone images of vahanas or guardian animals flanking the structure, while free-standing pillars are erected in front of the shrine with an image of the deity's vahana. A column with a statue of the Malla ruler in respectful attitude stood in front of the patron deity. Open areas for ritual performances, mandaps, halls for community gatherings, and water taps or fountains were built for the city in the square by successive generations of rulers.

Bhaktapur is by far the most peaceful and lovely example of city architecture in Nepal. It remains less crowded and devastated by 'modernisation'. But the city suffered greatly in the 1934 earthquake when almost ninety percent of the buildings were damaged. Commendable renovation and reconstruction by a dedicated German conservation team over twenty years has brought back some of Bhaktapur's original glory. It is difficult to date many of the buildings in the **Durbar Square**, for many of them have been renovated or reconstructed over the centuries. In a curious way it does not seem to matter whether the buildings were built four hundred years ago or yesterday; their beauty is timeless.

The three cities have been declared by Unesco as World Heritage Sites. While the Durbar Squares (of Kathmandu, Patan, and Bhaktapur) are almost identical in concept, the joy of the individual cities lies in walking through the by-lanes and side streets to see its attractive domestic architecture which is still functional and vibrant with life. Nowhere else in the subcontinent, except perhaps in Kerala (India), can one trace the evolution of royal and religious art from domestic architecture, from homes and houses still inhabited and used by the people.

The next period in the story of the Valley is the conquest and unification of the area under the Shah dynasty of Gorkha. This tiny hill town (between Pokhara and Kathmandu) was the home of the Gorkhas who ventured out to control the three Malla capitals. By the end of the eighteenth century, with the capital at Kathmandu, the Gorkha kingdom stretched from present-day Shimla in the west to Sikkim in the east. After a hard-fought war against the British East India Company in 1813 (who wielded power across the rest of the subcontinent), the kingdom under the Shahs continued to remain independent, burdened only with the token presence of a British Resident.

In 1844 a young rebel named Jung Bahadur Kunwar staged a coup, upturned the monarchy, and established the rule of the Ranas (traditionally Prime Ministers to the Kings). It was this enthusiastic ruler who visited (Queen Victoria in) Britain in 1850 and brought back with him a passion for neo-classical architecture, with whitewashed walls, Corinthian columns, arches, triangular-roofed windows, and stucco do-dahs. His passion soon gained popularity in the Valley and today in the three cities one can see traditional architecture rubbing shoulders with (degenerate) examples of British neo-classical structures of the late nineteenth century.

In 1951, the deposed Shah ruler was reinstated to the throne of Nepal (with a little help from its neighbour—India) and it is his grandson Birendra who is the present (titular) monarch of a democratic Nepal. With the advent of modernisation, commercial ventures, and tourism, the architecture of Nepal has (as it has in the rest of the subcontinent) taken a turn for the worse, combining mismatched concepts from the west (the present royal palace in Kathmandu!) with the very poorest contemporary styles in concrete and glass. But the charm of the Valley lies in the three cities; the traditional domestic and religious architecture in parallel with the proud hospitable character of the people and the beauty of the landscape.

Domestic architecture of Kathmandu is primarily in brick and timber; slim baked, burnt-orange clay bricks and the deep resonate texture of carved *sal*-wood windows, doors, beams, and balconies. The houses are two or three storeys high, with a tiled sloping roof, common in areas where rain and snowfall are high.

The public façade of a typical house is formal, with the large expanse of the brick wall clearly demarcated horizontally by the divisions of the wooden beams of the flooring. The sloping roof is supported by wooden beams that protrude like a canopy and are held in place by external wooden brackets or struts. The structural wooden beams and brackets, which play such a vital role in maintaining the stability of the brick construction, is included in the decorative scheme of the building, and their function is often camouflaged by artistic carvings. The ribbon beams, floor dividers, dissolve into great naga bodies that coil around the frame of the building, the brackets become flying celestial figures, and beams are decorated with intricate geometric patterns.

Carved window.

In the sacred (square) temple the two-or-three-tiered sloping roof was given a sharper gradient and acquired a form identified in south-east Asia as the pagoda. Each floor was proportionately smaller and the roofs followed a graded line to the summit capped by a gilded kalash. To uphold the steep angle of the sloping roof rafters, brackets and external struts were added, which soon fell under the wood-carver's chisel, assuming the form of divine figures, celestial nymphs, and erotic couples who blessed the building with prosperity and guarded it from destruction. Around the rim of the temple roof or tiers of roofs is hung a line of bells with long leaf-shaped tongues that capture the slightest breeze which sets off the most delicate tinkling chime. The rim of each storey is framed by a thin curtain cloth which ripples with the breeze, extraordinarily enhancing the architecture by making it appear to be in perpetual movement, like a colossal spinning prayer-wheel.

To the basic design of the building comes the addition of (necessary) windows, doorways, and balconies. Here again the architectural purpose of providing openings for entrance, air, and ventilation is given an artistic dimension far beyond functional expectations. The doorways and windows have wooden frames whose entire surface is carved. In order to 'set them into' the brick surface the frame expands like a giant butterfly and incorporates support brackets and protrusions that hinge into the wall. In a temple or palace these flying hinge brackets are embellished with wonderful guardian nymphs and mythical creatures. The door-or window-frame is sometimes carved in a sequence of parallel planes. Other homes have verandahs with carved wooden pillars.

The windows are often shielded with a wooden screen that allows light and ventilation while providing a certain privacy to the inmates (necessary because the houses are built so close together). The lattice windows are truly exceptional for each house, palace, or temple seems to have a different design. Wooden strips, the size of the window, have slots into which the cross beams of the screen are fitted. Each piece is carved to form, when joined together, an intricate design or motif. So whether the window is circular, rectangular, or square, the wooden pieces are interlocked with hinges (without the use of expensive metal nails) to create a unique pattern. The **Wood Carving Museum** of Bhaktapur has a magnificent collection of windows and frames, but one has only to walk through the towns to see the imaginative outburst of window designs in the homes of the poor and the unknown.

While the homes are dark and dingy within, the outward façade offers the residents an opportunity to look out onto the streets where all the action takes place, where the religious processions and festivals are celebrated. So the window and the ornate balcony play a crucial role in the life of the people and are given the most careful consideration by the wood-carver and architect. Sometimes a house or group of houses are built around, and look inward into a quiet, enclosed courtyard sheltered by the inner walls of the homes.

When walking through Patan and Bhaktapur try to catch a glimpse of these created open spaces. Above is the canopy of the sky, on all sides, the houses have carved windows and doors that lead into the courtyard, and the open area is studded with little shrines for daily prayer, a well or a sacred image. Most gorgeous among the courtyard enclosures are those belonging to the city palaces off the Durbar Square at **Kathmandu**, **Patan**, and **Bhaktapur**. Whether it is a potter's home in Bhaktapur, the royal palace in Patan, or a temple in Kathmandu, the glory of this traditional architecture is the perfect conversion of functional structural details of brick-timber architecture into aesthetic ornamentations of the most sophisticated kind.

Kathmandu

Kathmandu city is the capital of Nepal and lies on the western side of the Valley. The Vishnumati river frames the west and runs north to south, with the Bagmati forming the southern boundary. Kathmandu is separated by a short bridge across the Bagmati river from the city of Patan. As the capital, Kathmandu has converted many of the old palaces and Rana establishments into official buildings. The King's palace is to the north with a road leading to Kathmandu's huge maidan. South-east of the park is the road leading to Singha Durbar (once the largest residential palace of the Ranas, now the Government Secretariat), the road to Bhaktapur, and the bridge road to Patan. Off the western side of the central park is the maze of the old bazaar, and Asan where vegetables, cloth stores, wholesalers of beads, and tourist shops are crowded together in narrow lanes. New Road on the western side of the maidan leads straight to the magnificent **Durbar Square**.

The area is extremely crowded and requires a little time for orientation. To your right (north) is a huge white neoclassical structure, above which can be seen the many-tiered pagoda spires called **Lalitpur, Bhaktapur**, and **Basantapur Towers** (the city of spring, i.e. Kathmandu). To the left, just where the Square opens out, is the ornate doorway to the **Kumari Bahal**. The doorway leads into one of the most elegant courtyards in the

Plan of Kathmandu Durbar Square.

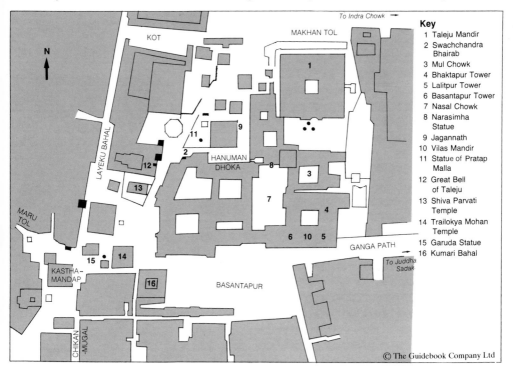

To Indra Chowk →

MAKHAN TOL

KOT

N

LAYEKU BAHAL

MARU TOL

KASTHA-MANDAP

CHIKAN-MUGAL

BASANTAPUR

HANUMAN DHOKA

GANGA PATH

To Juddha Sadak

Key
1 Taleju Mandir
2 Swachchandra Bhairab
3 Mul Chowk
4 Bhaktapur Tower
5 Lalitpur Tower
6 Basantapur Tower
7 Nasal Chowk
8 Narasimha Statue
9 Jagannath
10 Vilas Mandir
11 Statue of Pratap Malla
12 Great Bell of Taleju
13 Shiva Parvati Temple
14 Trailokya Mohan Temple
15 Garuda Statue
16 Kumari Bahal

© The Guidebook Company Ltd

country. All four sides are lavishly decorated with carved wooden windows, brackets, and doorways. It is here that the living virgin goddess lives. In this tradition a young girl of the Shakya community, carrying auspicious physical signs, is chosen to be the goddess and remains here, appearing only to bless the populace and the royal family on festive ocassions. When she reaches puberty her role as the living representative of the patron goddess Taleju ends and a new little girl is brought to this gorgeous (prison?) home.

Stepping back into the Square one can see the charming, apparently haphazard, alignment of temples and shrines. They follow, we are told, a sacred invisible mandala which (over the centuries) dictated where the temples to the various deities should be built. Moving behind, past the pagoda-like **Trailokya Mohan Temple**, are smaller shrines and the stone statue (one of the finest in the Valley) of the faithful Garuda. Due west, the path opens out into another square dominated by the huge form of the **Kasthamandap**, one of the oldest structures in Kathmandu, from which the city derived its name. Its broad sloping tiled roofs and pillared hall dominate the surroundings. All around are temporary stalls of vegetable-sellers seated on the ground and shops in every nook and cranny, with little paths leading into the bazaar labyrinth punctuated only with little street shrines and lanes of houses with wonderful details of wooden windows and doorways.

Back in the Square opposite the **Kumari Bahal** (due north) is the delightful rectangular temple to **Shiva and Parvati,** easily identified by the statues of this divine couple lovingly peering out of the upper floor window at the street below, looking down just as ordinary people do from their humble homes. Past the Shiva–Parvati temple on a path that curves a little eastwards, one comes into another square called **Hanuman Dhoka**. It is so called because at the far right is a pedestal with an indistiguishable orange pasty figure of the much-honoured monkey companion (of Lord Rama of the Ramayana epic), Hanuman. He stands to the left of the entrance to the palace. The **Palace** consists of several courtyards, few of which are open to the public, but do go in. Just past the ticket entrance to your left is a powerful image of the half-lion, half-man incarnation of Vishnu, **Narasimha**, disembowling a demon. This statue guards the entrance and the **Nasal Chowk**, a huge courtyard dominated by the towering spires of the **Basantapur Tower** to the south, a circular tower to the north, and the Bengal hut roof to the east. You can climb up the Basantapur tower to experience the interiors of such traditional architecture: the steep wooden staircase, the window views from the other side, the dark rooms and passageways patterned with wooden roof beams and clay-tiled floors. Back in

Nasal chowk, at the north-eastern end, is the **Mul Chowk**. It is not open to the public but it is well worth risking a pleasant smile to the guard to get a peek at another lovely courtyard with richly carved wooden decorations on the windows and columns.

Out in front of the Hanuman statue, the large, tiered pagoda form is dedicated to **Jagannath**, Vishnu, Lord of the Universe. The idol within bears an inscription dating it to 1563. Walking around it to the column with the **Statue of Pratap Malla** one can see the elegant form of an octagonal **Krishna Temple**, then the drum house with enormous drums that were played on ceremonial occasions. Moving further north, a few steps ahead is the gigantic (4 metre high) figure of **Kalabhairab**, the terrifying lord of Time or **Swachchandra Bhairab** (Time the only true test of honesty), a form of Shiva in front of whom none can tell a lie.

Following the path north-eastwards, past other little shrines, one can catch a glimpse of the dramatic form of the great **Taleju Mandir**. Though entry is restricted only to the Royal family and Brahmins on special days, it is a magnificent structure to be admired at a distance. Raised high on a series of platforms, the temple is built on a concealed mandala. The square temple is surmounted with the classically pitched sloping roof in tiers upheld by beautiful figurative bracket struts and gilded details.

Swayambhu

Two kilometres west of Kathmandu is a hill with the oldest and most venerated Buddhist stupa in the Valley. According to mythology it marks the place where the sacred lotus of wisdom grew, before the valley was created. The stupa is reached by a stairway from the eastern side or a motorable road and stairway on the western side. To the east, right in front of the stupa, is a large (1.5 metre), long gilded Vajra, the holy thunderbolt, the power of Buddhist Dharma. The stupa is huge, rising above the cramped area of shrines, its gilded stepped spire raised majestically to the sky, the region of pure light, wisdom. Below, on the square base, are the painted, ever-watchful eyes of wisdom surveying all directions. Around its base is a ring of prayer wheels and five cardinal Buddhas enshrined in niches. The western one, Amitabha, the Buddha of boundless Light, is the centre of much of the worship here. North-west of this niche is the small but

Prayer flags.

venerated gilded temple to the goddess Harita to whom devotees bring their children to seek protection from illness and death.

Bodhnath

The most awe-inspiring site in Kathmandu is the beautiful and gigantic Stupa of Bodhnath. It stands seven kilometres east of Kathmandu where there are several Tibetan monasteries and settlements. A narrow passage provides entrance into the sacred area which is dominated by the colossal whitewashed form of the stupa (with a diameter of over 100 metres). It is like an earth mound, rising up to the all-seeing eye. The gilded spire is embraced by the canopy of the sky. As you walk in pradakshina, clockwise around the stupa, or around on one of its tiered platforms, you feel (satisfactorily) dwarfed by its presence, as insignificant as a fluttering prayer flag against the solid stable form of the Stupa of Bodhnath (the Lord of eternal, universal wisdom).

Pashupatinath Temple, Kathmandu.

Pashupatinath Temple

On the same eastern side of Kathmandu is one of the most sacred Hindu sites of worship. The temple is dedicated to Pashupatinath, Shiva the Lord of animals. According to mythology, Shiva, creator (and hence destroyer) of the universe came to this forested area to frolic amidst the creatures of his creation. Disguised as a stag he wandered freely till he was captured by the antlers by Man and forced to assume the form of the linga, now worshipped in the temple. The temple is (exclusively) open to Hindus and consists of a courtyard with many small shrines, an enormous, gilt-plated (delightful) Nandi in front of the shrine. The central temple has four doors open to the directions from which the four-faced linga of Pashupati watches over his cherished universe. The temple, in its pagoda-like form, is heavily gilded with gifts from rich supplicants for earthly wealth and has lost its original simplicity and charm. To the eastern side flows the Bagmati river, and it is here that cremation of Hindus takes place in the holy presence of Pashupatinath, the Creator and Destroyer of all. Across the bridge is a row of lovely little shrines, and a place which serves as a viewing point for foreigners who are not allowed into the temple precincts. Further over the hill, through the woods, is another sacred Hindu site dedicated to the goddess Gujeshshwari, consort of Shiva.

Patan

This city, once called Lalitpur (the beautiful city, which it is), lies across the Bagmati river, south-east of Kathmandu. The distance between the two Durbar Squares is approximately seven kilometres and at Patan it is located in the heart of the city. The road from Kathmandu enters the Mangal Bazaar. To the immediate right (southern-most side) is a small doorway into the palace building and **Sundari Chowk**, appropriately called the beautiful courtyard. The courtyard is faced on all four sides by brick walls fitted with the loveliest windows, and at its centre is an exquisite pond. Called **Tusa Hiti**, it is an ancient royal bath guarded by the serpentine coils of huge stone nagas encircling it. The inner face of the pond is lined with miniature shrines with quality sculptures of deities, and at one end is a gilded water spout in the shape of a conch. The design and divine presence of deities makes it appear more like a ritual pond rather than a royal bath tub (but who knows what the Malla kings considered themselves to be?). Outside in the square, moving northward, is a Krishna Temple, the ceremonial bell, the Hari Shankar Temple (dedicated to the compound concept of Shiva and Vishnu), the stone Krishna Temple, the Biswanath Temple (the oldest shrine here), and finally in this line is the most important patron deity (of businessmen), Bhimsen. Opposite it is an ornamental Licchavi water spout called Mangal Hiti.

The stone **Krishna Temple** is worthy of comment for it looks

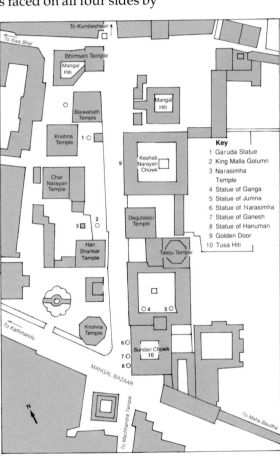

Plan of Durbar Square, Patan.

different from the traditional pagoda-type shrines and has some interesting decorative elements. It was built by Siddhi Narasimha Malla and took six years to complete (1637). It has a pillared verandah which provides light and breeze, while the roof follows the conical shikhara form of northern Indian temples. There are brackets and running stone friezes depicting various stories from the Ramayana and Mahabharata epics, and legends about Krishna, the divine lover. Most unusual and intriguing are the floral stone panels (on the lowest floor) which evoke memories of Akbar's **Fatehpur Sikri** wall decoration, of Mughal flowers on carpets and brocades.

To see how metal repoussé work and ornamentation (a famous craft in the Valley which has degenerated into a tourist industry) is incorporated into religious architecture, wander behind the Bhimsen Temple to **Kwa Bahal**. Entrance from the street is through a narrow passage from which you can hear inmates of the monastery chanting prayers. The entire façade of this living shrine, dedicated to the Buddha, is covered with sheets of embossed, gilded copper, protective images of Buddhist deities, and wonderful birds flying off from the rooftops.

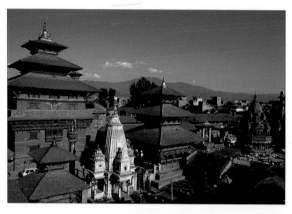

Durbar Square, Patan.

South-east from the Durbar Square, along a narrow lane with excellent examples of domestic architecture and metal cottage industries, is the unique terracotta shrine of **Maha Baudha**. Unfortunately the shrine courtyard is congested with encroaching houses and the structure was damaged quite severely in an earthquake, but it must be seen for nothing like it exists in the Valley today. It is said that this temple was built as a *petite* copy of the **Mahabodhi Temple** at **Bodh Gaya** (Bihar, India), the sacred site where the Buddha attained enlightenment. The temple, like its prototype, has a shikhara roof, but the entire surface of the brick temple is covered with a sheath of decorative terracotta tiles (*see* **Vishnupur**, West Bengal, India) and miniature niches enshrined with images of the Buddha.

Bhaktapur

To get to Bhaktapur (19 kilometres from the heart of Kathmandu city) one has to travel to the eastern quarter of the Valley on a road fringed by rich green paddy-fields (the staple food) and two-storeyed village brick houses that dot the undulating countryside. Along one way is Thimi, a lovely potter's village. Here one can see artists engaged in ancient traditional skills, making pots and clay images. There are three important squares to be seen at Bhaktapur: the **Durbar Square**, its extension, the **Taumadhi Tol,** and the **Tachapal Tol**.

Following the damage caused by the 1934 and 1988 earthquakes, the Durbar Square looks far less congested than those of the other two cities. From the entrance gate on the north side are two magnificent statues of Bhairab (Shiva, the awesome one) and Durga (killing the bull demon, Mahisha). Opposite are four rather small insignificant-looking shrines built by the Malla kings as replicas of four of the most sacred Hindu sites in India (Jagannath in Orissa, Rameshvara in Tamil Nadu, Kedarnath and Badrinath in Uttar Pradesh). Here, in order to spare the royal family from having to undertake arduous pilgrimages, the gods are close at hand right outside the palace!

To the right is a large building with a sign advertising the **National Art Gallery** with a collection of stone sculptures, thankas, primitive and contemporary painting on the first floor. Outside, moving eastward, is a free-standing column with the statue of Bhupatindra Malla, the huge Taleju bell in front of (the temple) entered through the gorgeous Golden Gate or **Sun Dhoka**, one of the finest samples of gilded copper-work from which Hindu deities emerge from a bed of ornamental designs.

Following the west-east movement comes the **Palace of 55 Windows** (now fewer in number), and beside it is a wonderful (reconstructed) octagonal **Chasalin Mandap**. It is one of the most elegant structures in the Valley: with an innovative transformation of an octagonal building up to a circular roof and the flowing line of the roof tiles bending with their own weight like petals of an upturned lotus. At the end of the square are a few more shrines and two large guardian lions.

Branching southwards from the octagonal pavilion is a water tap, a replica of the **Pashupatinath Temple** (so that the

Durbar Square, Bhaktapur.

ruler did not have to go to Kathmandu!), and the road that turns east to the **Taumadhi Tol**. Towering over this square at one end is the magnificent **Nyatapola Temple**. Set high above ground level on a stepped pyramidal base guarded by powerful mythical creatures, stands the temple with its five-tiered roof, complete with painted wooden sculptured details, a resplendent home for the goddess Mahishasuramardini, the destroyer of the demon (asura) who appeared as the bull, Mahisha.

To the east of the square is the goddess's partner, in a gilded triple-roofed shrine, **Kasi Biswanath**. Dedicated to Bhairab and, as the name suggests, is the home of Shiva, Lord of the Universe who resides in Kashi (**Varanasi**, India). The wide open areas and side lanes around the square are crammed with people when the temple festivals, like the Bisket chariot procession and competition, takes place. A walk southward leads to the wonderful **Potter's Square** where millions of pots and clay vessels are made, fired, and sold by the local potters from their homes.

A pleasant walk north-eastward past some incredibly beautiful examples of restored traditional houses, lanes, and market squares is **Tachapal Tol**. One side of the square is dominated by the elegant **Dattatreya Temple** dedicated to the Hindu trinity and has a little white statue of Indra peeping out from the upper floor window. Behind the temple is a lane leading to the **Wakupati Narayan Temple**, dedicated to Vishnu. It is a small, delightful, gilded temple set within an enclosed courtyard. Just behind the Dattatreya Temple is the **Wood Carving Museum** established in recent years. The museum has an exceptional collection of carved wooden windows and doorways collected from different parts of the valley. The display is arranged within its courtyards and rooms. The much advertised Peacock Window is the pride of the collection. The museum is a perfect homage to the wood-carvers who, over the centuries, made the Valley a unique world heritage site that urgently needs to be cared for and protected.

Kedarnath

1
2

Badrinath

3

Golden Gate
(Sun Dhoka)

King Malla Column ●

Taleju Bell

Palace with the
Fifty-five Windows

4

to Potter's Square

Pashupatinath
Temple

Nyatapola
Temple

1 Statue of Bhairab
2 Statue of Durga
3 National Art Gallery
4 Chasalin Mandap

© The Guidebook Company Ltd

TAUMADHI TOL

Tachapal Tol

Kasi
Biswanath

Plan of Durbar Square, Bhaktapur.

WHAT'S IN THE NEIGHBOURHOOD

It is impossible to adequately describe how much there is to see in the Kathmandu Valley. Short trips can be made to the colossal (fifth century) reclining figure of Vishnu on his bed of serpent coils in the tank at **Bodhanilkantha**, the lovely fortified town of **Kirtipur** (to the south-west), the ancient shrine at **Changu Narayan** (to the north-east), and the quiet temple grove of **Dakshin Kali**, south-west of Kathmandu, where animal sacrifices are still performed. A visit to the Valley would be incomplete without a darshan of the awesome mountains from **Nagarkot**, **Shivpuri**, or **Pokhara**. Today the tourist industry is well-equipped to assist the eager adventure traveller on treks to see nature's grandest creations: the young Himalaya, the exotic, fragile rhododendron forests, and the highest peak on our planet, Mount Everest.

HOW TO GET THERE

Kathmandu has an international airport linked to India, Europe, and the Far East. Within the Valley there are buses, taxis, cycles, and rickshaws for hire but surely the best, most educative way to appreciate the architectural heritage of the region, is on foot— and the distances are pleasantly short. There is a full range of hotels from very cheap guest-houses to luxury five star hotels to very charming middle range accommodation in Kathmandu.

The best time of year to travel in the Valley is from September to April. If you are trekking then come between February and April or September to November (it rains between June and August, and the winter months are very cold). The 13th April is the first day of (one calendar) New Year and it is springtime when the three cities are alive with celebrations and temple festivals. Buddha Jayanti, the great Buddhist festival marking the birth of the Buddha and also his enlightenment and final Parinirvana, is held on the full moon night of May. In the later part of the year around Indrajatra, Durga puja, Divali (September-November) and Shivratri in (February-March) are important, colourful Hindu festivals drawing devotees from all parts of the Valley.

Taxila

At first sight Taxila may prove a disappointment. The ruins are shallow, the ancient cities hardly distinguishable above the ground, and literally nothing remains of the fertile land once so favourably described by Greek scholars and early travellers. But a visit to Taxila is a sort of pilgrimage for it stood at the cross-roads of three critical trade routes into India, to Central Asia and West Asia, and on to Europe. Ideas, concepts, technologies, and innumerable influences were traded here.

Modern historians (much to the horror of fundamentalists) are finding that there was greater interchange of ideas in the ancient world than had been previously thought. The cross-fertilisation of cultures that occurred early in human history did so much to remove the 'purity' and monotony of mono-cultures. What we inherit today is a synthesised cumulative experience which came to us through the ages from such hybridisations that one finds at Taxila.

To Taxila came some great historical personalities like Alexander the Great from Macedonia and the Mauryan Emperor Ashoka from the Gangetic plains of eastern India. Long after these personalities were dead the routes of communication remained alive and open. Here, in the third century BC the philosophy of the Buddha came into contact with Greek and Parthian ideals. At Taxila, images of the gentle Buddha of the eastern Himalaya are dressed in Greek robes and sandals. It is this intangible, very subtle but vital aspect of human culture that one honours at Taxila.

The valley within which Taxila is situated is only 18 kilometres long and 8 kilometres broad at its mouth and stands 550 metres above sea level. On the eastern side of the valley are the Murree hills, to the north and south are two of its spurs, Sarda and Margalla, and a rocky ridge of limestone, the **Hathial**, divides the valley into two unequal parts. From the hills flowed streams and rivulets that fed the valley making it, in the words of Hiuen Tsang the seventh century Chinese scholar, 'a land of rich harvests, flowing streams and fountains, abundant flowers and fruits'. All this has gone, the hills around Taxila are bare and raw, brown and barren with meagre vegetation most of the year.

Nothing remains of the early part of Taxila's history during the Stone and Copper Ages. In the fifth century BC the region formed part of the Persian empire. During the next three hundred years it benefited from efficient Persian administration and

(opposite) : Ruins of Sirkap, Taxila.

witnessed the introduction of Aramaic which was centuries later to influence the development of the local Kharoshthi script.

In the spring of 326 BC Alexander, the ruler of Macedonia, descended to the plains of the Punjab, having conquered most of the Persian empire. Greek accounts describe Alexander's encounter with the city of Taxila. The most amusing story concerns Onesikritos, his staff philosopher.[22] He was asked to meet local sages and understand their world-view. One sage ticked him off, telling him to remove his clothes and show some humility; another asked why Alexander had come; he had not been invited. Yet another sage of Taxila remarked, 'I commend the King [Alexander] because, although he governs so vast an empire, he is still desirous of acquiring wisdom, for he is the only philosopher in arms that I have ever seen'. Leaving his newly carved empire in the hands of administrators, Alexander wished to return to Greece, but died on the way home.

Within a decade Taxila was incorporated into the expanding Mauryan empire with its capital at Pataliputra (Modern Patna, Bihar, east India, many thousand kilometres away). Young Ashoka was sent to Taxila to look after this northwestern frontier city when he was still a prince. Roads and roadways were built, trees were planted, traveller's lodges and wells built along the way, and Mauryan administration was introduced into the valley. When Ashoka became emperor and was converted to the way of the Buddha, the impact was felt in distant Taxila, as indeed it was in far-away Shri Lanka. The state religion was introduced into Taxila and the earliest city here (within the Bhir Mound in the southernmost part of the valley) was adorned with its first Buddhist monument, the great **Dharmarajika Stupa**. From its name it would appear that the stupa contained some relics of the Buddha (the only true Dharma-raja, King of the Law of Dharma), perhaps a gift from the newly converted emperor to the town which he had ruled as a prince.

Dharmarajika Stupa, Taxila.

The stupa is (15 metres high and 50 metres in diameter) raised on a platform. Around it is a passage for pradakshina and in the outer circle is a ring of smaller stupas. The original stupa was renovated and expanded over the centuries and perhaps even plastered and gilded with the addition of images of the Buddha placed in niches at the cardinal points.

North of this complex of stupas and votive shrines donated by wealthy patrons is a monastery with cells and peaceful courtyards for the monks. Found among the ruins, hidden like hoards of treasure, were large heaps of coins, a gold-mine for the historian reconstructing the economic and political life of the people of Taxila.

For the next eight hundred years or more Buddhist shrines continued to be built in Taxila. In Buddhist literature Taxila, or more correctly Takshashila, grew to be a famous university (like **Nalanda**), attracting scholars and students from all parts of the Buddhist world, even as far away as China. It was celebrated in the ancient world as a prestigious centre of learning where students could receive instruction in almost any subject, from mathematics to medicine, astrology to philosophy.

Over the hill of the Dharmarajika Stupa (to the north-west) on a spur of the rocky Hathial outcrop stands the **Memorial to Kunala**, an imposing stupa and monastery. According to Hiuen Tsang, Emperor Ashoka returned to his capital in Pataliputra, and his son Kunala was sent to govern Taxila. It happened that he had actually been sent there at the behest of a lustful stepmother smarting from her spurned advances to the young prince. Unknown to Ashoka, the miserable stepmother sent a messenger to Taxila with orders carrying the emperor's insignia, to punish the young prince. According to Hiuen Tsang the stupa and monastery marks the site where the prince with the beautiful eyes was blinded. This story and many variations of it are to be found in Greek literature.

Statue of the Buddha, Taxila.

The **Kunala Stupa** is raised on a triple-tiered base with pillars and mouldings, and was once coated with plaster or dressed in stone. West of the stupa are the remains of the monastery which consists of a courtyard surrounded by a verandah and cells for the monks to live in. An annexe or extension to the monastery appears to have been built further up the hill. This cloister too has the usual open courtyard with windows to let in light and breeze. There are several cells, some with little niches on the walls for lamps and books. From the Hathial outcrop one gets an excellent view of **Sirkap** below. This city marks the next historical stage of development at Taxila.

After the brief period of Mauryan rule lasting only three generations, the Greeks again invaded the region, but this time from their home town in Bactria. A wave of Greek ideas flowed once again through the valley of Taxila. From the hilltop of Hathial one can see one of the most beautiful Bactrian contributions to Taxila, the city of **Sirkap**. The long rectangular city plan is surrounded by a city wall five kilometres long. Right down the centre is a wide 700 metre long main street, with shallow ruins of walls of buildings divided into city blocks. Each block was given a religious structure, a stupa or shrine set within an enclosed courtyard. Behind the line of shops on the main street and shrines were the residential homes of the city dwellers.

Walking from north to south along the main street, the first monumental structure that would have dominated the view is the large **apsidal shrine** (to the east in the fourth block, between the fifth and sixth streets). This shrine has one rounded side that follows the form of the circular votive stupa at the eastern end. The apsidal shrine was a kind of chaitya prayer hall, similar in design to that found in western India (**Ajanta**, Kanheri, Bedsa, and Karle). The next block has a small very early stupa dated by historians to the first century BC, its circular dome decorated with plaster-work decorations. The next block has the famous **Shrine of the Double-Headed Eagle**. This is a very interesting first century shrine with many decorative motifs from Greek and Indian architectural tradition. On the façade is a row of Corinthian pilasters with foliage sprouting from the capitals

Map of Taxila Valley.

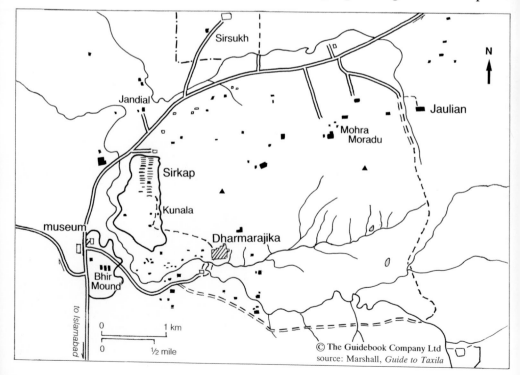

© The Guidebook Company Ltd
source: Marshall, *Guide to Taxila*

separating little niches in three contrasting styles. Seated on top of the central niche is the double-headed eagle from which the shrine derives its name. The stupa was of familiar shape and form with a base drum or dome decorated with plaster-work.

At the southern end of the street is the so-called Royal Palace and the homes of the rich and famous. There is a maze of rooms, courtyards, verandahs, and within the rooms were excavated a large number of carved soft stone dishes, goblets, toilet trays, now on display in the Museum at Taxila. The Greek artists also worked with local metalworkers to produce images cast in bronze and copper.

Jaulian is on a road north-eastward (7 kilometres away) from Sirkap on a rugged hilly outcrop. A description by Sir John Marshall, one of the chief archaeologists of Taxila, captures the aura of this site:[23]

> It is upwards of forty years since I visited Taxila [in 1913] and I still remember the thrill I got from the sight of the buried cities. At the time I was a young man, fresh from archaeological excavations in Greece and filled with enthusiasm for anything Greek; and in that far-off corner of the Panjab it seemed as if I had lighted all of a sudden on a bit of Greece itself....I felt then, as I have never ceased to feel since, that there is something appealingly Greek in the countryside itself; in the groves of wild olive on the rocky slopes, in the distant pine-clad hills below Murree, and in the chill, invigorating air that blows from the snow-field beyond the Indus.

Mohra Moradu, Taxila.

Clambering up the road to the second century AD stupa and monastery of Jaulian one cannot but concur with Sir John. The olive trees are an instant reminder of a distant Mediterranean land and of the rich culture that travelled miles across Europe and the Middle East to settle in the western plains of the Indian subcontinent. A narrow entrance leads into the courtyard of the lower stupa. It is a brick construction covered over with plaster and adorned with rows of plaster images of the Buddha. Above, approached by a short flight of stairs, is another stupa (once about 20 metres high) with miniature stupas surrounding it. The main stupa is profusely decorated with pilasters, niches with Buddhist images, attendants, and animals. The costumes and robes worn by the sculptured figures, their facial type, and aesthetic delineation are distinctively Greek. To the west of the main stupa is the monastery with nearly thirty cells for monks, and here too the walls have been adorned with scenes from the life of the Buddha.

WHAT'S IN THE NEIGHBOURHOOD

The **Museum** at Taxila must be one of the loveliest in the world, with a pretty garden of trees, flower-beds, and fountains that look out at the breath-taking view. The museum is not very large but has a fine collection of objects unearthed during excavations. There is a model of Taxila which gives an idea of the layout of the various cities of Bhir Mound, Sirkap, Jaulian, Sirsukh, and Mohra Moradu. There is a vast coin collection that records the various historical periods of Taxila's history: from Persian times, to Alexander, the Mauryan empire, Bactrian Greeks who were followed by the Shakas, Parthians, Kushans and, finally, the destruction of Taxila by the invading hordes of White Huns.

The Museum also has an excellent collection of Gandharan art delineating the changing artistic trends over the long period of Taxila's occupation. Beautiful carved stone images of the Buddha and the Boddhisattvas are followed by figures made of more easily malleable plaster, creating images almost repetitive and sterile in form.

HOW TO GET THERE

Taxila is 35 kilometres from Islamabad, the modern capital of Pakistan, and a little over 32 kilometres north–west of the city of Rawalpindi. There are organised tours, buses, and cars that ply up and down the Grand Trunk Road. There is little in the way of hotels or restaurants at Taxila and most people like to go on a one day picnic trip. The best time of the year to visit is during the winter months (October to March) when it is cool and the long walks along hill tracks is a pleasant sojourn into the past.

Mohenjodaro

No one understood the significance of the excavations at Harappa until Mohenjodaro was discovered. Even when the announcement of the rediscovery of this five thousand year old city was reported in the *Illustrated London News* in September 1924, no one quite comprehended the extent of the civilisation nor the extent of its sophistication.

Today, after nearly sixty years of excavations both in India and Pakistan, more than 400 similar ancient urban centres have been uncovered. They stretch from as far as Kabul in the west to Delhi in the east, and to the far south to Gujarat (**Lothal**) and Maharashtra in India, with a huge cluster of towns around Mohenjodaro. This makes it a more extensive civilisation than any other comparable one in Mesopotamia or Egypt.

This civilisation was named after the Indus River Valley in which the first most important cities were discovered. Mohenjodaro, one of the largest metropolises, was built on the west bank of the river. The course of the Indus river has moved, as it must have done for centuries, and is now nearly five kilometres from the ancient embankment. But the river once played a vital role in the development and evolution of Mohenjodaro, providing vital drinking water, water for domestic use, to carry away the refuse and sewage of the densely populated habitation. Many historians, acknowledging the vital role that the river played in city life, have suggested that one of the causes of the collapse and gradual abandonment of Mohenjodaro may have been the moving away of the river. There is ample evidence also of the annual flooding of the river that brought rich alluvial soil downstream. This provided the farmer with fertile topsoil so essential for the bumper harvests (rice and cotton for textiles) necessary to maintain the city economy.

At Mohenjodaro there is a **Museum** with some reconstruction drawings and plans that provide a provocative picture of the city of Mohenjodaro in its prime. It may be useful to study them before venturing on a tour of the deserted streets of the ancient township. The relationship of the river and the city becomes clear when one sees how the water system was used as a means of communication from one region of the civilisation to another and for transporting essential supplies of foodgrain from neighbouring villages to the city dwellers. Food was brought in by boat and carried through the broad roads by bullock cart. It was stored in what the archaeologists first called the civic granary, an enormous platformed, well-ventilated structure for storage. Since nothing that looks like money was found at these sites it was believed that the system of exchange was through barter, and grain was the source of wealth on which the entire economy was founded. This notion was further supported by the position of the granary in an apparently prestigious area of the city of Mohenjodaro where it could be well-guarded and function as a sort of treasury.

From outside the museum you can see the highest mound in the area, topped by a ruined stupa. It was this stupa that initially attracted archaeologists to the region, motivated by their interest in establishing the growth and expansion of the Buddhist world in the early centuries of the Christian era. What they actually found, which no one had quite expected, was a city that pushed back the history of the subcontinent to 2500 BC. The stupa is still the landmark and occupies its elevated position because no excavations were ever carried out below it. To the west of the stupa is apparently the most important zone of the city in which the **Granary**, the **Great Bath** are located, along with other large buildings that may have served administrative purposes.

Beside the granary is the brick structure called the Great Bath. It consists of a large rectangular pool two metres deep with steps leading into it from the narrower ends. The bricks here have been tightly packed and lined with bitumen to make the pool waterproof. Around the pool are cloister-like rooms that are now believed to have served

Plan of Mohenjodaro.

some religious purpose. The elaborate water supply system and drainage network for the Great Bath make it one the most intriguing structures at Mohenjodaro.

Mohenjodaro is not the original name, of course, but one given by local villagers referring to the 'mound of the dead', the tower and hillocks of abandoned debris of bricks that they and their forefathers had noticed in the surroundings. The site is impressive, for the excavations are deep revealing the high walls of the buildings, in contrast to these at **Lothal** where only the shallow foundations appear above the ground.

It is estimated that the ancient city of Mohenjodaro once occupied an enormous area of four square kilometres, of which only a small portion has been excavated and left uncovered. Large trenches were dug and work begun to study the stratification of the city. What astounded the archaeologists was its symmetric plan. It was built on a rectangular grid with broad roads several metres wide running north to south. From these main roads, side streets and smaller service lanes created a systematic web providing access to every house in the city block, and each was connected to an underground drainage system. Walking through the main streets and into the bylanes one can visualise life in Mohenjodaro five thousand years ago. The streets busy with bullock cart traffic and pedestrians. The narrow lanes, like the crowded bazaar lanes of Lahore, lined with awnings that kept the sun out, keeping them relatively cool. The houses in the apparently wealthier zone of the city have been excavated and reveal enormous blank, windowless outer walls, a style still practised in these desert areas to prevent hot dusty air from entering the homes. Many of the houses are two or more storeys high, in typical brick and timber construction still in use today. The baked bricks used for construction are of a regular standard size. This is another incredible feature of this civilisation: almost all the 400 cities within the 1000 mile radius made use of a similar type of brick. The plans of the houses are different but have areas for bathing with

Plan of State buildings, Mohenjodaro.

drainage shutes and living spaces, often with a central courtyard within for domestic privacy and housework. Stairways lead up to the roof (which no longer exists) but must have provided, as indeed it does in many homes today, a place in which to sleep and rest during the cool nights of summer and a pleasant recreational area on sunny winter days.

While excavating the city the archaeologists found over 79 feet of deposits and evidence of several successive reconstructions and layers of habitation. Along the city walls, buildings and wells are tell-tale marks of stratifications revealing how each subsequent stratum of (inferior quality) building was added to the last, recording for posterity the story of Mohenjodaro from its creation to its decline—an uninterrupted period of occupation for over one thousand years.

Sir Mortimer Wheeler's excavation reports records that:[21]

Stratified potsherds and other objects were recovered literally by the ton; four weeks after the beginning, twelve wagon loads of selected pottery were sent back to base, and more followed.

Seal with figure wearing horn crown surrounded by animals, National Museum, New Delhi.

The **Museum** at Mohenjodaro has an instructive collection of the artifacts found in the houses of the great city. Large collections of wheel-thrown pottery finely worked with a red and black slip, with designs and motifs of birds and flowers are a lively heritage of the past. The shapes and sizes of the pottery give some indication of their use: enormous storage pots a metre or so high, tiny little vessels that look like a child's make-believe kitchen set, pots for cooking, serving, and small-mouthed containers for oils and precious liquids (perfumes?). There are hundreds of clay toys for children of animals, bullock carts, and of people at work which provide an animated account of life in the ancient metropolis.

A fine collection of beads in semi-precious stones and some gold jewellery were found at the site. Semi-precious stones that were not from the region led historians to speculate about overland trade with other cultures: lapis lazuli and turquoise from Persia and Afghanistan. The recovery of seals at Sumer has confirmed that the people of the Indus Valley had trade contacts with their contemporaries in Mesopotamia.

Most intriguing of course are the seals, some steatite (a kind of soft stone) ones which bear inscriptions and beautiful carved figures of animals, of humped bulls, unicorns, tigers, and strange men wearing bull horn masks and seated cross-legged on a throne. While the script is still an enigma and has not so far been deciphered, the seals were undoubtedly used by traders to mark their goods before sale and export, some probably used as family insignia or a religious talisman.

Nothing much is yet known about the religion of the people of Mohenjodaro but there are many conjectures. Some say that the seated mask-wearing male on the seals is a prototype of Shiva, a prominent deity of the Hindu pantheon. Others say that the large stone objects (that look more like a pestle and mortar for pounding grain) are signs of phallic worship in this ancient culture, a custom that continues to be practised by present-day Hindus. Others point to the female figurines and talk of mother goddess worship. It may perhaps have been a wonderful culture which had no formal religion; a truly liberal people who, unlike us, spent little time and resources on warfare, on arms and weapons, and the destruction of others; who instead crafted their valuable supply of metals to make tools, jewellery, and exquisite masterpieces of sculpture and on building well-planned cities that attracted thousands of people to come and live and partake of their sophisticated culture for centuries.

WHAT'S IN THE NEIGHBOURHOOD

There are several other contemporary sites around Mohenjodaro where some excavation work has been done. **Kot Diji** is 40 kilometres east of Mohenjodaro; **Chanhu-daro** (128 kilometres south of Mohenjodaro) bears evidence of a later phase of the civilisation, and it would appear that the inhabitants had to move away from the older metropolises and set up shoddy settlements in nearby areas where conditions, economic and environmental, were still favourable. **Lothal** (Gujarat, India) is a well-kept site that also exemplifies how the southern sites of the Indus Valley culture endured much longer than those directly on the Indus basin. The city of Harappa in the state of Punjab (which can be reached from Lahore) was unfortunately devastated by poor excavation practices and robbers, and is not as exciting a site as Mohenjodaro.

HOW TO GET THERE

There is now an hour long flight to Mohenjodaro from Karachi. Local guides meet the daily flight and can take visitors around. A longer rail route is available. The winter months (October to March) are best suited for the visit and long walks. There is a small rest-house near the museum at Mohenjodaro.

Lahore

Lahore holds yet another key to understanding Islamic architecture in the subcontinent. Like **Delhi** (the capital of India), the city provides visual reminders of its parental heritage, of its occupation by a series of rulers since the eleventh century. But like two children of the same parents they are very different, each with their own personality and temperament. Throughout their shared history Lahore and Delhi have been inseparable, but distinctive in character.

Today Lahore is the largest city of the state of Punjab in Pakistan, with an elegant mixture of the old, the colonial, and the new. For the monarchs who ruled from Delhi, Lahore was a crucial buffer zone. It was necessary for invading armies from the west to take this city first before they could break through to Delhi. But a protective barrier is also a gateway, and Lahore was the first to come into contact with new ideas and creative influences. Great poets and artists settled here rather than further within the Indian peninsula.

The raids and establishment of a court at Lahore began in the eleventh century (in recorded history) first by Ghazni and later by Mohammed Ghori. Ghori's kingdom in the subcontinent was left to his trusted slave and able military assistant Qutub-ud-Din Aibak, with his capital in Delhi where he built the famous **Qutub Minar**. But it was in Lahore that the celebrated poet Amir Khusrao held court. For the Khalji, Tughluq, Sayyid, and Lodi dynasties, Delhi was the centre of power and the administration of Punjab was delegated to their appointed Viceroys. Throughout the thirteenth and fourteenth centuries Lahore was relentlessly invaded from the north and north-west. Finally, when Delhi came under the rule of Sultan Ibrahim Lodi, the Governor of Lahore invited Babur (reigning in Kabul) to join forces and take Delhi. Babur spent time in Lahore before capturing Delhi after a decisive battle at Panipat in 1526. After this experience, Mughal rulers (and, for a brief period, Sher Shah Suri who ousted Humayun, the second Mughal Emperor, from the Delhi throne) never forgot the critical importance of Lahore and spent time and effort in strengthening its forts and embellishing its environment.

The exiled Humayun, returned to Lahore in 1555 but died soon after he reclaimed the Delhi throne. His young son Akbar (14 years old at the time) was crowned emperor at Kalanor in the Punjab and proceeded immediately to Lahore. Being an

(opposite) :
Wazir Khan's Mosque.

intelligent man, he sensed the perfect positioning of an older citadel constructed by his predecessors and built the new **Lahore Fort** at the same site, with its northern side facing the River Ravi. Akbar based himself here while he was expanding his empire in the subcontinent.

As the Mughal empire grew so did its fame, and artists and poets flocked to Akbar's ateliers in Lahore. The first Portuguese Jesuits came here to visit the great emperor who had grown so interested in world religions. Akbar, desperate for a son and heir, sought the blessings of the Sufi saint Shaikh Salim Chisti at a retreat outside Agra. A son was born named Salim and to commemorate the saint and the child a new fort was built called **Fatehpur Sikri** (near Agra, India). Prince Salim grew up in Lahore, spending much time in his father's court and artistic workshops, developing a love for all things beautiful.

It was in Lahore that Prince Salim set eyes upon Anarkali ('Pomegranate Blossom' she was Akbar's favourite dancing girl). Akbar, legend has it, was furious and had the lady entombed outside the fort. Whether this story is fact or fiction, a modest tomb stands in Lahore believed to have been built, by the lovesick prince (in 1615). The gravestone in the **Tomb for Anarkali** bears the tragic inscription,

Tomb of Asaf Khan, Lahore.

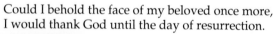

Could I behold the face of my beloved once more,
I would thank God until the day of resurrection.

The tomb was converted into a church during British occupation and now the building serves as an archive (with a collection of old prints) within the compound of the Government Record Office.

Jahangir (as Salim was known when he succeeded Akbar) continued to live and love Lahore even after he ascended the throne in 1605. Rather than busy himself with the problems of the empire he spent many pleasure-filled winters in Lahore, leaving it only in the hot summer months to go to the glorious garden city of **Srinagar** (amidst the Kashmir hills, which Akbar had added to the empire).

Once a passionate lover, always a lover, Jahangir had many passions. Just beyond Lahore (35 kilometres to the west in Shaikapura), Jahangir built a lovely pavilion in the middle of an artificial lake, and a tower called **Hiran Minar** in memory of his pet deer (*hiran*). The small lake is filled by an elaborate water system and the embankment has an open pavilion at the centre of each of its four sides. A ramp leads from the shore to the three-storeyed arched building at the centre of the lake, where the emperor sat and watched the forest and its animals. The octagonal building with its thick walls is incredibly cool and the arched doorways open on all sides catch every breath of passing breeze.

Jahangir's Tomb

Jahangir's love of Lahore is further underlined by his expressed desire to be buried in **Dilkush**, the gardens (of the heart's delight) that he had gifted to his wife Nur Jahan. Jahangir died in 1627 while on his way from Lahore to Kashmir, and according to his wishes was brought back to Lahore to await burial. His beautiful and powerful wife Nur Jahan had built a rather special tomb for her father (**Itimad-ud-Daulah's Tomb** in **Agra**) and **Jahangir's Tomb** is of similar design. It stands on the bank of the Ravi across from the fort in a vast (55 acre) enclosed garden. The square tomb (85 metres on each side) is single-storeyed, with four tall, very graceful minars at each corner. The minars have a lively zig-zag play of coloured inlaid marble-work and are topped by small white kiosk-like domes. The long, flat-roofed ground floor is punctuated by a line of arches which open into a corridor that runs around the building. The tomb chamber is

Minaret, Jahangir's Tomb, Lahore.

set at the centre of the building, through a passageway of painted walls and mosaic marble floors. A staircase leads up to the open court of the roof, and this is where the tomb has been placed in accordance with the emperor's wish to be buried under the canopy of the sky and stars in the manner his great-grandfather Babur. From the paintings and accounts of Jahangir's reign one gets the impression that the emperor loved birds and flowers. One must imagine that the gardens around Jahangir's tomb were once filled with flowering trees and plants, the songs of birds, and the gay abandon of fluttering butterflies. Today the garden presents a pathetic sight of neglect and disinterest.

The royal garden tombs of the Mughal emperors are all as dissimilar as their individual personalities: Babur was buried in a modest tomb in Kabul, **Humayun's Tomb** in **Delhi** is an elaborate affair: an octagonal building of red sandstone, marble highlights with a huge white marble dome. **Akbar's Tomb** in **Sikandra, Agra** is a spectacle. A five-storeyed, terraced, red sandstone structure with arches and no dome, the cenotaph perched on the top floor in an open white marble-screened terrace. Jahangir's Tomb is far more modest than either his father's or grandfather's garden tomb and larger but less ornate than **Itimad-ud-Daulah's Tomb** (his father-in-law), and is of a style that was never repeated. On the roof platform of the tomb is the marble cenotaph of Jahangir beautifully inlaid in black with the ninety-nine glorious names of God. The cenotaph was once surrounded by beautiful marble screens believed to have been robbed in later centuries to decorate the **Golden Temple** in Amritsar.

West of the tomb's forecourt is a another, the **Tomb of Asaf Khan**, the brother of Nur Jahan and father of Mumtaz Mahal (for whom the **Taj Mahal** was built in Agra). The tomb today has lost most of its beauty and is poorly maintained, but it was a classic traditional, domed octagonal structure with bright tile-work decorations and highlights.

Nur Jahan survived her husband Jahangir by 18 years and these were spent in intrigue and trouble. Jahangir had named his son Shah Jahan (who built the Taj Mahal) as his successor, but he was not Nur Jahan's son. At the time of Jahangir's death, her own candidate grabbed the throne and fortified Lahore only to be displaced a few days later by Shah Jahan, who rushed back to Lahore to quell the rebellion and convey to Nur Jahan that she had backed the wrong horse. Nur Jahan, though in disfavour, continued to live well, being an excessively powerful and wealthy woman, and set about building her husband's tomb and her own. The **Tomb of Nur Jahan** is a sorry sight; no fit place for the legendary beauty, who wielded so much power and influence in her lifetime and virtually ran the empire on behalf of the pleasure-seeking, passionate Jahangir. It stands forlorn today near the railway track, desolate and uncared for, stripped of its original decorative work and pomp.

Lahore Fort

Shah Jahan had his capital at Agra and Delhi, but he had a special place in his heart for Lahore, the city of his birth. He visited Lahore despite his preoccupations with his great architectural projects in Delhi and Agra. The 400-mile long route that linked the three capitals was lined with trees, and Shah Jahan enjoyed travelling from one home to another.

The **Lahore Fort** that one sees today is a happy blend of what Akbar originally built along with additions and renovations introduced by Jahangir and Shah Jahan. The rule of thumb that (does not always work but which) art historians use to distinguish the various styles is: anything in red sandstone is Akbar's or Jahangir's and anything covered in marble, heavily inlaid, is attributed to Shah Jahan's opulent taste.

The fort was more or less rectangular in shape (380 by 330 metres) with the long northern side facing the Ravi River. The modern entrance to the fort is through the regal **Alamgir Gate** built by Aurangzeb, Shah Jahan's son who succeeded him. A modern ramp leads the way into a wide open courtyard, and at the north-western corner is an entrance to the **Moti Masjid**, the Pearl Mosque, for the private use of the royal family. This elegant little mosque is said to have been built by Shah Jahan and has a courtyard with a tiny tank for ritual ablutions and delicate arches marking the mirhab. Back into the main courtyard to the east is the grand **Diwan-e-Am** where the emperor gave his public audiences. A marble and red sandstone balcony at the rear end was built by the Emperor Akbar, and it was here that he sat before the august gathering that came to pay their respects.

A passageway leads behind the Diwan-e-Am to a row of palatial buildings built along the northern side of the fort facing the river, and it is important to see how the view was incorporated into the architectural scheme. The building directly behind the Diwan-e-Am is **Jahangir's Quadrangle** with elaborate sandstone pillars and brackets that spring from their sides in the shape of mythical animals. The central area may once have been a lovely

Plan of Lahore Fort.

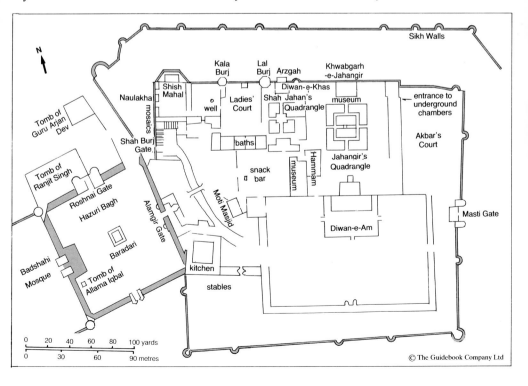

ornamental garden of the type so often depicted in Mughal miniature paintings. At the northern end of the quadrangle is the **Khwabgarh-e-Jahangir**, Jahangir's house of dreams. Unfortunately the dream-like quality of the building is lost as it has been converted into a museum (with a dreary display) that houses an interesting collection of paintings and manuscripts.

South of the museum is the **Hammam**, the once opulent royal baths, but the marble floors and painted walls have been denuded. The museum beside the Hammam has an armoury and picture collection. Outside the museum is **Shah Jahan's Quadrangle**, with a row of rooms on the east side and **Shah Jahan's Diwan-e-Khas** along the north side. This elegant pavilion of marble screens, mosaic floors, and wide arches served the emperor as a place where he met special guests and family members. One can only imagine the reception such guests would have received with exquisite Persian carpets on the floor, richly embroidered bolsters and brocade cushions to recline on, with refreshments served in jewelled vessels and jade glasses. At the corner of the Diwan-e-Khas is an octagonal tower called **Lal Burj**, the red tower, also covered with tile mosaics and screen-work. The murals on the walls are of a later date but add to the richness of the building.

Following the northern line, the next courtyard is the **Ladies Courtyard** where the emperor met with his harem: mothers, daughters, many wives, and ladies-in-waiting. The **Ghusl Khana** is another royal bath with an elaborate system for hot and cold running water and areas where the ladies could elaborately groom themselves. Standing at the corner is the twin tower of the Lal Burj, termed the black or **Kala Burj**, which is closed for security reasons as it stands in ruins.

The next courtyard is the last in the line and is the most beautiful contribution made by Shah Jahan to the Lahore Fort. The courtyard has lovely mosaic flooring and all around are lavishly decorated pavillions from which one could once catch a glimpse of the river and enjoy the cool water-swept breeze. **Shish Mahal** is the palace of mirrors, adorned with tiny concave mirrors set in gilt and carved plaster-work as part of an elaborate ceiling design. At night, when the lamps and torches were lit in the pavillion, the mirrors reflected the flickering lights like a sky with a million dazzling stars. The pillars of the pavillion are equally lovely with ornamental bases and inlay-work. Some of the adjoining pavillions are decorated with murals, others adorned with stucco-work.

The wide open courtyard is characteristic of Mughal palacial architecture. The courtyard served several purposes, while the surrounding rooms and verandahs offered comfortable sheltars, when required. Looking over the eastern corner of the courtyard is the little gem-like pavillion called **Naulakha**, literally meaning nine lakhs, perhaps the sum of money spent to build this costly pleasure cove. The structure has a curved roof in the style of the Bengal hut (of bamboo) and is tastefully decorated with very special inlay-work along the pillars and walls. The more intricate the design the more elaborate the process, and in some of the inlay-work here a single flower is made up of several tiny pieces of semi-precious gems: jade-greens, agate-reds, and lapis lazuli blues. From the window of the pavillion one can look out onto the main square and see the graceful domes rising from the enormous **Badshahi Mosque**, the **Tomb of Ranjit Singh**, and the gilded dome of **Guru Arjan Dev's Memorial** which mark the next stage of the story of Lahore.

One of the exits of the fort is from the east side through the Elephant Gate where one can see the **Shah Burj** (Gate), the royal gateway. This eastern end of the fort wall was once covered with vibrant ceramic tiles. The tile-work of the fort is beautiful and is a feature not to be easily found in the forts of Delhi or Agra (but can be seen in the **Gwalior Fort** in India). This technique of decorating monumental buildings was once profusely used in Persia and parts of Pakistan (such as Multan). The mosaics have been arranged in patterns with angels and combat scenes, elephants and camels, floral and geometric designs.

Ceramic tile-work, Lahore Fort.

Badshahi Mosque

Walking back to the Alamgir gateway, the path opens out into a huge open courtyard, with the fort on one side and the dramatic stairway to the **Badshahi Mosque** on the other. This area is called the **Hazuri Bagh** and within it, to one side, is the **Tomb of Allama Muhammad Iqbal**, the great poet who died in 1938. His poetic works are still read, admired, and studied in schools and colleges throughout Pakistan and also India, inspiring great emotions of patriotism and independence: speaking as they do of a time of colonial oppression and the liberating spirt of freedom.

Shah Jahan had three sons, the eldest, the favourite and heir to the throne was the aesthete, Dara Shikoh, who was murdered by his younger brother Aurangzeb, perhaps the better warrior and statesman. Aurangzeb inherited a much poorer treasury from his father who must have spent millions on the construction of the **Red Fort** (Delhi), the **Taj Mahal**, renovating the **Forts** of **Agra** and **Lahore**, amongst other projects. Aurangzeb rightly felt such extravagant expenditure to be wasteful and the only really major building venture he undertook (apart from the construction of his wife's tomb in **Aurangabad**, India) was the enormous **Badshahi Mosque** at Lahore. It was the largest mosque in the subcontinent, built to accomodate 60, 000 people in prayer. A grand stairway leads to the entrance gate and a huge open

Badshahi Mosque, Lahore.

courtyard paved with red sandstone. The experience of space and freedom here is incredible, with the magnificent blue sky above to remind one of God's eternal grace. The western face of the building is exalted, with grand arched openings. There is a delightful return to the traditional play of pink sandstone and white marble highlights in the exterior decorations. The hall within has plastered walls and ceilings with bold floral designs in almost a poor imitation of the grand marble effects achieved by Aurangzeb's father. Above the western façade rise three bulbous marble-covered domes, adding a majestic grace to the Badshahi Mosque, the mosque of the King of Kings.

During the reign of Jahangir, one of his sons had taken refuge with the Sikh Guru Arjun Dev. Although Akbar had patronised this religious group and even granted them the land on which the **Golden Temple** was built in Amritsar, Jahangir was not pleased by his son's act of rebellion. Tragically, he had the Guru killed, and this act alone is said to have fired lasting animosity between Sikhs and Muslims. After Aurangzeb a line of weak Mughal rulers were unable to control the empire and bits of the territory fell to aspiring young rulers. Lahore became the target of raids and convulsed by strife, till it was finally captured by the Sikhs and ruled (1799-1839) by Ranjit Singh whose tomb stands near the entrance to the fort beside the memorial he built to Guru Arjun Dev.

Detail from Badshahi Mosque.

Wazir Khan's Mosque

In the days when the Mughals held court in the Fort an entire city and a maze of bazaars grew up outside the fortified palace (in the southern quarter of Lahore) to furnish the needs of the imperial lords and their courtiers. Indeed, the Mughal emperors encouraged the nobility to built their homes and gardens around the fort in Lahore. Today the market area near the fort is a delightful place. The narrow streets are lined with shops, crowded with people and goods, and the sun never seems to find a place to fall on the ground below. Like the caravanserais of old, these traditional marketplaces are neatly organised into specialised areas, with a jewellers' street, another for the sale of cloth, and yet another brimming over with burnished brassware.

Amidst this riot of colour and exotic sensations is one of the most beautiful sights of Lahore, **Wazir Khan's Mosque**. Wazir Khan was a favoured member of Shah Jahan's court in Lahore and he had this exquisite mosque built, a likeness of which cannot be found anywhere in the Indian subcontinent. The mosque stands in a congested courtyard (300 metres from Delhi

Wazir Khan's Mosque.

Gate) and follows the traditional form of a mosque. Its distinctive beauty lies primarily in the ceramic tile decoration which cover its minarets, walls, and doorways. The coloured tiles attain their brilliance from the mineral content of the glaze and under severe temperatures obtain an incomparable lustre and vibrance. Mesmerising turquoise, the deepest ink-blue, sunflower yellow, and new-leaf green along with shades of brick red and earth browns make up the colour scheme, while the motifs range from the tree of life to arabesques. The use of tile mosaic work in architecture was a heritage from Persia and was used only for a brief period in India before the Mughals made full use of the abundance of natural coloured stones and semiprecious gems to adorn their buildings. But the effect of the glow and radiance of tile decoration (as in Wazir Khan's Mosque) is bold and daring whereas the delicate inlaid stone-work on a monumental scale (as in the Taj Mahal) tends to be soft and diffused. What is remarkable is that both these very disparate styles were in vogue in the court of Shah Jahan.

WHAT'S IN THE NEIGHBOURHOOD

There is lots to see and do in Lahore but one of the prettiest places is the **Shalimar Gardens**, built by Shah Jahan outside the city (to the north-east), but now well within the city limits. The garden was not built near the river, as was the practice in other cities like Srinagar, but fed by a great canal constructed by the emperor to feed the Mughal capital. The garden consists of three terraces with water running through them. The lowest terrace is of the traditional *charbagh* variety while audience halls and residential palaces were constructed on the second terrace, so that when the emperor came to this faraway garden he and his harem could spend some time here amidst the scintillating waters, fountains, and orchards. We are told that Shah Jahan was so fond of this garden (which has lost much of its grandeur and sophistication) that he preferred to stay here rather than travel all the way to the Lahore Fort.

Along the Mall (now called Shahrah-e-Quaid-e-Azam) there are some lovely old colonial buildings in an elegant style: **Aitcheson College**, the **High Court**, the **GPO**, and the **Museum** with the Zamzama cannon in front. The **Museum** has a good collection of miniature paintings, manuscripts, and carpets. The Gandharan sculptures are priceless and include the **Fasting Buddha**, an extremely powerful image. The Buddha, undertaking vigorous penance, is depicted in this sculpture with every bone in his body, muscles, and blood-vessels visible through the skin, as if transparent. He is portrayed deep in meditation, his eyes lost in their dark cavities as if reaching inwards to find the meaning of life within his inner being.

HOW TO GET THERE

Lahore has an international airport connected to countries around the world. There are trains, buses, and an internal air service to other cities of Pakistan. Cars, three-wheeler rickshaws, and even horse carts can be hired for a tour of the city. The best time of the year to visit is in winter, between November and March, after which it gets very warm and dusty.

Shri Lanka

The island of Shri Lanka lies like a little emerald on the dark waters of the Indian Ocean. This lush tropical island (644 kilometres from the equator) has been the home of animals such as the elephant and the leopard, which inspired so much of the sculptural art of the region and can still be seen roaming wild in the jungles of the south-east. Exotic birds shared this jungle haven, and recent archaeological evidence confirms that this paradise has supported human life for over 10,000 years.

This tiny island (435 kilometres long and 225 kilometres at its maximum width) emerges from the sea on a bed of gneisses and schists, granite-layered with crystalline limestone and quartzites. Here and there great stone boulders erupt from their bed of green jungle and stand serene and powerful against the blue sky. The palace retreat of **Sigiriya** was built on a mighty stone boulder that protrudes 200 metres above the plains, and the colossal images of the Buddha at **Gal Vihara** owe some of their special beauty to the lovely streaked grey granite outcrop from which they were carved.

The hilly region of the island is concentrated in the centre of the southern part. From here nature worked for centuries to bring rich deposits of gems down to the lowlands and valleys. Ratnagiri, the city of gems, to the south-west of the island is still one of the largest producers of precious and semi-precious stones in the world: blood red rubies, sparkling blue sapphires, burnt yellow topaz, crystal-green alexandrites, royal purple amethysts, and quartzes.

The ancient inhabitants of the island who found the gems did not have to go far to sell them. For over two thousand years merchants braved the seas from the east and west to buy these coveted miracles of the earth. Favourable monsoon clouds that swept in from the south-west brought traders from India, Persia, and the Arab world many centuries before the Christian era. Roman coins have been found in several places on the island and trade links with China and south-east Asia continued for centuries. The island also found its place in the literature of the ancient world, Tambarpanni, the copper-red land, which the Greeks called Taprobane. The prefix Shri connotes all that is auspicious, gracious, and prosperous. Lanka, the kingdom of Ravana in the epic Ramayana, where the hero Rama came to rescue his wife, Sita. In the Hindu Puranas the island, Lanka was believed to be a tiny piece of Maha-Meru (the mountain that

(opposite) :
Seated Buddha,
Anuradhapura.

upholds the world) which had fallen into the sea. It was given to Kubera (lord of riches and wealth) who built a radiant jewel palace there in which he 'lived, was adored and worshipped by all'. Serendib (from which words like serenity and serendipity came to English) was the affectionate pseudonym given to this idyllic place by the seafaring Arab traders.

In the sixteenth century, over-sea trade interests brought the Portuguese and then Dutch to this gem and spice island. Shri Lanka was thus the first region in the subcontinent to be

colonised by the Europeans. First came the Portuguese colonists, then the Dutch, and finally the British who, after taking Kandy in 1815, ruled the whole island. Today, almost fifty years after attaining independence from foreign rule, a complex culture flourishes in the island with a mixed population of Sinhalese, Tamils, Moors, Burghers, Buddhists, Hindus, Muslims, and Christians.

The south and south-west areas are relatively wet, receiving two monsoons a year, and the tropical jungles have endowed the inhabitants with much-prized timber for building purposes. Even today domestic architecture, as in many parts of southern India (Kerala), is constructed of clay bricks, timber beams, and pillared verandahs, thatched or tiled sloping roofs.

Nineteenth century engraving, Anuradhapura.

The plains of the north and north-east are comparatively dry and it was here that one of the island's greatest contributions to civilisation were made—an effective, sustainable water system still in use today. Far back, at the beginning of the Christian era, rulers of the land realised the importance of water conservation and evolved a practical system of tanks and canals protected by forests and green gardens. For agricultural irrigation and domestic use the tanks stored rainwater that poured over the island during the brief rainy months of the year, manifesting the thought of the great twelfth century ruler Parakrama Bahu: 'Let not one drop of water reach the sea without first serving man.' The island has several rivers that flow down from the hills across the plains to the sea, but it was this network of tanks (*wewa*) that brought the greatest prosperity to the people. The perennial water source supported the magnificent building projects at **Anuradhapura**, **Polonnaruwa**, and **Sigiriya** centuries before the scene of action moved to the pretty hill capital of Kandy and later to the present-day west coast capital of Colombo.

Anuradhapura

This ancient capital was built in the middle of the northern plains of Shri Lanka. It is honoured today as the greatest Buddhist site on the island. The story of how the gentle religion of the Buddha came to the island begins more than two thousand years ago at a place (eleven kilometres east of Anuradhapura) called **Mihintale** or the mountain of Mahinda. Here, amidst the forested rocky hillside and mango trees, King Devanampiyatissa out hunting deer met prince Mahinda (Mahindra), son of the Mauryan Emperor Ashoka, who had travelled all the way from the eastern Gangetic plains of India bearing with him the Buddha's message of peace. To mark the the place where the Shri Lankan ruler was converted to the way of the Buddha, the lovely **Amba** (mango) **Sthala** (place) *dagoba* was constructed in the third century BC and all around it other religious structures were built. Nearby is the **Aradhana Gala** from where Mahinda is said to have offered his first sermon, and high above the Dagoba is a huge flat-topped boulder referred to as **Mahinda's Bed** where the pilgrim ambassador from India is believed to have slept and meditated. At the summit of the Mihintale Kanda is the large first century BC Maha Seya Dagoba where a strand of the Buddha's hair is said to be enshrined. From here one can get a superb view of the plains of Anuradhapura and its magnificent dagobas.

View of Mihintale.

After the Buddha's death, according to sacred Buddhist scriptures, his bodily remains (*saririka*s) were divided and enshrined in various places in artificially-created funerary mounds that came to be called stupas. The great stupas of **Sanchi** (Madhya Pradesh, India) and the now extant one at Amaravati (Andhra Pradesh, India) follow a pattern of development from enormous solid hemispherical earth mounds that were sheathed with stone slabs. Around the earth mound was constructed a protective fencing. Since the stupa was solid, ritual circumambulation of the holy relic was performed by entering the fencing gateways built at the four cardinal points and walking around the circular path keeping the right shoulder always closest to the stupa. The entire stupa acquired symbolic meaning. The round earth mound, which carried in its hidden mass the 'seed of dharma', the relics of the Buddha or a saint, the finial on the stupa a square fence with the symbolic tiered umbrella of dharmic protection pointing the way to the steps of heaven and salvation. In Shri Lanka the stupa is called a dagoba, derived by combining two Sanskrit words *dhatu*, relic and garbha, womb chamber, and carries the same import of meaning and symbolic significance. It is believed that the most sacred dagobas in Shri Lanka do actually contain the body relics—hair, bone, or tooth of the Buddha—which arrived on the island in mysterious and miraculous ways. A typical Sinhalese dagoba has three parts, representing the three planes of existence, set on a circular mandala ground plan. The moulded base or platform, the earth mound that evolved into poetic forms: the bell-shape, bubble shape, the lotus shape, and the rice mound shape. Above this solid mass rose the finial, a condensation of the harmika railing and the umbrella into a compact stepped (the thirteen steps to salvation) abstract form. The four cardinal points were often guarded, in a manner similar to the Amaravati stupa, by pillared shrines into which were added images of the Dhyani Buddhas who protect space and project the spread of Dharma and wisdom. The entire stupa

Plan of
Anuradhapura.

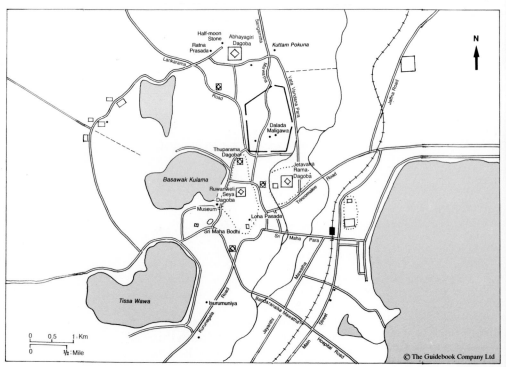

was enclosed by a railing which provided space between the railing wall and stupa body for circumambulation by the pilgrims. This space could be filled with concentric circles of pillars that support a roof around the dagoba and the structure was referred to as a *vatadage*. Apart from these supreme religious Buddhist structures, there were viharas (*vihares*) in which the monastic order could live in accordance with the Buddha's philosophic attack on the abominable caste system. 'Just as rivers flow into the ocean leaving behind their various identities, so do various castes and classes form a single community when they join the order.' The best and oldest examples of Buddhist architecture in Shri Lanka are to be found at Anuradhapura.

Anuradhapura served as the capital of the ancient kingdoms of Shri Lanka for nearly 1400 years and was ruled by more than 250 kings. Today the township is dominated by the **Tissa Wewa** to the south and the huge **Basawak Kulama Tank** just north of it. The ancient monuments of Anuradhapura are aligned in a great arch around these waterscapes. The Tissa Wewa is believed to have been built by the newly converted king Devanampiyatissa in the third century BC and served as the major source of drinking water for the town.

To the south of the Wewa is the **Isurumuniya Rock Temple**, jammed between boulders of rock containing some exquisite sculptures of lovers and embracing couples. Nearby is a group of ponds, two of which are decorated with playful relief sculptures of elephants frolicking in a lotus pond. The thick growth of lotus flowers pushed about by the enormous elephants are reminiscent of similar scenes to be found in the painted murals of **Ajanta** and the bas-reliefs at **Sanchi** (India). It's those smiling elephant eyes that are unforgettable: a snatch of humour so characteristic of early Buddhist art in the subcontinent.

Today the vast expanse of ruins at Anuradhapura has been fenced off and preserved as a sacred relic of the past, but a few areas are still the centre of active worship. Most honoured amongst them all is the sacred **Shri Maha Bodhi Tree**. This pipal tree with delicate heart-shaped leaves has grown from a sapling brought to the island in the early centuries of the pre-Christian era from **Bodh Gaya** (India), from the very tree under which the Buddha meditated and attained nirvana twenty-five centuries ago. The Shri Maha Bodhi Tree is a sacred symbol of the teachings of the Buddha, of the need for meditation and discipline. For the human animal, unlike any other species on this planet, is ruled by greed and lack of self-restraint. The key to eternal joy and freedom from this endless cycle of desire was found by the Buddha under the Bo tree. He asserted a powerful positive belief in human beings, 'that no god can do anything for humankind, salvation [*moksha*, nirvana] can only be attained through education, self realisation, self-conquest and self-emancipation', thereby leaving us the masters of our lives, the protectors of this planet.

The Shri Maha Bodhi Tree is enclosed by gold-plated fencing and a platform, the *bodhighara*, around which many young shoots have taken root. Pilgrims come from far and near not to worship but to honour this tree, offering it flowers, incense, and water. It is after all the tree of wisdom (bodhi), reminding us that the onus of salvation lies entirely within ourselves.

Ruwanweli Seya Dagoba, Anuradhapura.

Just north of the Maha Bodhi Tree is the **Loha Prasada**, a mass of 1600 granite columns laid out in neat rows of 40 by 40. This is all that remains of a magnificent nine-storey residence for monks who attended on the Bodhi Tree. It was originally built in the second century BC and had a thousand rooms, possibly built like a terraced pavilion with diminishing storeys not unlike the Dharmaraja Ratha of **Mahabalipuram** (Tamil Nadu, India). The pillars were sheathed in metal plates studded with gems or covered in plaster and painted; the roof had copper tiles which gave it its name: Brazen (*loha*) palace (*prasada*). West of this graveyard of columns is the former British residency, beside the Basawak Kulama Tank, now converted into the Archaeological Museum.

North-east of the museum is the great **Ruwanweli Seya Dagoba**, a second century BC stupa. Each of the four cardinal points is marked by a gateway and the dagoba is held up above the ground by a ring of sculpted stone elephants who, according to mythology, carry the weight of the world on their reliable shoulders. Scattered around the monument are stone images of the Buddha and the ruler Dutugemunu, who is credited with having started building the Dagoba in his lifetime (though it was incomplete when he died in 144 BC).

Directly north of the Ruwanweli Seya is the oldest stupa on the island, the **Thuparama Dagoba**. It is the oldest for it is believed to enshrine the collar-bone of the Buddha, a holy relic brought by Mahinda as a gift from Emperor Ashoka to Devanampiyatissa who enshrined it here. This third century BC dagoba was further renovated in subsequent centuries and enclosed with a ring of wooden, and later stone, pillars as a vatadage. Its bell-shaped form and whitewashed appearance are a result of later-day reconstructions.

Most magnificent in physical size and concept is the **Jetavanarama Dagoba**. Its gigantic earth mound is nearly 122 metres high with a diameter at the base of over 113 metres, making it almost as enormous as the pyramids of Egypt and certainly the largest Buddhist structure in the subcontinent. Nearby are some ruined monasteries, palaces, and the ancient Temple of the Tooth, **Dalada Maligawa**.

Further north is another complex of monasteries and dagobas. The most intriguing is the **Abhayagiri Dagoba**, the earth mound (literally, with grass and scrubs growing out of its immense hemispherical form). This dagoba was created under the instruction of King Abhaya in 88 BC and reconstructed in subsequent centuries to its present height of 110 metres with an equal diameter. North-west of this grand dagoba is the **Ratna Prasada**, the Gem Palace, a monastery of enormous pillars built in the second century, and guarded by a lovely sculptured naga king holding the auspicious pot of plenty, flowing over with floral branches of prosperity. Nearby is the Queen's pavillion at the entrance of which is the loveliest moonstone in Shri Lanka. The entrance to Buddhist and Hindu homes, religious buildings, and ritual areas was considered an important architectural feature. The doorway leads men and gods into the building, and keeps evil forces outside. It is therefore not unusual to find entrance-ways, the floor in front, the door-jambs, and the lintel above elaborately adorned with auspicious signs and symbols. Here the steps descend to the ground in a series of horizontal planes, the wide, sweeping area before the first step paved with a semi-circular (hence moon) stone. This stone was carved, in accordance with its circular form, with a series of concentric panels carrying the usual symbols of good fortune and spiritual well-being radiating out from the central hub of the sacred lotus flower, the supreme symbol of purity and goodness. There are ringed processions of cheerful creatures—the mighty elephant, the swift horse, the loyal hard-working bull, the gentle deer and the hansa, aquatic birds—who can distinguish good from evil.

East of the Abhayagiri Dagoba is one of the loveliest water pools in the area, called the **Kuttam Pokuna** or the twin ponds, believed to be third century ritual bathing pools for monks. The smaller of the two ponds is fed by water that flows dramatically through the gaping mouths of mythical creatures. The larger pond, almost twice the size of its twin, is similarly surrounded by moulded, stepped embankments and the sheer geometry of the tanks are poetic.

WHAT'S IN THE NEIGHBOURHOOD

Mihintale, eleven kilometres east of Anuradhapura, is a dramatic walk up a great rock site, which marks the introduction of

Buddhism into the island. Thirty-two kilometres south-east of Anuradhapura is the magnificent fifth century, 13 metre (second tallest in the island) standing **Aukana Buddha** figure in a brick shelter. The Buddha statue carries many of the characteristic features of Sinhalese Buddhist sculpture which had, quite early in its historical development, broken away and synthesised many stylistic traits from the Indian prototype.

The Buddha stands serene and straight with feet firmly on the ground. The size and proportions are such that there is little in India that even matches the awe-inspiring grandeur of these Shri Lankan Buddha images. As in Buddhist images at Sarnath and Mathura, the Buddha wears a single piece of cloth draped around the body leaving one shoulder bare and the other covered so that the cloth falls in great folds from the left shoulder. The folds of the garment in the Buddhist Gandharan school (north-western region of the subcontinent) were depicted realistically in accordance with the Greco-Roman tradition. In Sarnath the artist treated the cloth as if it were a veil, revealing the pulsating warmth of the body below; and the flexed relaxed posture of the Buddha was almost feminine in its gracefulness. In the Aukana image the folds are like a decorative pattern, rising in a precise sweep of waves bunched at the left shoulder and falling again like a sheet over the arm.

HOW TO GET THERE

Anuradhapura is 206 kilometres north-east of Colombo. There are trains, cars, and buses that ply this lap of the route of the cultural triangle. There are a few guest-houses and hotels in which to stay overnight. Anuradhapura is a 101 kilometre journey from **Polonnaruwa** via a centre point rest-cum-hotel complex at **Habarana** where you could base yourself for day trips to both these sites. The beautiful city of **Kandy**, via the rock-cut caves of **Dambulla**, is 138 kilometres south of Anuradhapura.

Polonnaruwa

After the island of Shri Lanka was attacked by the forces of the Tamil king, the great Rajaraja Chola, in the eleventh century, the capital of the new kingdom was set up in Polonnaruwa and Anuradhapura was left to ruin. When the Cholas were overthrown there was a resurgence of Buddhism and some effort went into preserving the beauty of Anuradhapura, but the new city was the centre of all creative attention. Polonnaruwa continued to be occupied from the eleventh to the fourteenth centuries with additions and enlargements made by each successive generation. The greatest of all was the Sinhalese ruler Parakrama Bahu I (AD 1164-97) who built the spectacular artificial lake called **Parakrama Samudra** (the sea of Parakrama) which feeds acres of paddy-fields in the area.

The Quadrangle
Some of the most beautiful monuments of Polonnaruwa are clustered in an enclosure called **Dalada Maluwa**, the **Quadrangle** on the east bank of the mighty inland sea. Entrance is through a gateway, possibly of two storeys when complete, equipped with a low basin for washing the feet before entry into the sacred complex. A large circular building to the left is the remains of an attractive Vatadage, possibly built before Polonnaruwa was made the capital. The circular sanctuary stands on a base, and above rises the inner platform of the second terrace, its podium carved with a frieze of lions and animated dwarfs. Above this rises the ornamental railing of the pradakshina path, punctuated by pillars that must have supported the roof of the vatadage. This area is reached by a short flight of stairs at the four cardinal points leading up to the now ruined brick wall of the low stupa shrine with images of the Buddha looking out towards the four directions. The Vatadage is a beautiful structure, representative of all that is lovely about Sinhalese—Buddhist architecture: the simplicity of its massive proportions, the active play of decorative elements with plain abstract surfaces, and the ingenuous grandeur of the overall concept.

Right opposite the circular Vatadage is the **Hatadage**, the House of the Eight Relics, which once enshrined on the top floor important relics of the Buddha. It is a unique structure entirely built of finely cut and well-fitted blocks of dressed stone. The podium on which it stands is guarded by a line of seated lions. The walls of the low building are plain except for a sunken relief pattern of hansas and an inscription of King Nissanka Malla. To the east of the structure is the 'stone book', the **Gal Pota**, an inscription by the same king regarding his victorious military expeditions in India.

North of the Hatadage is the Chapter House and beside it, in the corner, is the **Sat Mahal Prasad**, the seven-storeyed palace. It is like a classical, pyramidal, terraced form symbolic of Mount Meru, representing the successive hierarchic configurations of the divine mountain. The building is closely related to the temples of Angkor of Cambodia and those of Thailand.

On the opposite side of the Hatadage are other equally intriguing buildings. The **Atadage**, the home of the Tooth Relic and, next to it in the corner, is a platform which once housed the figure of the reclining Buddha, and beside it is the **Lata Mandapaya**. This hall (mandap) served king Nissanka Malla as a congenial setting from which to listen to the chanting of prayers. Throughout the Buddhist world the lotus flower, growing on its long stem above the stagnant waters, is a symbol of purity and grace; a reminder that we too should remain pure like the flower though surrounded by slime and inertia. The lotus flower usually appears on the capital of pillars, as motifs for wall sculptures and paintings, and as the pedestal of purity that raises the divine Buddha above the realm of gross existence. Here, at the Lata Mandapaya, the long shafts of the pillars are fashioned like tapering curvaceous lotus stems rising out of the floor to support a wooden roof that no longer exists. This gallery of carved granite pillars makes one feel as if one were a diminutive lilliputian walking the waters of a pond where giant, curling lotus stems hoist the flower buds above like a canopy to capture the sunlight of wisdom.

In the south-west corner of the Quadrangle is the **Thuparama**, an Image House or shrine. The principal image is enclosed within a square chamber, but the outer walls of the building with little niches, pilasters, and stucco work are like a distant

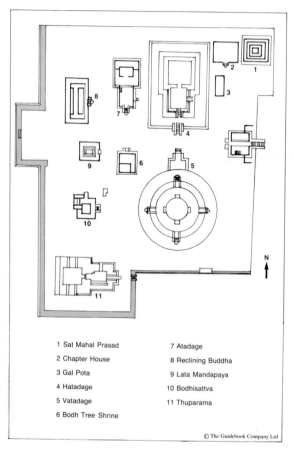

1 Sat Mahal Prasad
2 Chapter House
3 Gal Pota
4 Hatadage
5 Vatadage
6 Bodh Tree Shrine

7 Atadage
8 Reclining Buddha
9 Lata Mandapaya
10 Bodhisattva
11 Thuparama

© The Guidebook Company Ltd

Plan of Dalada Maluwa, Polonnaruwa.

relative of the Chola temples of Tamil Nadu of the eleventh century. Many more such examples can be seen in the **Hindu Temples** north of the Quadrangle.

To the south are the remains of the **Citadel**, the inner capital. The **Royal Palace** of Parakrama Bahu was possibly a mighty seven-storeyed brick and timber structure with palatial rooms, audience halls, and chambers. Opposite the palace is the **Council Chamber** and what remains of this triple-terraced structure. A lively frieze runs around the building and the parade of elephants is especially charming. There are two flights of stairs leading up to the main chamber and the entrance is marked by a decorative, auspicious moonstone of concentric circles, guarded by mythical creatures and grimacing (grinning?) lions. The long hall is pillared and the ministers would have sat in rows, their designated positions determined by status and postion.

From the Council Chamber there is a path which leads to the **Kumara Pokuna**, a stepped pond believed to be the royal bath fed by underground conduits from the Parakrama Samudra.

Outside the royal citadel and administrative area, moving northward, are other religious structures of ancient Polonnaruwa. **Menik Vihara** has a ruined dagoba, an image house for Buddhist statues. **Rankot Vihara** has the largest dagoba (55 metres high) in Polonnaruwa and beside it is a tank for the monks to bathe in. Further north is the amazing **Lankatilaka**, an enormous image house (52 metres long and 17 metres high). It is an important example of an architectural setting built for colossal images of worship. At the far end of the hall stands a brick image of the standing Buddha; a vaulted roof would once have covered the sanctum. The central hall in front of the image was plastered and still carries traces of brightly-coloured murals on the walls. The large open hall offered enough space for communal worship and the performance of rituals. Perhaps this is what the original site of **Gal Vihara** would have looked like.

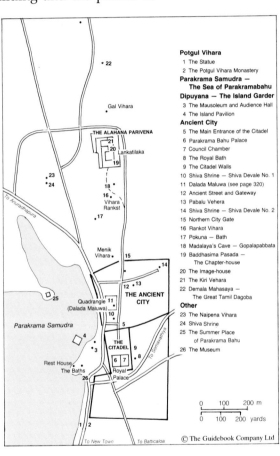

Plan of Polonnaruwa.

Potgul Vihara
1 The Statue
2 The Potgul Vihara Monastery
Parakrama Samudra —
    The Sea of Parakramabahu
Dipuyana — The Island Garden
3 The Mausoleum and Audience Hall
4 The Island Pavilion
Ancient City
5 The Main Entrance of the Citadel
6 Parakrama Bahu Palace
7 Council Chamber
8 The Royal Bath
9 The Citadel Walls
10 Shiva Shrine — Shiva Devale No. 1
11 Dalada Maluwa (see page 320)
12 Ancient Street and Gateway
13 Pabalu Vehera
14 Shiva Shrine — Shiva Devale No. 2
15 Northern City Gate
16 Rankot Vihara
17 Pokuna — Bath
18 Madalaya's Cave — Gopalapabbata
19 Baddhasima Pasada —
    The Chapter-house
20 The Image-house
21 The Kiri Vehera
22 Demala Mahasaya —
    The Great Tamil Dagoba
Other
23 The Naipena Vihara
24 Shiva Shrine
25 The Summer Place
    of Parakrama Bahu
26 The Museum

© The Guidebook Company Ltd

Gal Vihara

It is here, a few kilometres north of Polonnaruwa, that you can see the largest sculptural masterpieces of Shri Lanka. The statues are carved out of a long granite wall which forms the backdrop. Along the rock face there are tell-tale marks where wooden beams upheld the brick and timber structure of the image house in which these enormous images were probably enshrined. There are four magnificent images carved out of the rock, each more special than the next. The southern-most depicts the Buddha seated in lotus pose with his palms resting on his lap, one over the other. The face of the Buddha reflects all the tranquillity of a person deep in meditation, and around the head of curls is a halo of light sparkling with the radiance of inner wisdom. The next image is within a rock-cut cave where the seated Buddha is surrounded by various deities, including Brahma and Vishnu. In the rock-cut cave there are the remains of mural paintings that would have brightened the interiors of the rock shelter and glowed in the light of oil lamps. The third figure is the Standing Buddha with his arms folded across his chest. It is an unusual and rare pose.

Standing Buddha, Gal Vihara.

Possibly the artists of Gal Vihara were creating in the drama of these gigantic rock images the moving tale of the Buddha who attained nirvana after years of meditation and was honoured by the gods for his superhuman achievement in conquering desire. Then how he walked and contemplated on what he should do with his heaven-born wisdom, his decision to preach and teach the world that Buddhahood is everyone's birthright. Finally, the last stage, when the Buddha attains complete release from the endless cycle of life (at the time of his death), the Parinirvana, the great enlightenment. The last statue is colossal, as if the size is indicative of the magnitude of the concept and depicts the (14 metre) figure of the reclining Buddha. The Buddha lies on his side with his head resting on one palm on a bolster that sags slightly under the weight. The other arm follows the curve of his body and his feet are held together (to attention), capturing the great moment before physical death and eternal life.

WHAT'S IN THE NEIGHBOURHOOD
Further north from Gal Vihara are some interesting sites. There is the **Demala Mahaseya** where Parakrama Bahu attempted to build 'the largest dagoba in the world' but didn't. Nearby is the **Jetavana Monastery** complex with the lovely **Lotus Bath**, a tiered, stepped tank in the shape of a many-petalled flower. Also within this much ruined complex is the **Tivanka Image House**, sometimes called the Northern Temple, with a huge image of the Buddha in the very Indian triple-flexed pose, and some of the oldest mural paintings in the island of Shri Lanka adorn its walls.

HOW TO GET THERE
Polonnaruwa is 216 kilometres from Colombo via the lovely rock-cut caves of Dambulla. Habarane is 45 kilometres from Polonnaruwa and is a convenient half-way place at which to stay. Anuradhapura is a 101 kilometre journey from Polunnaruwa via the half-way point of Harbarana.

Parinirvana of the
Buddha, Gal Vihara.

Sigiriya

Imagine nature's beauty and the artist's sense of drama and its converse: the drama inherent in nature and the artist's creation of beauty. Set them together in one site and that is Sigiriya. The sight is spectacular, to say the least. A high rock boulder rises like a large mushroom 182 metres above the plains. It was this solitary outcrop with nothing nearby that overlooks or overshadows it, that was chosen as the site for a fifth century palace abode, one of the loveliest in the world. The climb up to the palace on the flat top of the boulder is a difficult one and the engineering skills required to realise such a project are quite mind-boggling. It was a fitting dwelling place for Buddhist monks who, in accordance with their tradition, sought out lonely retreats for silent prayers and meditation.

Then came fanfare and royal commotion. Kasyapa, the eldest son of the reigning ruler of the fifth century, feared that his younger brother might inherit the throne. His younger brother, Mogallan, was the son of a royal mother while Kasyapa's mother was a commoner. Kasyapa took matters into his own hands, imprisoned his father, whom he later had murdered, and frightened his brother into escaping to India. Alone and unchallenged, but wary of trouble, Kasyapa set about constructing his new palace on the exalted lonely outcrop of Sigiriya. The project took seven years to complete and in AD 477 Kasyapa installed himself in this 'pie in the sky'. Only to lose everything eleven years later to his brother Mogallan who returned from India and defeated him in battle near the modern village of Habarane. Mogallan returned the capital to Anuradhapura, leaving the monks and nature to look after this beautiful Lion Rock. Kasyapa has been branded by history as a 'parricide' and 'a mad genius'. A visit to Sigiriya only confirms that there must have been something exceptional and singular about a king who ventured to live there.

To the west of the Sigiriya rock face are the **Water Gardens**, a series of terraced landscaped ponds and fountains. The fountains play on the power of gravity and water is forced out from the moats on either side. From above, the view from the palace of the Water Gardens and the green plains below is breathtaking, the work of an ingenious engineering wizard.

Then comes the approach to the rock face; halfway up the boulder is an overhanging rock pocket. The walls of the **Gallery** have been plastered and adorned with fifth century mural

(opposite) :
Entrance to Sigiriya.

paintings, the likes of which are hard to find. These world-renowned paintings of sensuous, bare-breasted flower-girls or sky nymphs have been compared to the murals of **Ajanta** (India). The technique and concept of mural painting at both sites are similar. The drawing was apparently almost freehand, for there are many corrections and changes in the position of hands and body posture to be seen through the overpaint. There is also something truly original about this work. The female forms are gifted with heavy, nubile breasts, tiny waists 'hardly greater than the girth of the neck', and long tapering arms like graceful tendrils of creepers. Their perfect oval faces have heavy-lidded sensuous eyes, sharp aquiline noses, full lips, and heads encompassed with elaborate crowns and flowers in the hair. The bright play of colours and bold drawings are truly a mark of the sophistication of early Sinhalese painting. The subject of the frieze is the parade of these opulently jewelled celestial maidens advancing in pairs or singly, to shower sprays of flowers onto the approaching dignitaries (of whom you are one). Today only a few of the maidens have survived the two thousand five hundred year journey in time. There can be no doubt about the celestial origin of the ladies for they are swimming in clouds, in the paintings the heavenly mist rising up to their waists. There can be no scepticism about their sensuous impact either for further up the picture

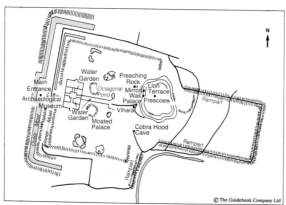

Plan of Sigiriya.
Below: Water
Gardens, Sigiriya.

gallery is the **Mirror Wall** with burnished, plastered walls covered with poetic graffiti recording the songs of praise of early visitors who were struck by the beauty of the celestial creatures:

> Ladies like you make men pour out their hearts,
> You also thrill the body, making its hair stiffen with desire.

The picture gallery leads out onto a wide open terrace. Here the rock face was carved in the shape of a crouching lion. The massive paws frame the staircase from which the ascent to the plateau palace begins. The colossal sphinx-like form of the lion (sinha, hence Sigiriya) collapsed long ago. But the idea of a lion entrance and the palace standing atop the lion's back is wonderful, with the faintest touch of the bizarre.

The plateau on top of the hill covers an expanse of over four acres and consists of a ruined **Summer Palace** where you can see the plots of rooms and stately halls. At one end is a magnificent water tank and other storage reservoirs.

A small Archaeological Museum is situated near the main entrance to the site.

HOW TO GET THERE

Sigiriya is 67 kilometres from Polonnaruwa. There is a rest-house near the site and a few hotels have come up to accommodate visitors who wish to stay, but most people come here as part of a one day tour.

Most visitors arrive at Colombo, the capital of Shri Lanka, which has an international and domestic airport. Colombo is an interesting place to stay with wonderful hotels, sites and museums. Anuradhapura, Polonnaruwa and Sigiriya are the three points of the tourist golden triangle. There are regular tours and tourist facilities for these sites. Anuradhapura is 206 kilometres from Colombo, and 101 kilometres from Polunnaruwa and Sigiriya is 67 kilometres from Polonnaruwa. There is so much to see at these three sites that is worth budgeting for lots of time to enjoy the monuments and to take it all in.

Painting from Sigiriya.

Travel Information

Travelling in the Tropics is a wonderful experience. The best time to travel is generally between October and April or as indicated at the end of each chapter. Advice on preparing for a trip, health matters, clothing, and travel tips are common to all the countries of the subcontinent.

How to get there
All the countries of the subcontinent, with the exception of Bhutan, are linked by international flights from North America, Europe, West Asia, South-East Asia, and the Far East. Bombay and Karachi also have flight connections with Africa.

Within the countries of this region, the major cities are connected by the various national carriers: for instance Royal Nepal Airlines Corporation (RNAC) have flights from Karachi (Pakistan); Bombay, New Delhi, and Calcutta (India); Dhaka (Bangladesh); and Colombo (Shri Lanka) to Kathmandu. Likewise Indian Airlines, Pakistan International Airlines (PIA), and Air Lanka have flights from their respective major cities to the neighbouring capitals. Bhutan's fledgling national airline, Druk Air, has flights to Paro from New Delhi, Kathmandu (Nepal), and Calcutta.

Internal Travel
Both national and private airlines provide a good network of flights and reasonable frequency within the various countries of the subcontinent. Indian Airlines prides itself on being the second largest domestic airline in the world, but its services have recently been augmented by new, privately-owned, internal airlines. Likewise, private carriers are operating both major trunk routes and smaller feeder services in Nepal and Pakistan.

Airline security in the subcontinent is generally strict and thorough. What can be taken on board as hand luggage often varies with international convention. Batteries of any type are not allowed: they are often removed from cameras. In some airports the local police security disallow lap-top computers, taperecorders, radios, and pocket knives. All hand baggage is X-rayed but most airports allow film to be inspected by hand. Some airports, such as Bombay, Colombo, Karachi, and Delhi also X-ray checked-in baggage.

The extensive rail network in the subcontinent makes this one of the most convenient, economical, and enjoyable ways of travelling within the various countries. Pakistan Railways operates good trains on major trunk routes but one of the great experiences of travel in the region is a journey on Indian Railways. The vast network and frequency of trains makes travel not only pleasurable (we hope) but in many cases most suitable for reaching some of the more remote sites in the country. Vijayanagar in central Karnataka, for example, is only 13 kilometres from Hospet which is connected by an extremely convenient overnight train from Bangalore. The return is also overnight. Likewise, Mohenjodaro in southern Pakistan is only eight kilometres from the local station, and the overnight train from Karachi is met by horse-drawn tongas for the pleasant one hour journey to the site in the early morning. In Shri Lanka the train service is more limited, and there are no passenger trains in Nepal.

In all parts of the region the most direct way of reaching many of the sites detailed in this book is by road. All areas have bus services of varying standards of comfort and efficiency. In many cases this is the only way of reaching a site by public transport. For long distances a combination of train and bus travel is the most economical and convenient. Long bus journeys are generally uncomfortable. On many long routes 'video coaches' operate, subjecting all the passengers to the conductors favourite film. Some state transport corporations and tourist organisations operate air-conditioned buses on trunk routes and stop every two to three hours at roadside restaurants. It is advisable to book in advance for longer journeys. A few travel companies and hotels organise round-trip excursions by coach to nearby towns and sites. For instance, many hotels and private agencies in Delhi operate same day return trips to Agra and Fatehpur Sikri; although both cities deserve more time than these introductory tours provide.

Car rental in the region takes two forms. The facility to hire self-driven cars is fairly recent and is limited to major cities. Hiring a car with driver is not only cheaper but generally more convenient as the driver often doubles as a guide, and this is possible in almost any town although the standards of maintenance in some of the smaller towns might raise a few questions or eyebrows.

Visas

All countries in the region require tourists to have a valid passport and most nationals require visas to enter each of the countries. If spending a long time in the region and planning to visit more than one country, a multiple-entry visa is advisable and best sought when making the original application.

Time Zones

Pakistan is five hours ahead of GMT. India, despite its size, is a single zone 5 ½ hours ahead of GMT, as is Shri Lanka. Nepal is 5 ¾ hours ahead of GMT, Bhutan six hours.

Security

While extremely wealthy in its cultural heritage there are many poor people in the subcontinent, so be kind to them and don't flash your wealth or patronise them. Begging should not be encouraged. Travel in South Asia is, happily, still remarkably safe. Money, passports, tickets, and valuables should be kept on one's person all the time. Don't leave items lying unlocked in hotel bedrooms or public places that might invite attention. Travelling by train or bus demands special alertness.

A few special precautions are advisable. It is best, for instance, to avoid those areas in the subcontinent that are facing political difficulties.

Health

Everything thrives in the tropics so a few precautions are necessary for travel in the subcontinent. A few simple precautions for personal health:

Yellow fever certificates are required for all travellers arriving from Africa, Latin America, and Papua New Guinea. Other vaccinations, although not officially required, are advisable. Typhoid, polio, and tetanus are important but a meningitis vaccine is required only when visiting infected areas, information about which will be available with local travel clinics. Infectious hepatitis can largely be avoided by taking a gamma globulin injection just before leaving for the subcontinent. While cholera is endemic in Bangladesh and there are occasional outbreaks elsewhere in the region, immunisation is not mandatory. An anti-rabies vaccine is now available and advisable if travelling off the beaten track. A booster or fresh course of injections is necessary if bitten by a dog or any wild animal.

Malaria is widespread throughout the region. Opinion on what pills to take is constantly being revised, so advice from a local travel clinic must be sought before starting a journey. It is important to begin the course before arriving and continue it for at least six weeks after leaving an infected area.

Most modern medicines are available over the counter in drugstores but it is wise to travel with a reserve stock. If any prescription drugs are required, bring enough for the duration of the trip. It is sometimes best to keep two stocks—one in hand baggage and the other in checked-in baggage.

A small health kit should include a remedy for upset stomachs, some antiseptic cream, lip salve, mosquito-repellant cream, suntan lotion, water-purifying tablets in case bottled water is not available, antiseptic lotion, Elastoplast, etc. Many travellers develop minor problems on their second or third day as a result of 'climate shock' due to heat exhaustion rather than contaminated food and water, but if an upset stomach persists seek medical advice. Many people advise drinking a lot of fluids (boiled and filtered water with a little salt and sugar) and keeping to a diet of rice and yoghurt for a couple of days.

The standard advice is to drink only boiled, bottled, or mineral water, eat unpealed fruit, avoid fresh salads and, despite the delicious cuisine of the subcontinent, go easy for the first few days.

Accommodation

The range of accommodation throughout the subcontinent is impressive. The grand palace hotels of Udaipur and Jaipur are matched by great hotels built at the turn of the century such as The Galle Face in Colombo, the Taj Mahal in Bombay, and The Grand in Calcutta. Newer, modern five star and deluxe properties have been built in most major cities over the past three decades, giving the region some of the best hotels in the world; and at prices that often match those elsewhere in the world.

In smaller towns the choice is more limited. Moderately priced hotels are generally good value. In some areas of India, such as Rajasthan, a new category of Heritage Hotels has been created to list converted family homes, old forts, castles, and similar properties. Lodges, often run by government tourist development corporations, are generally good value. During the peak season, which for most of the subcontinent is from October to April, advance reservations are advisable. Budget hotels are available in most towns and YMCAs or YWCAs operate in the major towns of India, Pakistan, and Shri Lanka.

In almost all large towns, near railway stations, and the international airports there are touts on the lookout for an unsuspecting tourist. It is advisable to make travel arrangements only after checking out the various options and seek advice from hotel travel counters.

Communications

Most towns have direct-dial facilities for both local and international calls. Many markets now have privately run public call booths which are extremely reasonable. Most hotels however mark up their communication tariffs by at least 100 percent, and sometimes up to 250 percent, so the rates should be checked before use. Almost all hotels now have fax facilities and many still have telex lines.

The postal service varies but it is generally secure and reliable. Postcards and letters can take up to two weeks to reach Europe and parcels take their own time. Sending a registered parcel from any of the countries in the region is a lengthy process. Customs forms are usually required and occasionally a copy of the invoice of whatever is being sent.

Most major international courier companies and many local ones operate in the subcontinent, offering both domestic and international services.

Photography

The subcontinent is a photographer's paradise.

Taking photographs of airports, railway stations, bridges, military installations, and from the air is prohibited in all countries of South Asia.

You can freely photograph all monuments mentioned in the book with a hand-held camera. However, permission is required to take photographs in museums and for the use of a tripod and flash at most sites. Monuments with fragile, ancient mural paintings like Ajanta need to be especially protected from flash photography that damage them. So even if you can take a photograph of these paintings, and the guard on duty is not looking, please don't.

Special permission for professional photography (with tripod and flash), movie camera, or video is obtained from the Pakistan Archaeological Department (Islamabad) and The Archaeological Survey of India (next to the National Museum, Jan Path, New Delhi). Permission cannot generally be given at the site. When taking photographs of people use the standard 'do unto others what you don't mind being done to yourself/ your wife/ family'. People in the subcontinent are kind and forgiving, and do not mind having their photograph taken, but care must be taken in Muslim areas and at bathing ghats.

Colour print film is now readily available in all major cities of the region but the price and vintage varies. Most hotel shops are more expensive than the nearby market. Only a limited range of slide film is generally available and Kodachrome only rarely. Bring a good supply of film: some photographers suggest at least twice the amount you expect to use. If travelling in summer keep film cool. Film left over at the end of a trip makes a welcome present for someone who has been of assistance.

Visiting the monuments

Most monuments (under the care of the respective Archaeological departments) are open from sunrise to sunset. There is usually a small token entrance fee (not outrageous rates as one has in Europe) to the monument/museum. Archaeological

Museums in Pakistan and India are closed on Fridays. Many monuments tend to be crowded on public holidays and weekends. To enjoy the monument be prepared to walk, so dress comfortably, carry the minimum (bottled water), wear good walking shoes, and go with an enquiring and receptive mind.

Etiquette

The subcontinent is governed by tradition which is both ancient and sacred. This is the land of the Buddha and Mahavir, the doctrine of ahimsa and Islam, the spiritual rather than the physical. So give all your leather articles (belts, boots, bags) a rest and wear cotton and natural materials for a change. To stay cool and elegant cover yourself with light cotton clothes, protecting your limbs (long sleeves, full trousers, full length skirts) from the grace of the sun. People tend to cover their heads from the glare and the heat. Travelling between October and April in the daytime is relatively warm while nights tend to be chilly. Northern India, Nepal, Pakistan, and Bhutan are cold from mid-December through to mid-February when warmer clothing is required even during the day.

Respect and modesty are appreciated throughout the region. Most people are extremely warm and travellers should not be alarmed by questions about their personal life, family, job, or income. Many of the monuments mentioned in this guide were at one time a place of worship, or are still in worship, or are monuments of international importance and require respect. Please do not smoke, eat, or drink within the precincts of the monuments and dress modestly and respectfully.

When visiting a temple, mosque, or gurudwara it is important to leave all footwear outside and walk barefoot. Some shrines also ask for leather belts and bags to be left outside with an attendant. In Sikh gurudwaras and mosques during prayer the head should be covered. You may make an offering to the shrine of flowers which can be purchased near the monument.

Glossary of Architectural terms

amalaka stylised fruit associated with regeneration, incorporated at the summit of northern Indian *shikhara*s as a support for the *kalash*.
antarala passage or vestibule leading to the sanctum of temple.
ashrama monastic retreat.

bagh (Arabic/Persian) garden, usually formal, as in *charbagh*; a garden subdivided into four equal sections.
bahal monastery; term for *vihara* in Nepal.
baoli well; step well; elaborate underground labyrinthine water system.

chaitya sacred spot or object; shrine with *stupa*.
chakra wheel.
char four: Also *charbagh* four part garden; *charminar*, building with four minarets.
chhatri canopy or kiosk.
chorten funerary reliquary.
chowk court; courtyard; square.

dagoba derived from Sanskrit for relic chamber or *stupa*.
dargah (Persian) precinct, especially shrine of holy man.
darshan vision of divine grace; pilgrimage; homage.
darwaza (Persian) door, gate, or portal, especially of monumental proportions, usually prefixed with a name, e.g Dilli Darwaza meaning the Gate that leads to Delhi.
daulat khana (Persian) literally 'abode of majesty': king's palace enclosure; treasury.
dharamsala the home of dharma; a monastic abode.
dhvaja standard, banner, or flag; hence, *dhvaja stambha*, flag-staff.
dikpala regent of the cardinal directions of space; hence *ashta dikpalas*, regents of the eight directions of space.
diwan (Persian) royal court or hall of audience, hence *diwan-e-am* (of public audience), *diwan-e-khas* (of private audience).
durbar (Persian) royal assembly.
dvara door, hence *dvarapala*, door-keeper.

garbha-griha literally 'womb chamber': inner sanctum of temple.
ghat approach; steps down to a river, embankment, hilly area.
giri hill.
gompa monastery.
gopura gatehouse to temple.
gumpha Orissan term for excavated cave.
gurukul the home of the guru, where students came and lived and studied with the teacher.

hammam (Arabic) bath of the Turkish or Roman type.
harmika finial of *stupa*.
haveli mansion; merchant's house.

iwan (Arabic) vaulted hall or recess opening out to a courtyard.

jagamohan term used for *mandap* in temples of Orissa.
jali lattic or filigree-patterned screen.
jami/jama masjid Friday or congregational mosque; see *masjid*.
johar voluntary mass self-immolation.

kalash water pitcher, vase, used as a symbol of plenty; immortality.
kirtimukha literally 'Face of Glory': a grotesque mask; also called *grasamukha*, protector of worshipper from evil.

linga mark: the phallic symbol of Shiva; the mark of potential cosmic creativity; fertility.

madrassa (Arabic) literally 'reading place' : school of Islamic learning associated with a mosque.
maidan open field in fort or palace, hence civic park.
mandala magical diagram; a visual aid to prayer.
mandap hall or pillared pavillion, of which the following are the most important types: *ardha-* (immediately before the sanctuary, when larger than an *antarala*); *bhoga-* (gift); *gudha-* (walled); *kalyana-* (for the ceremonial wedding of a god in the south); *maha-* (main element of a southern temple before the *vimana*, usually detached); *megha-* (multi-storey space of a Jaina temple); *mukha-* (portico when larger than a *praggriva*); *nat-* (dance hall); *ranga-* (open hypostyle, often detached and usually *navaranga*; *sabha-* (for assembly, equivalent to *maha-* and usually *rang*).
markara mythical crocodile whose ever-watchful, wide-open eyes protect the building.
masjid (Arabic) mosque, hence jami/jama masjid, Friday mosque, and nagina masjid, 'jewel mosque'; palatial chapel.
mihrab (Arabic) niche in principal wall of mosque marking the direction of Mecca.

naga serpent deity.
namaz prayer (in mosque).
naubat khana (Arabic/Persian), place for beating drums to mark the hours and important court events.

pitchwai cloth painting used as a curtain hung in front of the image of the principal deity in a temple.
pol gateway; entranceway.
pradakshina patha circumambulatory path or passage around a shrine.
puram/pur city, usually prefixed by a proper name, hence Kanchipuram.
purna-kalash 'bowl of plenty'.
purnima full moon; auspicious night.

qibla (Arabic) axis of prayer; wall of mosque facing Mecca.

rang-mahal literally means painted palace but generally used figuratively to mean pleasure palace.
ratha temple chariot, sometimes used for shrine.
rauze mortuary complex of tomb or funerary mosque in a compound.

sabha assembly.
sangha order of monks, especially Buddhist, hence *sangharama* (abode of the Buddhist order; monastery).
shah (Persian) king, but used in general to convey exaltedness.
shaikh (Arabic) elder; chief; holy man; descendant of the companions of the Prophet.

shastra traditional science; theoretical treatise.
shikhara northern temple superstructure; crowning cupola of southern temples.
shish-mahal palatial house, its walls decorated with mirror mosaic.
simha lion.
stambha pillar; post, column.
stupa tumulus; burial or reliquary mound.
sufi Muslim mystic or hermit.
surya sun: *surya mandir*, sun temple; *surya-vamsha*, descendants of the sun.
swayambhu self-existant; that was born of the Self.

thanka Buddhist cloth hanging; portable icon for Buddhists of Bhutan, Ladakh, and Tibet.
tirtha literally, 'fording place': place of spiritual regeneration; temple; hence Tirthankara, 'ford-maker'.
toran ceremonial portal, gateway.

vahan(a) vehicle or mount of god.
vajra thunderbolt; in Buddhist lore it is symbolic of power, hence: *vajrasana*, seat of the thunderbolt; *vajrapani*, the *bodhisattva* who holds the thunderbolt.
vastu residence, hence *vastushastra*, traditional science of architecture and *vastu-purush-mandala*, diagram for the residence of the Purusha; the formula for sacred building.
vatadage used in Shri Lanka for enclosed *stupa* or *dagoba.*
vedika railing, especially of sacred enclosure.
vihara residential quarters of monastery.
vimana storeyed building with receding terraces, used in South India for the temple building and roof (equivalent to northern *mulaprasada*).
vyala lion; leopard; mythical guardian animals depicted in temple precincts.

yaksha/yakshini masculine and feminine tree spirits.
yatra/jatra procession.

Glossary of Iconography

Abhaya Hand gesture of protection.

Agni Lord of Fire. Depicted in human form surrounded by flames, or just as a flame worshipped as part of all major Hindu rituals, as the purifier of the world, keeper of the hearth, etc. One of the principal deities in Vedic literature.

Ananta The infinite. A term applied to **Vishnu** and others.

Apsaras Celestial nymphs, seen flying above the gods, showering flowers, carrying umbrellas, garlands, etc.

Ardhanareshvar *See* **Shiva**.

Arjun One of the five Pandava brothers, heroes of the Mahabharata.

Avalokitesvara Bodhisattva. *See* **Buddhist Art**.

Avatars of Vishnu *See* **Vishnu**.

Balakrishna Baby Krishna. *See* **Krishna** under **Vishnu**.

Balarama Brother of **Krishna**, worshipped alongside him.

Bhagavat Gita Song of the Divine One. Part of the Mahabharata epic. A philosophical discussion between **Arjun** and **Krishna** that encapsulates the essence of Hindu philosophy.

Bhagavat Purana Puranic literature devoted to *Vishnu* relating the story of *Krishna*. The manuscripts are often illustrated with paintings.

Bhairava *See* **Shiva**.

Bhumidevi Bhumi, personification of the Earth goddess. *See* **Vishnu**; *also* Bhudevi, wife of Vishnu.

Bodhi tree *See* **Buddhist Art**.

Bodhisattva Potential Buddha, renouncing Nirvana to remain on earth for the benefit of humanity, to show others the Middle Path.

Buddhist Art

HINAYANA PERIOD Third to first centuries BC. The Buddha in this period is given no human form. His presence is represented by symbols.

> **Bodhi Tree or the pipal tree** *Ficus religiosa*. A large tree with spreading branches and heart-shaped leaves. It was under this tree that the Buddha attained enlightenment or nirvana.

> **Dharma chakra** The Wheel of Dharma. The word Dharma has many meanings: duty, the way, the path, action, and ideal. The wheel is used to suggest concepts of movement, time, progress, and change moving towards immortality and perfection.

> **Footprints** The presence of the holy one in Buddhist or Hindu iconography is symbolised by footprints with auspicious markings.

> **Stupa** After the Buddha died his body was cremated and the remains divided into portions. A stupa, or funerary mound, was built over the remains in various parts of the country, and these are objects of veneration and places of pilgrimage for Buddhists.

> **The empty throne** Symbol of honour.

SOME INCARNATIONS OF THE BUDDHA The Buddha appeared in several forms in his previous lives, gradually acquiring the strength and moral stature to attain Buddhahood or enlightenment. These stories are narrated in the Jataka tales:

Chadanta Jataka A white elephant with six tusks—and two wives. To his jealous wife he willingly sacrificed his tusks and died.

Mahakapi Jataka In the form of a monkey, the Buddha willingly sacrificed his life to save his companions.

Mriga Jataka A golden deer, whose bravery converted the hunter to the path of non-violence or *ahimsa.*

LIFE OF THE BUDDHA To commemorate the Buddha's life on earth, a few important events often figure in Buddhist narrative sculptures:

Maya's dream The Buddha's father was Suddhodana, the Raja of Kapilavastu, a state in modern Nepal. His mother Maha Maya dreamt of a white elephant, which was interpreted to mean the birth of a 'gift to humankind'—either a great king or saint. Mother Maya is often portrayed lying on a bed surrounded by attendants, with a tiny elephant hovering above.

Birth of the Buddha In sculpture, mother Maya is shown standing near a tree, with the baby Buddha appearing from her side. According to the story, Maya desired to go to her father's home for the delivery. On the way there they came to a grove of Sal, called Lumbini. Stopping to rest, she went into labour and the Buddha was born.

Yasodhara and Rahul Gautama (Buddha) married Yasodhara, and to them a son, Rahul, was born. After the Buddha's attainment of nirvana, Yasodhara and Rahul both joined his religious order.

Buddha sees the cruelties of life Gautama's father strove hard to prevent his son from leaving the palace for fear that he might become an ascetic. Gautama managed to leave the palace in his chariot and in the streets of the city encountered illness, poverty, and death. He then resolved to discover the meaning of life and the path that would end the cycle of human misery.

Buddha leaving his palace In sculpture this scene is depicted by a horse, Gautama's faithful steed Kantaka, leaving the palace. In Hinayana sculpture the horse is shown riderless, but the umbrella symbolises the Buddha's presence. Celestial creatures carry the feet of the horse so that no one in the palace can hear the sound of its hooves and thwart the Buddha in his resolve to renounce the world and all his earthly possessions.

Nirvana Enlightenment; the awakening of true Awareness that releases one from the cycle of life. Gautama wandered for many days and months, visiting teachers and scholars, and searching for an answer to the riddle of life. He understood that mere learning or asceticism would not provide an answer. At Bodh Gaya in Bihar he meditated. He was tempted by Mara, and rain and thunder, in attempts to break his concentration. Beautiful women, the daughters of Mara, reminded him of his palace, wife, and son, but he persevered.

Seated the yogic posture, in the lotus pose or *padmasana*, for meditation, the Buddha finally attained enlightenment. In sculpture he is shown seated in the *padmasana* posture with his hands placed on his lap, one palm above the other in the *dhaya mudra.*

Mahaparinirvana The great and final liberation of the Buddha from the cycle of incarnation. At the time of his death the Buddha attained immortality.

Bhumisparsa mudra The Buddha in meditation, tempted by Mara, reaches out with one hand and touches the ground, calling upon Mother Earth to witness the magical moment of his conquest of temptation and desire. The Buddha is shown seated with one hand touching the earth. Below him, Mara and Mother Earth are usually personified.

BODHISATTVA Potential Buddha, often depicted as a prince wearing a diadem and rich jewels to portray the 'richness' of the soul.

Avalokiteshvara Bodhisattva A being who is capable (*eshvara*) of enlightening insight (*avalokita*). In the legend we are told that he renounced the attainment of Buddhahood out of compassion and will continue to preach till the last being has been brought to enlightenment. He is often shown in sculpture supported by a lotus pedestal, wearing jewels and rich attire. His face, however, is lost in silent meditation.

Avalokiteshvara Padmapani (or Bodhisattva Padmapani) The Buddha stands holding a lotus, *padma*, the ultimate symbol of purity.

Vajrapani In one hand he holds a *vajra* or thunderbolt—often like a rod with a small sphere at either end.

Maitreya Buddha The Buddha who is yet to come.

Chamunda *See* **Devi**.

Chand The personification of the Moon.

Churning of the Ocean Often depicted in painting and sculpture, this refers to an episode at the beginning of time when the ocean was churned (like milk); ambrosia and all goodness appeared and the gods and demons fought to attain such powers. *See* **Kurma Avatar** under **Vishnu**.

Dakshinamurthi *See* **Shiva**.

Devi A general term for the female principle, female goddess (Sakti, the power). It is in the union of male and female, of two opposites, that the holistic concept of Hindu philosophy is to be understood.

Devi stands on a lotus pedestal, carrying a lotus in one hand. In her benign and terrifying form she may have a number of arms relaying her various attributes.

Chamunda The goddess here also has a terrifying expression. She is the destroyer of evil and wears a garland of skulls. She is in the posture of an ascetic and has starved herself in her meditation and penance. Snakes, scorpions, and the like adorn her emaciated body. The goddess, we are told, was created by *Durga* to combat the demons Chanda and Munda, from whom she derives her name.

Durga The inaccessible one.

Kali Bhadrakali and Mahakali are the forms that the *Devi* assumes to destroy evil. Her form, with many arms, weapons of war, and her terrifying expression frightens away her opponents (evil-doing enemies) and also destroys the fear of her devotees.

Mahishasuramardini Devi is created with all the powers of the gods to slay the demon bull Mahisha. She is often shown with several arms, beheading Mahisha who transforms himself from a bull into the form of a man but is eventually killed.

Uma/Parvati Shiva's wife, carrying a lotus in one hand, is often depicted seated or standing by Shiva's side.

Dharmachakra Wheel of Dharma; *see* **Buddhist Art**.

Ekadanta *See* **Ganesh**.

Ganesh Ganapati, Vighnesvara or Vinayaka, the Remover of Obstacles and son of **Shiva** and **Parvati**.

Birth of Ganesh Parvati created Ganesh from dirt off her body. He served as her guard. On one occasion Shiva attempted to enter Parvati's bathing area and was stopped by Ganesh. Unknowingly, Shiva cut off the head of his son. Parvati, in her fury, demanded the return of her son's life, and Shiva replaced Ganesh's head with an elephant's head obtained from a herd nearby.

Ganesh has two wives, Buddhi and Siddhi, personification of wisdom and attainment of desire, respectively.

Ganapati One of his names as Lord of the *ganas*, or chief of the army of the gods. He is also said to have aided Vyasa in the composition of the Mahabharata.

Ekadanta Refers to Ganesh's elephant head being represented in iconography with one broken tusk.

Ek is one, the only supreme being; *danta*—tusk or tooth—is a symbol of strength and power. Hence Ekadanta is the all-powerful one. As one of India's most popular deities, he is worshipped at the commencement of every activity or venture.

There is a story that the Moon (Chand) looked down at the elephant-headed baby and started to laugh. Ganesh snapped his tusk and hurled it at the Moon who began to lose his brightness. Ganesh stopped the process, but the curse had been given and forevermore the moon will wax and wane

Ganesh is shown standing, sitting, and dancing. Due to his now rotund belly, he is rarely depicted in yogic posture but on a seat or throne. Ganesh's trunk turns towards the left (very rarely to the right). Apart from jewellery, Ganesh, like his father Shiva, wears a snake tied as a belt around his waist or across his chest, like the holy thread worn by caste Hindus. Ganesh has as his companion vehicle, or *vahana*, a rat that aids him in finding a way past all obstacles.

Ganga Personification of the goddess of the sacred river Ganga. The saint Bhagiratha prayed for her presence on earth to wash away the sins and ashes of the dead. Ganga descended with all her force, and Shiva took the weight of the mighty river on his head, the waters were lost in his curls, subdued by his presence. The river flows from the central Himalaya, through the northern plains of India, to the east where it meets the Bay of Bengal.

Garuda Mythical bird, the companion *vahana* (vehicle) of **Vishnu**, shown carrying his Lord or with human arms folded in prayer.
Gopi(s) Female cowherds and wives who sport with **Krishna**.
Govardhan Mountain that Krishna lifted. *See* **Krishna** under **Vishnu**.

Hanuman Monkey chief, the faithful companion and devotee of **Rama** in the Ramayana.
Hari Hara *See* **Shiva**.
Hinayana Period *See* **Buddhist Art**.

Indra Lord of the firmament and sky, thunder and lightning. He holds a *vajra* (thunderbolt) in one hand and rides on a huge white elephant resembling a white cloud. This Vedic deity was superseded by **Krishna** and others in later periods.

Jain From the term *jina*, meaning the victor, comes the term Jaina or Jain, meaning followers or sons of the victor.

Mahavir Jain was, like the Buddha, born of a princely family. He left home and took to a life of severe asceticism. His teachings revolve around the notion of life as a continuous stuggle against desires. He spread the message of peace and *ahimsa* (non-violence) as the path of deliverance from the cycle of life.
Jataka Tales A collection of 500 tales relating to the previous incarnations of the Buddha. *See* **Buddhist Art**.

Kali *See* **Devi**.
Kaliya Serpent that Krishna subjugated. *See* **Krishna** under **Vishnu**.
Kalki Avatar of Vishnu. *See* **Vishnu**.
Kalyanasundara *See* **Shiva**.
Karttikeya *See* **Skanda**.
Krishna Avatar of Vishnu. *See* **Vishnu**.
Kurma Avatara *See* **Vishnu**.

Lakshmi The goddess of wealth emerging from the ocean and bathed by two elephants (Gajalakshmi). She represents all goodness. Lakshmi appears in all Vishnu's incarnations as Sita, wife of *Rama*, as Rukmini, *Satyabhama*, and *Radha* beside *Krishna*, etc. She carries lotuses, a pot of ambrosia, and other emblems.
Linga Phallic symbol of Shiva. *See* **Shiva**.

Mahabharata Epic poem about the fortunes of the Pandava family.
Mahishasuramardini *See* **Devi**.
Maitreya The Buddha who is yet to come.
Matsya Avatar *See* **Vishnu**.

Naga, Nagadeva A race of sacred serpents who rule the underworld. They represent the water, the earth, and all the treasures derived from the earth. As snakes are crucial to farmers in loosening the soil and destroying rats who eat the grain, snake worship is common in almost all parts of India. They are portrayed alone, often with hoods and jewellery or entwined as couples (*naga* and *nagini*), and along with other deities like *Shiva*, *Ganesh*, etc.

Often seen with human heads and arms and snake-like bodies, they are said to be immortal, having tasted the ambrosia from the *Churning of the Ocean* (*see* above). They bring prosperity, marriage, and offspring to their devotees.
Nandi Bull. Companion (*vahana*, or vehicle) of Shiva.
Narasimha Avatar of Vishnu. *See* **Vishnu**.
Narayana Epithet of **Vishnu**.
Nataraja *See* **Shiva**.
Natesa *See* **Shiva**.

Parasurama Avatar of Vishnu. *See* **Vishnu**.
Pashupati Shiva, lord of all creatures. *See* **Shiva**.
Pipal tree *See* **Buddhist Art**.

Radha Krishna's young lover. *See* **Krishna** under **Vishnu**.
Rama Avatar of Vishnu. *See* **Vishnu**.
Ravana King of Lanka, who kidnapped Sita and was defeated by *Rama* in the Ramayana. Depicted with ten heads, he is described in literature as a brave and well-read man. Unfortunately, his weakness (lust) was the cause of his downfall.
Rukmini Wife of Krishna. *See* **Krishna** under **Vishnu**.

Saraswati Goddess of learning and of all knowledge and wisdom. Her symbols are a book (palm leaf), holy beads, a *vina* (stringed musical intrument), and the lotus. She is assigned to Brahma as his companion.
Satyabhama Wife of Krishna. *See* **Krishna** under **Vishnu**.
Sesha The serpent that floats on the sea of eternity. *See* **Anantasesha** under **Vishnu**.

Shiva   A supreme deity, one of the trinity of *Vishnu, Brahma*, and *Shiva*, symbolizing preservation, creation, reabsorption, and re-creation (achieved sometimes through destruction).

MANIFESTATIONS OF SHIVA:

(i)   Without form, the Supreme Being with no beginning and no end.

(ii)   The luminous pillar or *linga* (phallic symbol), the emerging form that is limitless in its power.

   The pillar appears in a story from the Shiva Purana, when Vishnu and Brahma contest supremacy. Shiva turns into a never-ending luminous pillar, Brahma and Vishnu strive to find the end of the pillar and in failing to do so underline Shiva's supremacy.

   The *linga* rests on a *yoni* stone, symbolizing the female principle. The *linga* is often rounded or faceted. In rare cases a face or many faces appear on its side, as in the Pashupati temple in Kathmandu.

(iii)   The third is the human form that Shiva assumes for the benefit of his devotees.

   Shiva is described firstly as an ascetic wearing the skin of a tiger or a simple loin-cloth. Snakes twine around his wrist and neck. like jewels, for he is also Lord of the Underworld. In his hair Shiva wears the crescent moon as a jewel to symbolise this aspect as 'conqueror of time and all that changes'. He wears a *datura* flower in his matted sage-like hair. As in all depictions of deities, Shiva has many forms and many arms, limbs, and heads to manifest his various attributes.

Ardhanareshvara   A composite figure, half-man and half-woman, *Shiva* and *Parvati* united to symbolise the reconciliation of opposites to create a holistic entity. The male half wears a different headdress, clothing, and jewellery. The female side curves gracefully, relaxed and in repose.

Bhairav   'The terrible' form of Shiva, with an awesome expression, as an ascetic with little clothing accompanied by a dog.

Dakshinamurti   The ascetic and teacher, Shiva is seated in yogic posture, surrounded by animals and devotees.

Gangadhara   Shiva is said to have borne the weight of the great river *Ganga* as it fell down onto the earth. Ganga is depicted as a female goddess often perched in Shiva's hair, much to the annoyance of *Parvati*, Shiva's jealous wife.

Hari Hara   Composite image of *Vishnu* and *Shiva*.

Kalyanasundara   Shiva as a handsome prince at the time of his marriage to *Parvati*.

Nataraja   Shiva dancing the dance of creation. He often stands with one leg raised, the other trampling on Apasmara, the symbol of ignorance. He is often depicted with four arms: one carries a flame (destruction), the second a *damru* (a little drum that beats out the rhythm of creation), the third hand in *abhaya mudra* (protection), and the fourth pointing to his foot (denoting salvation from ignorance). His hair spreads out in waves, and there is often a halo of fire around his swirling form.

Pashupati   Lord of All Creatures. Shiva usually has his trident in one hand and a deer in the other.

Shiva–Parvati   Seen often as husband and wife, seated with their two children, *Ganesh* and *Karttikeya*, and their animal companions (*Nandi*, Shiva's bull, Parvati's tiger, Ganesh's rat, and Karttikeya's Peacock).

Somaskanda Shiva, Parvati, and son Skanda. *See* **Skanda.**

Tripurantaka In reference to a legend in which Siva, with his bow and arrow, destroyed the three cities of the demons.

Vishapaharana Shiva with a blue throat. He saved the world by swallowing the poison of the ocean. This stained his throat, hence Nilkanta (*nil* means blue, *kanta* means throat).

Skanda (Karttikeya or Subrahmanya) *Shiva's* son and the lord of Shiva's army, Skanda rides on a peacock. He was born of Shiva's seed, carried away by *Agni* (Lord of Fire), and brought up (in one version) by *Ganga* (the river). He is described as a youthful, handsome boy, who is as radiant as the Sun.

Stupa Buddhist funerary mound.

Subrahmanya *See* **Skanda.**

Surya The lord of the sun rides across the sky on a chariot drawn by seven horses (the seven colours of the rainbow), usually carrying two lotuses in his hand. He wears high boots, and the armour covering his chest has given rise to a belief that his image is of foreign origin. He is accompanied by his charioteer, the lame Aruna. His female companions or handmaidens include Rajni, Usha, and Chhaya—radiance, dawn, and shade, respectively. Usha and Pratyusha drive away the darkness with their bows and arrows.

Tara Buddhist goddess of compassion.

Tirthankara(s) There are ten regions of the universe, each with 24 Tirthankaras in each of the three ages—past, present, and future. They take the part of teachers who, by example, lead the way to salvation. Adhinatha, Parsvanatha, and Mahavir (*see* **Jaina**) were three of the Tirthankaras.

Tripurantaka *See* **Shiva.**

Trivikrama *See* **Vishnu.**

Uma *See* **Devi.**

Vajra Thunderbolt.

Vajrapani Bodhisattva with the thunderbolt. *See* **Buddhist Art.**

Vamana Avatar of Vishnu. *See* **Vishnu.**

Varaha Avatar of Vishnu. *See* **Vishnu.**

Venugopal Krishna, the flute player.

Vinayaka *See* **Ganesh.**

Vishapaharana *See* **Shiva.**

Vishnu In ancient lore Vishnu was one amongst the Vedic deities. but subsequently was elevated to form part of the trinity of Brahma, *Shiva*, and Vishnu.

Vishnu is shown in three positions, standing, sitting, and reclining. When he is standing with one hand raised in the *abhaya* hand gesture, he is offering protection to his devotees. In one hand Vishnu carries the *shank*, or conch, used to blow the call to battle, the sound of salvation. In his other hand is the *chakra*, or disc, a circular wheel with spokes that is flung at the enemy, cutting off their heads and arms, the symbol of protection. He also carries the lotus of creation and a wooden club, the symbol of destruction. Vishnu's consorts are *Lakshmi*, who sits to his right, and *Bhumidevi* on the left. They are the attributes of wealth and the prosperity of the earth, and carry a lotus and a lily, respectively.

Anantasesha The image of Vishnu reclining on the serpent Sesha that floats on the sea of eternity. *Lakshmi* is seated beside Vishnu and *Bhumidevi* is often shown pressing his feet. The serpent Adisesha has a hood of one or more heads, with a body that coils to provide a bed or seat for Vishnu. Brahma is said to have emerged on a lotus from the belly of Vishnu, also called Padma- (lotus) nabha- (navel) swamy (Lord).

The *vahana* of Vishnu is Garuda, identified with the Brahminy kite, a large, beautiful chestnut-coloured bird found in India.

INCARNATIONS OR AVATARS OF VISHNU   In every cycle of decadence Vishnu is said to come to earth to save her from destruction. Vishnu is seen sometimes surrounded by his ten avatars.

Matsya Avatar   Vishnu appears in the form of a huge fish, or half-fish and half-man.

The legend tells of a sage who caught a small fish and put it in a bowl. The fish grew too big for the bowl and the lake, and had to be taken out to sea. This fish saved the universe that was overwhelmed by a deluge. The fish avatar is also said to have saved the Vedas and holy books from the floods.

Kurma Avatar   Vishnu appears as a tortoise that served as a gigantic pedestal in the episode referred to as the *Churning of the Ocean*. The gods and demons churned the ocean at the beginning of time as one churns milk to make butter. By churning the ocean, good and evil rose to the surface, and ambrosia—the formula for eternal and youthful life—was brought forth from the waters. In order to churn the mighty ocean, the gods needed a churning rod. For this they used a mountain, and Vishnu, as a tortoise, provided the support to hold the rod in place.

Varaha Avatar   From the deluge at the origin of the earth Vishnu, in the form of a giant boar, lifted up the earth (goddess) out of the waters of creation.

Vishnu's form is often shown as half-man with a face of a boar that has picked up the earth, *bhu*, personified as a little goddess (Bhuvaraha).

Narasimha Avatar   Vishnu appears with a lion's head and human body, usually with the evil man Hiranyakasipu, who is being torn apart and devoured on his lap. The story relates that Hiranyakasipu obtained many boons from the gods and declared himself infallible. No one, neither man nor beast, could kill him, no weapon could injure him, neither by day nor by night, outside or within the house. Perturbed by his power, the gods requested Vishnu to destroy Hiranyakasipu. Vishnu assumed the form of half-man and half-lion, and at dusk, at the threshold of the house (neither inside nor outside), he tore the demon to pieces.

Vamana Avatara (Trivikrama)   In sculpture and painting Vamana, or Vishnu, is usually depicted as a dwarf or small man who is receiving a gift from King Bali. In order to teach Bali a lesson Vamana asks for a gift of three paces of land. How much land can the dwarf take in three paces thinks Bali and agrees to make the gift. Vishnu steps out of the Vamana form and places one foot to conquer the earth, another that stretches from earth to heaven, and looks for a third pace. Bali, realising Vishnu's greatness, offers his head, acknowledging defeat. In sculpture Vishnu is shown stretching out his leg to take the three paces (*tri* meaning three plus *vikrama* meaning victory). The repentant Bali was then appointed lord of the underworld.

Parasurama   Very rarely to be seen, Vishnu in human form holds a *parasu* (battleaxe) in one hand. Born a Brahmin, he took to the ways of a *kshatriya* (warrior) and slew his mother for her lustful ways.

Rama   This avatar of Vishnu is the hero of the epic Ramayana and, with his wife Sita and brother Lakshmana, is widely so depicted in sculpture and painting. Rama usually holds a bow, Sita stands to his right, and Lakshmana, a little shorter than Rama, often carries a bow. Hanuman, the monkey lord, is often shown with this group.

Krishna Is usually depicted with the attributes of *Vishnu*: the conch and the disc. He wears a peacock-feather crown, a flaming yellow dhoti, garlands and flowers. His skin is said to be dark like the blue-black rain clouds, symbolic of his goodness.

His lover as a cowherd was *Radha*. Krishna's chief wives are Rukmini and *Satyabhama*. From childhood in Mathura and Brindavan (UP), Krishna went to live in Dwaraka (Gujarat).

Krishna reappears in the Mahabharata epic. He plays the charioteer and philosopher guide to *Arjun* during the great battle to explain the *Bhagavat Gita* (Song of the Divine One) which encapsulates the essence of Hindu philosophy.

Balkrishna Krishna as a child often depicted dancing with a butter ball, crawling about and playing.

Kaliyakrishna and Goverdhana Krishna's childhood as a cowherd is described in many scenes: with his mother *Yasodha* killing the demon horse, conquering the serpent Kaliya, breaking away from the cart and mortar, stealing butter, dancing with a butter ball, playing with the *gopis* and girls of the village, lifting up Mount Goverdhana to protect cows and humans from the storm sent by Lord Indra.

Venugopal An avatar of Vishnu as the boy cowherd, Venugopal—Krishna as the player of the *venu* (flute)—plays music, luring his followers, the cowherds and cows.

In order to free the world from oppression, Krishna was born to kill the wicked King Kamsa. The king had imprisoned Devaki, prophesied to be the holy mother. Her child was smuggled out at birth and given to *Yasodha* to look after. This scene is depicted as a stormy night, with a child being carried away in a basket. King Kamsa is dashing a child to the ground, in an attempt to kill all infants he thinks might destroy him.

Buddha Also considered to be an avatar of *Vishnu* (incorporated in the medieval period).

Kalki The avatar of *Vishnu* that is yet to come, at the end of this *kaliyuga* (time cycle) when the world dissolves into decadence. Virtue and justice disappear, then Kalki (horse and rider) will come and free the world of evil.

Yaksha/Yakshi Celestial, supernatural beings, associated with wealth and prosperity. Usually female forms holding flowers or branches of trees that blossom at their touch.

Yamuna The river is personified as a goddess riding on a tortoise carrying a pot of her holy waters.

Yashodha Krishna's mother. *See* **Krishna** under **Vishnu**.

yogi one who practices the discipline of *yoga*; fem. *yogini*, also refers to manifestation of the great goddess.

Further Reading

Allchin, B. and F. R, *The Rise of Civilisation in India and Pakistan*. Cambridge: 1982.
Allen, Charles, *Lives of the Indian Princes*. London: 1984.
Anderson, M.M., *Festivals of Nepal*. London: 1971.
Aran, Lydia, *The Art of Nepal*. Kathmandu: 1978.
Archer, W.G. and Senarat Paranavitana, *Ceylon: Paintings from Temple, Shrine and Rock*. 'UNESCO World Art Series'. Paris: 1958.
Banerjee, N. R., *Nepalese Architecture*. Delhi: 1980.
Bernier, Ronald, *The Nepalese Pagoda—Origins and Style*. New Delhi: 1979.
Brown, P., *Indian Architecture (Buddhist and Hindu)*. 2nd ed., Bombay: 1942.
Brown, P., *Picturesque Nepal*. New Delhi: 1984.
Conze, E., *Buddism : Its Essence and Development*. Oxford: 1951.
Coomaraswamy, A.K., *History of Indian, and Indonesian Art*. London: 1927.
    Mediaeval Sinhalese Art, 1st ed. London: 1908; rpt. New York: 1956.
Dago Tshering (ed.)., *Bhutan Himalayan Kingdom*. Thimphu: 1979.
Davies, P., *Splendours of the Raj: British Architecture in India 1660-1947*. London: 1985.
    Penguin Guide to the Monuments of India. Islamic, Rajput and European vol. 2 . Harmondsworth: 1989.
Deheja, V., *Early Buddhist Rock Temples*. London: 1972.
Deva, K., *Temples of North India*. New Delhi: 1969.
Edmunds, Tom Owen, *Bhutan: Land of the Thunder Dragon*. London: 1988.
Gajurel, C.L. and K.K. Vaidya, *Traditional Arts and Crafts of Nepal*. New Delhi: 1984.
Gascoigne, B., *The Great Moghuls*. London: 1979.
Harle, J.C., *The Art and Architecture of the Indian Subcontinent*. Harmondsworth: 1986.
Hickman, Katie, *Dreams of the Peaceful Dragon: A Journey into Bhutan*. London: 1987.
Jorn, W., *The Traditional Architecture of the Kathmandu Valley*. Kathmandu: 1977.
Kramrisch, S., *The Art of Nepal*. New York: 1964.
    The Hindu Temple, 2 vols. Calcutta: 1946.
    Indian Sculpture. Calcutta: 1933.
Lord, J. H., *The Jews in India and the Far East*. Westport: 1976.
Marshall, J., *Taxila.*, 3 vols. Cambridge: 1951.
Marshall, J., and A. Foucher, *The Monuments of Sanci.*, 3 vols. New Delhi: 1940.
Michell, G., *Penguin Guide to the Monuments of India: Hindu and Buddhist* vol. 1. Harmondsworth: 1989.
Miller, Babara. S., (trans.) *Bhagavad Gita*. Harmondsworth: 1962.
Mitra, D., *Buddhist Monuments*. Calcutta: 1971.
    Udayagiri and Khandagiri. New Delhi: 1960.
Mookerjee, A., *The Tantric Way*: 1977.
Nath, R., *History of Sultanate Architecture*. New Delhi: 1978.
O'Flaherty, Wendy Doniger, (ed.,) *Hindu Myths*. New York: 1975.
Pal, Pratapaditya, *Art of Nepal*. Los Angeles/Berkeley: 1985.
Paranavitana, Senarat, *Art and Architecture of Ceylon, Polonnaruwa Period*. Colombo : 1954.
    The Stupa in Ceylon. Colombo: 1946.

Sarkar, H., *Studies in Early Buddhist Architecture of India*. Delhi: 1966.
Schmidt, K. Khan, *5000 Years of Art in Pakistan*. Utrecht: 1963.
Sewell, Robert. A., *Forgotten Empire : Vijayanagar*. New Delhi: 1987.
Shah, U. P., *Studies in Jaina Art*. Banaras: 1955.
Sivaramamurti, C., *Indian Art*. New Delhi: 1974.
   The Art of India. New York: 1977.
Spear, P., R. *A History of India*, vol. II., Harmondsworth: rpt. 1978.
Smith, V. A., *A History of Fine Art in India and Ceylon*. Oxford: 1911.
Snelling, John, *The Buddhist Handbook*. London: 1987.
Thapar, R., *A History of India*, vol. I., Harmondsworth: rpt. 1978.
Toy, S., *The Strongholds of India*. London: 1957.
   The Fortified Cities of India. London: 1965.
Zimmer, H., *The Art of Indian Asia*, 2 vols., New York: 1955.

The Archaeological Survey of India publishes an excellent (inexpensive) series of booklets to many of the major sites in India.

The Odyssey Guide series (The Guidebook Company, Hong Kong) have individual guides to India; Delhi, Agra & Jaipur; Bombay; Goa; The Museums of India; The Hill Stations of India; Pakistan; The Kathmandu Valley and Shri Lanka.

References

1. John Marshall, *Illustrated London News*, Sept. 1924.
2. Sacred Nitnem: Jaap Sahib, Author's translation.
3. *Tuzuk-i Jahangiri*, 2 vols, trans. Nur al-Din Muhammad Jahangir, rpt., Delhi: 1968.
4. R. Heber, *Narrative of a Journey through the Upper Provinces of India, 1824-25*, vol II. Calcutta: 1825.
5. Parasuram Caturvedi, (ed.), *Mirabai ki Padavali*. Varanasi: 1973.
6. Huge Davenport, *Udaipur: The Trials and Triumphs of the Mewar Kingdom*, Jaipur: 1975.
7. Ibid.
8. *Babur Nama: Memoirs of Babur* (tr.), rpt., New Delhi: 1970.
9. Ibid.
10. M.S. and D.S. Randhawa, *Indian Sculpture: The Scenes, Themes and Legends*. Bombay: 1985.
11. T.S. Burt, *Journal of the Asiatic Society*, 1839.
12. Author's rendition of the myth.
13. Ibid.
14. E.B. Havell, *Ancient and Medieval Architecture of India*. London: 1915.
15. Beal, S., *Life of Hiuen Tsang*. London: 1911.
16. Romila Thapar, *Ashoka and the Decline of the Mauryas*. rpt., New Delhi: 1963.
17. Ainslie T. Embree, *Sources of Indian Tradition*. vol I., rpt., New Delhi: 1988.
18. Ronald Latham, *Marco Polo: The Travels*. trans., Harmondsworth: 1958.
19. N.S. Ramaswami, *Mamallapuram: An Annotated Bibliography*. Madras: 1980.
20. Mortimer Wheeler, *My Archaeological Mission to India and Pakistan*. London: 1976.
21. Ibid.
22. John Marshall, *Taxila*. 3 vols., Cambridge: 1951.

Index